PENNSYLVANIA

GETTING STARTED GARDEN GUIDE

Grow the Best Flowers, Shrubs, Trees, Vines & Groundcovers

Quarto is the authority on a wide range of topics.

Quarto educates, entertains and enriches the lives of our readers—enthusiasts and lovers of hands-on living.

www.quartoknows.com

First published in 2014 by Cool Springs Press, an imprint of Quarto Publishing Group USA Inc., 400 First Avenue North, Suite 400, Minneapolis, MN 55401 USA. Telephone: (612) 344-8100 Fax: (612) 344-8692

quartoknows.com
Visit our blogs at quartoknows.com

Cool Springs Press titles are also available at discounts in bulk quantity for industrial or sales-promotional use. For details contact the Special Sales Manager at Quarto Publishing Group USA Inc., 400 First Avenue North, Suite 400, Minneapolis, MN 55401 USA.

Library of Congress Cataloging-in-Publication Data

Weigel, George.
  Pennsylvania getting started garden guide : grow the best flowers, shrubs, trees, vines & groundcovers / George Weigel.
     pages cm
  Includes bibliographical references and index.
  ISBN 978-1-59186-620-6 (sc)
  1. Gardening--Pennsylvania. 2. Plants--Pennsylvania. I. Title.
  SB453.2.P4W45 2014
  635.09748--dc23
                              2014012728

Acquisitions Editor: Billie Brownell
Senior Art Director: Brad Springer
Layout: Danielle Smith-Boldt

Printed in USA

PENNSYLVANIA

GETTING STARTED GARDEN GUIDE

Grow the Best Flowers, Shrubs, Trees, Vines & Groundcovers

George Weigel

COOL
SPRINGS
PRESS
Home and Garden Experts™

MINNEAPOLIS, MINNESOTA

DEDICATION AND ACKNOWLEDGMENTS

Dedication

To Suze, my lifelong love, who's co-propagator of plants and my *other* two loves, daughter Erin and son Andy, who's grown the flock to include daughter-in-law Julie and a little sweet pea named Leona Pearl. Leona's an enthusiastic gardener too . . . she just doesn't know it yet.

Acknowledgments

Since gardening is such a regional endeavor, I liked the whole concept of state-by-state plant guides when I saw the original version of this book back in 2002. Liz Ball did that one—the *Pennsylvania Gardener's Guide*—and I was impressed. Who would've thought I'd be writing this all-new version in 2014?

I'd like to thank Liz for kindly referring me as her successor and for the valued advice on how to tackle this fact-packed project. Now that Liz is about as retired as any garden writer is apt to be, I wish her many happy, healthy years of gardening just for the pure joy of it.

I'd also like to thank Tracy Stanley and the production team at Cool Springs Press and especially editor Billie Brownell. Somehow Billie manages to juggle multiple book projects all at the same time and keep them all organized and flowing. I'd be crazy by now (or more so, as some would say).

I also appreciate the skilled look-over by horticultural editor [INSERT NAME TK], who made sure I had all of the ®s and ™s straight, not to mention correct spellings of botanical and cultivar names and a minimum of egregious factoid misfires (hopefully, none).

Finally, there's an army of info-suppliers out there that contributed bits and pieces over time to the plant database now taking up most of the memory capacity in my brain. Thanks to the many Master Gardeners, horticulturists, growers, garden-center folks, hort professors, public-garden staffers, Extension educators, home gardeners, and yes, even my own backyard bunnies and groundhogs, who assisted in compiling the critter-resistant information. At least my devoured pansies turned out to be good for *something* . . .

CONTENTS

WELCOME TO GARDENING

IN PENNSYLVANIA

After gardening for a while in Pennsylvania, don't be surprised if you find yourself reciting the old Dickens line, "It was the best of times, it was the worst of times."

On the one compost-stained hand, Pennsylvania has fairly plant-friendly weather, some of the world's best soil, and a climate that gives us four distinct seasons with an accompanying wide range of plant choices.

But on the other hand, we've got ravenous groundhogs, marauding deer, Japanese beetles, intermittent droughts and monsoons, an ever-increasing acreage of plant-killing "builder's soil," surprise frosts, invasive weeds, and assorted blights and fungi. Did I mention groundhogs?

Let's just say that gardening here can be challenging. It also can be one of the most rewarding and fun endeavors you'll encounter, all the while getting exercise in the fresh air. Who needs a health club when you can till, edge, dig, plant, and mulch? What's more, gardening is one of the best interests parents can pass along to an increasingly nature-starved, computer-fed new generation.

Unfortunately, few people have had any schooling in the fine art of yard care. Most Pennsylvanians end up winging it and learning by trial-and-error. Good thing you've found this book. We hope it'll give you the hands-on tips and best plants to save decades of money-wasting trial-and-error. If not, there's always concrete.

Pennsylvania's Gardening Heritage

Pennsylvania has a long, rich gardening history. Right from William Penn's 1681 founding of the colony, the state had plants ingrained in its DNA. Early Quaker, Mennonite, and Amish settlers gave high priority to gardening and nature, and Penn himself wanted his colony's first city (Philadelphia) to be a tree-abundant "greene countrie towne."

Philadelphia to this day has America's largest collection of public gardens (more than two dozen within an hour's drive), the nation's most respected community greening program, and the world's biggest, oldest indoor flower show (the Philadelphia International Flower Show).

Pennsylvania also was home to some of America's earliest horticultural icons. John Bartram, for example, became America's first "royal botanist" in 1765 and collected, catalogued, and grew hundreds of what were then unknown new-world species. The 46-acre Bartram's Garden in Philadelphia remains North America's oldest surviving public garden.

Philadelphian Bernard M'Mahon is credited with writing America's first garden book for Americans in the early 1800s, a how-to called *The American Gardener's Calendar*.

Philadelphians W. Atlee Burpee and David Landreth founded two of America's first seed companies, both of which are still selling seeds to 21st-century gardeners.

And the Painter brothers in Delaware County and the Peirce twins in Chester County built some of America's first tree collections, both of which also are still around today (respectively, the 650-acre Tyler Arboretum and what became the world renowned 1,050-acre Longwood Gardens).

Others added to the growing heritage, including Henry Phipps' grand Victorian-era conservatory in Pittsburgh (Phipps Conservatory), Milton Hershey's founding of one of the world's biggest rose gardens (Hershey Gardens in 1935), and J. Horace McFarland's eminent collection of early 20th-century garden slides (now part of the Smithsonian's Archives of American Gardens).

The bottom line is that Pennsylvania's gardening legacy stacks up favorably with any in the United States. Here's hoping some of that rubs off on you as you attempt to grow a decent hydrangea.

Weather and Climate

Pennsylvania's weather looks better on paper than in reality.

The state's average annual rainfall runs between 40 to 45 inches, the average summer high temperatures top out in the low to mid-80s, and the average lows run mainly in the 20s. Not bad. To get there, though, it's not unusual to go 6 or 8 weeks without a drop of rain, then see the entire 2-month supply fall in one afternoon. That's especially true when hurricane remnants blow up the East Coast in late summer.

Temperatures can be equally erratic. Most areas of the state see at least a few 100-degree summer days, and typical summers feature several 90-degree spells. In winter, lows have dipped to the minus-20s. Temperatures especially swing wildly in the spring and fall transitional seasons. The mercury can drop 60 degrees in a single day, going from an unusually balmy 80-degree fall day down to 20 degrees overnight when a Canadian cold front swoops down. Some of our worst tree damage has occurred when wet October "Nor'easter" snowstorms weigh down branches that haven't yet dropped their leaves.

Such change can be as jolting to gardens as it is to gardeners, as any flower-fancier who's draped sheets over the petunias in late May will tell you.

Yet for all of the bumps along the way, when Pennsylvania's weather turns nice, it can be *really* nice. Our spring wildflowers and native trees put on a glorious end-of-winter show that lasts for months. We get enough chill time over winter that it's possible to grow spring-flowering bulbs from February through June.

While summers can get hot and dry or hot and humid, they also can be pleasant. Rainfall usually happens often enough that it's possible to keep most plants growing full steam ahead with periodic hosings. It's seldom as oppressive as, say, Phoenix or Dallas.

As summer fades, skies turn blue and temperatures cool into the crisp 40s and 50s to produce spectacular fall-foliage shows. It's not just trees either. Numerous shrubs and fall-blooming flowers offer the possibility of a home landscape that blazes in autumn.

As in most of the United States, Pennsylvania winters have been warming. Lows aren't going below zero as often, and longer, warmer spells have increased our winter temperature averages and made winter-long snow covers rare.

When the U.S. Department of Agriculture revamped its Plant Hardiness Zone Map (a guide to average winter lows) in 2012, most of Pennsylvania moved a notch warmer on the scale. In other words, Harrisburg rated as Baltimore was, and Scranton rated where Harrisburg was.

There are some plants that one can grow more successfully now in Pennsylvania as the climate has warmed a notch.

A small space garden with kalanchoe in a container.

The upshot is that gardeners are finding that previously out-of-reach or "borderline-hardy" plants such as nandina, crapemyrtle, and even camellia are becoming better bets. Research at Longwood Gardens also found that plants are blooming earlier than before, northern species such as sugar maples and copper beeches are struggling more in our hotter summers, and some southern weeds and bugs are creeping into the region. (See more on the USDA map on page 21.)

The Lay of Pennsylvania's Land

Pennsylvania starts out at sea level in the coastal plains of the southeastern corner around Philadelphia, which is also the state's warmest region. Ridges and valleys dominate the state's midsection before the land rises at the Appalachian Mountains, dividing the western third of the state into a higher, cooler plateau. The extreme northwestern corner tapers back down into lakeside lowlands at Erie.

Pennsylvania is dotted with 250 lakes, untold streams and creeks, and several key rivers, ranging from the Delaware along the southeastern border, to the Susquehanna scissoring the center of the state, to the Allegheny and Monongahela that join to form the Ohio in the west at Pittsburgh.

Soil types vary markedly from region to region. Conditions are sandier in the coastal regions around Philadelphia and the Lake Erie shore. Then the land turns into rockier sandstone in the north-central Allegheny plateau and into poorer drained glacial hardpans in the northwestern and northeastern sections. Some of the nation's best agricultural soil is located in the Conestoga Valley of south-central Pennsylvania, while a reasonably productive shale and limestone mix covers most of the ridges and valleys in the state's midsection.

Pennsylvanians garden anywhere from postage-stamp-sized city gardens to extensive wooded plots in the countryside. The majority of us live somewhere between, in small towns and ever-creeping housing subdivisions in what used to be farmland or forest. Yet despite consistent housing growth, Pennsylvania still has plentiful rural areas and farms and remains one of America's most forested states with 17 million forested acres and 20 state-managed forests.

For the record, Pennsylvania's official state tree is the Eastern hemlock (*Tsuga canadensis*), and its official state flower is the mountain laurel (*Kalmia latifolia*).

Gardening in Pennsylvania

Although much of Pennsylvania's native soil is well suited for gardening, that's not what most gardeners have. Particularly in suburban subdivisions, common building practice has been to first clear the lots, and then grade for efficient water management and level building lots. In the end, several inches from the saved topsoil pile is spread back on top of the carved subsoil.

While that's good for homebuilding, it's not so good for plant life. Many a landscape plant has struggled and died in the resulting compacted, layered soil. For one thing, plant roots have a difficult time penetrating the packed soil below, leaving them shallow-rooted and more prone to drought. In rainy weather, water often backs up to rot roots when rain drains through the surface but can't percolate through the subsoil as quickly.

The Importance of Soil

For this reason, I can't stress enough how important it is to consider your soil before planting anything. If you're lucky enough to have relatively unscathed and well-drained soil, you can move right onto planting. But if you've got "builder's soil" or other rocky, clayish ground masquerading as soil, the solution is to improve it with organic material. Good choices include compost (homemade or from a municipal composting operation), mushroom soil (composted manure and sawdust or straw that's a byproduct of mushroom-growing), rotted leaves, dried grass clippings, spent straw, aged cow manure, store-bought humus, bagged "planting mix," or any combination of these.

Don't overdo it. You don't need to *remove* the soil you've got, just amend it by incorporating an inch or two of organic matter into the top 10 or 12 inches of loosened, existing soil. That'll give you slightly raised planting beds of loose, nutrition-enriched, better-drained soil that will increase your success rate.

I'd also suggest planting *beds* instead of planting *holes*. By improving wider areas, drainage is more consistent throughout, and plant roots can spread farther in all directions. The danger of planting in small holes with excessively improved soil is that it's akin to planting in a pot; the roots tend to circle within the "good stuff," and water will drain in but not out, backing up to rot roots within the planting hole.

Don't Call Me Dirt

So, how do you know if your soil is good or bad in the first place? Here are four ways to tell:

1. **Drainage test.** Before planting, dig a hole about as big as one of the rootballs of the plants you intend to plant. Fill it with water and give it 24 hours to drain. Then fill it again, and watch to see how many inches it drains per hour. If it's not going down by at least 1 inch per hour, you've got some "uncompacting" to do.

2. **Texture test.** Dig a tablespoon or so of soil and add enough water that you can roll it into a ball. If you can't form a ball, the soil is sandy and will drain quickly. Next squeeze the ball between your thumb and index finger to make a ribbon. The longer the ribbon before cracking, the more clay you've got. Less than 2 inches is good. More than 2 inches means the soil is clayish and will drain slower.

3. **Composition test.** Dig 2 to 3 cups of soil from 6 to 8 inches deep in your planting bed. Let it dry on newspaper for 24 hours. Use a sieve or colander to sift rocks, roots, and other debris out of the soil.

    Pour 2 cups of the sifted soil into a quart jar and add 1 tablespoon powdered detergent. Then fill the jar with water, seal, and shake vigorously for 3 minutes.

    After 1 hour, the biggest sand particles will settle into a bottom layer. After 2 hours, the slightly smaller silt particles will settle into a second layer. And after 24 hours, the smallest clay particles will settle into a third layer.

    Measure the thickness of each layer and the total depth. To figure the percentage of each layer, divide that layer's thickness by the total depth. (Example: If all three layers total 3 inches and 2 inches of that is the clay layer, then about 66 percent of your soil is clay.)

    Ideally, all three layers will be about the same. When any of the three exceed 60 percent, that type is undesirably dominant, and amending with organic matter is advised.

4. **Nutrition test.** This gives you a breakdown of your soil's nutrients and its acidity level, which is important for determining how well the plants can use soil nutrients. Kits and test strips are available at garden centers, but I'd suggest do-it-yourself tests offered by Penn State University.

Kits are available at county Extension offices and most garden centers inexpensively. Dig and mix your own soil sample, dry it overnight, and mail it in the provided bags to Penn State's soil-test lab. Online kits and more information are available at http://agsci.psu.edu/aasl/soil-testing/soil-fertility-testing.

The test report will tell you what fertilizer is needed at what rates and whether you'll need sulfur or sulfur compounds (to make the soil more acidic) or lime (to make it more alkaline).

Right Plant, Right Spot

The next important job is knowing the intricacies of your yard so you can match the right plants to the site. You can't just buy whatever plants you like and put them where you think they look good. Different plants have different needs. The more finicky ones will croak if you don't give them exactly what they want, but even the toughest plants thrive best in conditions they prefer.

The good news is that there are plants for every situation. It's far better to know your situation and then match plants accordingly than to do what most people do—go to the garden center the first sunny weekend in May and buy what looks good to them.

The more you know plants, the easier this will be. But even if you don't know a coneflower from a conehead, you'll get up to speed by consulting the plant profiles in this book.

Also important is knowing a plant's eventual size. The No. 1 landscaping mistake is putting too big of a plant in too little of a space. A rhododendron planted 1 foot from a wall will quickly end up looking squished on the back side and fat on the front. Shrubs planted too closely together not only will waste your money (why buy more than you really need?) but will soon become a work-creating, jumbled, crowded mess.

Three spacing guidelines to follow are:

1. **Don't space by how a plant looks now.** Go by the "mature" sizes listed on the plant tag. When planting next to a wall, take the mature width and divide that in half. Plant no closer than that distance. (Example: A holly that will get 8 feet wide should be planted a minimum of 4 feet away from a wall.)

   If two plants of differing sizes are being planted next to one another, add the two mature widths together and divide in half to determine the minimum spacing. (Example: A 6-foot-wide viburnum and a 4-foot-wide sweetspire should be planted no closer than 5 feet apart. 6 + 4 = 10. Then 10 divided in half equals 5.)

2. **Watch the heights.** If your windowsill is 3 feet off the ground and you don't want to obstruct the view, look for plants that top out at 3 feet tall, unless you don't mind regular trimming.

   In borders and foundation plantings, arrange your garden so that the tallest plants are in the back. In an island bed in which you'll be able to view your plants from all angles, go with the tallest plants toward the middle and the shorter ones around the perimeter.

3. **Know the property lines.** A leading cause of neighbor spats is plants hanging over property lines. To be on the safe side, use the same planting rule as when planting next to walls. Take the mature width of the plant, divide it in half, and plant no closer than that distance from the property line.

Planting Time

Most plants sold in containers can be planted anytime during the growing season, so long as the soil isn't frozen or soggy and you keep the new plants well watered until the roots establish. Plants sold "bare root" should be planted in early spring. Give new plants a good soaking once or twice a week the entire first season when it doesn't rain, then water in hot, dry weather thereafter according to each plant's water needs (described in this book's plant profiles).

The two best planting windows are in early to mid-spring (March through May) and in early fall (Labor Day through October).

If you're starting with turfgrass, use a hose or rope to mark the boundaries of the new bed. Then spray-paint to make a line on the grass. Be sure there are no buried utility lines anywhere nearby before doing *any* digging. Call Pennsylvania One-Call at 811 or 1-800-242-1776 to have lines located at no charge.

You've got three main options at this point:

Option 1 is to manually strip all of the turf using a spade to cut under and lift up a piece at a time. Once the turf is off, improve the soil with organic matter as described above. Use the stripped-off patches of turf to replace bare or thin spots in the lawn. This is free sod! Or compost it.

Option 2 is to use an herbicide to kill the turf. Be careful not to let the spray drift onto anything else that you don't want to kill. Once the turf has died, it can be removed or tilled into the soil. Organic matter can be worked into the soil at this time, too. Check the label to determine when it's okay to plant.

Option 3 avoids herbicides but is useful only when you're starting with reasonably good native soil. Lay 6-page sections of newspaper and 2 to 3 inches of mulch or wood chips directly over the turfgrass. The newspaper and mulch will smother the turf and cause it to compost in place. Allow six months of smothering time before planting.

How to Plant

There's more to planting than sticking your new plant in the ground with the root end down. "Operator error" kills and maims many a plant, especially with too-deep planting and overmulching. Here's a quick planting how-to:

For trees and shrubs, if you're not planting in a prepared bed, dig a hole 3 to 5 times as wide as the rootball but no deeper than the rootball's height. The goal is to plant it on solid ground so the soil doesn't settle underneath and allow sinking. Improve the hole's soil with no more than 10 percent organic matter as described above.

For container-grown trees and shrubs, fray out (tease apart) any circling roots before planting. If you can't free the roots by gently pulling them out, make three or four vertical cuts in the rootball to break up the tight mat.

For balled-and-burlapped trees and shrubs, set the plant in the hole and then cut off and remove all of the burlap—or as much as is possible without causing major root damage. Also cut apart and remove wire baskets and remove any rope or strings around the trunk or roots.

Either way, set plants so their root flare (the point where the base of the trunk starts to widen) sits an inch or two *above* grade. This helps prevent the plant from ending up too deep from minor soil settling. Planting below grade doesn't make the plant more stable or encourage deeper roots. Instead, it can suffocate plant roots and rot buried bark.

Look at the plant from all angles to make sure it's in the ground straight. Then backfill halfway with soil, tamp, recheck for straightness, water, then finish backfilling and tamp. Cover the ground with 2 to 3 inches of wood or bark mulch and then water again.

Pennsylvania's climate allows a diverse plant palette.

Staking is *not* necessary unless you've planted a rather large tree with a comparatively small rootball or if you've planted on a slope or in a windy area. If you need to stake, use a wide band or strap and two or three stakes to secure the tree at chest or shoulder level. Remove staking after no more than one year.

Most annual and perennial flowers perform best if you work a bit more organic matter—2 to 3 inches—into the top foot of your planting bed. Fertilize according to your soil-test report. Then use a trowel to dig individual holes, fray out any tightly matted rootballs, and set each plant in the ground at the same level as it was in the pot. Cover the ground immediately after planting with 1 to 2 inches of mulch.

Perennials are best planted in spring and fall, although they can be planted throughout the summer if kept watered. Most annuals are sensitive to cold and are best planted after all danger of frost. That varies from year to year and region to region, but on average, the spring frost-free dates range from early May in Pennsylvania's southeastern corner to late May in the mountain regions.

Mulching

Mulch is any material that goes on top of your garden beds. It retains soil moisture, chokes out weeds, moderates changes in soil temperatures, and prevents soil-borne pathogens from splashing onto leaves. Organic mulch also adds nutrients to the soil as it breaks down.

All mulches have their own particular pros and cons. A quick rundown:

- **Stone over black plastic or weed fabric.** This chokes out weeds well in the early going, but weed seeds eventually blow in and root between the stone on top of the fabric. This also can impede oxygen into the soil and interfere with water (both in and out). It's inorganic and doesn't add nutrients or organic matter to the soil over time.
- **Shredded hardwood mulch** (sometimes called "tanbark"). This ground-up tree wood is readily available, good at stopping weeds, and relatively inexpensive, but Penn State University studies found that it's also the best growing medium for artillery or "shotgun" fungus. That's a nuisance fungus that shoots hard-to-remove tarry black "dots" on house siding and fencing. Penn State research found that wood mulch mixed in a 60-40 ratio with mushroom compost virtually eliminates artillery fungus. However, that mix isn't widely available from mulch vendors (at least not yet). Penn State also found that cedar and cypress mulch are good at discouraging artillery fungus.
- **Bark mulch.** Tree bark (usually from pines and other evergreens) is more often sold in bags than bulk, but it's less prone to artillery fungus. It's also less prone to matting than shredded hardwood. Matting impedes rain absorption. Pine bark nuggets and mini-nuggets don't break down as fast as the finer-ground pine bark mulch, but they occasionally blow around in the wind. Some people also don't like the look of them.

- **Shredded leaves.** These can be used by themselves or mixed with wood chips. Leaves drain well and are excellent at adding nutrients and worm-friendly organic matter to the soil, but they break down quickly and need more frequent reapplication.
- **Wood chips.** Tree trimmings do a good job at choking out weeds, but not everyone likes the color or look. They can be free if a tree company is working in the area. One of their best uses is for pathways if you don't like the look in foundation beds.
- **Pine needles.** These also add organic matter as they break down, let the soil "breathe" well, and slightly acidify the soil. However, they're not readily available in Pennsylvania and tend to be expensive when they are. Pennsylvanians also aren't used to the "southern" look of pine-needle mulch.
- **Cocoa-shell mulch.** Other than having a chocolately fragrance at first, this is expensive, tends to blow around when dry, is potentially harmful to dogs and cats, and often rots as it breaks down.

Whatever mulch you use, 2 to 3 inches is enough around trees and shrubs. One to 2 inches is enough around perennial flowers, and 1 inch is enough around annual flowers. In all cases, keep mulch from touching plant stems and trunks so as not to encourage rotting.

Weed Control

It's much easier to prevent weeds than to try to eradicate them after they've been allowed to get out of control. Your first line of defense is to avoid bare dirt.

If you follow proper plant spacing, eventually your landscape plants will grow to touch one another and fill all of the space before weeds can get to it. In the meantime, keep the area in between mulched. Ditto for any other area where you don't have plants, lawn, decking, or sidewalks.

Another way to prevent weeds is to apply an annual or twice-a-year treatment of a weed preventer. These granular products are sold at garden centers and stop most (or many) weeds from germinating from seed. Weed preventers can be spread over flower and shrub beds since they don't affect most plants that are up and growing (including existing weeds). Check labels carefully to determine if any of your plants are sensitive to the chemicals in the weed preventer.

Once a weed is up, you have two options. You can either pull it or dig it (get roots and all so the weed doesn't resprout) or you can spray it with a weed-*killer*. Some weed-killers are specific enough that they kill only certain types of weeds, such as broad-leafed ones or grassy ones. Others will kill most anything green. Again, read the labels and make sure you're applying what you think you're applying.

Watering

Both over- and underwatering can kill plants. Different soils and weather require different amounts of water. The best guide is to water as you usually do for the length

Shade gardeners don't have to give up "drama" in landscape beds when they have a multitude of textures and forms.

of time you usually do, then give the water a half-hour or so to soak in. Then check the soil to see how wet it is underneath. Use a long stick or your finger to probe a few inches down into the root zone.

Wetting only the mulch or top inch of the soil will do your plants little good. Shallow waterings may even do more harm than good by encouraging surface rooting that's more prone to drought injury. The goal is to dampen the soil not only in the rootball itself but in the soil beside and below the roots. That encourages roots to grow out and down.

Most people underestimate how much water it takes to dampen the soil that deeply. The probe test will help you zero in on exactly how long you should water and at what rate. If you're overdoing it, you'll see puddles that aren't soaking in within a few minutes.

Keep in mind that weather influences water needs. Plants use far more water in hot, dry, windy conditions than they do in cool, cloudy weather.

Signs of not enough water are wilting leaves and browning around the leaf edges. If your leaves do that, the best time to water was yesterday.

A Few Design Pointers

Before you dig that first hole or whack back that first overgrown arborvitae, get to know your landscape. This is especially important if you've moved into an existing home. By doing "knee-jerk" relandscaping, you might realize too late that the "ugly" tree you just cut down shaded the patio in the evening or that "overgrown" holly was hiding the neighbor's cigarette-billboard collection.

Resist the urge to make wholesale changes right away. Correct the obviously horrific situations up front, but spend at least one growing season observing. Pay attention to where the sun comes up and goes down. Look to see where water pools after a rain. Where is it hot and dry vs. damp and shady? Are there windy spots? What existing plants do you like over the course of the whole season? What plants annoy you? Which ones are bug- or disease-riddled or demanding more maintenance than you're willing to give?

Moving into a new home is a different scenario. You'll probably be in a hurry to get something planted, especially if there's no shade or if your back patio stares out into the neighbor's back patio. Even then, don't rush things at the expense of thoughtful planning. Good judgment in the beginning will save you lots of expense and maintenance later.

Some other questions to ask yourself include:

- How do you use or want to use your yard? Do you need open space for the kids to play? Do you want a peaceful retreat? Are there plants where you want to walk or paths where you'd rather sit?
- What style of plantings do you like? Formal and neatly trimmed? Or a looser, more naturalistic look?
- What colors do you like?
- Are there views that need to be screened out? Or are there views you want to preserve and even accent?
- How much maintenance are you willing to put in?
- What about factors such as fragrance, plant origin, four-season interest, animal problems, bird- and butterfly-attracting, and growing edibles?

If you need some help figuring out any of that, look for models. Thumb through gardening magazines or books to get a feel for what catches your eye. Visit a public garden or two. Drive around a few neighborhoods. Snap a few pictures.

Finally, have fun! Enjoy the beauty you're creating. Be thankful for the health you've got to bend down and pull that weed. Take a minute to appreciate the fresh air, the scent of your flowers, and the sight of that blue sky that follows the hailstorm.

Don't worry if you don't get everything "right" on the first try. You can always move your mistakes. After all, a garden is never really done. And once gardening gets in your blood, you'll be glad that's true.

George Weigel

How to Use *Pennsylvania Getting Started Garden Guide*

The 170 plants profiled in this book were selected based on their ease of growth, exceptional ornamental value, and high success rate throughout Pennsylvania. Most are low-care, interesting in more than one season, and unlikely to run into bug, disease, or animal troubles. Unless otherwise noted in a "Zones" listing or discussion under a plant's profile, all of the plants will grow in all of Pennsylvania's USDA Cold Hardiness regions.

The profiles include each plant's botanical name and how to pronounce it, another common name (if any), bloom times and colors, and planning guidelines on height and width.

The graphic symbols include seven possible "added benefits" of the plants. These include:

 Native plant to the United States

 Attracts beneficial insects, such as butterflies and bees

 Drought-resistant

 Edible

 Attracts hummingbirds

 Critter-resistant, primarily to deer, rabbits, and rodents

 Fall color

Three other symbols are used to denote the light needs of each plant. The symbol of a full sun indicates at least 8 hours of direct sun is needed each day. A quarter shadow indicates six to eight hours of sunlight, not midday. The symbol that's half orange and half blue represents part sun/part shade, meaning shade in the afternoon or dappled or indirect light all day. The symbol that's bluish represents shade, meaning little to no direct sun all day.

 Full Sun

 Part Sun

 Part Shade

 Shade

Choosing and Growing the Plants

The majority of each profile describes the plant and gives you a real-life rundown on what you can expect from it, based on how I've seen the plants perform in Pennsylvania gardens.

Subsections tell you when, where, and how to plant; how to care for each plant, including watering, fertilizing, and pruning information; regional tips that are pertinent to Pennsylvania; and how to use each plant in your yard.

Don't overlook the "Try These" section, because it spells out the particular species and varieties that are likely to give you the best success and highest performance.

USDA Hardiness Zone Map

Cold-hardiness zone designations were developed by the United States Department of Agriculture (USDA) to indicate the minimum average temperature for an area. A zone assigned to an individual plant indicates the lowest temperature at which the plant can be expected to survive over the winter.

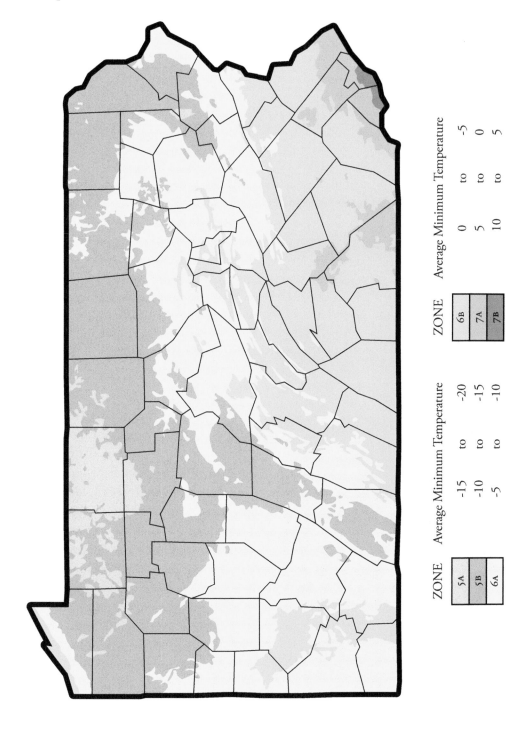

ZONE	Average Minimum Temperature
5A	-15 to -20
5B	-10 to -15
6A	-5 to -10
6B	0 to -5
7A	5 to 0
7B	10 to 5

ANNUALS

FOR PENNSYLVANIA

Annual flowers are ones that Pennsylvania gardeners primarily plant after the last frost of spring and then yank when fall's first frost ends their season-long bloom show. A few, such as snapdragon, dianthus,and dusty miller, are more cold hardy and can take a light April frost or two. Viola and pansy are the polar bears of annuals and can be planted either in early spring or in early fall to rebloom again the following spring throughout most of Pennsylvania.

Getting Started with Annuals

Annuals are commonly sold in plastic "cell packs" of three, four, or six small plants. Some of the best performers are sold singly (and more expensively) in 4- to 6-inch pots.

Begonias surround a water feature.

Many annuals also can be started from seed—either inside under lights or by direct-seeding them into the ground at frost-free time in spring. Zinnia, marigold, cosmos, larkspur, and cleome are five of the easiest to direct-seed outside.

Indoor-started seeds should go into a lightweight seed-starting mix 6 to 10 weeks before your area's last killing frost in spring, which typically ranges from early May in the Philadelphia area to late May in the colder northwest mountains. Keep the seedlings moist at all times, and grow them under plant lights or next to a sunny window in a cool room—ideally between 55 to 70 degrees. Give these young plants 7 to 10 days of increasing outdoor exposure before planting.

Because annuals are shallow-rooted, they'll need regular water at first. When rain doesn't happen, water annual flowers every 2 or 3 days for the first 6 weeks after planting. Then most will do fine with a soaking once or twice a week.

Keep the hose ever handy, though. If fiercely hot, dry weather causes annuals to wilt, they'll shut down flowering and possibly croak.

Most annuals flower best in full sun, although petunia, verbena, sweet alyssum, scaevola, flowering tobacco, and vinca bloom reasonably well in part-day sun. In less light, try even more shade-tolerant species, such as wax begonias, wishbone flowers, ivy geraniums, New Guinea impatiens, or browallia—or go with annuals that have colorful leaves (coleus, caladium, sweet potato vine, and polka dot plants).

A courtyard garden with Zonal geraniums.

Until recently, impatiens were the king of the annual shade garden. But a disease called downy mildew began wiping them out *en masse* recently, leading to a shift to mildew-resistant New Guinea impatiens and SunPatiens, or to other species altogether.

How to Maximize Bloom

Annuals appreciate fertile, moist, slightly acidic, and especially well-drained soil. It's helpful to work a ½- to 1-inch layer of compost, rotted leaves, or mushroom "compost" into the soil before planting. If you're starting with compacted ground, mix 2 or 3 inches of those organic amendments into the loosened top 10 or 12 inches of soil to create slightly raised planting beds.

Most annuals benefit from periodic applications of a balanced flower fertilizer (for example, 10-10-10 or 20-20-20) throughout their growing season. Some gardeners prefer granular fertilizers; others use liquid fertilizers applied through hose-end sprayers or mixed in watering cans. Also helpful is to work organic or pelleted, gradual-release fertilizer into the soil surface before planting.

Go easy on mulch. An inch of leaves, bark mulch, or bark chips is plenty. And keep it from touching the tender flower stems.

Annuals are best used in high-traffic spots where they deliver the most bang for the buck. Look to front-foundation beds, around patios, along walkways and especially in pots, hanging baskets, and window boxes. In containers, you'll likely need to water daily and fertilize at least every few weeks. Fertilizing at half-strength each week—"weekly weakly"—yields excellent results.

Snip off browned-out flowers ("deadheading") to keep the plants neat and to encourage continuing bloom. Otherwise enjoy the wall-to-wall color.

Annuals may be one-season wonders, but most of them make up for their short life span by blooming nonstop from the day you plant them until the day frost kills them.

Angelonia

Angelonia angustifolia

Botanical Pronunciation
an-jel-OH-nee-ah an-gus-tih-FOE-lee-ah

Other Name Summer snapdragon

Bloom Period and Seasonal Color
May to October; purple, lavender, pink, rose, white

Mature Height × Spread
12 to 18 inches × 12 to 15 inches

Angelonia is a fairly recent introduction to the arsenal of summer annuals and thus is not nearly so well known as "grandma favorite" marigolds, geraniums, and zinnias. To me, the flowers look a bit like orchids. Others say they resemble snapdragons. Don't let angelonia's dainty appearance fool you, though. This is one of the toughest performers in the heat and dry conditions of summer. The species comes in an ever-expanding range of colors and habits . . . some upright, some shorter and bushier, a few that are even somewhat spreading. The colors are mostly cool shades of purple, blue, pink, and white, plus a few bicolors. There are no hot reds or yellows. Yet. Angelonia makes an excellent cut flower.

When, Where, and How to Plant
Wait until all danger of frost is past to plant; a freeze will kill them. Angelonia blooms best in full sun but also gives a decent display in light shade. Improve lousy clay soil by working in an inch or two of compost before planting. Avoid planting near big trees, which will out-compete angelonia roots for moisture and nutrients. Angelonia also does well in pots and window boxes.

Growing Tips
Work a gradual-release fertilizer or granular, organic fertilizer into the soil at planting according to package directions. Look for one with roughly equal parts nitrogen, phosphorus, and potassium—the three numbers printed on the label. Then fertilize monthly with a liquid fertilizer formulated for flowers. Keep the soil consistently damp for best growth and flowering. When growing in a pot, fertilize at half-strength weekly. Water pots daily if it doesn't rain.

Regional Advice and Care
Most of the new cultivars bloom nonstop all summer and don't need to be deadheaded. But if any stems are sticking up with browned-out flowers, snip them off. If plants look "tired" by late season, cut back bare, leggy foliage, fertilize, and water well to refresh them until fall's first frost kills them. Yank them out at that point.

Companion Planting and Design
Dark purple angelonia looks particularly nice with pink shrub roses, or, for that matter, with any pink- or white-flowering summer shrub (spirea, butterfly bush, hydrangea, and so on). Use them in an edging along a walk or as a border along the driveway. Or spot them in any mixed garden, especially in a perennial border or cut-flower garden.

Try These
You won't go wrong with just about any angelonia variety you'll find at the garden center. My favorite is the compact Serena® series, which also happens to be one of the more available and less-expensive cell-pack types because it's grown from seed. Serenita® and Alonia® are two other very good compact types. The Angelface®, AngelMist®, and Carita® series are other excellent types that you might encounter in a variety of colors and growth habits.

Begonia

Begonia semperflorens-cultorum

Botanical Pronunciation
beh-GOHN-yah sem-per-FLOR-ens-kul-TOR-um

Other Name Wax begonia

Bloom Period and Seasonal Color
May to October; red, pink, rose, white

Mature Height × Spread
6 to 12 inches × 8 to 10 inches

Snooty gardeners might look down on the old-fashioned wax begonia as cheap and common, but those traits are precisely why this plant has been so widely used for so long. For starters, wax begonias grow in a wide variety of conditions. They'll perform in sun or shade, dry or damp, and they're one of the best competitors around big tree roots. Begonia's glossy leaves help it fight off drought and disease. Bugs aren't interested. Neither are animals, which is a big plus for deer- and rabbit-ravaged gardeners trying to grow an annual. The flowers are nickel-sized and lie open across the top of the glossy foliage; some varieties have dark leaves. Wax begonias are very compact growers, staying under a foot in both height and spread. What's not to love?

When, Where, and How to Plant
Wait until all danger of frost is past before planting. Space wax begonias closer than most annuals because they're such slow, compact growers—8 to 10 inches is good. Morning sun and afternoon shade is ideal, but wax begonias will tolerate *everything* from full sun to full shade, although their bloom is weaker in shade. An inch of mulch is plenty.

Growing Tips
Keep the soil damp for best growth. You'll need to water ones in full sun more often. Work a gradual-release fertilizer or granular, organic fertilizer into the soil at planting according to package directions. Then fertilize monthly with a liquid fertilizer formulated for flowers. If you're growing them in a pot, use half-strength fertilizer weekly and water daily.

Regional Advice and Care
Other than occasional watering, wax begonias take little care. They clean themselves and look fine without deadheading. About the only threat is the occasional slug that eats the leaves of shade-planted begonias at night. A slug repellent or scattering of sand over the soil surface usually stops that. Frost kills begonias in fall. Yank them out as you thank them for a summer of troublefree color.

Companion Planting and Design
Begonia's compact habit makes them ideal for lining the front of garden beds, especially along house foundations and walkways. They won't flop over into the lawn or sidewalk like some rangier choices. Red and white begonias pair well with golden summer bloomers (for example St. Johnswort, black-eyed Susans, and coreopsis), while pink and rose ones pair nicely with blue or purple summer bloomers (hydrangeas, butterfly bush, and caryopteris).

Try These
Even no-name, generic wax begonias are good, but even better are the Ambassador®, Cocktail®, and Doublet® series. Senator® begonias have dark leaves. If you're okay with the higher price, try the related and bigger Dragon Wing™ begonia (*Begonia coccinea*), which has red stems, red leaf undersides, and brilliant red flowers. Those are superb in pots and baskets. The Big® and Whopper® series are pot stars too. 'Gryphon' is a related beauty for the shade (pots or ground).

Blue Salvia

Salvia farinacea

Botanical Pronunciation
SAL-vee-ah far-ih-NAY-see-ah

Other Name Mealycup sage

Bloom Period and Seasonal Color
Early May to early November; blue, violet, white, blue-white bicolor

Mature Height × Spread
14 to 18 inches × 12 to 14 inches

Here's another good annual for the animal-plagued gardener. Blue salvia is bulletproof against both furry and buggy pests. And it's one of the best at producing in the hottest, driest, poorest-soil spot you've got. This Texas native is one of the last annuals to go down in a summer drought. Blue salvia is also tolerant of cool weather. It can withstand a light late-spring frost and even a frost or two in fall. The flowers are spiky and blue, although the species has violet and white versions. In warmer parts of the U.S., blue salvia is a perennial, but in Pennsylvania, it's an annual. I like these better than red salvia (*Salvia splendens*) because they bloom longer, bloom more consistently, and don't cry out to be deadheaded.

When, Where, and How to Plant
Plant after danger of spring frost passes, spacing plants about 1 foot apart. Full sun is best, although they'll do okay in some light shade. Blue salvia is tough under adversity, but planting in loose, damp soil gives peak performance. An inch of mulch is plenty.

Growing Tips
Water twice a week for the first 6 weeks, then once-a-week watering is fine when it doesn't rain. Work a gradual-release fertilizer or granular, organic fertilizer into the soil at planting according to package directions. Then fertilize monthly with a liquid fertilizer formulated for flowers. Fertilize blue salvias in a pot at half-strength weekly and water daily. Deadhead browned flower shoots.

Regional Advice and Care
Although blue salvia is sold as an annual, it may well survive winter, especially along the state's southern tier and in the Philadelphia area. Don't pull these in fall when they wither. Wait until spring and see if any shoots emerge from the base of the plants. If they do, cut off last year's dead stems and enjoy a free encore. If not, yank and plant new. Powdery mildew occasionally infects leaves and hampers bloom in damp weather, but the plants usually grow through it without treatment.

Companion Planting and Design
Pink shrub roses and blue salvia make a great sunny combination. Blue salvia also pairs well with the silvery foliage of annual dusty miller and with pink-flowering petunias or pink vinca. Consider locating plants throughout a perennial border to smooth over any gaps among the perennial blooming times.

Try These
'Victoria' is a readily available variety that's still among the best. 'Signum' and 'Rhea' are two other darker blue newer varieties, and 'Evolution' is slightly bigger and bushier (18 inches) with violet flowers. A sage cousin is *Salvia guaranitica* 'Black and Blue', which grows about 2 feet tall and wide, has dark blue flowers with black bases, and is the absolute *best* plant for attracting hummingbirds. Try that one in a deck pot.

Browallia

Browallia speciosa

Botanical Pronunciation
bro-AL-ee-ah spees-see-OH-sah

Other Name Bush violet

Bloom Period and Seasonal Color
May through October; blue, blue-violet

Mature Height × Spread
10 to 24 inches × 10 to 12 inches

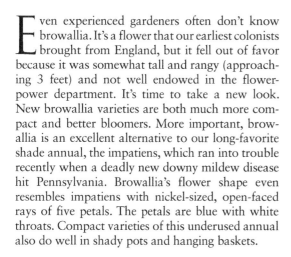

Even experienced gardeners often don't know browallia. It's a flower that our earliest colonists brought from England, but it fell out of favor because it was somewhat tall and rangy (approaching 3 feet) and not well endowed in the flower-power department. It's time to take a new look. New browallia varieties are both much more compact and better bloomers. More important, browallia is an excellent alternative to our long-favorite shade annual, the impatiens, which ran into trouble recently when a deadly new downy mildew disease hit Pennsylvania. Browallia's flower shape even resembles impatiens with nickel-sized, open-faced rays of five petals. The petals are blue with white throats. Compact varieties of this underused annual also do well in shady pots and hanging baskets.

When, Where, and How to Plant
Plant after danger of spring frost passes. Space about 1 foot apart. Browallia is best suited for morning sun and afternoon shade. They'll do okay in more light if kept watered, and they'll tolerate more shade at the expense of fewer flowers. An inch of mulch will be plenty. Browallia prefers somewhat acidic soil; add sulfur to the planting bed if your soil is alkaline (test first).

Growing Tips
Water twice a week for the first 6 weeks, then weekly if it doesn't rain. Work a gradual-release fertilizer or granular, organic fertilizer into the soil at planting according to package directions. Then fertilize monthly with a liquid fertilizer formulated for flowers. In a pot, feed them at half-strength weekly and water daily. Deadheading isn't needed.

Regional Advice and Care
Browallia doesn't like brutal heat. In the hot South, it usually shuts down blooming by August, but in Pennsylvania, it usually blooms nonstop from May to frost. During heat waves, water two to three times a week to counteract heat stress. Spider mites and whiteflies are occasional problems that can be treated with insecticidal soap.

Companion Planting and Design
Northern and eastern house-foundation beds are ideal. So is a pot or basket in any shady spot, such as under a covered deck, porch or patio. Good partners are other summer-blooming shade-lovers that bloom pink, white, or rose, including pink or white hydrangeas, variegated dogwood, and pink- or white-blooming abelia. *Begonia* 'Dragon Wing Pink' is a good annual companion.

Try These
The best browallia I've seen yet is Marine Bells®, a compact variety that stays under 1 foot and puts out dark purplish blue flowers that cover about 50 percent of the rounded plant most of the season. Also good is Blue Bells®, which is about twice as tall with equal flower coverage in a medium blue shade. Heirloom varieties can be started from seed, either directly in the ground or inside in late winter. These often reseed themselves outside but are taller and not as heavy in bloom.

Celosia

Celosia argentea

Botanical Pronunciation
seh-LOE-see-ah ar-GEN-tee-ah

Other Name Cockscomb

Bloom Period and Seasonal Color
May through October; red, gold, yellow,
yellow-orange, pink

Mature Height × Spread
6 to 20 inches × 10 to 14 inches

Celosia is an old-fashioned, sun-loving annual flower known in colonial days as "cockscomb." The classic color was red, and the plants readily reseeded themselves each spring, forming flower heads that looked like brains. More popular these days are types that produce 12- to 16-inch-tall plants with fat, plume-type flowers. Red is still the main color, but celosia also now comes in gold, yellow, pink, and yellow-orange. Give celosia a hot, sunny spot in the garden, and it'll bloom all summer. Forget shady spots and especially wet spots, which likely will rot its roots. Beyond that, celosia is a heat- and drought-tough plant that's seldom bothered by bugs or animals. It's also one of the best annuals for use as a cut or dried flower.

When, Where, and How to Plant
Plant in May after all danger of frost has passed. Sub-freezing temperatures will kill baby celosias. Space about 1 foot apart. Stick with full-sun locations. Prevent rotting by planting in slightly raised beds that have been improved by mixing an inch or two of compost into the top 10 or 12 inches of loosened existing soil. An inch of mulch is plenty.

Growing Tips
Water twice a week for the first 6 weeks, then once a week when it doesn't rain. Work a gradual-release fertilizer or granular, organic fertilizer into the soil at planting according to package directions. Then fertilize monthly with a liquid fertilizer formulated for flowers. In a pot, fertilize half-strength weekly and water daily. Deadhead browned celosia shoots to keep the plants looking neat.

Regional Advice and Care
Most newer varieties bloom more heavily and grow with less flopping and browning than older varieties. Staking usually isn't necessary. Many types can be started by direct-seeding into the garden in May—especially the heirloom cockscomb types. *Don't overwater*; that can lead to stem or root rotting. Rotting also may occur in rainy years in poorly drained beds. Assuming all goes well, celosia will bloom nonstop until frost kills them. Then yank them.

Companion Planting and Design
Red and/or gold celosia look good along the south- or west-facing fronts of houses, particularly those with red brick or yellow, burgundy, or maroon trim. Bands of celosia also do well lining sunny walks and driveways or skirting the base of tall evergreens such as arborvitae, spruce, and hollies. A mass of celosia is striking in a sunny island bed, where it makes a good summer replacement for a massed planting of spring tulips.

Try These
My favorite plume type is New Look®, a dark red bloomer that grows 14 to 16 inches tall and has dark leaves. Fresh Look Gold® is an excellent yellow-blooming, green-leaved, 14-inch, plume type. Cousin Fresh Look Red® is a similar red bloomer. For that old-time "brain" look, give me Prestige Scarlet®, which blooms a brilliant red on foot-tall plants.

Coleus

Solenostemon scutellarioides

Botanical Pronunciation
suh-len-oh-STEE-mon skoo-tul-air-ee-OY-deez

Bloom Period and Seasonal Color
Insignificant flowers; grown for foliage of burgundy, lime, copper, gold, velvety red, and endless choice of variegated multi-tones

Mature Height × Spread
8 inches to 3 feet × 12 to 18 inches

No annual flower offers better, brighter foliage than coleus. Who needs flowers when the leaves are deep burgundy edged in neon gold or a glowing two-toned lime? Breeders are actually trying to produce varieties that *don't* bloom so gardeners don't have to pinch off the ho-hum lavender spikes. Coleus used to be primarily a red-and-gold bicolor foliage plant that long was one of the Big 3 shade annuals along with impatiens and begonia. It's become even more popular lately due to the downy mildew disease that has struck impatiens and the explosion of new coleus colors, forms, and habits (including trailers). Although older, seed-grown varieties are still best in shade or half-day sun, many of the new introductions perform even better in sun than in shade.

When, Where, and How to Plant
Plant after danger of spring frost passes. Space smaller coleus 1 foot apart, bigger ones 18 inches apart. Check the label to determine whether your variety of choice is suggested for sun, shade, or both. Although coleus does well in a range of garden settings, their top calling is in pots.

Growing Tips
In the ground, water weekly when rain doesn't do the deed for you. Coleus are comparatively light feeders, but they appreciate a nitrogen-rich granular fertilizer or gradual-release fertilizer worked into the soil at planting and a "booster" dose or two of a liquid balanced fertilizer in season. In a pot, fertilize monthly and water daily. Cut back or cut off stems anytime they are growing too big. Primping won't hurt coleus.

Regional Advice and Care
Pot up a few coleus to grow as houseplants over winter before frost kills them. Coleus is among the easiest of all plants to root from cuttings. Some gardeners save a "mother" plant or two and start baby plants from the snipped tips inside toward the end of winter.

Companion Planting and Design
Many new coleus varieties are bushy enough and showy enough to make stunning flower pots by themselves—no partner needed! If you like trailers spilling down from your pots, pair coleus with yellow sweet potato vines or 'Limelight' licorice vine (*Helichrysum petiolare*). In the ground or in pots, dark-leafed elephant ears also make superb coleus mates. And for a knockout texture *and* color pairing, plant coleus with perennial golden variegated Hakone grass (*Hakonechloa macra*).

Try These
For garden beds, the 'Fairway' and 'Wizard' series are good performers and inexpensive. Give them shade, though, at least in the afternoon. I like the duck-foot types for their small, colorful leaves, but for big-leaf show-stoppers, give me Big Red Judy® (burgundy), 'Fishnet Stockings' (heavily netted gold and burgundy), and 'Watermelon' (red, cream, and green blend). Also excellent are Kong Rose™ and the whole Stained Glassworks™ and 'Solar' series.

Dusty Miller

Senecio cineraria

Botanical Pronunciation
sen-EE-see-oh sin-er-AR-ee-ah

Other Name Silver ragwort

Bloom Period and Seasonal Color
Insignificant flowers; grown for silvery gray foliage

Mature Height × Spread
8 to 15 inches × 10 to 12 inches

Some plants are stars of the garden show. Others are valuable "supporting actors." The latter describes dusty miller, a Victorian-era favorite whose silvery gray leaves improve the performance of just about any flower it's paired with. The classic combinations of red salvia and dusty miller and red begonias and dusty miller were used so often that many gardeners abandoned this Mediterranean native for overuse. But there's good reason for a dusty miller comeback. Actually there are three good reasons: 1) it's extremely drought-tough, 2) it seldom runs into bug, disease, or animal trouble, and 3) it's versatile enough to fit into any color scheme. You won't find a lot of variations as in many annual choices these days, but the basic few oldies are still goodies.

When, Where, and How to Plant
Dusty miller is fairly cold tolerant and able to survive a mild frost or two. It can be planted earlier than most annuals, two or three weeks ahead of spring's last frost (mid-April to early May). Space 10 to 12 inches apart. Full sun is best, light shade is still okay. Avoid wet soil, which can rot dusty miller's roots. An inch of mulch is plenty.

Growing Tips
Water twice a week for the first 6 weeks to establish the roots, then there's usually no need to water except in an extended hot, dry spell. Dusty miller is among the most drought-tough annuals. Work a gradual-release fertilizer or granular, organic fertilizer into the soil at planting according to package directions. Then fertilizer usually isn't needed. Pinch off any button-sized yellow flowers that form; they're not showy and detract from the silvery foliage.

Regional Advice and Care
Although dusty miller is sold as an annual, it often survives winter, especially along Pennsylania's southern tier and in the Philadelphia area. Don't pull these in fall! Let them stand over winter, and see if any new growth occurs in spring. If so, cut off last year's damaged stems and enjoy a free show. If no new growth occurs by May, discard these plants and buy new ones.

Companion Planting and Design
Dusty miller's silvery gray foliage is a neutral shade, so you won't go wrong with any partner. Plant it in a hot, dry area along with other sun annuals. Dusty miller looks especially nice paired with blue flowers (blue salvia, scaevola, or evolvulus), purple flowers (heliotrope or petunias), or pink flowers (vinca, pentas, or petunias). Plant a few for season-long foliage color in a perennial garden.

Try These
There's not much selection to pick from, but the few choices you'll find are good ones. 'Silver Dust' is a common 15-incher with velvety silver leaves. New Look® is my favorite with its silvery oak-shaped leaves and compact 10-inch size. And 'Cirrus' is a silvery white variety with dissected leaves.

Euphorbia

Euphorbia graminea

Botanical Pronunciation
yew-FOR-bee-ah grah-MIN-ee-ah

Other Name Annual spurge

Bloom Period and Seasonal Color
May to October; white, light pink

Mature Height × Spread
12 to 18 inches × 14 to 20 inches

This particular type of euphorbia (spurge) was unknown in U.S. gardens until the Proven Winners variety Diamond Frost® ('Inneuphdia') stormed onto the market in 2005. It and a line of successors have met with deserved rave reviews ever since for reliable and prolific mounds of airy white flowers all summer long. A single plant grows to the size of a basketball and produces a flower show reminiscent of the wedding-favorite baby's breath. Don't be fooled by the dainty flowers, though. Annual euphorbia is extremely tough in heat and drought, seldom runs into any setbacks, and has even become a popular holiday-season plant when paired with its euphorbic cousin, the poinsettia. This plant is also related to—but looks nothing like—the yellow-blooming perennial spurges.

When, Where, and How to Plant
Plant outside, 12 to 18 inches apart, after all danger of frost has passed. Annual euphorbia does equally well grown in pots or in the ground. It blooms best in full sun but performs reasonably well in light shade. Improve lousy clay soil by working in an inch or two of compost before planting. Mulching with an inch of bark is plenty.

Growing Tips
Using the package directions as your guide, work a gradual-release fertilizer or granular, organic fertilizer into the soil when planting. Euphorbias like to be fertilized monthly (use a liquid fertilizer formulated for flowers). Water once or twice a week for the first 6 weeks, then water is needed only during hot, dry spells. Water container plants every day or two. Euphorbia is one of the most drought-tolerant annuals. Deadheading is not necessary; the plant cleans itself as it keeps flowering.

Regional Advice and Care
Annual euphorbias can be potted and grown inside as a houseplant all winter. In spring, cut it back to a few inches and gradually acclimate it to the outside before replanting or repotting. In a few weeks, it'll start blooming for another season. Be aware that some people have skin allergies to the milky sap that's a hallmark of all euphorbias. Use gloves when handling any euphorbia if you're in that camp.

Companion Planting and Design
While annual euphorbia is stunning alone in a blue or black pot, it's become popular in black-and-white pot combinations along with such partners as black petunias, black sweet potato vines, and black elephant ears. In the garden, it pairs nicely with pink shrub roses, pink petunias, and any pink, blue, or purple bloomer or any dark-leaved shrub.

Try These
The original Diamond Frost® is excellent. The closely related *Euphorbia hypericifolia* 'Silver Fog' is more compact and even heavier in bloom. 'StarDust White Sparkle' is my favorite (most compact of all with heavy white blooming). *Euphorbia hybrida* Breathless Blush™ is an excellent light pink bloomer that also has dark spotted green leaves.

Geranium

Pelargonium × hortorum

Botanical Pronunciation
pel-ar-GO-nee-um hor-TOR-um

Other Name Zonal geranium

Bloom Period and Seasonal Color
May to October; red, pink, white, salmon, lavender, orange-red

Mature Height × Spread
12 to 30 inches × 14 to 24 inches

The geranium is such a well-known flower that it's one even non-gardeners can usually identify. That's ironic because, although people know the look, the plant is technically an annual called *Pelargonium*—which is different from the true perennial geranium that blooms primarily in lavender. Nonetheless, the geranium (let's go with the flow) consistently has been one of America's top five best-selling annuals for decades. People can't get enough of the unending variations, even though old-hand gardeners often turn up their nose at the plant as common, overused, and weak in flower-power. I'll admit, geranium is not one of my favorites, but somebody must like it because 150 million sell each year. The name "zonal geranium" comes from the dark, horseshoe-shaped coloration in its green leaves.

When, Where, and How to Plant
Plant outside after all danger of frost has passed. Geranium does best in pots and window boxes in full sun. In the ground, plant 14 to 18 inches apart and avoid wet spots, because poor drainage is a cause of root rotting. Work an inch or two of compost into the soil before planting. An inch of bark mulch to finish off will be just fine.

Growing Tips
Geraniums are heavy feeders. Work a gradual-release fertilizer or granular, organic fertilizer into the soil at planting according to package directions, then fertilize monthly with a liquid fertilizer formulated for flowers. Water once or twice a week for the first 6 weeks, then weekly throughout summer.

Water potted plants every day or two and fertilize every week or two. By far the biggest job is constantly snipping off the spent flower heads. Brown petals left dangling atop the plant look bad.

Regional Advice and Care
Geranium is slightly hardier than the average annual and often survives the first light frost or two of fall (down to about 25 degrees). Many gardeners save geraniums over the winter by storing them in an unwatered pot in the basement or even hanging them bareroot over attic rafters. Early spring cuttings are easy to start from the tips of a mother plant grown as a houseplant in winter.

Companion Planting and Design
A mass of red and pink geraniums looks nice, but to my eye, the best use is pairing geraniums with one or two other annuals in a mixed combination. Red ones pair nicely with yellow annuals (bidens, mecardonia GoldDust™, or zinnia Zahara Yellow™, for example), and pink ones look great with dusty miller or alyssum Snow Princess®.

Try These
The new "interspecific" hybrids are heavy blooming and heat tolerant. Look for the Caliente® and Calliope® series and many more interspecifics on the horizon. 'Sarita Dark Red,' 'Savannah Hot Pink', and Fantasia Violet™ are three top scorers in Penn State's Trial Gardens. For a part-shade hanging basket or window box, try the glossy-leaved trailing ivy geranium (*Pelargonium peltatum*).

Lantana

Lantana camara

Botanical Pronunciation
lan-TAN-ah KAM-mar-ah

Other Name Shrub verbena

Bloom Period and Seasonal Color
May to early November; red, orange, yellow,
gold, pink, bicolors

Mature Height × Spread
12 to 24 inches × 18 to 24 inches

     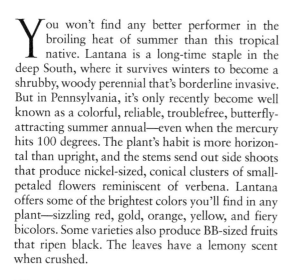

You won't find any better performer in the broiling heat of summer than this tropical native. Lantana is a long-time staple in the deep South, where it survives winters to become a shrubby, woody perennial that's borderline invasive. But in Pennsylvania, it's only recently become well known as a colorful, reliable, troublefree, butterfly-attracting summer annual—even when the mercury hits 100 degrees. The plant's habit is more horizontal than upright, and the stems send out side shoots that produce nickel-sized, conical clusters of small-petaled flowers reminiscent of verbena. Lantana offers some of the brightest colors you'll find in any plant—sizzling red, gold, orange, yellow, and fiery bicolors. Some varieties also produce BB-sized fruits that ripen black. The leaves have a lemony scent when crushed.

When, Where, and How to Plant
Plant after danger of spring frost passes in your hottest, sunniest spot. Lantana does equally well in the ground as in pots or hanging baskets. In the ground, most varieties will sprawl 18 to 24 inches, so give them more room than most annuals. Work an inch or two of compost into the soil before planting. Then mulch; an inch is enough.

Growing Tips
Water twice weekly for its first 6 weeks, then water as needed only in hot, dry spells. Lantana is one of the toughest annuals in dry weather. Work a gradual-release fertilizer or granular, organic fertilizer into the soil at planting according to the fertilizer directions. Then feed lantana once or twice over summer with a liquid fertilizer designed for flowers. Feed container plants at half-strength weekly and water daily.

Regional Advice and Care
Lantana usually lives through the first frost or two of fall, adding bright color to the fall landscape. Don't yank it out even when the plant finally browns. In warm winters in the warmest parts of Pennsylvania, lantana may push new growth from its roots in spring. If that doesn't happen by early May, *then* yank the dead plants. In season, don't hesitate to cut back any growth anytime it's getting too rangy. Mites occasionally cause stippling damage to leaves; spray insecticidal soap if that becomes intolerable.

Companion Planting and Design
Lantana is substantial enough to fill a pot or hanging basket by itself. It also looks good surrounding black-leaved elephant ears or hibiscus. In the ground, pair with other bright-colored annuals (zinnia, marigold, gloriosa daisy, nasturtium) or with red or gold perennials, such as black-eyed Susan, daylily, Shasta daisy, coreopsis, and mum. Lantana also perks up the base of evergreens.

Try These
Lucky™ 'Pot of Gold' is a searing gold bloomer that's earned several perfect scores in Penn State's Trial Gardens. 'New Gold' is another excellent tried-and-true golden bloomer. You won't go too wrong with any color in the Landmark™, Bandana®, or Patriot™ series.

Marigold

Tagetes species and hybrids

Botanical Pronunciation
ta-JEE-teez

Bloom Period and Seasonal Color
May through October; yellow, gold, red, orange, lime-white, bicolors

Mature Height × Spread
8 to 36 inches × 10 to 24 inches

The marigold has been used as a garden plant dating to medieval times when monks and nuns tied it to the Virgin Mary and began calling it "Mary's gold." No wonder the marigold has stood the test of time. It's one of the easiest annual flowers to start from seed, either inside or directly into the garden, and it's tough in heat, drought, and broiling sunlight. The familiar pincushion flowers sit atop sturdy stems that pop up from the green, lacy foliage. The colors are bright ones—red, orange, yellow, and lime-white—in addition to "Mary's gold." Double-petaled types are especially showy. Marigold has a unique odor described as "peppery" or "musky." Not everyone likes that trait, and some say it triggers their nasal allergies.

When, Where, and How to Plant
Wait until all danger of frost is past in May either to plant transplants or to plant seeds directly in loosened soil. Plant smaller transplants 10 to 12 inches apart, larger ones 12 to 14 inches apart. Stick with full-sun locations and well-drained soil that has been improved by working in an inch or two of compost. After planting, mulch with an inch or so.

Growing Tips
Water twice weekly for the first 6 weeks, then weekly when it's hot and dry. Marigolds aren't water hogs. They're also light feeders. Work a gradual-release fertilizer or granular, organic fertilizer into the soil at planting according to package directions, then fertilize once in midsummer with a liquid fertilizer made for flowers. Fertilize marigolds growing in a pot at half-strength every week or two and water daily. The biggest job is deadheading the browned flowers to keep the plants looking neat and to encourage continuing bloom.

Regional Advice and Care
Being Mexican natives, marigolds grow only during frost-free times. Don't rush to plant them before spring frost is done. Pull them out when fall's first frost turns them into brown blobs. You might need to stake taller African marigolds, but the more popular French types top out at a compact, no-stakes-needed 12 inches.

Companion Planting and Design
Marigolds hit their peak as massed displays in Victorian times. That's still impressive, but most people use marigolds these days in smaller clusters along sunny house foundations or along driveways and walkways. Also use marigolds to add color around the base of ornamental grasses and evergreens. They do well in sunny pots with a grass or spiky plant in the center and sweet potato vines trailing around the perimeter.

Try These
Go with the shorter French marigolds for their compactness. Good series include 'Aurora', 'Safari', Durango®, and 'Bonanza' (especially 'Bonanza Bolera', a maroon and gold beauty). If you're okay with taller 2-footers, try African types in the 'Taishan', Discovery™, and 'Inca' series. 'Lemon Gem' is a signet type (*Tagetes tenuifolia*) with edible petals.

New Guinea Impatiens

Impatiens hawkeri

Botanical Pronunciation
im-PAY-shenz HAWK-er-eye

Bloom Period and Seasonal Color
May through October; pink, red, rose, white, orange, lavender

Mature Height × Spread
12 to 30 inches × 16 to 24 inches

New Guinea impatiens is a relatively new find, hitting the U.S. market following a 1970 Asian plant hunting trip by Pennsylvania's Longwood Gardens and the U.S. Department of Agriculture. Good thing it came along because this impatiens species resists the downy mildew disease that has devastated America's top-selling annual, the bedding impatiens (*Impatiens walleriana*). Growers and gardeners alike began moving toward this cousin, which has longer, more slender leaves than bedding impatiens, but also does well in shady spots. New Guinea impatiens have the same open-faced flowers and most of the same colors as bedding impatiens, in nearly every shade except black and blue. Although the number of flowers per plant is fewer, New Guinea flowers (and plants) are bigger.

When, Where, and How to Plant
Plant in May after threat of frost passes. New Guinea impatiens do best in pots that get morning sun and afternoon shade. These are more sun-tolerant than bedding impatiens but they still prefer some afternoon shade. Deeper shade is fine, but flowering will be less. New Guineas like plenty of water but not so much that the soil stays wet and rots the roots. In the ground, plant in compost-enriched, slightly raised beds. Space plants 15 to 18 inches apart.

Growing Tips
Water in-ground plantings twice a week for the first 6 weeks, then once or twice a week throughout summer. Work a gradual-release fertilizer or granular, organic fertilizer into the soil at planting according to package directions. Then fertilize monthly with a liquid fertilizer formulated for flowers. Container plants should be fertilized at half-strength weekly and watered daily. Deadheading isn't needed.

Regional Advice and Care
The two keys to New Guinea success in hot Pennsylvania summers are picking the right site and regulating water. That's why growing them in pots usually yields the best results; pots drain well and can be moved if the light is too much or too little. Once you get the hang of the light and water needs, though, New Guineas can be showy, troublefree garden plants as well as pot stars.

Companion Planting and Design
Try edging or spotting them in northern and eastern foundation beds as a replacement for bedding impatiens. Or use them in deck or patio pots where the light is morning sun and afternoon shade. New Guinea impatiens are showy enough to fill pots on their own. No partner is needed.

Try These
Growers have begun selling affordable 4-packs of seed-started New Guinea impatiens in response to the downy mildew debacle. 'Divine' is such a series that's done well in the ground for me. SunPatiens® is a hybrid between New Guinea and bedding impatiens that's resistant to downy mildew and fairly sun-tolerant. Otherwise you'll find a ton of choices—including some with variegated and bronze leaves. Almost all have scored well in Penn State's Trial Gardens.

Ornamental Pepper

Capsicum annuum

Botanical Pronunciation
KAP-sih-kum AN-yoo-um

Bloom Period and Seasonal Color
May through October; white or lavender flowers; fruits of red, orange, yellow, gold, cream, black, purple

Mature Height × Spread
10 to 28 inches × 10 to 18 inches

This vegetable garden refugee comes with such attractive foliage and showy fruits that it's used in flower pots and ornamental gardens. The ornamental pepper is part of the same species as the grocery-store bell pepper and the hot pepper used in salsa. It's just a group separated out from the edibles because of good looks. You can eat the fruits of ornamental peppers, but beware: most of them are very hot and seedy. If you use ornamental peppers in the garden, be careful when handling. Oils from the fruits can sting your fingers and, worse yet, your eyes if you rub them after handling open fruits or seeds. Some varieties have purple, cream, and/or black foliage. But the brightly colored fruits are the true stars.

When, Where, and How to Plant
Ornamental peppers are tender (affected by cold), so wait until all danger of frost is gone to plant. They'll do well in pots or in beds; just give them *lots* of sun and well-drained soil. You can buy transplants or start your own from seed indoors 8 to 10 weeks ahead of planting time. In the ground, space 12 to 15 inches apart. After planting, top with an inch of mulch.

Growing Tips
Water twice a week for the first 6 weeks, then once or twice a week throughout the summer. Work a gradual-release fertilizer or granular, organic fertilizer into the soil at planting according to package directions. Fertilize once or twice more during the growing season with a balanced liquid or granular fertilizer. Taller varieties benefit from staking.

Regional Advice and Care
Peppers love heat. They'll thrive in July and August and add brilliant color as the fruits mature in early fall. Frost eventually kills them, so discard them when that happens, but not before saving some of the seeds collected from mature, shriveling fruit pods. Start the seeds inside the following spring. Or leave a few peppers in the ground over winter for the seeds to drop naturally. They'll often sprout on their own the following May.

Companion Planting and Design
Ornamental peppers make great accent plants in pots. In the landscape, they pair nicely with ornamental grasses, evergreens, and other hot-colored annuals that coordinate with the fruit colors. Garden centers often sell ornamental peppers for fall planting; their hot colors go well with mums, straw bales, and corn stalks.

Try These
I have three favorites. One is 'Black Pearl', which has nearly jet-black leaves and shiny, marble-sized fruits that mature from black to red. Another is 'Purple Flash', a beauty with two-toned purple-and-black leaves and round black fruits that ripen red. And third is 'Calico', which has purple, cream, and green variegated leaves and oblong black fruits that ripen red. There are many other great ones, though. Try what grabs your eye.

Pentas

Pentas lanceolata

Botanical Pronunciation
PENT-ahs lan-see-oh-LATE-ah

Other Name Star flower

Bloom Period and Seasonal Color
May through October; pink, rose, red,
lavender, white

Mature Height × Spread
1 to 3 feet × 12 to 18 inches

You'll find no better annual than pentas for attracting bees, butterflies, and to a lesser extent, hummingbirds to the garden. Once these warm-weather lovers kick into prime form in June, you'll almost always find pollinators buzzing around the umbrella-shaped flower clusters. Pentas get their common name from the star shapes of the pea-sized flowers that grow together to form the clusters. Despite running into almost no trouble from bugs or animals, pentas still aren't very well known. They've only recently become more common, most likely due to improved varieties that bloom heavier and grow to more compact sizes. If you've tried this one before and weren't impressed, give them a new look (which, by the way, is the name of a compact new pentas series).

When, Where, and How to Plant
Plant in May after all danger of frost has passed. Pentas are African natives that like it warm and sunny. Space 12 to 14 inches apart. Plant in slightly raised beds that have been improved by mixing an inch or two of compost into the top 10 or 12 inches of loosened existing soil. After planting, add an inch of mulch (keeping it away from the stems).

Growing Tips
Water twice a week for the first 6 weeks, then once a week when it doesn't rain. Work a gradual-release fertilizer or granular, organic fertilizer into the soil at planting according to package directions. Then fertilize monthly with a liquid fertilizer

formulated for flowers. In a pot, fertilize at half-strength weekly and water daily. Older, taller types benefit from staking.

Regional Advice and Care
Don't worry if you don't see many flower buds on plants at the garden center. Pentas start slow and bloom better as temperatures heat up. Snip off browned flower clusters to neaten the plant and encourage continued flowering. If plants get too tall for your taste or look tired by late summer, trim them back by up to one-third, then water and fertilize to rejuvenate. Pull them out when frost kills the plants in fall.

Companion Planting and Design
Pentas are excellent annual additions to a sunny bird or butterfly garden. The newer compact ones also are nice massed along the south- or west-facing sides of houses, and they add season-long color when located throughout a mixed border garden. They also do well as part of pot grouping when paired with an upright (ornamental grass or spiky centerpiece plant) and a trailer (such as sweet potato vine, licorice vine, or wandering Jew).

Try These
The foot-tall Graffiti® series (eight different choices) is the best I've seen so far for compactness and flower power. Also good is the Butterfly series, whose varieties grow a notch taller to about 18 inches, and the New Look® series, which grows about 12 to 14 inches tall.

Petunia

Petunia hybrids and selections

Botanical Pronunciation
peh-TOON-yah

Bloom Period and Seasonal Color
May to October; red, pink, purple, white, black, assorted pastels and bicolors

Mature Height × Spread
6 to 18 inches × 14 to 24 inches

No wonder everybody's planting this old-fashioned annual again. New generations of petunias are light years ahead of Grandma's petunias, which turned to mush after a rain and cried out for spent blossoms to be pinched off. The 1995 introduction of the Wave® petunia changed all of that, giving gardeners a weather-resistant, super-blooming petunia that spread vigorously with no pinching needed. Numerous varieties since have been as good or better, including improved versions of the original Wave®. The marked improvements have made the petunia Pennsylvania's sun annual of choice—especially in pots and hanging baskets. You'll find a wide assortment of colors, flower sizes, and growing habits these days (mounding, bushy, ground-huggers, and so on), and you won't go wrong with hardly any of them.

When, Where, and How to Plant
Plant outside after danger of frost has passed. Petunias are at their best in pots and hanging baskets, but they'll also perform well in a loose, compost-enriched garden bed. They bloom best in full sun but do reasonably well in part-day sun. Most new ones spread, so 16- to even 24-inch spacing in the ground is adequate. Wave® types and several others can be started from seed inside in late winter. Top with an inch of bark mulch.

Growing Tips
In the ground, work a gradual-release fertilizer or granular, organic fertilizer into the soil at planting according to package directions, then fertilize monthly with a liquid fertilizer formulated for flowers. Water once or twice a week for the first 6 weeks, then weekly throughout summer. In pots and baskets, water every day or two and fertilize every week or two with the same liquid flower fertilizer. Clip back growth that's getting too long or leggy.

Regional Advice and Care
Petunias are somewhat cold-tolerant and usually survive the season's first and last light frosts. The main in-season threat is the budworm, a caterpillar that bores into the base of flower buds and aborts flowering. Sprays of Bt solve it. Rabbits occasionally munch on young transplants, so use an animal repellent or temporary fencing if that's an issue.

Companion Planting and Design
Three petunias in a pot or basket yield a solid ball of color within weeks, and the show usually lasts all season. Petunias also are excellent in masses in any sunny foundation or border bed or lining a sidewalk or driveway. Plant a few atop retaining walls and let colorful arms drip down the stone or blocks.

Try These
My all-time favorite annual flower is Supertunia® Vista Bubblegum, a neon pink petunia that's nearly covered in flowers all summer. But lots of series have racked up nearly perfect scores in Penn State's Trial Gardens, including many Supertunia®, Surfinia®, 'Sanguna', 'Blanket', Whispers™, Potunia®, 'Famous', Opera Supreme™, Littletunia™, and Wave® progeny (Easy Wave®, Shock Wave®, and Tidal Wave®).

Scaevola

Scaevola aemula

Botanical Pronunciation
skay-VO-lah ay-MEW-lah

Other Name Fan flower

Bloom Period and Seasonal Color
May to October; blue, blue-purple, white

Mature Height × Spread
6 to 14 inches × 14 to 18 inches

Never heard of this one? That's because scaevola or "fan flower" is fairly new to our market, arriving here as an Australian import in the 1990s. It has done very well in Pennsylvania, tolerating our summer heat and humidity without complaint. Gardeners are drawn mainly by the flower color. Most scaevola varieties bloom blue or blue-purple. The only other color you'll find is white. The plant's habit is spreading and trailing, which is why most gardeners use this annual in hanging baskets or as a perimeter plant in a big pot. The flowers emerge from each leaf cluster along the stems, opening into a fan pattern. Look closely and you'll see that all of the petals grow curiously off to one side of the flower.

When, Where, and How to Plant
Plant after danger of spring frost. Scaevola blooms best in full sun but will do okay in part-day sun. Its best use is in hanging baskets or pots. If you plant in the ground, avoid poorly drained spots, because scaevola is prone to root rots in soggy soil. Head off rotting by planting in slightly raised beds that have been improved with an inch or two of compost. An inch of mulch added after planting is plenty.

Growing Tips
Water twice a week for the first 6 weeks, then water is needed only in hot, dry spells. Scaevola is drought-tough once established. During planting, work a gradual-release fertilizer or granular, organic fertilizer into the soil following the package directions. Then fertilize once or twice over summer with a liquid fertilizer formulated for flowers. Container plants should be fertilized with the same liquid product every two to four weeks and watered daily.

Regional Advice and Care
Scaevola is unlikely to run into bug or disease trouble, but the one thing that often troubles them in Pennsylvania gardens is the rascally rabbit. If you've got a bunny problem, keep your scaevola in a pot or basket. Fall frost will kill scaevola, so be brave and yank it and compost it after it browns. It's not coming back next year.

Companion Planting and Design
Scaevola is showy enough to make an attractive hanging basket all by itself. In a container, it pairs well with an upright pink annual, such as begonia Dragon Wing Pink™ or alternanthera 'Party Time,' or with a pinkish to reddish grass, such as fountain grass 'Rubrum' or 'Fireworks'. In the ground, use it at the front of a bed, backdropped by pink vinca or pink pentas.

Try These
The new Surdiva® series has been the best performer in Penn State's Trial Gardens. New Wonder® and Whirlwind® are other solid blue performers you'll likely find in garden centers. Bombay® is another good series. I like the rich color of Bombay Dark Blue®, and Bombay White® is the best white bloomer I've seen.

Sweet Alyssum

Lobularia maritima

Botanical Pronunciation
lob-yew-LAHR-ee-ah mahr-ih-TEE-mah

Bloom Period and Seasonal Color
May to November; white, pink, lavender

Mature Height × Spread
4 to 10 inches × 12 to 18 inches

Fragrance has been bred out of so many annual flowers in the quest for compact sizes, better bloom, and more colors, but the sweet alyssum is one that has still—for the most part—retained a sweet scent. The fragrance is mild and reminiscent of honey. Sweet alyssum plants are short, mounding, and somewhat spreading, making them popular choices for edging beds. The flowers form pea- to dime-sized dainty clusters that in cool weather nearly cover the small, narrow, silvery green leaves. Native to the Mediterranean, sweet alyssum tolerates drought reasonably well, although it likely will shut down flowering until cooler, damper weather comes along. Animals hardly ever bother it. Recently introduced varieties of sweet alyssum are marked improvements over older ones.

When, Where, and How to Plant

Direct-seed sweet alyssum into the garden in early May. Press the tiny seed into the soil surface and keep it damp. Last year's plants often reseed themselves, and "volunteers" can be transplanted as you like. Plant store-bought young plants 12 inches apart in full sun to part-day shade. Avoid wet spots. Ideally, plant in slightly raised beds that have been improved with compost. Mulch lightly; no more than an inch is needed.

Growing Tips

Sweet alyssum is a light feeder. Work a gradual-release fertilizer or granular, organic fertilizer into the soil at planting according to package directions, then fertilize once or twice during the growing season with a liquid fertilizer made specifically for

flowers. Water once or twice a week for the first 6 weeks, then water as needed only during hot, dry spells. In containers, water every day or two and use the liquid fertilizer monthly.

Regional Advice and Care

Don't worry if sweet alyssum shuts down flowering in the heat of summer. It'll resume when cooler temperatures return. If plants look brown or ratty in midsummer, give them a trim and a good soaking. Sweet alyssum often blooms beyond fall's first frost or two, so remove plants only after they've browned and collapsed. To encourage reseeding, wait until end of winter to remove plants.

Companion Planting and Design

Shrub roses and hydrangeas are ideal big brothers for sweet alyssum, which look like petite mounds of baby's breath flowers. Sweet alyssum also pairs nicely with bigger or bushier pastel annuals, such as blue salvia, elephant ears, *Perilla* 'Magilla' or 'Gage's Shadow', vinca, and zinnia. And it performs well in window boxes and pots as well as rock gardens and edging situations.

Try These

Snow Princess® is the best variety I've grown yet. It flowers well in the heat but really performs in fall, sometimes even into December in my garden. Frosty Knight® is another excellent new white bloomer, and Blushing Lavender® is a good lavender-flowered cousin. The 'Easter Bonnet' and 'Clear Crystal' series are two good performers that come in less expensive 6-packs.

Verbena

Verbena hybrids

Botanical Pronunciation
ver-BEE-nah

Bloom Period and Seasonal Color
May to October; purple, lavender, red, pink, white, bicolors

Mature Height × Spread
8 to 12 inches × 14 to 24 inches

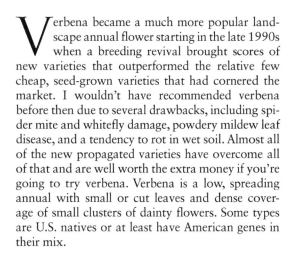

Verbena became a much more popular landscape annual flower starting in the late 1990s when a breeding revival brought scores of new varieties that outperformed the relative few cheap, seed-grown varieties that had cornered the market. I wouldn't have recommended verbena before then due to several drawbacks, including spider mite and whitefly damage, powdery mildew leaf disease, and a tendency to rot in wet soil. Almost all of the new propagated varieties have overcome all of that and are well worth the extra money if you're going to try verbena. Verbena is a low, spreading annual with small or cut leaves and dense coverage of small clusters of dainty flowers. Some types are U.S. natives or at least have American genes in their mix.

When, Where, and How to Plant

Good drainage is *essential*. That's why verbena does better in pots and baskets than in the ground. If you plant in the ground, avoid soggy spots and create slightly raised beds by working compost into the soil. An inch of mulch after planting is plenty. Plant container plants or in-ground in spring after danger of frost, in full to part-day sun.

Growing Tips

Work a gradual-release fertilizer or granular, organic fertilizer into the soil at planting according to package directions, then fertilize monthly during the growing season with a liquid fertilizer formulated for flowers. Water once or twice a week for the first 6 weeks, then weekly in dry weather. Water containers every day or two, and feed the liquid fertilizer every week or two.

Regional Advice and Care

Inferior verbenas often rot in rainy weather and get powdery mildew disease (whitish powdery substance on the leaves). Spider mites and whiteflies also suck the green color out of the leaves. 'Quartz' and 'Obsession', for example, are two common types I've given up growing for these reasons. Insecticidal soap can stop the bugs, but the best solution is to switch to a variety with better genes. Cooler spots or some afternoon shade is best in Zone 7 gardens.

Companion Planting and Design

If you're a beginner, try verbena in a hanging basket, where it partners nicely with petunias. That's the combo used in many municipal streetlight baskets. Verbena also makes a nice trailing plant in a pot with uprights, such as ornamental grasses, spiky cordyline, or tropical hibiscus. In the ground, verbena makes a good edging in front of boxwoods, yews, azaleas, and other evergreens.

Try These

You'll pay a little more, but stick with such series as Babylon®, Superbena®, Tapien®, Tukana®, Lanai®, 'Aztec', 'Lascar', and 'Costa del Sol'. Also try the reseeding native, the 3-foot-tall *Verbena bonariensis*. A few verbenas overwinter in warmer parts of Pennsylvania and are sold as perennials, such as the purple-flowering 'Homestead Purple'.

Vinca

Catharanthus roseus

Botanical Pronunciation
kath-ah-RAN-thus RO-see-us

Other Name Madagascar periwinkle

Bloom Period and Seasonal Color
May to October; pink, white, rose, red, lavender

Mature Height × Spread
6 to 16 inches × 12 to 15 inches

Have a broiling hot, sunny, dry spot where you'd like to add summer flowers without watering every 2 minutes? Annual vinca is your answer. If these Madagascar natives can thrive in mall parking-lot islands surrounded by asphalt and exhaust-spewing cars, they'll likely do well in your hot yard. Vinca is an upright plant with dark green, glossy leaves and five-petaled, pinwheel flowers that look a lot like impatiens. Recent breeding has given us numerous flower colors and new varieties with blooms nearly the size of quarters. It's very showy. Newer varieties also are better at overcoming the main vinca threat of root-rotting fungal disease. A few new varieties (Cora Cascade™, for example) have a more trailing habit, giving a new option for sunny hanging baskets.

When, Where, and How to Plant

Vinca is *very* sensitive to cold temperature and needs warmer greenhouse temperatures than most annuals. If you see yellowish leaves on a plant at the garden center, that's a possible sign of chill stress from which the plant may never fully recover. Wait until all danger of frost is past to plant. Space 1 foot apart in full sun. Plant in very well-drained soil. Adding an inch of mulch after planting is good.

Growing Tips

Water twice a week for the first 6 weeks, then vinca needs a drink only occasionally in hot, dry weather. These are very drought-tough but will rot in poor drainage or wet soil. Work a gradual-release fertilizer or granular, organic fertilizer into the soil at planting according to package directions. Then fertilize monthly with a liquid fertilizer formulated for flowers. In a pot, fertilize half-strength weekly and water every day or two. Pull them out when frost kills them in fall.

Regional Advice and Care

Cold temperatures and soggy soil are the two biggest enemies. Don't be too quick to plant annual vinca outside. Late May is not overly conservative. Avoid wet locations, plant only in well-drained soil, and don't overdo it with the sprinkler. Vinca seldom runs into bug or animal issues.

Companion Planting and Design

Mix vinca with other heat-lovers in a west- or south-facing foundation bed, in a full-sun island garden, or along a hot driveway or sidewalk. Juniper, holly, spruce, and boxwood are good evergreen partners. Butterfly bush, blue mist shrub, spirea, and crapemyrtle are good shrub partners. And lavender, purple coneflowers, purple salvia, switchgrass, and Russian sage are good perennial partners. Vinca do very well in sunny pots too.

Try These

Give me the Titan™ series for its big flowers and hefty, 14-inch, bushy plants. The Nirvana® and Cora™ series are also solid performers in a variety of colors. For less expensive 4- and 6-packs, I've been pleased with the Pacifica series, which includes the excellent red-flowered 'Pacifica Red'. Also worth trying are the Heatwave and Cooler series.

Zinnia

Zinnia species and hybrids

Botanical Pronunciation
ZINN-ee-ah

Bloom Period and Seasonal Color
May to October; red, gold, orange, yellow, pink, lime, lavender, bicolors

Mature Height × Spread
8 in to 4 feet × 12 to 24 inches

A long-time favorite that hit its heyday in Victorian times, the zinnia is one of the tallest, showiest annual flowers. It also makes one of the best cut flowers. Our fore-gardeners no doubt used lots of zinnias because they're one of the easiest flowers to grow from seed. Classic old varieties grow to 3 and even 4 feet tall and produce showy pompon flowers at the top. Recent breeding has focused on shorter, heavier-blooming, disease-resistant types that tend to have more daisylike flowers. All do well in heat and sun, and all still make great cut flowers. The common zinnia (*Zinnia elegans*) is native to Mexico, but the narrow-leaf *Zinnia angustifolia* is also native to the southeast United States as well.

When, Where, and How to Plant
Zinnia doesn't like cold, so wait until all danger of frost has passed to plant transplants from the garden center or plant seeds directly into the ground. Zinnia also can be started inside from seed in late March under lights. Plant in full sun and well-drained soil, ideally in compost-improved raised beds. Space 12 to 18 inches apart. An inch of mulch is plenty.

Growing Tips
Water twice a week for the first 6 weeks, then zinnia needs water only occasionally in hot, dry spells. Work a gradual-release fertilizer or granular, organic fertilizer into the soil at planting according to package directions. Then fertilize monthly with a liquid fertilizer formulated for flowers. In pots, fertilize at half-strength weekly and water every day or two. Deadhead spent flowers. Yank plants when frost kills them in fall.

Regional Advice and Care
Zinnia is susceptible to leaf spotting and mildew as well as root-rots in wet soil. Head off disease by planting in sun and well-drained soil and giving adequate space between plants. A better solution is to try one of the new disease-resistant varieties. Prevent rotting by avoiding wet spots or poorly drained soil and by avoiding overwatering. Head off occasional Japanese beetle damage by spraying Neem oil or handpicking them.

Companion Planting and Design
Zinnia is a must in any cut-flower garden. It attracts hummingbirds and is a good choice in a sunny pollinator garden. Masses of zinnia provide inexpensive color to sunny island gardens, or seeds can be interplanted with other annuals and reseeding perennials to create a meadow garden or cottage garden.

Try These
The Zahara™ and Profusion series are the two best to date with vibrant colors, compact size (12 to 18 inches tall), and virtually no disease. My single favorite zinnia is Zowie Yellow Flame™, a 2-footer with orange-red flowers that have yellow matchstick-like tips. The Magellan™ series has classic, double-petaled flowers on foot-tall plants. And good, old-fashioned taller types include 'Benary's Giant', 'Oklahoma', and 'Dreamland'.

BULBS

FOR PENNSYLVANIA

You'll usually find this group of plants sold in mesh bags or packages *inside* a garden center as opposed to growing in pots outside. The common denominator among bulbs, corms, rhizomes, and tubers is that these are all fleshy plant parts that are planted in the ground—usually when they're dormant and leafless. Leaves and flower stalks emerge from the buried part weeks to months later.

True bulbs are swollen organs that have small, living plants already growing inside; examples include tulip, daffodil, and hyacinth. Corms are fat, flat, scaly, or fibrous stems whose leaves and flowers emerge from nodes on the corm; their examples include crocus, gladiolus, and freesia. Tubers are enlarged roots that send out shoots and roots from nodes along their surface; they include dahlia, cyclamen, and perennial (tuberous) begonias. And rhizomes do the same thing, except they're swollen underground stems instead of roots; examples include canna, ginger, and most iris.

For simplicity's sake, I'll refer to this whole group as "bulbs."

Spring or Summer? Hardy or Not?

Bulbs can be grouped by when they bloom (spring-flowering or summer-flowering) and by whether they'll survive if left outside in the ground all year (hardy or non-hardy).

Spring-flowering bulbs include the "big three" of tulip, daffodil, and hyacinth as well as a raft of smaller and lesser-planted species, such as crocus, Siberian squill, glory-of-the-snow, Grecian windflower, and snowdrop.

Spring bulbs are planted in fall.

Tulips and muscari in spring.

Soon after, the bulbs put down roots, and their hormonal "clocks" start ticking. After the appropriate amount of winter chilling, bulbs send up leaf shoots and then flower stalks that bloom anywhere from February (snowdrop and winter aconite) to June (ornamental onion). Then they die back and go dormant the rest of the season.

Summer-flowering bulbs are best planted in spring. These put down roots and then grow leaf shoots and flower stalks soon after. They die back at the end of the season and spend the winter in dormancy. Most summer bulbs bloom for several weeks at various times during the summer.

Almost all spring bulbs are winter-hardy. That means you plant them once and leave them in the ground to come back year after year.

Most summer bulbs, however, are *not* winter-hardy in Pennsylvania. They'll flower the first season after planting, but if you don't dig them and store them dormant inside over winter, they'll turn to mush in the frozen soil. The main exception is the lily. Most lilies are winter-hardy statewide and can be left in the ground over winter.

Allium spaerocephalum

Other popular summer bulbs that need to be lifted and stored soon after fall's first light frost include gladiolus, dahlia, canna, calla, caladium, freesia, and tuberoses (*Polyanthes tuberosa*).

Planting and Using Bulbs

All bulbs appreciate loose, fertile, well-drained soil that's slightly acidic to neutral in pH. Cold, wet clay is *the* fastest way to kill them. Lessen that threat by working an inch or two of compost, mushroom soil, rotted leaves, or similar organic matter into the loosened top 10 or 12 inches of existing soil to create slightly raised planting beds. Always plant bulbs with the pointed end facing up.

Bulbs tend to be grossly underused in Pennsylvania gardens. That's because spring-blooming ones have the distinctly un-American trait of requiring patience between planting and bloom, and most summer ones require the work of repeated planting, lifting, storing, and replanting.

You'll get the biggest impact by planting bulbs in clusters instead of single rows. Try them in front of foundation beds or in any front yard garden, around the bases of trees, around mailboxes, along fences, and in borders. Spring bulbs interplant nicely with perennials, which take over the space when the bulbs go dormant by late spring. They do well in pots too.

But arguably the best feature of spring bulbs is that they have the good sense to flower when Pennsylvanians can use it most—at the end of a cold, gray winter.

Canna

Canna × generalis

Botanical Pronunciation
KAN-nah jen-er-AL-iss

Bloom Period and Seasonal Color
Summer; red, orange, yellow, pink

Mature Height × Spread
2 to 8 feet × 1 to 2 feet

If you're looking for something big, bold, and bright, you won't find many plants that do all three better than cannas. The wide, strappy leaves rival banana foliage in size; the plants grow a hefty 4 feet and up; and the bloom colors are sizzling red, orange, and yellow. Although often called "canna lilies," cannas are actually summer-blooming rhizomes (not true lilies) hailing from the tropics and subtropics. Their flowers just *look* like lily flowers. In their native Mexico and other Zone-8-and-warmer climates, cannas are durable perennials that make traffic-stopping, roadside hedge plantings. In Pennsylvania, we have to content ourselves growing cannas as annuals; that is, dig them in fall to store over winter or buy new ones each spring.

When, Where, and How to Plant
Cannas like three things above all else: heat, sun, and moisture. Wait until mid- to late May to plant them outside. A sunny wet meadow or boggy area is ideal, although cannas are tough enough and versatile enough to do reasonably well in dry conditions and nearly any soil type. Cannas also do well in pots and will grow as aquatic plants in water gardens.

Growing Tips
If you're starting with your own dormant, saved rhizomes, loosen the soil to 10 or 12 inches, work in an inch or two of compost, then plant the rhizomes so the tips are just below the surface. Otherwise, plant store-bought plants at the same depth as they're growing in their pot. Cannas are heavy feeders, so give them a monthly dose of a fertilizer formulated for flowers throughout the growing season. Keep the soil consistently damp for best growth and flowering. Cut off the flower stalks after the flowers have browned.

Regional Advice and Care
Get a jump by starting rhizomes in pots inside in early to mid-April. Give them gradually more light outside over 7 to 10 days before planting. Japanese beetles sometimes chew holes in canna leaves and eat flower buds. Neem oil is an effective control. When fall's first frost knocks back canna foliage, cut plants to 2 or 3 inches, dig and dry the rhizomes in shade for a few days, then store them in paper bags inside (ideally at 45 to 55 degrees F) over winter.

Companion Planting and Design
Cannas are most often used as centerpiece plants in large flower pots. They're especially effective in pots around swimming pools and sunny decks, underplanted with other bright-colored summer annuals, such as lantana, petunias, marigolds, and sweet potato vines. Or use them in a mixed border garden or as backdrops to shorter annual flowers.

Try These
My favorite two are 'Tropicanna' (orange flowers and brilliant yellow-and-green striped foliage) and 'Wyoming' (orange flowers and dark foliage). 'Bengal Tiger' is similar to 'Tropicanna' and 'Dark Knight' is a red bloomer with dark foliage.

Crocus

Crocus species

Botanical Pronunciation
KRO-kus

Bloom Period and Seasonal Color
March to April; purple, lavender, yellow, white, assorted two-tones

Mature Height × Spread
4 to 5 inches × 4 to 6 inches

These short, upward-facing, cup-shaped flowers are beloved not only for their bright colors but because they're among the earliest bloomers in spring. Most are up and flowering by March, often poking through the last of the melting snow. Although technically a corm (a flat, scaly stem that looks something like a squashed acorn), crocus is Pennsylvania's fourth best known spring bulb, after tulip, daffodil, and hyacinth. Crocus corms are readily available in garden centers and home centers each fall, both in the most common colors of purple, lavender, or yellow or in multi-colored mixes. The 4-inch-tall, narrow, grass-like leaves emerge in late winter, followed by 3 to 4 weeks of flowers. By mid-spring, the plants collapse into dormancy, where the corms remain hidden until the following season.

When, Where, and How to Plant
Plant crocus corms from mid-September through November. Crocus does best in full sun but also grows well in part shade, including under shade trees. Prevent rotting by improving the soil with compost and planting in slightly raised beds. Plant two corms to 3 inches deep and 4 to 6 inches apart with the tiny, emerging nodes pointing up. Cover the bed with 1 inch of bark mulch or chopped leaves.

Growing Tips
Fertilizer isn't needed at planting if you've added compost. Crocus is not a heavy feeder, but for peak performance, scratch a balanced, granular fertilizer formulated for bulbs into the soil surface early each fall. Water immediately after planting to settle the soil; otherwise, no watering is needed.

Regional Advice and Care
Let the foliage die back to the ground in spring, then either rake it off or toss a light layer of mulch on top. As long as the leaves are green, they're "recharging" the corms for next year's blooms. Crocus occasionally are eaten by rabbits, and buried corms are sometimes eaten or moved by rodents. If you run into that, use animal repellents or cover the planted bed with chicken wire, covered lightly by mulch.

Companion Planting and Design
Crocus look best when they're planted in masses or clusters as opposed to straight lines. Assuming all goes well, the planting will fill into sheets of color that gradually expand each season. Plant annual flowers among and even over top of crocus corms in May after crocus goes dormant for the season. Crocus corms also can be planted into lawns; just try to delay the season's first mowing until the crocus foliage has begun to yellow. Crocus is also one of the best choices for "forcing" into bloom in pots inside over winter.

Try These
If rodents are a problem, try "Tommy" crocuses (*Crocus tommasinianus*). Three good varieties of those are 'Ruby Giant', 'Barr's Purple', and 'Lilac Beauty'. Large-flowering crocuses (*Crocus vernus*) are the showiest and deer-resistant, but they're also apparently tastier to rodents.

Daffodil

Narcissus species

Botanical Pronunciation
nar-SISS-us

Bloom Period and Seasonal Color
Late February to June; gold, yellow, white, various pastels, two-tones

Mature Height × Spread
4 to 24 inches × 6 to 12 inches

If you're a bulb beginner, start here. Daffodils are virtually failproof, they hardly ever run into bug or animal trouble, and they're among the best bulbs at coming back year after year. Unlike tulips, which often peter out after a few years, daffodil patches usually spread and improve with age. Daffodils have strappy leaves and flower stalks topped by distinctive two-part flowers, short cups or trumpets projecting from a fan of petals. Choices number in the thousands, ranging from 4- to 6-inch miniatures to 2-foot-tall heirlooms and with bloom times from late winter through early June. Colors are mostly gold or yellow but also white, apricot, peach, and other pastels. Some daffodils are fragrant, especially the Jonquilla and Tazetta types.

When, Where, and How to Plant
Plant daffodil bulbs mid-September through November, about 6 inches apart and three times as deep as their height (3 to 8 inches down, depending on type). Mulch with 1 to 2 inches of bark, shredded wood, or chopped leaves after planting. Daffodils perform best in full sun, but they also make an excellent spring groundcover under shade trees, provided they get 8 hours of light a day. Plant in slightly raised, compost-enriched beds.

Growing Tips
Fertilizer isn't needed at planting if you've added compost. Scratch a balanced, granular fertilizer formulated for bulbs into the soil surface early each fall. Watering is not needed, other than right after planting to settle the soil.

Regional Advice and Care
Don't worry if daffodils send up leaf shoots in winter. There's no need to cover them. At worst, you'll end up with some brown leaf tips. Let the foliage die back to the ground in spring. Don't cut, braid, or otherwise mess with green leaves, which "recharge" the bulbs for next year's bloom. If your planting gets crowded, dig up bulb clumps after the leaves die back, separate individual bulbs, and replant them immediately 6 inches apart. Daffodils are mildly poisonous (causing nausea), so don't let pets or children eat any parts.

Companion Planting and Design
Use daffodils to edge or flank evergreen plants, which make an excellent backdrop to highlight the bright gold, yellow, and white blooms of a daffodil colony. Daffodils also interplant well with mid- to late-season perennials, such as daylilies, coneflowers, black-eyed Susans, mums, and hostas. The daffodils poke up, flower, and enter dormancy as the perennial foliage takes over the space. Annual flowers can be planted among or over top of dormant daffodils in late spring.

Try These
Daffodils have so many variations that the American Daffodil Society breaks them into 13 different divisions. You won't go wrong with any. I particularly like the short, early, golden/yellow bloomers 'Hawera', 'Tete-a-Tete', and 'February Gold'. 'Ice Follies', 'Dutch Master', and 'Carlton' are three taller oldies-but-goodies.

Dahlia

Dahlia species and hybrids

Botanical Pronunciation
DALL-ee-uh

Bloom Period and Seasonal Color
Late summer to early fall; red, pink, orange, yellow, white, bicolors

Mature Height × Spread
2 to 4 feet × 1 to 2 feet

This large family of mega-bloomers has a somewhat finicky reputation because it's prized by collectors and often grown in formal, labeled displays in botanical gardens. Although dahlias can run into several bug and disease problems, they usually pay off with big, gorgeous flowers—at least in the first season. To keep them going year after year in Pennsylvania gardens, dahlia tubers need to be dug, overwintered inside, and replanted each spring. Native to Central America, dahlias will freeze and rot over winter if left in the ground, except possibly in well-drained beds in the southeastern corner of the state. Dahlias bloom from late summer into early fall, making them the best bulb-family choice for late-season color. They also make ideal cut flowers.

When, Where, and How to Plant
Dahlias are best planted using dormant tubers bought in spring from garden centers or catalogs. Wait until mid- to late May to plant. Plant the tubers with the "eyes" (little bumps) facing up, about 3 to 4 inches deep and 1 to 2 feet apart. Full sun and raised beds are perfect. A site in light shade is okay. Control weeds and retain soil moisture with a 2-inch soil covering of bark, wood mulch, or chopped leaves.

Growing Tips
Most dahlias benefit from staking to keep the plants from flopping when the flowers open. Place the stakes first, then plant the tubers to avoid unfortunate stabbing incidents. Fertilize monthly with a granular organic fertilizer or with a flower fertilizer rich in phosphorus and potassium (something such as a 5-10-10 ratio). Keep the soil consistently damp.

Regional Advice and Care
Pinch off the tips of the main shoots when plants reach 1 foot to encourage compact growth and improved branching. Watch for mites, leafhoppers, and aphids feeding on the leaves. Spray with insecticidal soap to control them. Snip off browned flowers to neaten plants and to encourage more blooms. When frost browns the foliage in fall, cut plants to the ground, and dig the tubers. Dry them in the shade for a week, brush off excess soil and store inside over winter in peat moss or sawdust in boxes or paper bags, ideally at 45 to 55 degrees F. Don't let the stored clumps touch one another.

Companion Planting and Design
Dahlias work best in small groups in the middle or back of a mixed border garden, where they'll be the late-season stars. Combine them with spring and early-summer perennials so there's something going on until the dahlias kick in by August and September.

Try These
Selection is *huge*. The American Dahlia Society lists 16 different dahlia types (pompon, water lily, cactus, peony, anemone, for example) and 15 different colors. Go with the colors and forms that grab you. Me? I'm partial to the "dinner-plate" varieties that put out flowers as wide as 8 to 10 inches.

Glory-of-the-Snow

Chionodoxa forbesii

Botanical Pronunciation
kye-ahn-oh-DOCKS-ah FORBS-ee-eye

Bloom Period and Seasonal Color
April; purplish blue, pink

Mature Height × Spread
5 to 6 inches × 4 to 6 inches

W hy, oh, why is this glorious little bulb so underused? The only thing I can figure is that people just don't know it, even though it has been in plant catalogs since the late 1800s. Glory-of-the-snow puts out masses of 6-inch-tall, star-shaped flowers early each spring and, unlike the much better known tulip, gets better with age. Colonies fill in and slowly creep outward to make stunning purplish blue carpets for 2 to 3 weeks each spring. Yet glory-of-the-snow stops short of turning invasive. You won't find it popping up in unwanted spots or rooting out into the lawn, for example. Care is almost nil. It'll bloom in partly shaded sites. And even the deer, bunnies, and rodents don't bother it. What's not to like?

When, Where, and How to Plant

Plant bulbs mid-September through November, about 2 to 3 inches deep and spacing 4 to 6 inches apart. Full sun is best, in slightly raised beds that have been improved by mixing an inch or two of compost into the loosened top 10 to 12 inches of existing soil. Cover the bed with 1 inch of bark or wood mulch or chopped leaves.

Growing Tips

Fertilizer isn't needed at planting if you've added compost. In early fall, mix in a balanced, granular fertilizer formulated for bulbs into the soil surface. Water immediately after planting to settle the soil; otherwise, there's no need to water.

Regional Advice and Care

Glory-of-the-snow almost takes care of itself. Your main job is raking off the foliage after it's browned in late spring. But the leaves are small and narrow enough that they almost disappear after they collapse while heading into dormancy by late spring. I don't even bother raking. I just toss a little fresh mulch over the bed, and call it a day. If you'd like to enlarge your planting, dig up and separate the bulbs right after the leaves turn brown, and replant them immediately in their new home.

Companion Planting and Design

A massed groundcover colony of glory-of-the-snow under trees or shrubs makes a colorful and glorious spring carpet. Use it to add early-season life under shrubs that are just starting to leaf out, such as shrub roses, hydrangeas, or dwarf lilacs. The other good use is in bands at least 2 feet wide along the front of any garden or as an edging along a walkway or patio. In that setting, replant the space with summer annual flowers after the glory-of-the-snows have died back. Glory-of-the-snow also is a good choice for "forcing" into bloom in pots over winter.

Try These

The straight species is perfectly fine, but the variety 'Blue Giant' has slightly bigger flowers and more pronounced white centers. 'Pink Giant' is a pale lavender-pink variety. The closely related *Chionodoxa luciliae* (also known as *C. gigantea*) blooms in lavender-blue and has a white-blooming variety ('Alba').

Hyacinth

Hyacinthus orientalis

Botanical Pronunciation
HYE-yah-sinth-us or-ee-en-TAL-iss

Bloom Period and Seasonal Color
April; purple, blue, pink, rose, white, creamy yellow

Mature Height × Spread
8 to 12 inches × 6 to 12 inches

  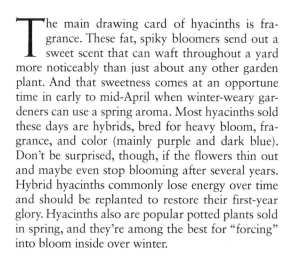 

The main drawing card of hyacinths is fragrance. These fat, spiky bloomers send out a sweet scent that can waft throughout a yard more noticeably than just about any other garden plant. And that sweetness comes at an opportune time in early to mid-April when winter-weary gardeners can use a spring aroma. Most hyacinths sold these days are hybrids, bred for heavy bloom, fragrance, and color (mainly purple and dark blue). Don't be surprised, though, if the flowers thin out and maybe even stop blooming after several years. Hybrid hyacinths commonly lose energy over time and should be replanted to restore their first-year glory. Hyacinths also are popular potted plants sold in spring, and they're among the best for "forcing" into bloom inside over winter.

When, Where, and How to Plant
Plant hyacinth bulbs mid-September through November, about 6 inches apart and 6 inches deep. Mulch after planting with an inch of bark, shredded wood, or chopped leaves. Potted, blooming hyacinths also can be planted outside in spring. Hyacinths bloom best in full sun but will do reasonably well in part shade. Plant in slightly raised beds that have been improved by mixing in an inch or two of compost.

Growing Tips
Fertilizer isn't needed at planting if you've added compost. Scratch a balanced, granular fertilizer formulated for bulbs into the soil surface early each fall. Hyacinth blooms are so heavy, especially when weighted with water drops after a rain, that you may want to stake them to prevent drooping. Water immediately after planting to settle the soil, then watering is not needed.

Regional Advice and Care
Deer usually don't bother hyacinths, but rabbits and rodents occasionally sample the buried bulbs and young shoots. Try animal repellents if you have animal trouble. Or cover the planted bed with chicken wire topped lightly by mulch. Let the foliage die back or at least begin to yellow before cutting it after bloom. Some people have skin allergies to hyacinths; wear gloves when handling if you're not sure. If eaten, hyacinths can cause vomiting or diarrhea, so don't let pets or young children eat any parts.

Companion Planting and Design
Purple and dark blue hyacinths pair nicely with golden daffodils, which overlap bloom times. Because of their fragrance, hyacinths are best used next to patios, near windows, along walks and any area within nose range. Or interplant with mid- to late-season perennials, such as daylilies, coneflowers, black-eyed Susans, mums, and hosta. As the hyacinths wind down, the perennials will take over the show.

Try These
'Blue Jacket', 'Peter Stuyvesant', 'Midnight Mystique', and 'Delft Blue' are some of the best purples and blues/purples. Try 'Jan Bos' if you like deep pink. 'Pink Pearl' is a nice two-tone lighter pink. And if you lean toward yellow, 'City of Haarlem' is a creamy bloomer, while 'Yellow Queen' is deeper yellow.

Lily

Lilium species and hybrids

Botanical Pronunciation
LIL-ee-um

Bloom Period and Seasonal Color
Summer; white, red, orange, pink, rose, numerous bicolors, pastels

Mature Height × Spread
1 to 6 feet × 12 to 18 inches

A long-time garden favorite, the lily is a winter-hardy, summer-blooming bulb that acts like a perennial flower. Plant lilies in spring, and they'll come back to flower year after year, then die back each fall. Lilies come in a huge array of colors and shapes, from foot-tall "pixies" to bright orange or red "Turk's cap" types to 4-foot-tall classics with trumpet-shaped blooms. Most lilies are at least mildly fragrant. The flowers appear in clusters atop stiff, upright stems that have glossy, strappy, laddered leaves. Lilies make some of the best cut flowers; just snip off the pollen-laden anthers to avoid staining tablecloths. The white Easter lily, which can be planted outside in spring, is a top-selling potted plant. A few lilies are natives of the United States.

When, Where, and How to Plant
Lilies can be planted as dormant bulbs in spring or as live plants spring through fall. Dormant bulbs go 6 to 8 inches deep and 1 foot apart. Transplants should be planted at the same depth as they were in the pot. Find a full sun spot in slightly raised, compost-enriched beds. Top with 2 inches of bark mulch or chopped leaves.

Growing Tips
Water after planting, then watering is needed only during very hot, dry spells. Fertilize early each spring and early each fall with a granular fertilized made for bulbs or flowers. Taller types might need to be staked. Place the stakes first, then plant to avoid stabbing the bulbs. In ensuing years, stake right after the shoots emerge for the same reason. Snip off the tops of flower stalks after the blooms fade.

Regional Advice and Care
Lilies are winter-hardy, so there's no need to dig and lift the bulbs as you would with dahlias, gladioli, and cannas. The biggest threat to lilies is munching by rabbits. Use repellents or surround plantings with chicken wire to discourage them. Use Neem oil to repel occasional chewing damage from beetles and insecticidal soap if aphids become a problem. Cut plants to the ground after frost browns the foliage in fall.

Companion Planting and Design
Lilies interplant well with spring bulbs such as tulips, daffodils, and hyacinths. They also pair nicely with perennial flowers, especially if you color-coordinate them with species that overlap bloom times, such as garden phlox, purple coneflowers, and Russian sage. Shrub roses make other good partners. Lilies look best when planted in clusters. Fragrant ones are ideal next to patios, walkways, and windows.

Try These
There's no shortage of good choices. 'Star Gazer' is the best known hybrid, but 'Anastasia' is a similar type in a soft white-pink blend. Try orange or red tiger lilies if you lean toward bright stuff, and if you're keen on fragrance, it's hard to beat 'Casa Blanca', a white Oriental type.

Ornamental Onion

Allium species

Botanical Pronunciation
AL-ee-um

Bloom Period and Seasonal Color
May to June; purple, lavender, white, yellow

Mature Height × Spread
1 to 4 feet × 6 to 12 inches

Bugged by rodents, rabbits, deer, or other bulb-eating pests? Allium's your answer. Hardly anything bothers this large family of late-spring-blooming bulbs because of its oniony scent and taste. *You* likely won't notice the scent though, unless you take a close sniff of a wounded leaf or bulb. Ornamental onions send up strappy leaves in spring, followed by stiff flower stems that can reach upwards of 4 feet. Rounded flowers of assorted sizes and colors (purple and lavender are most common) ultimately open at the stem tips. These are some of the most eye-grabbing garden plants—almost like something out of a Dr. Seuss book. They're a must in a children's garden. Some are U.S. natives. Bonus—their young leaves can be chopped for use in soups or salads.

When, Where, and How to Plant
Plant bulbs mid-September through November, ideally in full sun. Hot, dry sites are fine. Plant two to three times as deep as the bulb's height and 6 to 12 inches apart, depending on the variety's size. Slightly raised beds that have been improved by mixing in an inch or two of compost are ideal. Cover the planted bed with 1 inch of bark or wood mulch or chopped leaves.

Growing Tips
Fertilizer isn't needed at planting if you've added compost, but it helps to incorporate a balanced, granular fertilizer formulated for bulbs into the soil early each fall. Watering is not needed, except possibly in an exceptionally hot, dry spell as the flower stems and flower buds are forming. Do *not* water in summer when the plants are dormant.

Regional Advice and Care
Let the foliage die back to the ground in late spring. Leaves "recharge" the bulbs for next year's bloom, so don't cut, braid, or otherwise mess with leaves while they're still green. Ornamental onion leaves typically die back while the flowers are still colorful. It's fine to remove browned leaves then and remove the flower stalks later after they dry and the flowers turn brown.

Companion Planting and Design
Pair with pink- or purple-blooming late-spring perennials, such as salvia, baptisia or dianthus. You'll then need something to take over the space in July when ornamental onions finally die back for the season. There are three options: Plant annual flowers in the gaps; place flower pots on top of the newly empty space; interplant with summer-blooming bulbs, such as lilies or cannas, or with fall-peaking perennials, such as mums or asters.

Try These
My favorite is 'Globemaster', a whopper that produces softball-sized purple balls at the top of 3-foot stems. 'Gladiator' and 'Ambassador' are similar big ones. *Allium christophii* produces purple balls of dainty star-shaped flowers on 18-inch stems and *Allium schubertii* is a 2-footer that looks like a purple star exploding. 'Drumstick' looks like, well, upright drumsticks with purple tips.

Siberian Squill

Scilla siberica

Botanical Pronunciation
SILL-ah sye-BEER-ih-kah

Bloom Period and Seasonal Color
April; dark blue

Mature Height × Spread
5 to 6 inches × 4 to 6 inches

Not many flowers bloom in a rich, cobalt blue color. If that's your fancy, Siberian squill is the ideal early-spring bulb choice. This demure April bloomer first sends up 4-inch strappy leaves and then masses of dime-sized, six-petaled flowers that hang down like little blue lampshades. Each blue petal has a darker blue stripe running through it. Siberian squill gets better with age, producing spreading colonies that make striking carpets of blue for 2 to 3 weeks every spring. It's one of the most shade-tolerant spring bulbs, which makes it a good option under trees. Although the colonies spread, they're not overly aggressive and don't root their way into adjacent lawns. Animals let Siberian squill alone, so there's no need to worry about repellents or replanting.

When, Where, and How to Plant
Plant squill bulbs mid-September through November, about 3 inches deep and spaced 4 to 6 inches apart. A full-sun site is best, but these bloom reasonably well even in shadier spots, such as woodland edges. Plant in slightly raised beds that have been improved by mixing in an inch or two of compost. Cover the bed with 1 inch of bark or wood mulch or chopped leaves.

Growing Tips
Fertilizer isn't needed at planting if you've added compost. Mixing a balanced, granular fertilizer formulated for bulbs into the soil surface early each fall is a good idea. Water immediately after planting to settle the soil; otherwise, you don't need to water.

Regional Advice and Care
About all you'll need to do is rake off the foliage after it's browned in late spring. Even that's not necessary since Siberian squill has such small leaves that they almost disappear after they collapse while going dormant. Just toss a little fresh mulch over the squill bed, and it'll look perfectly neat. If you'd like to spread out your planting, dig up and separate bulbs right after the leaves turn brown, and replant them immediately in their new home.

Companion Planting and Design
Use Siberian squill in masses or bands at least 2 feet wide along the front of any garden or as an edging along a walkway or patio. Replant the space with summer annual flowers after the squill dies back. Squill also makes an excellent, albeit fleeting, groundcover under trees and flowering shrubs. Especially nice is a mass of them under a pink- or white-blooming tree that blooms at the same time, such as flowering cherry or one of the "Little Girl" magnolias ('Ann', 'Betty', 'Jane'). Siberian squill also is a good choice for "forcing" into bloom in pots over winter.

Try These
The straight species is perfectly fine, but the variety 'Spring Beauty' has even richer, deeper blue blooms. 'Alba' has white flowers instead of blue. The closely related *Scilla bifolia* 'Rosea' has narrower flower petals of pale pink and is mildly scented.

Tulip

Tulipa species and hybrids

Botanical Pronunciation
TEW-lip-ah

Bloom Period and Seasonal Color
March to May; every shade except blue
and black

Mature Height × Spread
6 to 24 inches × 6 to 10 inches

The tulip is the diva of the bulb world, so beloved that it spurred a colonial-era Dutch investment furor called "tulipmania." Gardeners still know and love this spring icon, but the tulip comes with two big down sides: Deer, rabbits, and rodents enjoy eating them as much as we enjoy looking at them, and most of them go downhill within a few years. That doesn't mean they're not worth trying. Get around the first problem by using animal repellents, scare tactics, or chicken wire laid over the planted bed. Solve the second by treating tulips as annuals. That's what public gardens such as Longwood and Hershey Gardens do to achieve their jaw-dropping displays—they yank tulips after bloom and replant fresh each fall.

When, Where, and How to Plant
Plant tulip bulbs mid-September through November. Smaller ones go 4 to 6 inches deep, larger ones 8 inches deep. Space 6 to10 inches apart, in masses or clusters of at least a dozen instead of lined up single-file like soldiers. Full sun is best in slightly raised, compost-improved beds. Top the beds with 2 inches of bark mulch or chopped leaves.

Growing Tips
There's no need to fertilize if you're planting new each fall. To get tulips to come back year after year, try the Darwin hybrids and *kaufmanniana, fosteriana*, and *greigii* types. A balanced, granular fertilizer formulated for bulbs mixed into the soil surface early each spring and again early each fall is ideal.

Watering is not needed, other than right after planting to settle the soil.

Regional Advice and Care
Also important in getting tulips to come back year after year is letting the foliage die back to the ground in spring. So long as the leaves are green, the bulbs are "recharging" for next year. Don't cut, braid, or otherwise mess with the leaves at least until they yellow. Clip off the flower stalks after the blooms fade.

Companion Planting and Design
Spot clusters of tulips around high-traffic locations, such as along the front of the house, around the mailbox, under front yard trees, and along the driveway or front sidewalk. Tulips also do well in window boxes and pots and make a huge impact when massed in a garden that's later replanted with summer annuals. Or interplant with nearly any mid- to late-season perennial (these will take over the space later). Plant still more at the base of tall evergreens.

Try These
The selection is huge, from 6-inch March bloomers to classic 2-foot May "single lates." Flower shapes include pointed lily types, fringy-edge types, and my favorite, *viridiflora* types, that have green "flames" lapping up the petal undersides ('Verichic' is a great choice). I also like 'Golden Apeldoorn' (yellow Darwin type), 'Christmas Dream' (vivid pink), 'Negrita' (dark burgundy-purple) and 'Orange Emperor' (an orange early-season shortie).

Evergreens and Conifers

FOR PENNSYLVANIA

Evergreens are landscape plants that hold their foliage all winter. Some of them are needled plants, such as pine, spruce, and juniper, while others are plants with wider leaves that don't drop in fall, such as rhododendron, holly, and boxwood. Conifers are plants that bear cones. Almost all are needled and *look* like they're evergreens, but a few drop their needles in fall. (More on that shortly.) All of these add up to make a diverse category ranging from groundhugging mats to towering 100-foot trees.

Using Evergreens and Conifers in the Landscape

Many of the plants in this section have nothing in common botanically, other than they all have roots growing out the bottom. Instead, I've grouped these by how they're *used*, since a plant-selection starting point for many gardeners is whether a plant is evergreen or not.

Being evergreen is a particular advantage in two key settings around the yard: for blocking out unwanted views all year long, and for hiding exposed block foundations or other "uglies" around the yard. So even though a flowering bush such as an azalea could be grouped with the shrubs or pines could easily fit in with the trees, evergreen choices are lumped here for your January-to-December convenience.

The job of screening out unwanted views and sounds (such as busy streets, the neighbors' pool, the truck terminal next door) generally falls to tall conifers. These are mostly needled plants that typically grow taller than wide—often to 50 feet or more in 20 to 30 years.

Many a buyer of larch, baldcypress, or dawn redwood, though, has been surprised when their "evergreen" turned bronze in fall and dropped every last needle, only to fill back in the following spring. These are examples of conifers that *aren't* evergreens.

The rest of Pennsylvania's "evergreen" stable is very good at growing into a dense, living, year-round wall. Most of these (fir, pine, spruce, arborvitae, holly, falsecypress, Japanese cedar, and Leyland cypress, for example) grow best in open, sunny spots—the exact site where so many new homeowners are looking to add privacy in bare, new subdivisions.

Tall evergreens also make excellent, heat-bill-saving windblocks in winter, especially when planted along the north and northwest sections of a property.

Yew branch, *Taxus baccata* 'Repandens'

And many needled evergreens make attractive standalone specimens, especially ones with a weeping habit or colorful foliage.

One side note about needled evergreens—although they don't drop their foliage each fall, they *do* drop some of their needles each year. Needled evergreens shed their older needles from their inner branches as new needles grow on expanding branches toward the tree's tips.

Around the House

Most broadleaf evergreens and shrubbier types of needled evergreens see most of their use around house foundations, in mixed gardens or spot-blocking utility boxes, heat pumps, and the like.

They became almost obligatory ringing houses in the twentieth century, mainly because people thought it necessary to hide cinder-block foundations. That explains why it's so common to see so many Pennsylvania homes skirted with boxy yew hedges and wall-to-wall azalea "gumdrops." Now that most homes are built with attractive stone bases or siding that runs to the ground, there's less argument to support planting evergreens all the way around.

The downside of underdoing it with evergreens is that if you don't have enough, the property looks barren all winter. My advice is there's room for all. Mix evergreens and flowering shrubs so you'll have a pleasing blend of flowers in summer but sufficient greenery in winter. Choose based on your size needs, the growing conditions of the particular site, and whatever colors and textures grab your eye.

One other evergreen bonus is that many of them can be snipped for use in holiday home decorating, from sprigs of holly berries to boughs of fir prunings to an entire Christmas tree grown in a big backyard. Whatever the ultimate purpose, there's an evergreen to fit the bill.

Arborvitae

Thuja occidentalis

Botanical Pronunciation
THEW-yah ok-sih-den-TAY-liss

Other Name White cedar

Bloom Period and Seasonal Color
Pea-sized brown cones; foliage is green, lime, or gold

Mature Height × Spread
18 to 50 feet × 4 to 10 feet (dwarfs available)

Other than possibly yew, arborvitae is the most common evergreen in Pennsylvania landscapes. Tall types are typically lined up like green soldiers every 4 feet apart along property lines, where they make a dense screen planting in tight spacing. Although this type can grow upwards of 50 feet tall and 12 feet across, arborvitae shears well and can be kept to the size needed to get the privacy job done. The American or Eastern arborvitae (*Thuja occidentalis*) is the traditional choice, but the Western arborvitae (*Thuja plicata*) is catching on lately since it's less attractive to deer. Both are native U.S. plants with soft needles that grow in overlapping fans. Besides tall uprights, dwarf and 4-foot globe types are available, as well as gold-tinted versions.

When, Where, and How to Plant
Plant arborvitae in spring or early fall as a burlap-wrapped, field-dug plant or from spring through early fall as a container-grown plant. Full sun is best in damp, loose, mildly acidic soil. Loosen soil three to five times as wide as the rootball but only as deep. Arborvitae usually adapts to lean, rocky and/or compacted soil and to fairly dry or wet spots. Avoid soggy spots. Cover the ground after planting with 2 to 3 inches of wood chips or bark mulch kept a few inches away from the trunk.

Growing Tips
Water deeply once or twice a week for its first full growing season. Water weekly for the next 2 years during hot, dry spells. Then water probably won't be needed except in a drought. Fertilizer isn't

necessary unless growth or foliage color is poor. If you're suspicious, test the soil for nutrients and pH (acidity level).

Regional Advice and Care
Shear to control its size from early spring through July. Never cut back to bare branches; cut only to wood with live needles attached. Deer *adore* arborvitae (especially in winter), so keep repellents handy, protect with fencing, or plant Western arborvitae. Watch for bagworms, which are needle-eating caterpillars that feed on the cone-like sacks hanging from arborvitae branches. Handpick and destroy the sacks or spray plants with Bt (*Bacillus thuringiensis*) in June when bagworms first hatch.

Companion Planting and Design
Besides border plantings, clusters of arborvitae are good for screening selected views wherever height but limited width is needed in sunny to partly sunny areas. Dwarf or golden ones make good sunny evergreen specimens. Globe types are good boxwood alternatives under windows or along driveways.

Try These
'Smaragd' ('Emerald Green') is widely available and good at sending up a single lead shoot. 'Degroot's Spire' is a particularly narrow form. 'Green Giant' is a bigger, faster-growing Western type where deer are near. 'Holmstrup' is my favorite dwarf upright (6 feet by 4 feet). And Mr. Bowling Ball™ and 'Hetz Midget' are good 4-foot globe types.

Azalea

Rhododendron species and hybrids

Botanical Pronunciation
roe-doe-DEN-dron

Bloom Period and Seasonal Color
Late April into June; pink, white, red, lavender, salmon flowers

Mature Height × Spread
3 to 6 feet × 4 to 8 feet

Evergreen azaleas are species of Asian rhododendrons that are widely planted in Pennsylvania landscapes, typically sheared into balls along house foundations. People love them for the showy, broadly tubular flowers that nearly cover the plants in late April to mid-May. They also hold their fingernail-sized leaves all winter. The azalea's popularity has led to an almost endless choice of hybrids and varieties, including some that get bronze fall foliage and at least two lines that rebloom in fall (Bloom-a-Thon® and Encore®, both of which are winter-hardy in Zones 6 and 7). Beautiful in bloom though it is, be aware the azalea has a high death rate due to factors including too-deep planting, root rot in compacted clay soil, excess mulch, drought, and damage from deer and lace bugs.

When, Where, and How to Plant
Azaleas are picky about planting. Morning sun and afternoon shade is ideal, but plants need moisture under trees. Full sun is okay, if the soil is kept well watered (but never soggy). Azaleas demand loose, fertile, well-drained, acidic soil. Azalea collectors suggest improving poor soil by adding 25 percent coarse sand and 25 percent compost, plus planting in slightly raised beds. Tease out the roots of container-grown plants before planting an inch or two above the soil's grade. Mulch after planting with 2 to 3 inches of wood chips or bark kept a few inches away from the trunk.

Growing Tips
Water deeply once or twice a week for the first full growing season, then weekly during hot, dry spells.

Scatter a balanced, granular, organic, or gradual-release fertilizer formulated for acid-loving plants over the bed in early spring and early fall. Scratch sulfur into the soil surface in spring and fall to adjust alkaline soil.

Regional Advice and Care
Azaleas tolerate shearing but are best thinned and their size controlled with hand-pruners right after they finish blooming. Azalea is a deer favorite, so be ready with repellents or fencing, especially in winter. A serious pest is the lace bug, which sucks chlorophyll out of the leaf undersides most of summer and especially in full-sun settings, causing a stippled, brownish look. Spray insecticidal soap under the leaves to control. Azaleas are toxic to pets and somewhat toxic to people if they're eaten.

Companion Planting and Design
Siting along eastern and northern house foundations is a good use. Azaleas are striking when massed in a damp, wooded setting or spotted throughout a shade garden. Liriope, sedge, and Japanese forestgrass are good, grasslike textural partners.

Try These
I'll defer to evergreen azaleas recommended by the Pennsylvania chapter of the American Rhododendron Society, including 'Dayspring', 'Delaware Valley White', 'Elsie Lee', 'Hardy Gardenia', 'Herbert', 'Hershey's Bright Red', 'Louise Gable', 'Madame Butterfly', 'Martha Hitchcock', 'Pleasant White', 'Rosebud', 'Sandra Ann', and 'Treasure'.

Baldcypress

Taxodium distichum

Botanical Pronunciation
taks-OH-dee-um DISS-tih-kum

Other Name Swamp cypress

Bloom Period and Seasonal Color
Russet-bronze fall foliage and rounded, 1-inch brown cones

Mature Height × Spread
40 to 70 feet × 25 to 35 feet

This is one of those conifers that *looks* like a needled evergreen but that drops its foliage over winter (hence "bald" in the plant's nickname). Baldcypress is a slender, pyramidal tree with half-inch-long, soft, green needles that turn russet-bronze in fall before dropping. The trunk has fibrous, copper-colored bark that offers winter interest. The most useful feature of this eastern U.S. native is that it doesn't mind extended periods of wet or even flooded soil, giving a tree option where most other species would die. In wet areas, baldcypress usually sends up knobby projections called "knees." That's normal. Don't worry or try to cut them off. Just be aware that though baldcypress looks evergreen, it's not the choice if you're looking for screening in winter.

When, Where, and How to Plant

Here's a tree for your wettest area, although baldcypress is surprisingly tolerant of dry soil too. Plant burlap-wrapped, field-dug plants in early spring or early fall or container-grown plants from spring through early fall. Full sun is best in damp, loose, acidic soil. Loosen soil three to five times as wide as the rootball but only as deep. Add sulfur if a soil test shows your soil is alkaline. Cover the ground after planting with 2 to 3 inches of wood chips or bark mulch, carefully keeping it a few inches away from the trunk.

Growing Tips

Water deeply once or twice a week for the first full growing season, then soak the soil well every 2 or 3 weeks in hot, dry weather. This is one plant you can't overwater. Fertilizer usually isn't needed, but sulfur may need to be scratched into the soil surface in spring and/or early fall if yellowish needles indicate the soil is too alkaline.

Regional Advice and Care

Baldcypress is an underused, medium-fast grower, typically growing 1 to 2 feet per season. Pruning isn't needed, other than to eliminate crossing branches or to remove dead lower branches that may occur as the tree ages. It's easily winter-hardy throughout Pennsylvania and seldom runs into any bug, disease, or animal troubles.

Companion Planting and Design

Baldcypress is perfect for tall, growing-season privacy or for clustering in wet, sunny meadows. It's also a good choice for along sunny stream banks that sometimes flood and as a backdrop for lakes and ponds on larger lots. In smaller lots, try one or a few as specimens in any wet spot or next to a water garden.

Try These

'Cascade Falls' and 'Fallingwater' are two weeping baldcypress varieties that can be trained and/or pruned into upright, house-corner specimens out front or used as a water-garden backdrop specimen. 'Peve Minaret' is a slow-growing dwarf upright (about 6 feet tall and 3 feet across in 10 years) that's small enough for mixed gardens and sunny foundation corners.

Blue Atlas Cedar

Cedrus atlantica 'Glauca'

Botanical Pronunciation
SEE-druss at-LAN-tih-kuh GLAU-kah

Bloom Period and Seasonal Color
2- to 3-inch blue-green cones mature light brown; year-round powdery blue foliage

Mature Height × Spread
40 to 60 feet × 30 to 40 feet

Zones 6 and 7

The powdery blue needles on this elegant evergreen make blue atlas cedar a favorite specimen in Pennsylvania's Zones 6 and 7. The needles are stiff, 1 to 1½ inches long, and as consistently blue in summer's heat as in January. The upright form starts out as a fairly narrow and open pyramid, growing twice as tall as wide and about 1 foot a year. Like people, its growth rate slows and it "fattens out" as it ages, winding up around 40 feet tall and 30 feet across. The weeping form ('Glauca Pendula') grows wider than it is tall and is especially striking when trained over pergolas, arbors, and even the garage. Both types can be espaliered or shaped into whatever living sculpture strikes your fancy.

When, Where, and How to Plant
Blue atlas cedar transplants best as a container-grown plant as opposed to a burlap-wrapped, field-dug plant. Plant from spring through early summer in full sun and damp, loose soil. Mildly acidic to mildly alkaline soil is fine; atlas cedar isn't as picky about pH as many evergreens. Loosen the soil three to five times as wide as the rootball but only as deep, avoiding any soggy spots. After planting, mulch with 2 to 3 inches of wood chips or bark kept a few inches away from the trunk.

Growing Tips
Water deeply once or twice a week for the first full growing season, then water is needed only in a prolonged drought. Once established, atlas cedar is drought-resistant. Fertilizer usually isn't necessary unless growth or foliage color is poor. Do a soil test if either of those signs occurs.

Regional Advice and Care
Prune in late spring to early summer (if needed) to eliminate crossing branches, to shape the plant as desired, or to remove dead lower branches that may occur on older trees. Avoid cutting back into bare branches; only cut to wood with live needles. Bagworms (caterpillars in conelike sacks hanging from the branches) occasionally feed on needles. Handpick and destroy the sacks or spray tree with Bt (*Bacillus thuringiensis*) in June. Voles sometimes gnaw bark at a tree's base. Wrap hardware cloth or screening loosely around the base when trees are young.

Companion Planting and Design
The upright form is best used alone in a sunny spot, where it'll stand out as a frontyard, house-corner, or back-corner star. Train a weeper to drape over a patio pergola or large, sturdy arbor. Either form can be espaliered along a property line or a large, empty, sunny wall. Cheddar pinks or pink creeping phlox add delightful spring color around a blue atlas cedar base. Leadwort makes a color-coordinated, dark blue groundcover.

Try These
'Glauca' is the blue-needled upright, 'Glauca Pendula' is the blue-needled weeper, and the straight species *Cedrus atlantica* has green needles.

Boxwood

Buxus species and hybrids

Botanical Pronunciation
BUCKS-us

Bloom Period and Seasonal Color
Inconspicuous white flowers in April to May; foliage green or blue-green all year

Mature Height × Spread
3 to 10 feet × 2 to 6 feet

Boxwood has no showy flowers, no eye-grabbing texture, and no flashy fall foliage. So why do we plant so many of them? It's probably because boxwood is such a versatile and functional plant that—given the right spot—gets the job done reliably and without much work other than an annual trim. Boxwood is most commonly grown as a round, broadleaf evergreen used to line sidewalks and house foundations. Upright types are useful for framing doorways or for adding privacy along borders where space is tight. Boxwood also is fairly shade-tolerant and not attractive to deer, two other selling points for a lot of homeowners. Most varieties and hybrids are cold-hardy throughout Pennsylvania, except for littleleaf boxwood (*Buxus microphylla*), which is iffy in Zone 5.

When, Where, and How to Plant
Boxwood tolerates a range of light, although morning sun and afternoon shade is ideal, especially in Zone 7 locations. Keep the soil damp in hot, sunny spots. Courtyards, east-facing walls, and similar wind-protected sites guard against winter leaf damage. Avoid heat pockets, such as along hot asphalt. Plant container-grown plants spring through early fall in loose, well-drained soil. Keep mulch, about 2 to 3 inches of wood chips or bark, away from boxwood's trunk.

Growing Tips
Water deeply once or twice a week for the first growing season, then weekly during hot, dry spells. Trim in spring or summer. Test the soil to determine if nutrients or pH-altering amendments are needed. Otherwise, regular fertilizer usually is not needed.

Regional Advice and Care
Boxwoods are often trouble-free but not quite bulletproof. Extreme heat and cold are two cultural issues. Leaf miners, mites, and scale are potential bug problems. An apparent disease known as "boxwood decline" has long caused sporadic trouble, not to mention a new blight disease that debuted in Pennsylvania recently. Boxwood is mildly toxic to pets and people when eaten.

Companion Planting and Design
The neat, trimmed look of boxwood makes it a favorite in any formal design. It's a natural around Colonial-style homes as well as in herb gardens, knot gardens, and for edging walkways. Boxwood holds its own from tree-root competition and pairs well in wooded, dry shade settings with liriope. In foundation plantings, pair boxwood with tulips, daffodils, and hyacinths for spring color and then with petunias, alyssum, and begonias for summer color.

Try These
Good 3- to 4-foot rounded types are 'Justin Brouwers', 'Glencoe' (Chicagoland Green™), 'Green Velvet', 'Green Ice', and 'Green Mound'. 'Green Mountain' is a compact pyramid that's good for flanking doors (5 feet tall by 3 feet wide). 'Elegantissima' is similar in size but has attractive white-and-green variegated foliage. 'Dee Runk' is an excellent tall and narrow type (8 to 10 feet tall by 2 to 3 feet across).

Cherrylaurel

Prunus laurocerasus

Botanical Pronunciation
PROO-nus lore-oh-SAIR-ah-siss

Bloom Period and Seasonal Color
April through May; pinkish white flowers;
glossy green leaves

Mature Height × Spread
3 to 16 feet × 4 to 18 feet

Zones 6 and 7

   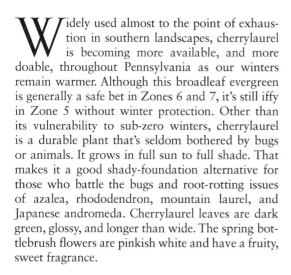

Widely used almost to the point of exhaustion in southern landscapes, cherrylaurel is becoming more available, and more doable, throughout Pennsylvania as our winters remain warmer. Although this broadleaf evergreen is generally a safe bet in Zones 6 and 7, it's still iffy in Zone 5 without winter protection. Other than its vulnerability to sub-zero winters, cherrylaurel is a durable plant that's seldom bothered by bugs or animals. It grows in full sun to full shade. That makes it a good shady-foundation alternative for those who battle the bugs and root-rotting issues of azalea, rhododendron, mountain laurel, and Japanese andromeda. Cherrylaurel leaves are dark green, glossy, and longer than wide. The spring bottlebrush flowers are pinkish white and have a fruity, sweet fragrance.

When, Where, and How to Plant
In spring, plant cherrylaurel in loose, compost-enriched, well-drained, mildly acidic soil. Avoid soggy spots. Any light from sun to shade is okay; just keep the roots damp in hot, dry spots. Cherrylaurel also is good in the root competition and dry shade under trees. Unravel the roots of container-grown plants before you plant. Then cover the ground using 2 to 3 inches of mulch (wood chips or bark) kept a few inches away from the trunk.

Growing Tips
Water deeply once or twice a week for the first growing season, then water is needed only during very hot, dry spells. Cherrylaurel has good drought-tolerance once the roots are established. Scatter a balanced, granular, organic or gradual-release fertilizer over the bed in early spring.

Regional Advice and Care
Plant in courtyards, east-facing walls, and similar wind-protected sites to guard against winter leaf damage, especially in colder regions. Or spray plants once or twice over winter on above-freezing days with an anti-transpirant if leaf-edge browning is a problem. Erecting a burlap barrier may help adventurous Zone 5 gardeners nurse a cherrylaurel through winter. Cherrylaurel can be sheared after blooming to maintain desired size, but using hand pruners to thin excess branches and shorten too-long ones is less traumatic and yields a more natural look.

Companion Planting and Design
Compact varieties make good shade evergreens along northern and eastern house foundations. Clusters of cherrylaurel do well amid the roots and shade of a grove of trees, especially underplanted with dry shade-tolerant perennials, such as barrenwort, coralbell, foamybell, variegated Solomon's seal, and sweet woodruff.

Try These
You'll likely find a few limited choices in garden centers, such as the classic 'Otto Luyken' (3 to 4 feet tall by 6 to 8 feet across) or 'Mt. Vernon' (a foot smaller both ways). 'Schipkaensis' is a 4- to 5-footer that's common in Zone 7. And for a similar leaf and flower look but in a 10- to 15-foot-tall evergreen hedge, look for Portuguese laurel (*Prunus lusitanica*). It's a Zone 7 and possibly Zone 6 option.

Fir

Abies species

Botanical Pronunciation
AY-beez

Bloom Period and Seasonal Color
Bluish cones; year-round green, blue-green, silvery green foliage

Mature Height × Spread
15 to 50 feet × 10 to 30 feet

Fir makes an elegant tall evergreen choice with its slim, upright habit and flat, blue-green to silver-green needles. The needles are also softer than pine and spruce. Those ingredients add up to make fir our favorite Christmas tree species. Like a lot of evergreens, numerous dwarf forms are available for landscape choice, plus versions that weep, grow in rounded forms, or that have gold-green or white-banded needles. Fir is suited to cool, mountainous regions, so it tends to do best in cooler Zone 5 and 6 regions of Pennsylvania as opposed to its upper range of Zone 7. It's *not* a fan of hot, urban areas, where it also dislikes air pollution. The white fir (*Abies concolor*) and Fraser fir (*Abies fraseri*) are U.S. natives.

When, Where, and How to Plant
Try to match that cool mountainside homeland. Avoid hot spots and wet clay. Plant field-dug, burlap-wrapped plants or container-grown ones in spring in acidy, well-drained, and even rocky or gravelly soil. Loosen soil three to five times as wide as the rootball but only as deep. Mulch with 2 to 3 inches of wood chips or bark, keeping it a few inches from the trunk.

Growing Tips
Water deeply once or twice a week for the first growing season, then soak weekly during hot, dry spells. Fertilizer isn't necessary unless growth or foliage color is poor. If you're suspicious, do a soil test for nutrients and pH (acidity level).

Regional Advice and Care
White (concolor) fir is the most heat- and drought-tolerant of the fir clan, so start with that in warmer areas. Other than excess heat and poorly drained soil, fir is unlikely to run into bug or disease trouble, although it's not immune to deer and the usual cast of mites, bagworms, needlecast, and such. If pruning to control its size is needed, wait until early summer and lightly trim off most of the new growth. Remove lowest branches at any time if they die as the tree ages (but don't leave stubs).

Companion Planting and Design
Fir makes a good, tall screen planting or windbreak, especially lined along the north and northwest sections of a landscape. Standalone firs make attractive specimens in larger front or back yards. Fir's bluish to silvery foliage pairs well with pink- or blue-blooming shrubs (abelia, blue mist shrub, spirea) or perennials (purple coneflower, cheddar pinks, dark blue iris). Dwarf types are useful as sunny foundation specimens.

Try These
Fraser fir is sleek and has silvery needle undersides, while Korean fir (*Abies koreana*) and its silvery 'Horstmann's Silberlocke' variety make showy specimens. Nordmann fir (*Abies nordmanniana*) is denser, bigger, and dark green. All of these do better in Zones 5 and 6 than in the warmer Zone 7. Douglas-fir (*Pseudotsuga menziesii*) is dense, fast growing, and widely used but isn't a true fir; plus it's increasingly disease-prone.

Heavenly Bamboo

Nandina domestica

Botanical Pronunciation
nan-DEE-nah doe-MESS-tih-kah

Other Name Nandina

Bloom Period and Seasonal Color
Small, creamy-white flowers May to July; red, purple, or burgundy cool-season foliage

Mature Height × Spread
2 to 6 feet × 2 to 8 feet

Zones 6 and 7

The durability, colorful foliage, and fall to winter fruits of this broadleafed evergreen have made heavenly bamboo a long-time landscape staple from Baltimore southward. It's also been used in the Philadelphia area, but warmer weather has expanded its use throughout Pennsylvania, except for the colder Zone 5 regions. Other than its dislike for single-digit temperatures, heavenly bamboo is virtually trouble-free and versatile in diverse conditions, from sun to shade and in dry, damp, or poor soil. The leaves are twice as long as wide and offer red to purple-burgundy coloring in fall, winter, and early spring. Many varieties produce clusters of pea-sized red fruits in fall and winter. Despite its nickname, heavenly bamboo is *not* a true bamboo and won't run all over the yard.

When, Where, and How to Plant
Plant heavenly bamboo from spring through early summer most anywhere except in soggy spots. Although very adaptable, ideal conditions are loose, damp, and well-drained soil in an area protected from winter wind. Untangle the roots of container-grown plants before planting, then mulch with 2 to 3 inches of wood chips or bark kept a few inches away from the trunk.

Growing Tips
Water deeply once or twice a week for the first growing season, then water is needed only in a prolonged drought. Heavenly bamboo has excellent drought-resistance once the roots establish. Scatter a balanced, granular, organic or gradual-release fertilizer over the bed in early spring.

Regional Advice and Care
It's not unusual for heavenly bamboo leaves to brown around the edges (or worse) in cold, windy winters. Trim off any dead tips back to live growth at winter's end; new foliage will appear by mid-spring. Plants that are getting leggy or too big also can be trimmed back as desired at winter's end. Limit winter wind damage by planting heavenly bamboo in courtyards, east-facing walls, and similar wind-protected sites. Or protect in winter with a burlap barrier.

Companion Planting and Design
Compact varieties are perfect for low-care, minimal trim use around house foundations in both sunny and shady exposures. Heavenly bamboo competes well with tree roots, so it's useful in dry shade under trees where most plants struggle. Masses of them hold soil in place on banks, while a line of them makes a colorful driveway or sidewalk alternative to boxwood.

Try These
The species is upright (typically 6 feet by 4 feet) and fruits well but tends to get "bare legs." Gulf Stream™ is upright but denser with red fall foliage. 'Harbour Dwarf' is lower and more spreading in its habit with ample red fall fruits. Moon Bay™ is a mounded 3-by-3-footer with reddish fall foliage and few to no fruits. The compact, mounded 'Fire Power' is my favorite for its fire-engine-red winter color, but I've never seen it produce fruits.

Hinoki Falsecypress

Chamaecyparis obtusa

Botanical Pronunciation
kam-ee-SIPP-ar-iss ob-TOO-sah

Other Name Hinoki cypress

Bloom Period and Seasonal Color
Pea-sized brown cones; year-round green or gold foliage

Mature Height × Spread
6 to 30 feet × 4 to 8 feet (dwarfs available)

Get Hinoki falsecypress off to a good start and give it ample room to grow, and this is one plant you may never need to water, spray, or trim. Compact types are especially good choices for the low-care gardener. This Japanese native has rounded, overlapping fans of soft needles that are mostly dark green. Some varieties have golden or gold-green foliage. Growth habits range from tall, open and skinny plants to fatter, denser pyramids to miniatures that grow into little buns or cushions. Most are fairly slow growing and look best unpruned to display their natural loose, irregular, or twisted shapes. If you like tightly sheared balls or pyramids, get a yew and whack away. Hinoki falsecypress would rather grow in its own individual "character."

When, Where, and How to Plant
Plant Hinoki falsecypress in spring or early fall as a balled-and-burlapped, field-dug plant or from spring through early fall as a container-grown plant. Full sun is best in a damp, loose, acidic location. Hinoki falsecypress adapts to dry or poor soil and grows in part shade, although with a more open look, but avoid soggy spots. Loosen soil three to five times as wide as the rootball but only as deep. Two to 3 inches of wood chips or bark mulch, kept a few inches away from the trunk, should be added after planting.

Growing Tips
Water deeply once or twice a week for the first full growing season, then water as needed only in a prolonged drought. Hinoki falsecypress has excellent drought-resistance once its roots establish. Fertilizer isn't necessary unless growth or foliage color is poor. If you're suspicious, do a soil test for nutrients and pH (acidity level).

Regional Advice and Care
Hinoki falsecypress does well in all parts of Pennsylvania, tolerating both our coldest Zone 5 winters and the hot, humid summers of Zone 7. Plants hold their needle color well in winter winds. Pest problems are rare, and deer aren't particularly fond of Hinoki falsecypress, although they'll sometimes browse the species in winter. Use repellents if that's the case.

Companion Planting and Design
Compact uprights such as 'Nana Gracilis', 'Gracilis Compacta', and 'Kosteri' are good door-flanking alternatives to the mite-prone dwarf Alberta spruce. Taller uprights are options for screening in tight areas or for softening big empty walls. Dwarf types make good rock garden plants, and the whole Hinoki family should be a top consideration in any Asian garden or water-feature setting.

Try These
'Nana Gracilis' (6 feet by 4 feet) is my favorite evergreen and a Pennsylvania Horticultural Society Gold Medal Award winner. 'Nana Lutea' (4 by 3) and 'Tetragona Aurea' (8 by 4) are gold-needled, dwarf uprights. 'Crippsii' is golden and bigger (more like 15 by 8 in 20 years). 'Gracilis' and 'Ericoides' are tall, narrow, green-needled, faster-growing uprights (12 to 15 feet by 6 to 8 feet).

Holly

Ilex species and hybrids

Botanical Pronunciation
EYE-leks

Bloom Period and Seasonal Color
White flowers April to May; red fall fruits; year-round green, blue-green, or green-gold foliage

Mature Height × Spread
4 to 40 feet × 4 to 20 feet (narrow varieties also available)

Evergreen hollies come in a variety of shapes and sizes, explaining why this plant family is so widely used throughout Pennsylvania landscapes. Best known are the spiny, broadleafed, red-fruiting types that grow into dense, 6- to 10-foot shrubs. But evergreen options also include the native American holly (*Ilex opaca*), a narrow, 30- to 40-foot-tall tree; the native inkberry holly (*Ilex glabra*), a mounded, 3- to 6-footer with smooth leaves, pea-sized black fruits, and tolerance for shade and wet sites; and the Japanese holly (*Ilex crenata*), which looks like and is used like a boxwood. Female plants produce fruits and require a male with overlapping bloom time to pollinate them. Note that hollies (including the berries) are moderately toxic to people and pets.

When, Where, and How to Plant
Hollies prefer damp (but not soggy), well-drained, acidic soils. Check the soil pH before planting and add sulfur if needed. Full sun is best, but most hollies still do well in part shade. Plant burlap-wrapped, field-dug hollies in spring and container-grown ones anytime from spring through early fall. Loosen soil three to five times as wide as the rootball but only as deep. Apply a mulch after planting to a depth of 2 to 3 inches using wood chips or bark kept a few inches away from the trunk.

Growing Tips
Water deeply once or twice a week for the first growing season, then every 2 or 3 weeks in hot, dry weather. Keep the ground damp until the soil freezes to head off winter leaf damage. Scatter a balanced, granular, organic or gradual-release fertilizer formulated for acid-preferring plants over the bed in early spring.

Regional Advice and Care
In cold, windy areas, plant hollies along east-facing walls or similar protected sites. If leaves are browning in winter, spray on above-freezing days in December, January, and February with an anti-transpirant, or erect a burlap barrier. Chinese holly (especially the spineless *Ilex cornuta* variety 'Burfordii') and *Ilex* × 'Nellie Stevens' are two of the most heat-tolerant types for warmer Zone 7 areas. Hollies shear well to maintain their size; the best timing is spring through midsummer.

Companion Planting and Design
Tall American hollies make good screen plantings or specimens. Compact uprights such as Dragon Lady™ and Red Beauty® are excellent choices for house corners. The rounded, smooth-edged Japanese and inkberry hollies are naturals around house foundations or as low hedges or driveway and sidewalk edging.

Try These
Blue hollies, especially 'Blue Princess' and the accompanying male 'Blue Prince', are my favorite "big-shrub" varieties that also do well in dry shade under trees. Red Beauty® is my favorite upright at a slow-growing 8 by 4 feet. 'Hoogendorn' is a good compact Japanese holly. Longwood Gardens' research rated 'Densa', 'Bright Green', 'Shamrock', and 'Nigra' as the best inkberries.

Japanese Cedar

Cryptomeria japonica

Botanical Pronunciation
krip-toe-MEER-ee-ah jah-PON-ih-kah

Bloom Period and Seasonal Color
Small brown cones; year-round green, blue-green, or yellow-green foliage

Mature Height × Spread
25 to 50 feet × 12 to 20 feet (dwarfs available)

The short, densely spaced, soft needles on this Japanese evergreen give it a fine-textured look. That, along with its sleek habit, make Japanese cedar an attractive choice for something different from the more common spruce, fir, and pine. Japanese cedar isn't a true cedar, but it's similar in cold-hardiness, which is no problem in Pennsylvania's warmer Zone 6 and 7 regions but somewhat iffy in Zone 5. The usual habit is about twice as tall as wide, growing fairly quickly to 25 to 30 feet tall and 10 to 12 feet wide in 20 to 25 years. Dwarf and miniature versions are available that grow into 3- to 4-foot mounds. Japanese cedar's dense foliage tends to thin with age, and needles typically turn bronze to purplish over winter.

When, Where, and How to Plant
Plant balled-and-burlapped, field-dug Japanese cedar plants in spring or container-grown plants from spring through early fall. Full sun is best in damp, loose, acidic soil, but this plant also does well in part shade, albeit with a bit more open habit. Just avoid soggy spots. Loosen soil three to five times as wide as the rootball but dig the hole only as deep. Mulch after planting with 2 to 3 inches of wood chips or bark, keeping all mulch a few inches away from the trunk.

Growing Tips
Water deeply once or twice a week for the first growing season, then water is needed only occasionally in very hot, dry spells. Its drought-resistance is good. Fertilizer isn't necessary unless growth or foliage color is poor. If you don't know, test the soil for nutrients. Add sulfur if the soil is too alkaline.

Regional Advice and Care
Japanese cedar does fine out in the open in Zones 6 or 7 but benefits from a protected site or warm microclimate in colder, windy areas. Some varieties retain their green color over winter better than others. Ditto with their dense habit. Japanese cedars accept shearing better than many evergreens, but they look best with little to no pruning. If trimming or pruning is done, do it lightly in spring through early summer. Deer, bugs, and disease seldom are problems.

Companion Planting and Design
Because it tends to become less dense with age, Japanese cedar is better used as a specimen evergreen or in triangular groupings as opposed to lining up as a border screen. Dwarf types are good choices around water gardens, in rock gardens, or mixed with bright perennials in sunny border gardens.

Try These
'Yoshino' (a Pennsylvania Horticultural Society Gold Medal Award winner) and 'Kitayama' (20 to 30 feet by 10 to 12 feet) are top varieties for denseness and holding color. 'Black Dragon' is a compact upright (10 by 6) that's dark green and ideal sited at house corners. 'Elegans Nana' (blue-tinted) and 'Globosa Nana' (green) are 4-foot, mounded choices.

Japanese Plum Yew

Cephalotaxus harringtonia

Botanical Pronunciation
seff-ah-loe-TACKS-us HAR-ing-tone-ee-uh

Bloom Period and Seasonal Color
Purplish berrylike cones; year-round dark green foliage

Mature Height × Spread
3 to 12 feet × 5 to 10 feet

Zones 6 and 7

Japanese plum yew looks a lot like a common yew with its dense, bushy habit and dark green, soft, flat needles. But this underused Japanese native offers one big advantage over yew—deer don't like it. Beyond the apparent taste difference, look closer and you'll see that the needles of Japanese plum yew are noticeably wider than yew. The cones are different too, looking like plum-purplish berries, which gives the plant its nickname. Japanese plum yew comes in two main shapes—a horizontal type that makes a good, waist-high groundcover under trees and a narrow, vase-like type that grows about 10 feet tall and 6 feet across. It's also durable in a range of conditions, from damp to dry soil and from sun to shade.

When, Where, and How to Plant
Japanese plum yew is one of the few shade-preferring evergreens. It'll take full sun, but the needle color isn't as rich green. Avoid brutally hot, windy spots (no parking-lot islands, for example, though it's unlikely you'd have that). *Always* avoid soggy spots. Otherwise Japanese plum yew isn't picky. Plant spring through early fall, ideally in damp, well-drained, mildly acidic soil. Loosen soil three to five times as wide as the rootball but only as deep. Mulching is good, so after planting top with 2 to 3 inches of wood chips or bark (but keep it a few inches away from the trunk).

Growing Tips
Water deeply once or twice a week for the first full growing season, then you'll likely only need to water in a bad drought. Once established, Japanese plum yew has good drought-resistance. Fertilizer usually isn't needed unless growth or needle color is poor and a soil test indicates a nutrient is lacking.

Regional Advice and Care
Japanese plum yew performs better in the heat than common yew, but it's not as tough in the cold. It's reliably winter-hardy only in Pennsylvania's Zones 6 and 7 regions. It may survive Zone 5 winters, but a protected, warmer microclimate is recommended for Zone 5'ers wanting to try this plant. Like yew, Japanese plum yew shears and prunes well. The best timing is spring through midsummer.

Companion Planting and Design
Mass spreading types to make a dense, evergreen groundcover in a tree grove or wooded area, especially one plagued by deer. Spreaders also can be used around shady foundations if they're kept trimmed. Use uprights to flank a shady doorway, as vertical accents in a mixed garden, or as screen plantings in a tight, shady area.

Try These
'Duke Gardens' is the leading spreader (3 to 4 feet tall and 5 to 6 feet across), while 'Prostrata' is similar in habit but a notch smaller. Both won Pennsylvania Horticultural Society Gold Medal awards. 'Fastigiata' is the leading upright, growing a bushy, vase-shaped, 10-by-6-foot size. 'Korean Gold' is a similar upright with gold-green foliage.

Japanese Umbrella Pine

Sciadopitys verticillata

Botanical Pronunciation
sye-ah-DOP-ih-teez ver-tiss-ih-LAY-tah

Bloom Period and Seasonal Color
Small, light-brown clusters of cones at branch tips; green foliage all year

Mature Height × Spread
25 to 30 feet × 12 to 15 feet

This Japanese evergreen is a good choice if you're looking for at least one head-turning plant in the yard where people say, "Oooh, what's that?" Japanese umbrella pine isn't a true pine, but it has needles that spray out in a fan pattern from the branch tips as pines do. What's distinctive is that these needles are flat but noticeably fat and fleshy. Someone decided the look was like spokes fanning out in an umbrella and nicknamed it "umbrella pine." Japanese umbrella pine is a sleek (and pricey) upright, growing very slowly about twice as tall as wide. It does best in full sun in the cooler Zones 5 to 6 parts of Pennsylvania but prefers some afternoon shade in the hotter Zone 7 regions.

When, Where, and How to Plant
Although sunlight preferences vary slightly by zones, one thing Japanese umbrella pine wants everywhere is acidy soil and wind protection. Add sulfur if a soil test determines your soil is too alkaline. Avoid soggy spots. An ideal planting site is along the protected east exposure of a wall, fence, or windbreak. Spring planting is best; early fall is second best. Loosen soil three to five times as wide as the rootball but only as deep. Mulch after planting with 2 to 3 inches of wood chips or bark kept a few inches away from the trunk.

Growing Tips
Water deeply once or twice a week for the first full growing season, then water every 2 or 3 weeks during hot, dry spells. Fertilizer usually isn't needed unless growth or needle color is poor and a soil test indicates a nutrient is lacking.

Regional Advice and Care
It's normal for needle color to turn pale green over winter. Dark green color usually returns with warmer weather. Give plants adequate space so you don't have to prune and disturb the habit and texture. If you must prune, do it spring through midsummer and use hand-pruners to shorten overly long branches back to more internal branch junctures. Deer occasionally browse branches in winter, so use repellents or erect a fence if you're in deer country.

Companion Planting and Design
Japanese umbrella pine is a star. Use it alone in key views—centered in a window, at a house corner, or as a water-garden backdrop, for example. Use it with low partners that accent its base, such as golden coreopsis, dwarf red daylily, or dwarf blanket flower, instead of taller bushes that obscure and detract from the plant's habit and texture.

Try These
The straight species was good enough to earn a Pennsylvania Horticultural Society Gold Medal Award. It's a slow-grower and somewhat expensive, so buy a small one and be patient. 'Joe Kozey' is more compact and slow-growing than the species. 'Wintergreen' holds its green needle color well all winter.

Juniper

Juniperus species

Botanical Pronunciation
joo-NIP-er-us

Other Name Eastern red-cedar

Bloom Period and Seasonal Color
Blue berrylike cones on females; year-round green, blue, silvery green, or gold foliage

Mature Height × Spread
1 to 50 feet × 6 to 20 feet

Juniper is another common landscape evergreen that comes in multiple sizes, shapes, and needle colors. Options range from ground-hugging mats that scarcely reach a foot tall to vase-shaped bushes that grow 4 to 6 feet tall and 6 to 10 feet across to our native Eastern red-cedar (*Juniperus virginiana*), which is a pyramidal tree that can grow 40 to 50 feet tall and 12 to 20 feet across. Juniper needles are short and stiff, some types more so than others. Color choices include green, blue, silvery green, and gold. Female plants offer the bonus of berrylike blue cones that birds eat in winter. All types do best in full sun and are among the best evergreen choices for your hottest, driest, lousy-soil sites.

When, Where, and How to Plant
Plant in spring or early fall as burlap-wrapped, field-dug plants or as container-grown plants from spring through early fall. Full sun is best in damp, loose, mildly acidic soil, but juniper tolerates a range of soils and sites *except* sogginess. Loosen soil three to five times as wide as the rootball but only as deep. Mulch 2 to 3 inches after planting with wood chips or bark; keep all mulch a few inches away from the trunk.

Growing Tips
Water deeply weekly for the first growing season, then you'll probably never need to water again. Juniper is exceptionally drought-tough. Don't fertilize unless growth or foliage color is poor. If you're not sure of your soil's fertility, conduct a soil test for nutrients and pH (acidity level).

Regional Advice and Care
The needles of some junipers turn purplish or bronze in winter. Juniper doesn't shear well, so hand-prune for best results. Never cut back into the needleless inner wood. Better yet, give plants ample room and skip pruning altogether. Deer aren't fond of juniper, but small rodents may chew the roots or trunks. Tip blight (stunted and browing tips) is possible on some varieties. Mites and bagworms are occasional bug threats.

Companion Planting and Design
Spreading and shrub types make ideal heat- and drought-tolerant evergreen groundcovers on sunny banks. Upright tree types are good for screen plantings along western and southern borders or as specimens in any hot, dry, open spot. Stick with low or dwarf varieties around house foundations . . . juniper tends to grow faster and get bigger than most people expect.

Try These
Juniperus conferta 'Blue Pacific' or 'Silver Mist' are blue/silver low spreaders. Japanese garden juniper (*Juniperus procumbens*) is an oldie-but-goodie green-needled spreader. Good shrub types are native Eastern red-cedar 'Grey Owl' (grayish green) and the Chinese junipers (*Juniperus chinensis*) 'Gold Lace' (gold) and 'Sea Green' (light green). *Juniperus communis* 'Gold Cone' is a narrow, 6-by-3-foot, gold-needled choice for sunny, skinny spots. *Juniperus squamata* 'Blue Star' is a 3-by-4-foot, steel blue "bun." Emerald Sentinel™ is my favorite tree-type Eastern red-cedar (it has prolific blue "berries").

Leyland Cypress

× *Cuprocyparis leylandii*

Botanical Pronunciation
koo-pro-SIP-ah-ris LAY-land-ee-eye

Bloom Period and Seasonal Color
Small brown cones; year-round green or green-gold foliage

Mature Height × Spread
50 to 60 feet × 10 to 12 feet

Zones 6 and 7

Leyland cypress answers the question, "What evergreen will give me the fastest privacy?" This green or green-gold, soft-needled evergreen can grow 2 to 4 feet a year. Although it's much taller than wide, Leyland cypress can still widen to 10 or 12 feet across by the time it reaches 50 to 60 feet tall. If you've got that space, let it zoom into a tall, living border fence. If not, be prepared to trim once or twice a year to keep it to the desired size. Leyland cypress has a more open, spray-type habit than the tighter arborvitae. It's not a true cypress but a hybrid of two American species—the Alaska-cedar and the Monterey cypress—that was first discovered in a British garden.

When, Where, and How to Plant
Leyland cypress is reliably hardy in Zones 6 and 7, but it's not cold-tough enough for a typical Zone 5 Pennsylvania winter. It's best planted in spring as a container-grown plant. Full sun is best in damp, loose, mildly acidic soil, but Leyland cypress tolerates light shade and poor, rocky, dry soil. It also tolerates salty soil and air pollution, making it a good urban performer. Avoid soggy sites and dig a hole three to five times as wide as the rootball but only as deep. Once it's planted, mulch with 2 to 3 inches of wood chips or bark, keeping it a few inches away from the trunk.

Growing Tips
Water deeply once a week for the first growing season, then water is needed only in very hot, dry spells. Leyland cypress has very good drought-resistance.

Fertilizer isn't necessary unless foliage color is poor (a soil test will confirm soil pH and fertility).

Regional Advice and Care
Other than avoiding sub-zero and soggy conditions, size control is the main issue. Leyland cypress is a very fast grower that can get gangly and quickly outgrow the intended space unless it's kept trimmed once or twice a year. Spring through midsummer is the timing. Fortunately Leyland cypress trims well, so long as you never cut back into the needleless, inner wood. Deer occasionally browse young Leyland cypress, and bagworms are a possibility.

Companion Planting and Design
Leyland cypress is almost always used as a tall, fast-growing evergreen screen planted along sunny property lines. Spaced 6 to 8 feet apart and in 4 to 6 feet from the line is ideal if that's the case. Leyland cypress also makes an attractive standalone specimen. Surround them with hot-colored perennials, such as black-eyed Susans, mums, golden coreopsis, blanket flowers, and daylilies.

Try These
The straight species is what's usually sold. 'Emerald Isle' is a variety with brighter green needles, 'Castlewellan' has green-gold needles, and 'Naylor's Blue' has blue-green needles. The choicest for specimen use is 'Gold Rider,' which is green-gold and slower-growing.

Osmanthus

Osmanthus heterophyllus

Botanical Pronunciation
oz-MAN-thus het-er-oh-FILL-us

Other Name False-holly

Bloom Period and Seasonal Color
Small white flowers September through
October; year-round green or green-and-white
variegated foliage

Mature Height × Spread
6 to 8 feet × 6 to 8 feet

Zones 6 and 7

Most people who see an osmanthus for the first time assume it's a holly. The leaves are broad, evergreen, and spiny, and they very much resemble an English holly. However, the leaves line up opposite one another, and the plant also blooms in fall instead of spring. The little white flowers aren't very noticeable, but their sweet scent is. Although false-holly (*Osmanthus heterophyllus*) is one of the cold-hardiest of the mostly Oriental *Osmanthus* clan, it's still unlikely to survive a Zone 5 Pennsylvania winter. It's not a bad idea to give it some winter protection even in Zone 6. The fall fragrance is the main attraction of the green-leafed type, but especially attractive year-round is the variegated variety 'Goshiki,' discovered by Pennsylvania's own Barry Yinger.

When, Where, and How to Plant
Plant osmanthus spring through early summer in loose, compost-enriched, well-drained, mildly acidic soil. Green-leaf types are best planted in full sun to part shade, while the variegated types are best in shade to part shade (no afternoon sun). Cover the ground after planting with 2 to 3 inches of wood chips or bark mulch kept a few inches away from the trunk.

Growing Tips
Water deeply once or twice a week for the first full growing season, then water is needed only during very hot, dry spells. Osmanthus has good heat and drought tolerance once its roots are established.

Scatter a balanced, granular, organic or gradual-release fertilizer over the bed in early spring.

Regional Advice and Care
In Zone 6, it's best to plant osmanthus in a spot that gives protection from winter wind to prevent browning of the leaf margins. If you're pushing the envelope in Zone 5, plant in a courtyard or similar wind-protected, warm-microclimate site and wrap young plants with a burlap barrier as an extra aid. There's no need to prune until osmanthus reaches the size you like, then snip or trim once a year in early spring to maintain the desired size.

Companion Planting and Design
Osmanthus makes a nice specimen next to a water garden, patio, or gazebo where the fall scent can be enjoyed. Several can be lined up to make a dense screen planting, especially where you'd like to discourage traffic (a feature of those spiny leaves). Trimmed osmanthus are good choices along eastern or northern house foundations. And since it does reasonably well in the dry shade and root competition of trees, plant one or more under a grove of trees.

Try These
'Goshiki' won a Pennsylvania Horticultural Society Gold Medal Award. Besides the green and creamy-yellow speckled foliage all year, the spring and fall foliage takes on hints of rosy-bronze. It doesn't produce the scent of the green-leafed species, but the leaf color makes it an excellent foundation shrub.

Pine

Botanical Pronunciation
PIE-nus

Bloom Period and Seasonal Color
Light brown cones; year-round green, blue-green, gold, or variegated foliage

Mature Height × Spread
25 to 75 feet × 20 to 40 feet (dwarf varieties available)

Pine is such a familiar species that many people refer to *any* evergreen as a "pine." Actually, the pine family is just one type of needled conifer that happens to show up in one variation or another almost everywhere on Earth. It's a highly adaptable species. Some pines are native to the United States, in particular the Eastern white pine (*Pinus strobus*) with its large, bushy habit and long, soft, slender, light green needles. But some pines have shorter, stiffer needles and narrow, upright habits. Others grow as short, rounded shrubs. Types that have golden, white-green, or gold-green variegated needles are prized specimens. Besides being useful in the landscape, pine seeds make good bird food, pine wood makes good lumber, and pine bark makes good mulch.

When, Where, and How to Plant
Balled-and-burlapped transplants can be planted in spring or early fall, or, from spring through early fall as a container-grown plant. Pick a site in full sun in damp, loose, mildly acidic soil, but pine tolerates poor, dry or rocky soil as well. Avoid wet spots. Loosen soil three to five times as wide as the rootball but only as deep. Mulch after planting, 2 to 3 inches of wood chips or bark, keeping all mulch a few inches away from the trunk.

Growing Tips
Water deeply once a week for the first growing season, then you'll probably never need to water again. Pine is very drought-tough. Fertilizer isn't necessary unless growth or foliage color is poor. If you have

questions about your soil, take a soil test to check nutrients and pH.

Regional Advice and Care
Northern native pines, such as Swiss stone pine (*Pinus cembra*) and Bosnian pine (*Pinus heldreichii*), suffer in the hottest Pennsylvania regions. Some pines, such as Austrian pine (*Pinus nigra*) and Japanese black pine (*Pinus thunbergii*), do well in salty soil while others do not (Eastern white pine and Swiss stone pine). Pines as a whole are carefree when all goes well, but the family is prone to a long list of woes, including sawfly larvae, scale, mites, bagworms, weevils, shoot moths, blight, and rust.

Companion Planting and Design
Pines are best clustered in open, sunny areas in large spaces. Stick with shrub types or standalone, upright specimens in smaller yards. Brightly colored, sun-loving perennials such as daylily, black-eyed Susan, and coreopsis are good partners, as are shrub roses, ornamental grasses, and St. Johnswort.

Try These
In Zones 5 to 6, I like Bosnian pine for its dense habit and salt and blight resistance and Swiss stone pine for its slow growth, narrow habit, and blue-green needles. Japanese black pine, Austrian pine, and Japanese white pine are good choices in Zones 6 to 7. Eastern white pine 'Fastigiata' is a worthy columnar native pine for smaller yards. The popular mugo pine (*Pinus mugo*) is too plagued by scale insects for my taste.

Rhododendron

Rhododendron species and hybrids

Botanical Pronunciation
roe-doe-DEN-dron

Bloom Period and Seasonal Color
May through June; pink, lavender, white, red, rose

Mature Height × Spread
3 to 10 feet × 4 to 10 feet

Rhododendron is the flowering evergreen family that encompasses azaleas. But when gardeners say "rhododendron," they're usually referring to the glossy, big-leaf plants that are covered with showy pastel flowers in late spring. Just so things aren't too simple for beginners, garden centers also sell small-leafed rhododendrons that *look* like azaleas. The popular 'PJM' (magenta) and the highly rated 'Olga Mezitt' (pink) are two examples. Names aside, the entire rhododendron family wants similar conditions—moist, acidy soil and good drainage. Although rhododendrons are usually considered to be shade plants, they bloom best in half-day to full sun. Give them what they want, and they can bloom happily for decades. Give them wet clay, and you'll see why they have such a high death rate.

When, Where, and How to Plant
Morning sun and afternoon shade is ideal. In full sun, keep the soil damp. In shade, less watering is needed, but plants don't bloom as well and grow "leggier." Loose, fertile, well-drained, and acidic soil is critical. Improve poor soil with 25 percent coarse sand and 25 percent compost to create raised beds. Fray out the roots of container-grown plants before planting. Plant an inch or two above grade, then mulch with 2 to 3 inches of wood chips or bark kept a few inches away from the trunk.

Growing Tips
Water deeply once or twice a week for the first season then weekly during hot, dry spells. Rhododendrons don't like drought. Scatter a balanced, granular, organic or gradual-release fertilizer formulated for acid-loving plants over the bed in early spring and early fall. Scratch sulfur into the soil surface in spring and fall to adjust alkaline soil.

Regional Advice and Care
Too many rhododendrons die from rotted roots in wet clay and excessive mulch. Many others die when they're inserted under existing big trees; give them compost and water help to overcome the tree roots' head start. Thin out excess or crossing branches and shorten too-long branches right after the plant blooms in spring. Use repellents or fencing if deer are nearby. Lace bugs and weevils are bug pests. Rhododendrons are toxic to pets and somewhat toxic to people if eaten.

Companion Planting and Design
Good sites: eastern and northern foundations; in the dappled sunlight of trees along a border, or along a partly shaded stream. Foamflower, liriope, lamium, creeping phlox, and fringe-leaf bleeding heart are good part-shade perennial partners.

Try These
Catawba types (*Rhododendron catawbiense*) such as 'Nova Zembla' (red) and 'Roseum Elegans' (lavender-pink) are U.S. natives. Consider native rosebay rhododendron (*Rhododendron maximum*) in a shady-native garden. Favorites recommended by the Pennsylvania chapter of the American Rhododendron Society: 'Caroline', 'President Lincoln', 'Scintillation', 'Vulcan's Flame', 'Chionoides', 'County of York', 'David Gable', 'English Roseum', 'Janet Blair', 'Ken Janeck', 'Percy Wiseman', and 'Yaku Angel.'

Russian Cypress

Microbiota decussata

Botanical Pronunciation
mye-kro-bye-OH-tah deck-oo-SAY-tah

Other Name Siberian cypress

Bloom Period and Seasonal Color
Medium green foliage in growing season,
brown-bronze in winter

Mature Height × Spread
12 to 18 inches × 6 to 10 feet

You've got deer. You've got shade. And you're looking for a low, spreading evergreen to cover lots of ground. That's a made-to-order situation for Russian cypress, sometimes called Siberian cypress or Russian arborvitae. Russian cypress sends out fan-shaped sprays of soft, medium-green needles that layer over one another about a foot high. The branch tips nod to give a graceful finishing touch to the plant. Plants spread outward 8 to 10 feet in a dozen years unless snipped. Native to Siberia, Russian cypress is very cold hardy and does best in the Zones 5 to 6 regions of Pennsylvania. One rap against it is the winter color. Those who like the plant say it turns "bronzy purple" in winter. Those who don't call it "dull brown."

When, Where, and How to Plant
Like most evergreens, Russian cypress demands good drainage. You *must* avoid wet clay. Plant spring through early fall in loose, acidic, compost-enriched soil, ideally in slightly raised beds. Russian cypress is less picky about sunlight. Full sun to part shade is ideal. It'll grow in shade but has a more open, less-vigorous habit. Mulch after planting with 2 to 3 inches of wood chips or bark kept a few inches away from the trunk.

Growing Tips
Water deeply once or twice a week for the first season, then you'll likely only need to water during hot, dry spells. Once established, Russian cypress has good drought-resistance and tolerates dry shade and root competition under trees. Fertilizer usually isn't needed unless growth or needle color is poor and a soil test indicates a nutrient is lacking.

Regional Advice and Care
In Zone 7 parts of Pennsylvania, Russian cypress is best used in morning sun but afternoon shade sites to limit heat stress. Once plants reach the desired spread, use hand-pruners to snip branches back to joints in spring or summer, making the deepest cuts from the layer underneath. Shearing won't harm the plant but it will destroy the layered look and nodding tips. Bugs and deer are unlikely, but Russian cypress may suffer root rot (from wet clay) or tip dieback (prune off browned tips).

Companion Planting and Design
An ideal spot is a group massed on a tree-planted or similar partly shaded bank, especially where the tips spill over the edge of a wall. But a Russian cypress groundcover is fair game anywhere, as long as the soil is well drained and the site isn't brutally hot. For color, plant a band of annual flowers or spring bulbs along the front edge of a Russian cypress bed.

Try These
You'll usually find just the straight species, which is fine. Celtic Pride™ supposedly has better winter color and resistance to tip dieback. 'Fuzz Ball' is a compact type occasionally offered, and 'Filip's Pretty Pride' is a newer compact type.

Sawara Falsecypress

Chamaecyparis pisifera

Botanical Pronunciation
kam-ee-SIPP-ar-iss pih-SIFF-ur-ah

Other Name Japanese falsecypress

Bloom Period and Seasonal Color
Brown cones; year-round green, blue, gold, or variegated foliage

Mature Height × Spread
10 to 50 feet × 10 to 20 feet (dwarfs available)

This family of Japanese soft-needled evergreens is similar to Hinoki falsecypress and also comes in a variety of looks. The species is an upright, green-needled tree growing to about 50 feet tall and 30 feet wide. Numerous variations include smaller trees, shrub types that are as wide as tall, and miniatures that grow as squat mounds. Needle colors include green, blue, and gold, plus variegated blends of those. Even the needle shapes have different looks, from flat fans that resemble arborvitae, to feathery needles that curl at the tips, to long, skinny, arching strands. The latter is what I'd suggest. These go by the common names of "green-thread" and "gold-thread" falsecypress and add eye-grabbing, fine texture to the landscape as well as evergreen color.

When, Where, and How to Plant
Plant Sawara falsecypress in spring or early fall as a burlap-wrapped, field-dug plant or from spring through early fall as a container plant. Full sun is best in damp—but not soggy—loose, acidic soil. Sawara falsecypress adapts to dry or poor soil and grows in part shade, although with a more open look. Dig to loosen soil three to five times as wide as the rootball but only as deep. Mulch after planting with 2 to 3 inches of wood chips or bark kept a few inches away from the trunk.

Growing Tips
Water deeply once or twice a week for its first season, then water is needed only in a prolonged drought. Sawara falsecypress has excellent drought-resistance once the roots establish. Fertilizer isn't necessary unless growth or foliage color is poor. A soil test for nutrients and pH (acidity level) will give you an idea of your soil's fertility, if you're suspicious.

Regional Advice and Care
Sawara falsecypress does well throughout Pennsylvania. Most types hold their needle color well in winter. An exception is the blue-needled 'Boulevard', which shows so many inner brown needles that many a gardener is convinced it's dying. Pest problems are rare, and deer aren't particularly fond of Sawara falsecypress, although they'll sometimes browse it in winter. Use repellents if that's the case.

Companion Planting and Design
Taller tree types are useful as screening along borders. Shrub types make nice specimens in sunny island gardens and do well in mixed plantings on sunny banks. Stick with compact shrub types and miniatures around house foundations so you don't end up with an overgrown look.

Try These
'Golden Mop', which grows about 6-by-6 feet and has a shaggy habit and thready golden needles, is my favorite. 'Filifera' is a green-thread small tree that grows 12 to 18 feet tall and 8 to 10 feet across. 'Filifera Aurea' is a gold-thread version of that. 'Plumosa' is a soft, green-needled, 30-foot tree type, and 'Squarrosa' is similar in size but with blue-green feathery needles.

Spruce

Picea species

Botanical Pronunciation
pie-SEE-ah

Bloom Period and Seasonal Color
Brown or red cones; year-round green, blue, or gold needles

Mature Height × Spread
35 to 80 feet × 15 to 40 feet (dwarf, spreading, and narrow types available)

Spruce is the most planted conifer in Pennsylvania landscapes, especially the blue-needled Colorado blue spruce tree (*Picea pungens*), the mite-prone dwarf Alberta white spruce (*Picea glauca 'conica'*) that flanks so many door-ways, and the tall, arching Norway spruce (*Picea abies*) that's widely used as a screen planting. It's certainly a varied and familiar species, coming in shapes from pyramids to weepers to creepers and in green-, blue-, or gold-colored needles. Some spruces are native to the U.S. (white spruce and Colorado spruce), and all hail from cooler parts of the world. Pennsylvania's Zone 7 is about as warm as most spruce tolerate. Nor do most care for alkaline soil, salty soil, soggy soil, or urban air pollution.

When, Where, and How to Plant
Spruce transplants best in spring as a field-dug, burlap-wrapped plant. Full sun is best in slightly acidic, well-drained and rocky or gravelly soil. Avoid hot spots—especially in Zone 7—and avoid wet clay everywhere. When it's time to plant, loosen the soil three to five times as wide as the rootball but only as deep. Then mulch with 2 to 3 inches of wood chips or bark, kept a few inches away from the trunk.

Growing Tips
Water deeply once or twice a week for the first season, then you'll likely need to water only in very hot, dry spells. Spruce is reasonably drought-tough. Fertilizer isn't necessary unless growth or foliage color is poor. If you want to be sure of your soil's fertility, take a soil test for nutrients and pH (acidity level).

Regional Advice and Care
Spruce is a species likely to fare worse in a warming climate. It may display browning or shedding needles during 90- to 100-degree days, especially in full sun, salty soils, and near asphalt. If pruning to control its size is needed, wait until early summer and lightly trim off most new growth. Remove the lowest branches anytime if they die as the tree ages (don't leave stubs). Adelgids, bagworms, and mites are bug threats. Some species are prone to needle-cast disease (dropping needles) and fungal cankers (a bark infection).

Companion Planting and Design
A line of tree-type spruce makes a good windbreak. Many spruce are sleek enough to serve as choice specimens in an open sunny yard. Consider weeping forms at house corners. Dwarf and miniature types are useful around house foundations and in rock gardens. Spreading types are a good option for an evergreen groundcover on a sunny bank.

Try These
Oriental spruce (*Picea orientalis*) is my favorite for its short needles, narrow habit, and red cones. Serbian spruce (*Picea omorika*) is a close second with its arching habit and blue-green needles. Weeping Serbian spruce 'Pendula Bruns' is a great skinny weeper. Colorado blue spruce 'Fat Albert' is a 12-by-8-foot, blue-needled, house-corner specimen.

Sweetbox

Sarcococca hookeriana var. *humilis*

Botanical Pronunciation
sar-koe-KOCK-ah hook-er-ee-AY-nah
HEW-mih-liss

Other Name Dwarf sweetbox

Bloom Period and Seasonal Color
Creamy white flowers March through April;
year-round glossy green leaves

Mature Height × Spread
12 to 18 inches × 4 to 10 feet

Zones 6 and 7

Sweetbox gets my vote as the most underused low evergreen for the shade. This particular sweetbox, *Sarcococca hookeriana* var. *humilis*, is a dwarf version that grows only 12 to 18 inches tall but sends out runners to make a dense, weed-choking colony of 4 feet and beyond. It's not overly aggressive, though. It doesn't climb, its growth rate is slow to medium, and runners are easy to dig out when the plant reaches the desired spread. The leaves are glossy, dark green, and slender, coming to a point like a small lance. Sweetbox is winter-hardy in Zones 6 and 7 but is iffy in Zone 5. An added bonus is the barely noticeable little white flowers that waft a sweet fragrance over the early-spring garden.

When, Where, and How to Plant
Plant sweetbox in spring through early summer in moist, compost-enriched, well-drained, mildly acidic soil. A moist, shady spot is perfect, but morning sun and afternoon shade is also fine. Avoid hot spots and full-sun locations. Mulch after planting with about 1 to 2 inches of wood chips or bark kept a few inches away from the trunk.

Growing Tips
Water deeply once or twice a week for the first season, then water every week or two during hot, dry spells. Although it prefers moist soil, sweetbox tolerates dry soil once its roots are established. Scatter a balanced, granular, organic or gradual-release fertilizer over the bed in early spring.

Regional Advice and Care
In Zone 6, guard against winter leaf damage by planting sweetbox in courtyards, along east-facing walls, or in similar wind-protected sites. Or spray an anti-transpirant on the leaves once or twice over the winter if leaf-edge browning becomes a problem. Sweetbox may survive Zone 5 winters, but it needs a protected area and maybe wintertime anti-transpirant sprays and a burlap protection, at least for the first two or three winters. Sweetbox can be pruned after blooming to maintain desired size. Dig out runners anytime to limit their spreading.

Companion Planting and Design
Sweetbox makes an excellent edging plant in shady areas, such as along a northern or eastern house foundation, along a shady walk, or along a shady stream. A patch of it also looks good around shaded sections of a water garden. A colony of sweetbox makes an attractive, fragrant underplanting for shrubs such as hydrangea, viburnum, and rhododendron.

Try These
Look for "*dwarf* sweetbox" on the label or for the word "*humilis*" at the end of the botanical name to be sure you're getting this compact version. The straight species can go 3 to 4 feet tall and isn't quite as winter-hardy. Dwarf sweetbox earned a Pennsylvania Horticultural Society Gold Medal Award.

Weeping Alaska-Cedar

Xanthocyparis nootkatensis 'Pendula'

Botanical Pronunciation
zan-thoh-SIPP-ar-iss noot-kah-TEN-siss

Other Name Nootka falsecypress

Bloom Period and Seasonal Color
Pea-sized, round, brown cones; year-round green foliage

Mature Height × Spread
25 to 35 feet × 8 to 12 feet

This durable but elegant upright evergreen makes one of the most graceful specimen plants in a Pennsylvania landscape. Native to the Pacific Northwest and northward to Alaska, the weeping Alaska-cedar is easily winter-hardy throughout Pennsylvania but is heat-tolerant enough to do well in a Philadelphia summer. Its medium-green, soft needles grow in fan shapes, and the branches of this type also have a gently weeping habit. Weeping Alaska-cedar isn't a true cedar, but botanists have had a hard time deciding exactly *what* species it is. Gardeners would tell you the soft, fan-shaped foliage reminds them of falsecypress or arborvitae. Regardless of what you call it, weeping Alaska-cedar grows slowly to an ultimate size of 25 to 35 feet tall and 8 to 12 feet across.

When, Where, and How to Plant
Plant weeping Alaska-cedar in spring or early fall as a burlap-wrapped, field-dug plant or from spring through early fall as a container-grown plant. Full sun is best in damp, loose, mildly acidic soil. But weeping Alaska-cedar adapts to poor soil, is reasonably drought-tough once established, and tolerates some shade. Avoid soggy spots. Loosen soil three to five times as wide as the rootball but only as deep. Mulch after planting with 2 to 3 inches of wood chips or bark kept a few inches away from the trunk.

Growing Tips
Water deeply once or twice a week for the first season, then water is needed only during unusually hot,

dry spells. Fertilizer usually isn't necessary unless growth or foliage color is poor. If you're suspicious, do a soil test for nutrients and pH (acidity level).

Regional Advice and Care
Limit heat stress to this northern native in Zone 7 by planting in an afternoon-shade site. Give your weeping Alaska-cedar enough space that you'll never need to prune it. If size control is needed, snip overly long branches in late spring to early summer or shear as lightly as possible to avoid ruining the plant's weeping habit. Never cut back into bare branches; only cut to wood with live needles. Diseases, animals, and bugs (except for the occasional bagworm) are unlikely.

Companion Planting and Design
This plant is a standalone star. Use it as the centerpiece of a rock garden or sunny island bed or off the front corner of the house (at least 6 feet out). Weeping Alaska-cedar also looks good backdropping a waterfall or pond. Sun perennials, such as coreopsis, daylilies, blanket flowers, black-eyed Susans, and mums, add seasonal color around an Alaska-cedar's base.

Try These
The straight species (as opposed to the weeping 'Pendula' variety) is bigger, wider, and more broadly pyramidal but still has slightly drooping branch tips. 'Aurea' is a yellow-needled form of that. 'Green Arrow' and 'Jubilee' are narrow weepers, growing to less than 6 feet wide.

Yew

Taxus species

Botanical Pronunciation
TACKS-us

Bloom Period and Seasonal Color
Pea-sized red fruits in fall and winter; year-round green or gold foliage

Mature Height × Spread
4 to 60 feet × 6 to 20 feet (narrow varieties available)

This is the evergreen most people shear into boxes or balls all around the house. The yew doesn't do anything terribly exciting, but it shows up in so many Pennsylvania yards because it's hard to kill, it's adaptable to everything from full sun to deep shade, and it keeps chugging along despite being butchered at any time into any shape. Left unpruned yews will grow into 40- to 60-foot-tall trees or large bushes that become more open with age. Yew needles are flat, soft, and dark green. Columnar and spreading forms are available in addition to the tree and shrub types. But be aware: the red berrylike fruits produced by female yews are toxic to people and pets, although not to birds.

When, Where, and How to Plant
Yew is one of the least finicky plants; if you just avoid soggy or salty spots, it'll likely live. The densest growth and best color is in full sun. Yew competes well in the dry shade and root competition under trees; it just grows slower and more open. Plant burlap-wrapped, field-dug yews in spring or early fall and container-grown ones anytime spring through early fall. Loosen soil three to five times as wide as the rootball but only as deep. Mulch after planting with 2 to 3 inches of wood chips or bark kept a few inches away from the trunk.

Growing Tips
Water deeply once or twice a week for the first season, then water likely won't be needed again. Yew is exceptionally drought-resistant. Fertilizer isn't necessary unless growth or foliage color is poor. If you're suspicious, do a soil test for nutrients and pH (acidity level).

Regional Advice and Care
Afternoon shade is best in the state's warmest regions; yews aren't happy south of Zone 7. Prune or shear spring through midsummer. Other than rotting in wet soil, the main threat is deer. Yew is a deer delicacy, especially in winter. Use repellents or fencing or plant the similar-looking but deer-resistant Japanese plum yew instead. Scale is an occasional bug threat (horticultural oil is a treatment).

Companion Planting and Design
Yew is an ideal hedge plant because it shears so well (cut wider at the base, narrower at the top). Taller types can be used for border screening (especially in shade), and spreading types make good evergreen ground covers under trees. Columnar types are useful for framing doors in tight areas. Yew is a good topiary plant too.

Try These
English yew (*Taxus baccata*) 'Repandens' is a top choice for massing under trees. Most types you'll find are *Taxus* × *media* hybrids between English yew and Japanese yew (*Taxus cuspidata*). Worthy ones include the spreading shrub types 'Densiformis' and 'Wardii', the bushy upright 'Hicksii', and the columnar ones 'Fastigiata', 'Flushing', and 'Beanpole'.

GROUNDCOVERS

FOR PENNSYLVANIA

Groundcovers are plants grouped in this chapter by their *use* instead of any common botanical trait. If it spreads out to thickly cover the ground, it qualifies as a "groundcover." By far, Pennsylvanians' groundcover of choice is turfgrass, used widely because it's highly tolerant of foot traffic and easy to "prune" with power equipment.

Garden centers have earmarked a few low-growing, fast-spreading perennial flowers that they sell in devoted groundcover sections in 25- or 50-plant trays. The Big Three are ivy, pachysandra, and periwinkle (vinca).

Plenty of other low, spreading perennials make excellent groundcovers though. You'll usually find them mixed in with other perennials, sometimes in the herb section (oregano and thyme, for example) or grouped under branded collections, such as Stepables® and Jeepers Creepers®.

But even bigger woody plants, including shrub roses, spreading juniper, leucothoe, Virginia sweetspire, and deutzia, make fine groundcovers. In other words, a groundcover doesn't have to be a ground-hugging perennial.

The Point of Groundcovers

From a practical standpoint, groundcovers keep soil from eroding, prevent weeds from overtaking bare ground, and absorb rainwater. They're also a key ally in the popular trend toward low maintenance. Singular masses of low-care groundcovers are much easier to maintain than mixed gardens with multiple species or landscapes with lots of annuals to be replanted each season.

But groundcovers also add beauty to the yard, whether that's a low, mounded bed of green to your eye or a colorful combination of variegated liriope and red-tinged barrenwort. Most of the time (especially if low care is your goal), it makes sense to pick one groundcover and mass it throughout a given

Sedum kamtschaticum

bed. When you interplant two or three vigorous spreaders, they tend to duke it out for the space and end up climbing over one another. While that chokes out weeds, the look crosses the line from "neat mass" to "jumbled mess."

That doesn't mean you can't mix groundcovers. You might need to "referee" to keep the different types in their intended space, but good pairing in the first place will limit that. Here's an example: ring a tree with a band of upright, grassy liriope and let spreading sweet woodruff fill the bed perimeter.

Lamium 'Beacon Silver'

Choosing and Planting Groundcovers

As with any plant, it's important to know your site and then pick a groundcover suited to those conditions. But there are groundcovers available for any site.

In a hot, sunny spot, look to plants that are at home in rocky spots or sunny meadows, such as creeping sedum, moss pink, vinca, creeping thyme, spreading juniper, shrub roses, and most grasses.

A moist, shady spot, however, calls for a different type of plant. Lamium, sweet woodruff, variegated Solomon's seal, crested iris, and pachysandra are examples of groundcovers more at home in those settings.

One of the toughest groundcover settings is in the dry shade of trees, where plants must contend with established tree roots as well as low light. Liriope, hardy ginger, barrenwort, variegated Solomon's seal, and leadwort are good choices there.

In the early years after planting, you'll have space between the plants. Some species fill in faster than others. Be vigilant to keep weeds under control until the plants fill in. Once established, most groundcovers need little to no water or fertilizer. Evergreen types may require no care at all, while leaf-dropping ones look good with a once-a-year weed-whacker "haircut."

Groundcovers are also useful in reducing the need for mulch. Low, spreading choices such as creeping sedum, creeping thyme, and sweet woodruff make low, carpet-like underplantings that stop weeds as well as mulch does.

And if you're trying to reduce mowing, a replacement bed of groundcover might mean more work and expense up front, but in the long run, you won't be chopping it 25 times a year.

Barrenwort

Epimedium species and hybrids

Botanical Pronunciation
ep-ih-MEE-dee-um

Other Name Bishop's hat

Bloom Period and Seasonal Color
Late March through May; rosy-pink, yellow, white flowers

Mature Height × Spread
8 to 12 inches × 18 to 24 inches

Barrenwort gets my vote as the most underused groundcover. This foot-tall European and Japanese import grows into a dense colony without being aggressive or invasive, its leaves and flowers are both subtly attractive, and even the deer and rabbits let it alone (usually). Its best feature, though, is that it's one of the toughest groundcovers in the dry shade and root competition under trees. Barrenwort does best in good soil and ample moisture, but it'll grow in your most barren spots (hence its name). The leaves are heart-shaped and often red-tinged in spring. The mid-spring flowers look like little hanging hats. Then the leaves turn yellow, bronze, or yellowish bronze in fall. Despite those attributes, barrenwort still isn't very widely used. You can change that.

When, Where, and How to Plant
Plant in spring or early fall, 15 to 18 inches apart. Barrenwort tolerates full sun, but afternoon shade to full-day shade is best. It'll also handle dry soil, rocky soil, and root competition, but it grows best in average moisture and compost-improved, slightly acidic soil. After planting, top the soil with 1 to 2 inches of bark mulch (keep it slightly away from the stems) and give a good soaking.

Growing Tips
Water weekly when conditions are dry the first season, then water is needed only in a prolonged drought. If you've improved the soil with compost at planting, no fertilizer is needed. Or you can scatter a balanced, granular, organic or gradual-release fertilizer over the bed early each spring according to package directions. To expand plantings, dig and divide clumps into fist-sized pieces with a knife early in fall, then replant the pieces at the same depth they were growing. Then water.

Regional Advice and Care
Some barrenwort species are semi-evergreen in Pennsylvania, but most will end up with brown leaves by winter's end. In early March before new growth begins, trim off last year's stems and leaves to about 2 inches to make way for fresh new growth and the flowers. Barrenwort is slow to get started. Be patient. It'll make a solid colony in a few years. Barrenwort seldom runs into any issues with bugs, diseases, or animals.

Companion Planting and Design
The number one use is massed by itself under trees. Barrenwort also is well behaved enough to use in patches in a shady perennial garden. Its heart-shaped leaves and mounding habit pair nicely with shade-tolerant grasses, such as Japanese forestgrass, Pennsylvania sedge, or the grass-like liriope.

Try These
I like the basic *Epimedium* × 'Rubrum', which has beautiful reddish new leaves and reddish yellow flowers. *Epimedium* × *perralchicum* 'Frohnleiten' is one of the more semi-evergreen types with attractive yellow flowers. *Epimedium* × *versicolor* 'Sulphureum' and 'Neosulphureum' are similar to 'Frohnleiten' and among the earliest bloomers. *Epimedium grandiflorum* 'Rose Queen' is a beautiful rosy pink bloomer with dark leaves.

Creeping Phlox

Phlox species

Botanical Pronunciation
FLOKS

Other Name Moss pink

Bloom Period and Seasonal Color
April through June; pink, red, lavender,
blue-violet, white, bicolor flowers

Mature Height × Spread
6 to 15 inches × 18 to 24 inches

I'm lumping three species under one catch-all name. The common denominators are that all are U.S. natives; all grow in low, spreading mounds; and all bloom profusely in April and May. Moss pinks (*Phlox subulata*) are the shortest (6 to 8 inches) and are the ones most often seen growing on front-yard banks and rock gardens. These bloom in a range of colors and are best in sunny spots. Creeping phlox (*Phlox stolonifera*) grows slightly taller, does best out of the afternoon sun, and blooms primarily in blue-purple colors. Woodland phlox (*Phlox divaricata*) grows 12 to 15 inches tall, is the most shade-tolerant type, and blooms mostly in blue. The leaves are small and narrow on all of these, and all are evergreen through most Pennsylvania winters.

When, Where, and How to Plant
Creeping phlox transplants best in early fall, although it usually does fine when planted in full bloom or soon after. Space 15 to 18 inches apart. Sunlight depends on the type you're trying (see the plant introduction). All types prefer well-drained and even sandy or gravelly soil. After planting, top the soil with 1 to 2 inches of bark mulch (kept slightly away from the stems) and give a good soaking.

Growing Tips
Although creeping phlox is prone to rotting in wet soil, it also doesn't care for drought either. Water weekly throughout the first season (when it doesn't rain), then give a good soaking once a week in dry weather. Creeping phlox is a light feeder, so a single, early-spring scattering of a balanced, granular, organic or gradual-release fertilizer is plenty. Dig and divide into fist-sized pieces in early fall if the bloom is going downhill. Shovel out and transplant any sections creeping beyond where you want.

Regional Advice and Care
Assuming your plants make it green through the winter, lightly rake out any dead tips or excess leaves in March. Dead stems can be trimmed back to live growth if winter hasn't been kind. Always keep at least 2 to 4 inches of stems. Creeping phlox also can be trimmed back after blooming if the growth is too bushy for your taste. Mites and powdery mildew are potential problems.

Companion Planting and Design
Moss pinks are ideal for massing on sunny banks or lining sunny driveways. More shade-preferring creeping phlox and woodland phlox are better choices on shady banks, spotted toward the front of shade perennial gardens, or in bands along north and east house foundations.

Try These
You'll find varieties galore, and most perform well. Go by the color you like. Some good moss pinks are 'Candy Stripe' (pink-and-white striped), 'Scarlet Flame' (rosy red), and 'Emerald Blue' (lavender-blue). 'Sherwood Purple' (blue-violet) is a classic creeping phlox, and 'Blue Moon' is one of the best woodland phlox.

Creeping Sedum

Sedum species

Botanical Pronunciation
SEE-dum

Other Name Stonecrop

Bloom Period and Seasonal Color
May through July; yellow, white, red, pink flowers

Mature Height × Spread
2 to 8 inches × 2 feet and beyond

As with creeping phlox, I'm lumping multiple species in this category. You'll find many different textures and leaf/flower colors in creeping sedum, but what's common is that all have fleshy, succulent leaves and grow in low, spreading mats. Creeping sedum blooms late spring to midsummer and is heroically drought-tolerant. It's also very short. Most types hug the ground at 4 to 6 inches, and some stay even lower. That habit is mainly what distinguishes creeping sedums from their better known cousin, the fall-blooming, pink-flowered, upright sedum 'Autumn Joy' and similar. Most creeping sedums are native to Europe and Asia, but one species—whorled stonecrop (*Sedum ternatum*)—is a U.S. native. That one actually prefers shadier and slightly damper conditions than most creeping sedums.

When, Where, and How to Plant
Plant in early spring or early fall in full sun, 15 to 18 inches apart. The exception is the native whorled stonecrop, which appreciates partial shade. All types prefer well-drained soil, to the point even of sandy, gravelly, or rocky soil. Improve clayish soil with an inch or two of compost or fine gravel. Go light on mulch; one inch is plenty, and keep it off the stems.

Growing Tips
Go easy on the water too. Water weekly the first season until the roots establish, then you should never have to water again. Fertilizer usually isn't necessary. If you want, you can toss some balanced, granular, organic or gradual-release fertilizer over the bed in early spring (follow package directions).

To expand your planting dig, divide, and transplant fist-sized pieces in early spring or early fall. Dig out sections creeping beyond where you want. Trim the tips off flowers after they brown.

Regional Advice and Care
The biggest threat to sedum health is root rot, especially in wet spells over winter. Work more compost or gravel into any dead zones and fill back in with divisions from surviving patches. Many creeping sedums are evergreen. At end of winter, lightly trim off any dead tips (if needed), and rake out any excess leaves. Keep at least 2 to 4 inches of stems. Bug, diseases, and animal troubles are not common.

Companion Planting and Design
Creeping sedum's short stature and drought-tolerance makes it a top choice for planting on green roofs. It's also a no-brainer in rock gardens, for massing on sunny banks, and for lining sunny walks, driveways, and west- or south-facing house-foundation beds. Its carpet-like habit also is ideal for use as mulch-replacing mats under shrubs, evergreens, and ornamental grasses.

Try These
My favorite is *Sedum rupestre* 'Angelina', which has narrow foliage of gold that turns coppery over winter. It's gorgeous year-round. *Sedum spurium* 'John Creech' has blue-green leaves and pink flowers. *Sedum spurium* 'Bronze Carpet' and 'Fuldaglut' have bronze-purple leaves and red flowers. *Sedum floriferum* 'Weihenstephaner Gold' has green leaves and orangish gold flowers.

Ferns

Multiple genera and species

Bloom Period and Seasonal Color
Grown for foliage; mostly shades of green, some with golden fall color

Mature Height × Spread
2 to 4 feet × 18 to 24 inches

Live in the woods with hungry deer lurking nearby? Start here. Ferns rate low on the deer menu, and most are at home in shaded, wooded environments. This huge family of plants is one of the oldest on the planet. They run the gamut from 75-foot tropical tree ferns to diminutive pond-dwellers. The plants unfurl like fiddles into leaves or "fronds" of assorted textures, setting one type apart from another. Leaf colors are mostly assorted shades of green, although the Japanese painted fern (*Athyrium nipponicum* 'Pictum') has striking leaves of metallic reddish purple, cream, and green, and the cinnamon fern (*Osmunda cinnamomea*) turns an attractive golden shade in fall. Most ferns in garden centers are U.S. natives. Some are evergreen.

When, Where, and How to Plant
Ferns are best planted in spring, though early fall is second best. Almost all ferns are ideally suited for full shade or at least afternoon shade. Avoid hot, sunny spots, where most ferns will brown out by midsummer. Plant 18 to 24 inches apart. Some are slower-spreading clump-formers; others spread quickly by underground rhizomes. Either way, they'll fill in eventually to make a dense colony. Mulch with 1 to 2 inches of bark or rotted leaves, and soak well after planting.

Growing Tips
Most ferns like damp, shady conditions. They'll tolerate dry shade under trees but may brown out in a hot, dry summer. Soak them weekly to prevent that during dry spells. Fertilizer isn't necessary, especially if you've improved the soil with compost before

planting. Ferns are best divided in early spring before new growth emerges. Divide into softball-sized clumps, replant, and water well.

Regional Advice and Care
Let evergreen ferns stand all winter, and clip off any weathered growth in early spring. Cut non-evergreen types back to the ground in fall, after frost kills the fronds, or early spring. A few less heat-tolerant types may suffer in summer in the warmer southeastern corner of the state. Examples include northern maidenhair fern (*Adiantum pedatum*) and the interrupted fern (*Osmunda claytoniana*).

Companion Planting and Design
Ferns are at their natural best massed under trees, lining wooded paths, surrounding a shady gazebo, or lining the boundary between the lawn and a wooded line. Shade perennials with rounded forms make good partners, especially hosta, false forget-me-not, and coralbell. Azaleas, rhododendrons, and smooth hydrangeas are good shrub partners.

Try These
I like the dainty, rounded leaves and spray form of the native northern maidenhair fern. If you like evergreens, try native wood ferns (*Dryopteris*) or the Christmas fern (*Polystichum acrostichoides*). The foot-tall Japanese painted fern is the most colorful and tolerates dry shade and tree-root competition well. The 3-foot native ostrich fern (*Matteuccia strathioptens*) is one of the fastest spreaders and tolerates more sun than most. The native lady fern (*Athyrium filix-femina*) is a graceful shade classic.

Hardy Ginger

Asarum canadense

Botanical Pronunciation
ah-SAR-um kan-ah-DEN-see

Other Name Canadian ginger

Bloom Period and Seasonal Color
May; non-showy purplish brown flowers

Mature Height × Spread
6 to 10 inches × 2 feet and beyond

First off, this is *not* the plant that produces the cooking spice ginger sold in grocery stores. That one's a fat-rooted tropical in a different genus (*Zingiber officinale*). This ginger is a low, spreading, shade-preferring groundcover grown for its dense, 6-inch-wide, heart-shaped leaves. It gets its common name from the scent of its roots (actually rhizomes), which have an aroma like ginger when bruised. Hardy ginger is a U.S. and Canadian native that has duller green leaves than the more popular European ginger (*Asarum europaeum*), which has glossy, dark green leaves. Another difference is hardy ginger dies back in winter; European ginger is evergreen through Pennsylvania winters. Both are trouble-free and likely would be more popular if sold in less expensive small sizes as ivy, pachysandra, and vinca are.

When, Where, and How to Plant

Plant in spring or early fall, 15 to 18 inches apart in shade to part shade. Hardy ginger usually wilts in full afternoon summer sun. It prefers cool, moist, rich, slightly acidic and "woodsy" soil but also does very well in the dry shade and root competition of trees. After planting, top the soil with an inch of bark mulch or leaves (kept slightly away from the stems) and give a good soaking.

Growing Tips

There's no need to fertilize, especially if you've improved the soil with an inch or two of compost at planting. Water once or twice a week throughout the first season to establish the roots, then give hardy ginger a drink only if it starts to wilt during a hot, dry spell. Dividing is optional; but if you'd like to speed up its spread, transplant divisions in early spring. Dig out any sections creeping beyond where you want.

Regional Advice and Care

Hardy ginger is slow to get started. Be patient. Once going, the rhizomes will spread to form a dense colony. Fall frost kills the native hardy ginger's foliage; gently rake out the dead leaves at winter's end. Cut out any ratty, winter-injured foliage of evergreen European ginger in early spring. Some people get a skin rash from handling hardy ginger, so use gloves if you're in that camp.

Companion Planting and Design

Interplant other spring woodland natives, such as Virginia bluebell, trillium, and bleeding heart, into hardy-ginger patches. The rounded leaves of hardy ginger also pair well with the grassy texture of Pennsylvania sedge and Japanese forestgrass. Or just plant hardy ginger by itself under trees and let it grow into a low-care mass—especially in deer country.

Try These

'Eco Choice' and 'Eco Red Giant' are improved varieties of hardy ginger with larger leaves and denser foliage. Go with the non-native European ginger if you prefer glossy leaves and an evergreen groundcover. Chinese ginger (*Asarum splendens*) is another glossy-leafed, evergreen type with silver-mottled foliage, but it's not reliably hardy in Pennsylvania's colder Zone 5 regions.

Lamium

Lamium maculatum

Botanical Pronunciation
LAY-mee-um mack-yew-LAY-tum

Other Name Spotted dead nettle

Bloom Period and Seasonal Color
Mid to late spring; pink, lavender, reddish purple, white flowers

Mature Height × Spread
6 to 10 inches × 15 to 18 inches

L amium offers two attractions—long-lasting spring flowers and colorful, silver-variegated foliage throughout the season. The flowers are hanging, hooded in shape, and about the size of a pinky fingernail. The leaves are about 3 inches across and in some varieties more silver than green. That bright foliage helps light the shade, which makes lamium a good alternative to the plain green leaves of pachysandra or ivy. Lamium fills in with its spreading clumps, but it stops short of crossing into invasiveness or rooting into the lawn. This plant is a different species from the more aggressive yellow archangel (*Lamium galeobdolon*), which blooms yellow and is best planted by itself in a difficult site, such as a shady bank or under big-rooted shade trees.

When, Where, and How to Plant
Plant in spring or early fall, 15 to 18 inches apart is good, in shade to partly shady sites. Lamium may wilt and even die back in full-sun sites. It prefers cool, moist, slightly acidic soil, but it handles under-tree plantings if it has occasional watering. Avoid planting in wet clay, which can rot the bases of the stems. After planting, top the soil with an inch of bark mulch or leaves (kept slightly away from the stems) and give a good soaking.

Growing Tips
If you've improved the soil with an inch or two of compost at planting there's no need to fertilize. Water once or twice a week during the first season to establish the roots. Do the same during hot, dry spells; otherwise, water is not needed.

If the patch is dense there's no need to divide, but dug-up divisions can be used to fill in any bare spots in early spring or early fall. Control sections that are creeping too far by digging out the runaways.

Regional Advice and Care
Lamium is variably evergreen in Pennsylvania, especially in Zones 6 to 7. See what you've got at winter's end. Trim off winter-killed or ratty foliage, and lightly rake out any excess leaves. Cut back as far as 2 or 3 inches after a brutal winter but never the whole way to the ground. Plants also can be lightly trimmed to remove browned flowers and any overly bushy growth in early summer. Slugs occasionally eat lamium leaves.

Companion Planting and Design
Lamium works best planted under or along evergreens (yew, azalea, boxwood, cherrylaurel, holly) in eastern and northern house-foundation beds. It also partners well with white-blooming smooth hydrangea (*Hydrangea arborescens*) under a grouping of small trees.

Try These
Pink Chablis® and 'Shell Pink' are two of the best pink bloomers. 'Purple Dragon' has eye-grabbing, deep reddish purple flowers. 'White Nancy' lights up the shade with its white flowers and silvery foliage. If you want to try the more vigorous, yellow-blooming yellow archangel type, look for the relatively well-behaved 'Hermann's Pride'.

Leadwort

Ceratostigma plumbaginoides

Botanical Pronunciation
sir-ah-toe-STIG-mah plum-ba-jih-NOY-deez

Other Name Plumbago

Bloom Period and Seasonal Color
August through September; blue flowers;
red fall foliage

Mature Height × Spread
8 to 12 inches × 2 feet and beyond

Here's another greatly underused groundcover. Leadwort is trouble-free, non-climbing, and has long-lasting, blue, open-faced, late-summer flowers reminiscent of impatiens. The nickel-sized green leaves turn glossy red in fall. All of that makes leadwort an excellent, low-care choice for late-season interest in yards that otherwise limp down the home stretch into winter. Three things, I think, keep leadwort from being one of our top go-to groundcovers. First, it's not evergreen like ivy, pachysandra, and vinca; second, it's usually not available in cheap, small sizes; and last, it's just not that well known. Don't let any of those stop you from trying at least a few plants in part-shade spots. Leadwort spreads and can be divided to create your own eventual inexpensive colony.

When, Where, and How to Plant
Leadwort does best where it gets morning sun and afternoon shade or in sunlight that's dappled by overhead tree leaves. It'll tolerate full sun if given an occasional soaking in hot, dry spells, and it'll tolerate deeper shade, although it'll grow less densely and flower less. Spring planting is best, but early fall usually works too. Space 15 to 18 inches apart. Ideally give leadwort loose, well-drained, and slightly acidic soil, but it does well in fairly dry spots. After planting, top the soil with 1 to 2 inches of bark mulch or rotted leaves (kept slightly away from the stems) and give a good soaking.

Growing Tips
Water weekly throughout the first season to establish the roots, then water is not needed, except in very hot, dry spells. Fertilizer is not needed, especially if you've worked an inch or two of compost into the soil at planting. Slice divisions into fist-sized pieces in early spring to help spread your colony. Any sections creeping beyond where you want can be shoveled out.

Regional Advice and Care
Leadwort is late to leaf out in spring (sometimes early May), so don't think it has died when it's still "sleeping." Leadwort leaves drop after frost in fall. Let tree leaves fall among the crowns of the bare plants over winter; these help insulate leadwort, especially in colder Zone 5 regions at the bottom end of leadwort's hardiness range. Just before new growth begins in spring, use a weed-whacker to trim the bare tips (at least 2 to 3 inches of stems), and lightly rake out excess tree leaves.

Companion Planting and Design
Use leadwort as an edging plant along shady or wooded paths or as a standalone groundcover massed under small to mid-sized trees. Another good use is underneath hydrangeas or azaleas along an eastern house foundation. Interplant spring bulbs, such as hyacinths or daffodils, for early spring color before leadwort leafs out.

Try These
You won't find any varieties or relatives . . . just the straight species of this Chinese native. That's okay; it's good enough as is.

Liriope

Liriope muscari

Botanical Pronunciation
lih-RYE-oh-pee muss-KAR-ee

Other Name Lilyturf

Bloom Period and Seasonal Color
August through September; lavender, blue-purple, white flowers

Mature Height × Spread
10 to 15 inches × 18 to 24 inches

Zones 6 and 7

Liriope is often mistaken for an ornamental grass because of its narrow, upright, strappy leaves and clumping habit. Actually, it's a grasslike, tough-as-nails perennial flower that puts out spiky flowers of lavender, blue-purple, or white in late summer. Liriope is commonly used in Zones 6 and 7 of Pennsylvania, but it's an iffy overwinter performer in the colder Zone 5 regions. A warm microclimate and an insulating layer of leaf mulch can help it through Zone 5 winters. Where hardy, liriope stays green all winter. Its foot-tall clumps spread to make a thick, versatile, weed-choking groundcover that asks for nothing more than an end-of-winter cutback. Plants are incredibly easy to divide and move, making it a choice that can be spread throughout the yard.

When, Where, and How to Plant

Liriope will work almost anywhere, although full sun and loose, well-drained soil is ideal. It won't bloom as well in shade, but the foliage is still texturally attractive. It'll even grow in compacted soil and in the dry shade and root competition of big trees. Plant in spring or early fall, spacing about 15 to 18 inches. One to 2 inches of bark mulch is plenty.

Growing Tips

Water every week or two when conditions are dry the first season, then you'll never need to water again. Liriope is extremely drought-tough. Fertilizer is not needed. To expand plantings, dig and pull or cut apart fist-sized clumps in spring or early fall. Replant pieces at their same depth, then water.

Regional Advice and Care

Liriope usually looks pretty good coming out of winter, faking gardeners into thinking no care is needed. However, once new shoots emerge from the base, last year's growth falls and eventually browns. It's much harder to clean up the look then. A better idea is to cut, weed-whack, or mow liriope down to 1- or 2-inch stubs at the end of winter *before* new growth emerges. Rabbits sometimes eat leaves of young plants. Use repellents or temporary fencing. Once plants age, damage usually stops. Avoid wet clay locations, which can lead to rotting at the base of the stems.

Companion Planting and Design

Liriope is excellent massed as a dry-shade groundcover under trees. It pairs nicely with the rounded or heart-shaped leaves of hosta, coralbell, false forget-me-not, or barrenwort in a part-shade garden. And it's excellent edging sidewalks, driveways, paths, and foundation beds or grown in a colony on a sunny to partly sunny bank.

Try These

'Super Blue' and 'Big Blue' are good lavender bloomers. 'Royal Purple' has purplish blue flowers, and 'Monroe's White' is a white bloomer. 'Variegata' has lavender flowers and striking white-variegated leaves for season-long color (best in shadier spots). 'Silvery Sunproof' has yellow-variegated leaves. Creeping lilyturf (*Liriope spicata*) is a cold-hardier cousin that spreads more aggressively by runners and works best used alone.

Pachysandra

Pachysandra procumbens

Botanical Pronunciation
paa-kih-SANN-drah pro-KUM-benz

Other Name Allegheny spurge

Bloom Period and Seasonal Color
April; pinkish white flowers

Mature Height × Spread
9 to 12 inches × 15 to 18 inches

Try this native version of the more common Japanese spurge (*Pachysandra terminalis*), the one you'll find in inexpensive trays in the groundcover section of garden centers. The most noticeable difference is that Japanese spurge has glossy leaves and flowers on the stem tips. Native Allegheny spurge has duller green leaves and flowers low on the plant. Japanese spurge also is evergreen and fast-spreading, which explains why it's one of Pennsylvania's Big 3 groundcovers while our native version rarely graces local gardens. On the plus side, native Allegheny spurge grows in well behaved clumps, it runs into fewer bug and disease troubles, and its leaves turn reddish in fall before dropping. Also, it attracts pollinating insects—a big plus in these pollinator-troubled times.

When, Where, and How to Plant
Plant in spring or early fall, 15 to 18 inches apart. Allegheny spurge does best in shade to part-shade spots in moist, well-drained, slightly acidic "woodsy" soil. It'll likely wilt and die back in full sun. Work an inch or two of compost into the soil before planting. After planting, top the soil with an inch or so of bark mulch or leaves (kept slightly away from the stems) and give a good drink of water.

Growing Tips
Water weekly or twice weekly throughout the first season to establish the roots, then water is needed only during hot, dry spells or whenever leaves begin to wilt. No need to fertilize.

Allegheny spurge is slower to spread than Japanese spurge. Clumps can be dug and divided in early spring or early fall into fist-sized pieces to help speed coverage.

Regional Advice and Care
Allegheny spurge is semi-evergreen and may keep at least some green foliage in some winters in warmer parts of Pennsylvania. At winter's end, trim off winter-killed or ratty foliage, and lightly rake out any excess fallen leaves. Cut back as far as 2 to 3 inches but never the whole way to the ground. If scale insects or fungal blight find your pachysandra patch, try cutting it back to 2 or 3 inches in spring. Then water to encourage fresh new growth. Blight also can be reduced by thinning an overly dense patch via division.

Companion Planting and Design
Allegheny spurge is most at home in a massed colony under a grove of trees. It also does well as a groundcover underneath shaded plantings of native shrubs, such as fothergilla, viburnum, smooth hydrangea, and Virginia sweetspire. And it makes a nice edging along a wooded path.

Try These
You usually won't find anything other than the straight species of Allegheny spurge, which is fine. If you run across it, try 'Kingsville', which is an interesting variety with silver-speckled foliage. If evergreen, glossy, and fast-spreading are more to your liking, though, go with Japanese spurge.

Periwinkle

Vinca minor

Botanical Pronunciation
VING-kah MY-nor

Other Name Myrtle

Bloom Period and Seasonal Color
April into May; blue, purplish blue, white flowers

Mature Height × Spread
6 to 8 inches × 2 feet and beyond

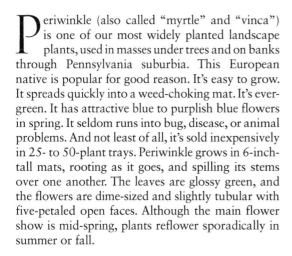

Periwinkle (also called "myrtle" and "vinca") is one of our most widely planted landscape plants, used in masses under trees and on banks through Pennsylvania suburbia. This European native is popular for good reason. It's easy to grow. It spreads quickly into a weed-choking mat. It's evergreen. It has attractive blue to purplish blue flowers in spring. It seldom runs into bug, disease, or animal problems. And not least of all, it's sold inexpensively in 25- to 50-plant trays. Periwinkle grows in 6-inch-tall mats, rooting as it goes, and spilling its stems over one another. The leaves are glossy green, and the flowers are dime-sized and slightly tubular with five-petaled open faces. Although the main flower show is mid-spring, plants reflower sporadically in summer or fall.

When, Where, and How to Plant

Periwinkle grows best in shade to partly shaded situations in damp soil, but it's versatile enough to do full sun and lousy soil too. Plant in spring or early fall, 10 to 18 inches apart (depending on how fast you want the planting to fill in). A labor-saving way to plant is to improve the soil with an inch or two of compost, then rake and top the ground with an inch of bark or rotted leaves and plant into the already mulched bed. Water well after planting.

Growing Tips

There's no need to fertilize. Water weekly during the first season when it's dry to establish the roots. Then water is needed only in extremely hot, dry spells. Speed the spread or expand your colony by dividing rooted pieces in early spring or early fall. Any stem section with roots growing out the bottom is fair game to transplant. Shovel out sections creeping beyond where you want.

Regional Advice and Care

Important—keep a new periwinkle patch well weeded in the early going! Once it fills in, it needs only occasional policing for weeds. But if you let creeping perennial or grassy weeds invade before the plot thickens, you'll have a difficult time bringing it back under control. Otherwise, just trim or shovel out periwinkle as needed. In fall or early spring, rake or blow out any fallen tree leaves thick enough that they're preventing sunlight reaching the periwinkle leaves.

Companion Planting and Design

Periwinkle is effective as erosion control on banks, especially when creeping under trees and taller shrubs, such as rhododendron, hydrangea, and cherrylaurel in shade, and rose, crapemyrtle, and blue mist shrub in sun. Interplant spring bulbs into periwinkle colonies.

Try These

Variegated periwinkle vines are popular choices for hanging baskets and pots. These also grow in the ground, although they sometimes seed around and get overly rambunctious. White-flowered versions ('Alba' and 'Jekyll's White', for example) occasionally show up in garden centers. Large periwinkle (*Vinca major*) is a bigger-flowered, taller-growing version that's an option in warmer Zone 7 parts of the state.

Sweet Woodruff

Galium odoratum

Botanical Pronunciation
GAY-lee-um oh-dor-AY-tum

Other Name Bedstraw

Bloom Period and Seasonal Color
May; white flowers

Mature Height × Spread
6 to 10 inches × 2 feet and beyond

Sweet woodruff is a low, creeping groundcover best known for its mildly vanilla-scented white flowers. A planting of it in bloom looks like snow in May. The rest of the season, sweet woodruff is a 6-inch-tall mounded mat of small, light green leaves. Native to European woodlands, the plant got its "bedstraw" nickname because it was commonly used to stuff pillows and mattresses. The leaves also have long been used as a garnish and as a key ingredient in German May wine. Sweet woodruff will keep creeping as long as there's bare space to fill (too efficiently for the liking of some), but it's easy to stop with a shovel and it doesn't climb. It drops its little leaves in fall and so isn't evergreen.

When, Where, and How to Plant
Plant about 15 to 18 inches apart in spring or in early fall. Sweet woodruff grows best in rich, loamy, damp, and slightly acidic soil, although it holds its own in dry conditions. It also tolerates clay soil and the dry shade and root competition under trees. Mulch lightly after planting (1 inch of bark or leaves is plenty) and give it a good soaking.

Growing Tips
Water weekly throughout the first season (when there's no rain) to establish the roots. Then water is needed only in very hot, dry weather. Even without any water, sweet woodruff may wilt and turn brown, but it usually bounces back when cooler, damper weather returns. No fertilizer is needed, especially if you work an inch or two of compost

into the soil at planting. Dig and divide fist-sized pieces in early spring or early fall to speed up coverage. Shovel out any sections creeping beyond where you want.

Regional Advice and Care
In March before new growth begins, lightly rake out any excess fallen leaves or other debris that's collected in the bare tangle of stems. This is also a good time to trim back or shovel out any growth going where you don't want it. The tiny flowers neatly disappear after bloom (no need for deadheading), but if you'd like to trim to neaten things anyway, right after flowering is the time. Bugs, diseases, and animal issues are very unlikely.

Companion Planting and Design
Sweet woodruff makes an excellent weed-choking, mulch-eliminating mat that fills in under shrubs and trees. It's especially effective under and around species that bloom at the same time, such as crabapple, serviceberry, azalea, rhododendron, and viburnum. In a woodland garden, it makes a nice underplanting for bleeding heart, Virginia bluebells, hosta, ferns, and spring bulbs, especially daffodils.

Try These
You won't find any alternative bloom colors or other variations, just the straight species. The *Galium* genus has about 400 members, but sweet woodruff is the only one that has been selected for widespread garden use.

Variegated Solomon's Seal

Polygonatum odoratum 'Variegatum'

Botanical Pronunciation
pol-ih-go-NAY-tum oh-dor-AY-tum var-ih-GAY-tum

Other Name Fragrant Solomon's seal

Bloom Period and Seasonal Color
Late April through May; white flowers

Mature Height × Spread
18 to 24 inches × 2 feet and beyond

This upright shade plant with the gracefully arching stems is a good example of a ground-cover that isn't a ground hugger. Variegated Solomon's seal typically grows 2 feet tall and spreads to form a thick colony that chokes out weeds better than short, mat-forming groundcovers. This 2013 Perennial Plant of the Year winner has green leaves with creamy white streaking. It lights up the shade and looks good all season. An added bonus is the bell-shaped white flowers. They're not terribly showy, but they do produce a sweet scent that most people describe as similar to that of lilies. The ladder-like, lance-shaped leaves turn yellowish in fall before dropping after frost. Look under the foliage in fall, and you also may notice small, round blue-black fruits.

When, Where, and How to Plant
Here's a good choice for your shadiest spot. Solomon's seal is native to wooded areas and colonizes nicely among the shade and root competition of trees. It grows best in damp, acidic, humus-rich soil, but it's versatile enough to tolerate dry shade and all but full-sun sites as well. Plant in spring or early fall, 18 to 24 inches apart. After planting, top the soil with 1 or 2 inches of bark mulch or leaves (kept slightly away from the stems) and give it a good soaking.

Growing Tips
Water weekly throughout the first season, then water is needed only in hot, dry spells after that. If you've improved the soil with compost at planting, no fertilizer is needed. To expand plantings, dig and divide clumps into fist-sized pieces in early spring, then replant pieces at the same depth. Then water.

Regional Advice and Care
No in-season care is needed other than occasional watering in droughty situations. Cut back stems to the ground anytime between the time frost browns the foliage in fall and when new growth emerges in spring. Slugs occasionally chew the leaves of Solomon's seal. Use slug traps, surround your planting with a band of gravel or sand (slugs hate to crawl over scratchy stuff), or go out at night with a salt-shaker to "season" the slimy pests to death.

Companion Planting and Design
Variegated Solomon's seal is at its best massed by itself in a colony under and around deciduous (leaf-dropping) trees. It's also effective in clumps in any woodland garden. And since it's tolerant of damp and temporarily wet sites, it's a good choice for a shady to partly shaded rain garden.

Try These
Variegated Solomon's seal is a European and Asian native, so if you're trying to go native, try the similar but green-leafed American native small Solomon's seal (*Polygonatum biflorum*). Also worth trying is the native false Solomon's seal (*Smilacina racemosa*), which has the same ladder-like, lance-shaped green leaves but which produces red fall fruits and showier white spring flowers.

LAWNS
FOR PENNSYLVANIA

What's Pennsylvania's most used plant? There's no question . . . turfgrass. These little blades of green show up around nearly every home, from puddle-sized condo patches to oceans of lawn flowing around countryside estates. Grass is our default groundcover, the plant that automatically goes on top of bare dirt until and unless we decide to do something else.

Grass has plenty of benefits. It prevents soil erosion and limits weeds. It allows rain to soak in and filters pollutants. It's inexpensive to install. It's great for foot traffic. It cools the ground and produces oxygen. It's familiar to maintain. And not least of all, it makes a neat carpet that appeals especially to the male of the human species.

Kentucky bluegrass

On the other hand, to maintain that pristine green carpet, homeowners spend hundreds if not thousands of dollars per year applying crabgrass preventer, weed-killer, grub control, and four to six shots of fertilizer. Or they hire a professional to do it for them.

Environmental groups argue that a lot of those fertilizers and chemicals end up polluting groundwater and killing aquatic life as far away as the Chesapeake Bay. Wildlife-friendly folks argue that lawns are nearly as barren to birds, bees, and other pollinators as asphalt and concrete.

And from a labor point of view, what other plant do we "prune" 25 times a year? And yet people want a lawn.

All Grass Is Not Created Equal

Those little green blades might all look the same, but they come in multiple species and hundreds of varieties within those species.

Check out Penn State University's turfgrass trials, and you'll see marked performances from one block to the next. The only difference is the variety. Golf courses, athletic fields, and other "high-end" users are buying the ruby-green good stuff, while

Joe Homeowner buys whatever is cheapest, then complains when his lawn gets bugs or it browns out at the first sign of drought.

To get off on the right foot, spend a little extra on better quality grass seed. If you're really serious, ratings are available from Penn State's trials by going to www.ntep.org/states/states.htm and clicking Pennsylvania on the state map.

Pennsylvania's climate is best suited for "cool-season" grasses– ones that go dormant in our cold winters and then green up during the growing season, especially spring and fall.

These include four main types:

- **Kentucky bluegrass,** a dark green, moderately fine-textured type that spreads quickly and densely, tolerates traffic well, and is reasonably good in droughts.
- **Perennial ryegrass,** another dark green and moderately fine-textured types that germinates quickly and tolerates traffic well but is a slower, clumping spreader.
- **Fine fescue,** which includes chewings fescue, creeping red fescue, and hard fescue. These are the finest-textured grasses and are excellent in drought and shadier spots but not as tolerant of foot traffic.
- **Tall fescue,** which has the coarsest texture of the four, is also the most tolerant of heat, drought, and foot traffic.

Fine fescue planted between steppingstones.

Since all have their pros and cons, most seed mixes include a blend of two or more of those. The breakdown typically varies depending on use, such as a higher percentage of fine fescue in a "Shady Lawn Mix" or more Kentucky bluegrass in a "Sun Lawn Mix." Turf-type tall fescue is often sold by itself so its coarser texture isn't as noticeable as when it's growing alongside fine fescue.

Starting a New Lawn . . . and Patching a Struggling One

The quickest way to start a new lawn or fix a dead one is to lay pieces of sod over the soil. Sod is already-growing grass, with roots and an inch or so of soil included, that comes in approximately 2- by 4-foot, carpetlike sections at garden centers.

Perennial ryegrass

The soil should be loosened first to at least 4 to 6 inches, then raked smooth. Sod sections are laid on top, bumped together, then tamped down and kept moist to encourage the roots to grow into the soil. It's more expensive than seeding, but you get instant results.

To start a new lawn from seed, prepare the soil the same way but then lightly rake grass seed into the surface. Some should stay at the surface, and some can be raked as deep as one-quarter of an inch (no deeper). Scatter seed at a rate similar to how you'd salt a steak (assuming you salt your steak). Tamp or lightly roll the seeded bed to encourage good soil contact and barely cover with a light layer of straw.

Water once or twice a day until the seed is up in 2 to 3 weeks. Late August through mid-October is one good grass-seed window, and late March through April is another. However, grass can be planted anytime during the growing season if you keep the seeded bed damp.

A soil test is a good idea before starting any new lawn. Do-it-yourself kits are available at county Extension offices and most garden centers. Test results will tell you whether you need to add lime or sulfur to correct pH levels (soil acidity) and how much (if any) nutrients are needed.

"Overseeding," which means adding grass seed to existing lawns, helps thicken lawns and makes them less prone to weed trouble. This is best done in early fall. Scratch the bare soil first with a rake or add seed after you've roughened the lawn by dethatching (that is, tearing up a spongy layer of dead roots with a rake-like machine) or by core aerating (using a machine that pulls finger-sized plugs of soil out of the ground to loosen compacted soil). Keep the soil damp until the seed germinates.

Caring for Your Lawn

Maintaining a perfect lawn takes frequent care and involves adding a variety of products throughout the year. But as you might notice from low-care public patches, grass will grow, stay green, and perform reasonably well (albeit with weeds) with nothing more than regular mowing. Take your pick where you fall on that spectrum—the coveted carpet, or as former PBS *Victory Garden* host Roger Swain calls it, "good-enough grass."

For carpet-growers, the season starts with a crabgrass preventer, applied when forsythia blooms fade. This stops the groundhugging "junk" grass that infiltrates thin lawns growing on poor, compacted soil. In cool, rainy springs, a second treatment may be needed 10 weeks later for season-long crabgrass control.

The first of four to six fertilizer treatments also goes down in early spring. Fertilizer manufacturers make this easy by selling "step programs" in which bags are numbered and mixed with herbicides and/or fungicides at appropriate stages. Fertilizers can be applied in granular form (most common) or sprayed on in liquid form.

Creeping red fescue

Most fertilizers are heavy in the nitrogen that turfgrass relishes for best green growth. Organic lawn fertilizers are also available for gardeners trying to avoid synthetic chemicals or opting for lesser, slower feeding rates with fewer applications.

The grubs of Japanese, June, and masked chafer beetles are major bug pests in Pennsylvania lawns. The fat, white, C-shaped larvae of these bugs feed on lawn roots, killing off whole patches that then pull up like unsecured pieces of carpet. Grub damage is most noticeable in late summer to early fall. Grub-killers are available to kill young grubs if you catch them in their root-eating act.

Chinch bugs and armyworms are among other bugs that damage Pennsylvania lawns.

Then there are lawn diseases, such as rust, red thread, brown patch, and dollar spot. These are often related to fertilizer (too much or not enough), weather, and poor soil. Fungicides are available to slow these.

And if that isn't enough to keep a carpet-grower busy, fall can bring assorted mushrooms and fungal "puffballs" to the soil, skunks can dig holes while searching for grubs, and weeds can elbow their way in.

To control weeds, some homeowners use one or two applications per year of granular broad-leaf herbicides for lawns. These are weed-killers that kill wider-bladed plants but not grass. Good-enough grassers dig or hand-pull bigger weeds, spot-spray creeping patches with a liquid broadleaf herbicide as needed, and/or tolerate weeds.

Dethatching and core aerating are jobs best done in fall if a lawn has developed a thatch layer thicker than 1 inch or if your soil is hard and compacted.

One other fall job that helps correct lousy soil is "topdressing." This involves spreading and raking a light, quarter-inch layer of compost or finely sifted soil over the lawn. This is enough to slowly build up poor soil and add organic matter and nutrition while not being so thick as to smother the existing grass.

Mowing and Other Good Things

Finally, there's the issue of mowing your lawn those 25 times a year or so.

Start by raising the mower height at least to 2½ to 3 inches. Most people cut the grass way too short, which dries the soil faster, reduces the lawn's storehouse of chlorophyll, and makes it easier for weeds to gain a foothold.

Second, cut often enough that you're never removing more than one-third of the grass blades at a time. Besides being less stressful on grass plants, this gives you smaller clippings that can be left on the lawn to decay and return nutrition and organic matter to the soil.

Third, keep the mower blades sharp. Dull blades bludgeon the grass tips instead of cleanly cutting them, making them more prone to moisture loss and disease.

Four more tips for maintaining a healthy lawn:

- Avoid cutting the grass when it's wet. Clippings mat, and you'll compact the soil.
- Avoid mowing when the lawn is going brown and dormant in a drought. Just stay off of it to the extent you can. Also don't fertilize when the lawn is dormant in a summer dry spell.
- Don't irrigate existing lawns. Unless you water deeply (which takes a lot of time and water), you'll encourage roots to grow close to the surface where the moisture is. Healthy lawns can survive 6 weeks of dormancy without water. The watering exception is first-year lawns, which should be kept damp until the roots fully establish.
- Before automatically adding lime or otherwise guessing at what your lawn may or may not need, retest the soil every few years to get a current read.

Using Turfgrass in the Landscape

A big, open patch of grass is a superb choice, for example, in the middle of the back yard where the kids play soccer or Dad hits plastic golfballs. It's also excellent for entertaining next to patios and pools, for pathways through landscaped beds, and for swales that guide rainfall away from basements.

A beautiful lawn can be very inviting.

Yet many a homeowner goes to heroic measures trying to keep grass alive when the shade and big roots of growing trees keep killing it off. Others risk life and limb mowing grass on too-steep banks instead of opting for the long-term lower care of trees, evergreens, and groundcovers.

And untold time and cost goes into expansive default lawns whose space could yield better payback, such as in fresh vegetables, flowers for pollinators, or the diversity that gives a yard four-season interest.

Turfgrass is excellent for getting soil-protecting vegetation in place quickly around a new home. But just because that's what you started with doesn't mean you can't dig up some of it in favor of more diversity.

The bottom line for me is that lawns play an important role in most landscapes. But like any other plant, it should go *where* it makes the best sense and be considered as *part* of the landscape, not *the* landscape.

ORNAMENTAL GRASSES

FOR PENNSYLVANIA

Pennsylvania is native territory to a variety of grassy plants, ones that push up soft, narrow blades from their roots. While some grasses are more suited to being mowed for foot traffic, most function better in their natural state, growing into upright clumps of varying heights that produce seedheads or plumy "inflorescences" at the top.

Growers have selected an ever-expanding variety of the more attractive ones from Pennsylvania and around the world for landscape use. Offerings range from foot-tall, bluish mounds to ones that grow 12 feet tall in a single year and look like corn stalks on steroids!

Grasses in the Garden

Gardeners tend to either love or hate ornamental grasses. Grass-lovers cite the variety of forms, the fall color, the swishing sound of grass blades blowing in a breeze, and especially the wispy, airy texture. Detractors usually say they just don't like that look, or they don't like how some grasses spread, or they don't like how brown blades blow around in winter if the lifeless clumps aren't cut, bundled, and tossed ASAP.

To each his own. I say try a few. Or not. Short ones make good edging plants, taller ones are great for hiding heat pumps and trash cans, and most of them make useful focal points that contrast nicely with all of the more commonly shaped rounded and spreading landscape plants.

As with any plant, know there is some effort involved no matter what you might have heard. (Do these sound familiar? "You can't kill grasses," or "They're no work at all!")

Most ornamental grasses are durable plants that seldom run into bug or disease trouble. Most tolerate drought and poor soil well. They don't need fertilizer or spraying. Even deer don't care much for them.

Yet grasses aren't immune to occasional leaf diseases. A few can get a bit frisky with roots that run, especially the seductive variegated ribbongrass (*Phalaris arundinacea* 'Pictum'), which should be avoided anywhere near other plants. And the main work demand is dealing with all of those blades once frost browns them out in fall.

Grassy Care Secrets

One way or the other, those brown blades need to be removed sometime before new shoots emerge the following spring.

Ornamental grasses offer textural interest and variety to the landscape.

The plants don't care whether you cut them in fall or spring. If you like the swishing sound in winter and like the texture of blades, albeit brown ones, by all means, let them stand until early spring. Birds appreciate dried, brown ornamental grass blades for nest-building.

If you'd rather see the clumps gone when the foliage browns, cut them right after frost. A work-saving trick is to use jute or sturdy string to tie the clumps around the midsection, then cut them 2 or 3 inches above the ground. The whole thing will topple like a tree in one neat bundle.

The compromise I use is to wait until so many of the blades are breaking and blowing around the yard by winter that it's getting messy. Then I cut and grind the blades in my chipper/shredder.

If you don't get rid of the spent clumps, you'll end up with an unsightly mix of new green shoots poking up through a crumbling brown mess. That's much harder to clean up than cutting in advance of new growth.

Most grasses grow in slowly spreading root clumps. They do best when they're dug and divided every 3 or 4 years or when the older centers began to die out. A few grasses prefer part shade, and many offer excellent attractive fall foliage. Beyond that, pick based on the sizes and the blade colors you prefer. If it turns out you don't like the look, odds are good your neighbor will take them off your hands for you.

Grasses mainly add subtle beauty to the landscape—attributes such as texture, form, light effects, and fall interest—as opposed to the blaring color of flowers.

Big Bluestem

Andropogon gerardii

Botanical Pronunciation
an-droe-POE-gon jur-AR-dee-eye

Bloom Period and Seasonal Color
Narrow, reddish plumes in August and September; burnt orange to copper-red fall foliage

Mature Height × Spread
5 to 8 feet × 3 to 4 feet

This tall, native grass once ruled the American plains. It's native to much of North America, growing from Mexico to Canada. Big bluestem makes a good landscape plant not only because it's at home in our soil and climate, but also for its upright habit and late-season color. Big bluestem's blades are a bit wider than most grasses and are blue-green for most of the growing season. By late summer, the 4- to 5-foot-tall clumps send up flowering stalks another foot or two that produce slender, slightly arching, reddish seedheads. Look close and you'll see the reddish color comes from tiny firecracker-shaped anthers that hang by thin filaments from the stems. In fall, the foliage turns a burnt orange to copper-red color that holds into winter.

When, Where, and How to Plant
Big bluestem is best planted in spring to early summer, 3 to 4 feet apart in full sun. It tolerates a wide range of soils from clay to sand and isn't picky about pH (moderately acid to moderately alkaline is fine). To plant, just loosen soil about 10 to 12 inches deep. Plant so that the crown (the point where blades emerge) is just above the soil line. Surround the clump after planting with 1 to 2 inches of wood chips or bark mulch. But keep mulch off of the crown to avoid smothering new growth.

Growing Tips
Water once or twice a week during the first season, then you'll likely never need to water again. Big bluestem is very drought-resistant. Fertilizer usually isn't needed; excess nutrients can actually lead to overly lush growth that flops over. Divide every three to five years in early spring by digging the clump with a spade, slicing at least fist-sized pieces from around the perimeter and discarding the older center section. Replant the newer sections.

Regional Advice and Care
Bundle and cut the foliage back to about 2 inches at the end of winter. If you don't like the dormant-season color or want to discourage possible seeding, do your cutback after fall's first killing frost. Other than that annual cutback and periodic division, big bluestem needs no other care. Bugs, diseases, and animal troubles are unlikely.

Companion Planting and Design
Big bluestem is ideal in its natural setting as a meadow plant mixed with native perennials, such as goldenrod, aster, blazing star, and coneflower. Its sturdy root system makes it useful for erosion control on a sunny bank. Or use it in sunny border or island gardens or for screening heat pumps and trash cans. Interplant with spring bulbs for early-season color before the new grass blades emerge.

Try These
You'll usually run into just the straight species, which is fine. 'Indian Warrior' and 'Red October' have more purplish fall foliage. 'Mega Blue' and 'Lord Snowden' have the best blue-tinted summer foliage. 'Red Bull' has bright red plume color.

Blue Fescue

Festuca glauca

Botanical Pronunciation
fess-TEW-kah GLAW-kah

Bloom Period and Seasonal Color
Tan seedheads in June and July; mostly year-round narrow silvery blue foliage

Mature Height × Spread
10 to 18 inches × 18 to 24 inches

Blue fescue looks like a blue pincushion. Plants grow in a tufted mound only about a foot tall. The blades are narrow—almost quill-like—and they're silvery blue, which is the plant's leading attraction. Blue fescue holds that color, too, through most winters in most of Pennsylvania, adding interest to the winter landscape. Native to France, blue fescue is a cool-season grass, which means it doesn't go dormant at fall frost like most ornamental grasses. On the flip side though, blue fescue sometimes starts to turn brown and go partially dormant during a hot, dry summer spell while most other grasses are reveling in the heat. In early summer, plants send up skinny stalks that produce dainty seedheads that change from blue-green to tan.

When, Where, and How to Plant
Plant blue fescue in spring to early summer or late summer through early fall. This is a compact, clump-grower, so 2 feet apart is good spacing (closer than most grasses). Full sun is ideal in well-drained soil. Avoid wet spots; blue fescue is prone to root-rotting in soggy clay over winter. Moderately acidic to moderately alkaline soil pH is fine. When you're ready to plant, dig a hole 10 to 12 inches. Position it so that the crown (the point where blades emerge) is just above the soil line. Surround the clump after planting with 1 to 2 inches of wood chips or bark mulch. Keep mulch off the crown.

Growing Tips
Water weekly during the first season then only during hot, dry spells if plants show signs of browning.

Fertilizer usually isn't needed. Divide every two to three years in early spring by digging the clump with a spade and slicing it in half or quarters. Cut no smaller than fist-sized pieces for replanting. Discard the center if it's dying.

Regional Advice and Care
Blue fescue tends to be a fairly short-lived grass, especially in poorly drained spots or when excessively mulched. Trim plants back to 4 inches at winter's end, even if the foliage is still blue. Also trim off the seedheads after they brown. Both of those cuts encourage longer plant life. Blue fescue performs best in the cooler Zone 5 and 6 regions of Pennsylvania. Plant in light afternoon shade and give some summer water to mitigate heat stress in Zone 7.

Companion Planting and Design
Blue fescue makes an excellent edging plant along sidewalks, driveways, and the front of sunny house-foundation beds. It offers contrasting spiky texture to rounded shrubs, especially pink- or blue-blooming sun-lovers such as shrub roses, dwarf butterfly bush, spirea, and blue mist shrub. Good flower partners are coneflower, phlox, cheddar pinks, and catmint (perennials), and petunia, vinca, dusty miller, and sweet alyssum (annuals).

Try These
'Elijah Blue' is the most common (and a good) variety. 'Boulder Blue' has arguably more vibrant silvery blue blades.

Feather Reed Grass

Calamagrostis × acutiflora

Botanical Pronunciation
kal-ah-mah-GRAHSS-tiss ah-kew-tih-FLORE-ah

Bloom Period and Seasonal Color
Buff-colored feathery plumes June
through November

Mature Height × Spread
3 to 6 feet × 2 to 3 feet

If you like your ornamental grasses upright instead of arching or floppy, here's your choice. Feather reed grass is as stiff and vertical as any type, growing into a tight bundle that's easy to keep 2 or 3 feet across. The green blades emerge in early spring, growing to 3 to 4 feet tall before sending up flowering stems that produce slender, feathery plumes in June. That makes feather reed grass one of the earliest grasses to set plumes, a result of it being a cool-season grass. The plumes start out a soft pinkish purple and mature to buff. The foliage isn't striking in fall (it goes from green to brown), but the plumes usually stick around in good shape through most of winter.

When, Where, and How to Plant
Feather reed grass is best planted in spring to early summer, 2 to 3 feet apart in full sun. It also does well in part shade and appreciates heat-mitigating afternoon shade in Zone 7 regions. Feather reed grass prefers damp, well-drained soil but tolerates clay as long as you avoid soggy spots. Moderately acidic to moderately alkaline soil is fine. Plant so that the crown (where blades emerge) is just above the soil line, in a hole about 10 to 12 inches deep. Surround the clump after planting with 1 to 2 inches of wood chips or bark mulch, keeping mulch off the crown.

Growing Tips
Water once a week during the first season, then water is needed only during hot, dry spells. Fertilizer usually isn't needed. Divide every three to four years in early spring by digging the clump with a spade, slicing at least fist-sized pieces from around the perimeter, and discarding the older center section.

Regional Advice and Care
Feather reed grass sometimes goes brown and semi-dormant in hot, dry summers. Occasional watering helps prevent that. Rust disease (red-orange streaking on the blades) is a possibility in wet or humid summers. Plants usually grow through rust; just cut and discard diseased foliage at season's end. Assuming foliage stays green until frost, bundle and cut the foliage back to 2 to 3 inches at the end of winter.

Companion Planting and Design
The stiff, upright habit of feather reed grass makes it a good choice in tight spots, such as in those 3-foot beds between buildings and walks or along small-lot borders. Its shade-tolerance makes it a top choice where you want a grass but don't have full sun. Feather reed grass pairs especially well with golden perennials, such as black-eyed Susans, coreopsis, goldenrod, and daylilies.

Try These
'Karl Foerster' is easily the most common and was a Perennial Plant of the Year. 'Overdam' is a 3-foot, white-edged type but is slightly less heat-tolerant. 'Avalanche' is a green-and-white-striped 4-footer with silvery plumes, and 'Eldorado' is a green-and-gold variegated 5-footer.

Fountain Grass

Pennisetum alopecuroides

Botanical Pronunciation
pen-ih-SEE-tum al-oh-pek-yur-OY-deez

Bloom Period and Seasonal Color
Pinkish purple or creamy white foxtail plumes
July through October; yellow-gold fall foliage

Mature Height × Spread
1 to 5 feet × 2 to 3 feet

Fountain grass gets its name from its loose, upright, arching habit, like a fountain spraying water. The blades are green and narrow, turning golden-yellow in fall. Foxtail-like plumes of pinkish purple or creamy white appear in July and last into fall. Plants are typically 2 to 3 feet tall, but foot-tall shorties are available. Most *Pennisetum alopecuroides* fountain grasses are winter-hardy to Zones 6 and 7 but iffy in Zone 5 winters. You'll also find *Pennisetum setaceum* fountain grasses, such as the popular burgundy-leafed 'Rubrum' and red-leafed 'Fireworks', but those aren't winter-hardy anywhere in Pennsylvania. Gauge winter-hardiness by where you find the variety at the garden center. If it's winter-hardy, it'll be in with the perennials. If not, it'll be sold with the annuals.

When, Where, and How to Plant
Plant in spring to early summer, 2 to 3 feet apart in full sun. It tolerates light shade and most soils (clay to sand, moderately acid to moderately alkaline). Plant so that the crown (where blades emerge) is just above the soil line, in a hole 10 to 12 inches deep. After planting, mulch with 1 to 2 inches of wood chips or bark. Make sure to keep mulch off the crown.

Growing Tips
After it's established, water only in very hot, dry spells, but water once a week during its first season. Fountain grass has very good drought-tolerance. You probably won't need fertilizer for it. Fountain grass is a slowly spreading clump-former that benefits from division every three or four years in early spring. Dig the clump with a spade, slice at least fist-sized pieces from around the perimeter and replant the sections, discarding the older center section.

Regional Advice and Care
Be aware that even "perennial" fountain grasses are borderline hardy at best in Zone 5 regions of Pennsylvania. A protected microclimate to mitigate winter cold may help nurse fountain grass through a Zone 5 winter. Bundle and cut the foliage back to 2 to 3 inches at the end of winter. If you don't like the dormant-season color or want to discourage possible seeding, cut it back after the first killing frost. Bugs, diseases, and animal troubles are unlikely.

Companion Planting and Design
Fountain grass makes an excellent mid-sized hedge when massed along a property line. Or use it to edge a sidewalk or driveway, planting grasses back 3 to 4 feet and underplanting them with sun-loving annuals, such as petunias, verbenas, or marigolds, or with low perennials, such as creeping phlox, creeping sedum, or hardy geraniums.

Try These
'Hameln' is a common (and good) 3-footer. 'Little Bunny' is a dwarf variety (15 to 18 inches tall), and 'Burgundy Bunny' is a similar size with red fall foliage. My favorite is a Zones 6 to 7 *Pennisetum orientale* species called 'Karley Rose', which grows 3 feet tall and has rosy purple summer plumes.

Hakone Grass

Hakonechloa macra

Botanical Pronunciation
ha-koe-neh-KLOE-ah MAY-krah

Other Name Japanese forest grass

Bloom Period and Seasonal Color
Pinkish seed heads late summer to
early fall; green, chartreuse, gold-
or white-variegated foliage

Mature Height × Spread
1 to 2 feet × 3 feet

Zones 6 and 7

This one's my favorite ornamental grass. In fact, I haven't run into anyone yet who *doesn't* like the fresh color and graceful cascading habit of Hakone grass, often called "Japanese forest grass" for its shaded, Oriental origin. This grass stays under 2 feet tall and comes in green, chartreuse, gold-variegated, and white-variegated versions. While most grasses prefer or even demand full sun, Hakone grass does best in afternoon shade. However, green-leaf Hakone grass does surprisingly well in full sun, while all types do fine even in full shade. Dainty pinkish seedheads form in late summer to add another dimension. This is also a grass that's very well behaved. It won't run all around a garden and can go many years without needing division.

When, Where, and How to Plant
Plant in spring to early summer, 3 feet apart in loose, damp, compost-enriched soil. Afternoon shade is ideal, but Hakone grass tolerates full shade to full sun. Green-leaf types are most sun-tolerant. Hakone grass also tolerates dry soil in shadier spots. Avoid heavy clay and soggy sites. Loosen soil to 10 to 12 inches before planting. Plant so that the crown is just above the soil line. Mulch with 1 to 2 inches of wood chips or bark. Keep mulch off the crown.

Growing Tips
Water once a week during the first season, then only in very hot, dry spells or if leaves start to brown. Usually no fertilizer is needed and neither

is division, unless clumps spread beyond where you want or are dying in the center. Divide in early spring by digging the clump, slicing fist-sized pieces from around the perimeter, and discarding the older center section.

Regional Advice and Care
Hakone grass is hardy in Zones 6 or 7 but iffy in Zone 5, where planting near a heated wall or other protected spot can make the difference. Cut foliage back to 2 inches in fall after plants brown or at the end of winter. Fungal leaf blight is a rare but possible disease. You'll have no worries with bugs or deer.

Companion Planting and Design
The cascading, bamboo-like texture pairs well with rounded forms, whether it's a shrub (hydrangea or nandina) or a perennial (hosta, coralbell, or false forget-me-not). Shade annuals, such as coleus, red New Guinea impatiens, and red begonias, are other good partners. Good edging sites include shady and wooded paths, eastern or northern house foundations, and streams and water gardens. Mass Hakone grass under trees as a groundcover. Dig a clump or two for use in summer flower pots.

Try These
The gold-variegated 'Aureola' is my favorite and was 2009 Perennial Plant of the Year. 'All Gold' is a beautiful chartreuse-leafed version. The entire species won a Pennsylvania Horticultural Society Gold Medal Award.

Indian Grass

Sorghastrum nutans

Botanical Pronunciation
sor-GASS-trum NOO-tanz

Bloom Period and Seasonal Color
Coppery yellow seed stems August through
October; yellow-orange fall foliage

Mature Height × Spread
3 to 5 feet × 3 to 4 feet

Indian grass is another U.S. native ornamental grass that, along with big bluestem (*Andropogon gerardii*), once made up a large part of the North American prairie. This is one of the more upright grasses, staying in a flop-resistant, tight vase of 3 to 4 feet. By August, plants send up seed stems another foot or two that produce narrow, feathery plumes that start out coppery yellow and end up a straw brown in fall. The straight species has half-inch-wide green blades, but the most popular varieties are blue-tinted ones. The foliage turns yellow to orange in fall, making it an attractive fall-interest plant. Indian grass is durable and not picky about sites, growing naturally from Canada to Mexico to Florida and tolerating even poor and clay soils.

When, Where, and How to Plant

Indian grass is best planted in spring to early summer, 3 to 4 feet apart in full sun. It tolerates a wide range of soils from clay to sand and isn't picky about pH (moderately acid to moderately alkaline is fine). Loosen soil down 10 to 12 inches to plant, setting the plant so that the crown (where blades emerge) is just above the soil line. Mulch after planting with 1 to 2 inches of wood chips or bark. Keep mulch away from the crown.

Growing Tips

Water once a week during the first season, then you'll likely never need to water again. Indian grass is very drought-resistant. Fertilizer usually isn't needed; excess nutrients can lead to overly lush growth that flops. Divide every three to five years in early spring by digging the clump, slicing fist-sized pieces from around the perimeter, and discarding the older center section.

Regional Advice and Care

Bundle and cut the foliage back to 2 inches at the end of winter. If you don't like the dormant-season color or want to discourage possible seeding, cut clumps back after fall's first killing frost. Indian grass sometimes self-seeds, so yank out any "babies" in spring that you don't want. Bugs, diseases, and animal trouble are unlikely.

Companion Planting and Design

Indian grass looks most at home in its natural setting—as a meadow plant mixed with native perennials, such as goldenrod, aster, blazing star, and coneflower. Its upright habit makes it a good choice along tight sunny borders, for edging patios, and for screening heat pumps and trash cans. Its durability and heat- and drought-tolerance make it a good candidate for use on sunny banks. Interplant with spring bulbs for early-season color before the new grass blades emerge.

Try These

Look for the blue-leafed 'Sioux Blue' variety that performed well in Longwood Gardens testing. That one's particularly disease- and heat-tolerant. 'Indian Steel' is another blue-tinted type with yellowish plumes. The straight species is fine too, especially if you prefer green over blue.

Little Bluestem

Schizachyrium scoparium

Botanical Pronunciation
skizz-ah-KEER-ee-um skoe-PAIR-ee-um

Bloom Period and Seasonal Color
Narrow coppery plumes in late summer mature silvery in fall; red, orange, yellow, purplish fall foliage

Mature Height × Spread
2 to 4 feet × 3 to 4 feet

The name might lead you to believe this is a cute edging grass, but little bluestem is actually a 4-foot-tall upright grass with green to green-blue foliage and narrow, copper-colored plumes in late summer. It's little compared to its cousin, big bluestem, which grows 5 to 8 feet tall. Other than size, these two are similar in appearance, although technically from two different species because of seedhead differences. Both are U.S. natives that hail from the prairie. Little bluestem is hardy throughout Pennsylvania, which is no wonder since it's found naturally from Canada to Florida in everything from occasionally damp, open fields to dry, rocky hillsides. Just give little bluestem plenty of sunshine, and it won't complain about lousy soil or lack of attention.

When, Where, and How to Plant
Little bluestem is best planted in spring to early summer, 3 to 4 feet apart in full sun. It tolerates a wide range of soils from clay to sand and isn't picky about pH (moderately acid to moderately alkaline is fine). Just make sure to avoid soggy sites. In a hole 10 to 12 inches deep, plant so that the crown (where the blades emerge) remains just above the soil line. Mulch after planting with 1 to 2 inches of wood chips or bark. Keep mulch off of the crown.

Growing Tips
Little bluestem is very drought-resistant. Water once a week during the first season, then you'll likely never need to water again. It's unlikely you'll need to fertilize; excess nutrients can lead to overly lush growth that flops. Divide every three to five years in early spring by digging the clump with a spade, cutting off fist-sized pieces from around the perimeter, tossing the older center section, and replanting what's left.

Regional Advice and Care
At the end of winter gather up and cut the foliage back to 2 inches. If you don't like the dormant-season color or want to discourage possible seeding, do your cutting back after fall's first killing frost. Bugs, diseases, and animal troubles are unlikely. Don't overdo it with mulch.

Companion Planting and Design
Little bluestem is at its best planted in masses or clusters along with native perennials such as goldenrod, asters, blazing stars, and coneflowers. One of its native homes is on hillsides, so consider it for sunny banks where you're trying to avoid mowing. It's also useful along sunny borders, sunny driveways, or for screening heat pumps and trash cans. Interplant with spring bulbs for early-season color before the new grass blades emerge.

Try These
The straight species is fine. 'The Blues' is a variety with blue-green summer foliage that turns burgundy in fall. 'Prairie Blues' has gray-blue summer foliage that turns orange-red in fall. And 'Standing Ovation' has blue-green summer foliage that turns a blend of orange, red, yellow, and purple in fall.

Prairie Dropseed

Sporobolus heterolepis

Botanical Pronunciation
spore-OBB-oh-lus het-er-oh-LEEP-iss

Bloom Period and Seasonal Color
Seed plumes mature from pink in August to light brown in fall; orange to copper fall foliage

Mature Height × Spread
2 to 3 feet × 18 to 30 inches

The name could use a PR agent, but prairie dropseed is better behaved and more attractive than it sounds. Although it *does* drop small seeds in fall, it's not invasive. Cutting the seedheads before they mature will end any chance of self-sowing if you're concerned. Prairie dropseed is a U.S. native that's shorter than most prairie grasses, topping out at 2 to 3 feet, with an arching habit. The foliage is narrow (almost hairy looking) and especially nice in fall when the blades turn from green to burnt orange. The late-summer, feather-duster-like seedheads mature from pink to light brown. Most unusual: this is a grass with fragrance. The seedheads have a scent that most people describe as reminiscent of cilantro or popcorn.

When, Where, and How to Plant
Prairie dropseed is best planted from spring to early summer, about 2 feet apart in full sun to light shade. It'll grow in damp, dry, rocky, sandy, or clay soil . . . pretty much everywhere except for soggy and shady sites. At planting time, loosen the soil 10 to 12 inches deep. Plant so that the crown (where the blades emerge) is just above the soil line. Surround plants after planting with 1 to 2 inches of wood chips or bark mulch. Keep mulch off of the crown, and don't overdo it.

Growing Tips
Prairie dropseed has great drought-resistance, so you'll likely water once a week during the first season; then you'll probably never water again. Fertilizer usually isn't needed and neither is division. Prairie dropseed doesn't die out over time in the center like many grasses, and it doesn't divide easily anyway.

Regional Advice and Care
This is a plant that asks for little more than to be cut back to an inch or two high each year, either after frost browns out the foliage or at the end of winter. If you don't want any chance of self-sowing, trim off the seed heads before they mature in fall. Or dig up any "babies" you don't want in early spring. Bugs, diseases, and animal troubles are unlikely.

Companion Planting and Design
Prairie dropseed is one of the best grasses if you're trying to convert a traditional sunny, open lawn space into a no-mow lawn (technically a "one-mow lawn.") It also makes a good edging plant along sunny walks and driveways, it can be spotted with sunny perennials throughout a rock garden, and it's a good choice for use on sunny banks. Mum, sedum, or aster are good fall-color partners.

Try These
The straight species is usually all you'll find at the garden center. You might run across 'Wisconsin', which reportedly has a heavier seed bloom than the species, or 'Tara', which is a compact variety.

Sedge

Carex species

Botanical Pronunciation
KAIR-ecks

Bloom Period and Seasonal Color
Small tan seed heads in summer; green, yellow, gold, blue, brown, variegated foliage

Mature Height × Spread
8 to 30 inches × 18 to 30 inches

Sedge isn't technically a grass, but the plants look like grass and are used like grass, so we'll mention it here. Sedges come in 1,000 different species and are found throughout much of the world, usually in damp settings. A few are eastern U.S. natives, in particular Pennsylvania sedge (*Carex pensylvanica*), which makes a beautiful, foot-tall lawn substitute or under-tree groundcover, and Tussock sedge (*Carex stricta*), a 2-foot spreader that prefers wet sites. Sedge's bladed leaves vary in width, some are very fine and thready, and in color, including green, yellow, gold, blue, assorted white- and yellow-variegated types, and even brown. Some have upright, fountainlike habits while others are short and tufted. And some are at least semi-evergreen, holding their leaves throughout winter.

When, Where, and How to Plant
Plant sedge in spring to early summer, 18 to 24 inches apart. Most types grow in full sun to mostly shade spots, although they appreciate ample moisture to sidestep browning in sunny spots. At planting, loosen soil to a depth of 10 to 12 inches. Position the sedge so that the crown (where the blades emerge) stays just above the soil line. Mulch after planting with 1 to 2 inches of wood chips or bark, making sure you keep mulch away from the crown.

Growing Tips
Water twice a week during the first season. Then water often enough to keep the soil consistently damp. But you can hold down watering by picking a damp spot in the first place. Fertilizer usually isn't needed. Divide in early spring to expand a colony by digging the clump, slicing apart fist-sized pieces, and replanting at the same depth. Otherwise division isn't necessary; sedges typically don't die out in the center as many ornamental grasses do.

Regional Advice and Care
A few sedges are winter-hardy only to Zone 6, so watch the plant tags or buy locally (garden centers usually carry only regionally cold-hardy choices). Other than keeping the soil damp, just cut sedge back to an inch or two at winter's end. For evergreen types, snip off foliage that has browned in winter wind.

Companion Planting and Design
Consider sedge for edging, massing, or groundcover use in damp to wet areas. Golden and variegated types make good accents, especially in partly shaded, damp sites or in eastern or northern house-foundation beds. Pennsylvania sedges deserve greater use as a native groundcover under trees. Sedge looks good edging water gardens (some grow *in* water gardens) and as a textural-interest addition to flower pots.

Try These
Besides the natives named already, try *Carex oshimenis* 'Evergold', a creamy yellow variegated 16-incher (hardy to Zone 6). *Carex elata* 'Bowles Golden' is a nice gold-leafed type (30 inches tall). *Carex morrowii* 'Variegata' and 'Ice Dance' are excellent white-variegated types. *Carex morrowii* var. *temnolepis* 'Silk Tassel' is a fine-bladed, 2-foot-tall textural star discovered by Pennsylvania's Barry Yinger.

Switch Grass

Panicum virgatum

Botanical Pronunciation
PAN-ih-kum vur-GAY-tum

Other Name Panic grass

Bloom Period and Seasonal Color
Pink to red summer seedheads; green or
green-blue foliage turns golden yellow
or burgundy in fall

Mature Height × Spread
3 to 8 feet × 3 to 4 feet

Switch grass is yet another U.S. native prairie grass that translates well into the home landscape, especially varieties that offer brilliant fall foliage of golden yellow to burgundy. The blades are medium in width and green or green-blue in summer. The plant's habit is mostly upright but with a gently arching, fountainlike finish. Some types are better at standing straight up than others, but generally, switch grass is one of the sturdiest at holding up when brown over winter. That makes it a good choice for those interested in giving winter cover and springtime nest-building material to birds. Switch grass sends up narrow flower stems in July or August that are topped with airy, dainty, almost "puffy" pink to red seedheads as opposed to plumes.

When, Where, and How to Plant
Switch grass is best planted in spring to early summer, 3 to 4 feet apart in full sun. Since it's sometimes found naturally in marshes, it tolerates damp soil better than most grasses. Switch grass also tolerates a range of soils from clay to sand and isn't picky about pH (moderately acidic to moderately alkaline is just fine). Avoid soggy spots. Plant so that the crown (where blades emerge) is just above the soil line in a hole 10 to 12 inches deep. After you plant, mulch using wood chips or bark (1 to 2 inches), but keep mulch off the crown.

Growing Tips
After watering once a week during the first season, you'll likely never need to water again, because switch grass has good drought-resistance.

Fertilizer usually isn't needed; excess nutrients can lead to overly lush growth that falls over. Divide every three to five years in early spring by digging the clump, slicing fist-sized pieces from around the edges, and discarding the older section from the center.

Regional Advice and Care
Gather up and cut back the foliage to 2 inches at the end of winter. If you don't like the dormant-season brown color or want to discourage possible self-seeding, do your cutback after the first killing frost. Switch grass occasionally self-seeds, so yank out any "babies" in spring that you don't want. Bugs, diseases, or animal problems are not common.

Companion Planting and Design
Switch grass makes a good, informal hedge along sunny borders . . . especially colorful in fall. Also use it in any meadow-garden setting (paired with sunny perennials), on sunny banks, or for screening heat pumps and trashcans. Interplant with spring bulbs for early-season color before the new grass blades emerge.

Try These
My favorite is the compact 'Shenandoah', which grows 3 to 4 feet tall and has red-tinged summer foliage that ends up rich burgundy in fall. 'Hanse Herms' is another good red-tinted, burgundy-in-fall variety. Good blue-tinted types include 'Heavy Metal', 'Northwind', 'Prairie Sky', and 'Cheyenne Sky'.

PERENNIALS
FOR PENNSYLVANIA

Perennial flowers are those that—at least in theory—return year after year. Most perennials die back to the ground in fall and then push up new growth and pop out new flowers the following season.

When I first found out about perennials, I thought, "Why would anyone plant anything *else* if you don't have to keep buying new ones each year?" Then I learned about the trade-offs. For one thing, most perennials bloom only four to six weeks out of the year, unlike annuals, which generally go nonstop from May to frost.

Then there's ongoing care, such as "deadheading" the spent flowers, dividing clusters that are spreading beyond their assigned areas, and replacing ones that petered out or that got eaten by deer, rabbits, or groundhogs.

The truth is that while perennials might take less care than some plants (vegetables, fruits, and roses, for example), they're not *exactly* no care. I'd rank them midway on the landscape-labor scale.

The Bright Side

Now that you're up on perennial pitfalls, let's look at why and how to use perennials. Under this broad category comes a very versatile and diverse group of plants. Perennials exist for every situation you'll find in the yard. Some of them laugh off even your hottest, driest, most barren spots, while others thrive in deep shade or boggy soil. Some bloom even as winter is still hanging on, while some late-season bloomers continue flowering into December. Some are short and clumpy. Others are tall and graceful. And the range of bloom colors, leaf colors, and

Rosa and *Lobelia*

Tiarella foliage

plant textures is limitless. A few perennials even hold their leaves all winter.

It all adds up to a palette that's tremendous fun for the artsy, creative gardener.

Working with Perennials

The British are masters at mixing and matching wide borders of multiple perennials that coordinate beautifully and hand off bloom to one another throughout the season. In Pennsylvania, perennials are more often used in smaller bands or clusters in mixed settings, typically paired with evergreens, shrubs, and trees.

Wherever you use them, the starting point is knowing the site (wet? dry? sunny? shady?) and then looking for specific perennials that match that site. In other words, you can't put whatever you like wherever you want. Sun-loving perennials, for instance, might never bloom in the shade, and species that prefer damp soil likely will fry next to the asphalt driveway.

Then it's a matter of skillfully pairing the suitable choices that catch your fancy. Some guidelines:

- In a border garden or foundation bed that's viewed from one angle (the front), layer your sizes from tallest in the back to shortest in the front. In an island bed viewed from multiple angles, place the tallest perennials in the middle and the shortest around the perimeter.
- Try to coordinate bloom and leaf colors. Plant so that neighbors look good color-wise with each other. A good strategy is to divide colors into two camps— "warms" (red, orange, gold, bright yellow, and burgundy) and "cools" (pink, blue, lavender, and most anything pastel). So long as you stick within each family, the colors won't clash.
- Spread out bloom times. Overcome perennials' limited bloom times by mixing species that bloom in spring and early summer with ones that bloom in late summer and fall.
- Contrast forms and textures. Avoid a boring, repetitive, "broken-record" look by pairing plants of different habits next to one another. For example, partner a rounded plant with a grassy one, or pair a ferny- or strappy-leafed plant with one that has broad or heart-shaped leaves.

Finally, don't be afraid to move your mistakes. One other benefit of perennials is that they dig, divide, and trade spots readily. So if you're not happy with how your first effort turned out, grab the shovel and try Plan B.

Think of it as "editing." And good exercise.

Aster

Botanical Pronunciation
AS-ter

Bloom Period and Seasonal Color
August through October; purple, lavender, blue-violet, white, pink

Mature Height × Spread
8 inches to 6 feet × 18 to 24 inches

Asters are late-season, daisylike flowers that should look familiar to most Pennsylvanians since so many members of this large plant family are native to the eastern United States. Asters are the tall purple plants commonly seen blooming in fields and meadows in early fall. At least a dozen species and untold varieties and hybrids have made their way into garden commerce. Heights range from 8-inchers to 6-footers, although most top out in the 2- to 3-foot range. Asters are one of Pennsylvania's Big 3 most-used fall perennials (along with mums and sedum), and for good reason. They're reliable returners, fairly long in bloom (four to six weeks for most), and come in a good selection of rich colors. They also make excellent cut flowers.

When, Where, and How to Plant

Asters are best planted in spring, although summer and fall planting are okay if plants are kept watered. Almost all species grow best in full sun. The exceptions are the native white wood aster (*Aster divaricatus*) and the native heart-leaf aster (*Aster cordifolius*). These do best in morning sun and afternoon shade. Plant asters 18 to 24 inches apart in well-drained, compost-enriched soil.

Growing Tips

Water weekly the first season, then asters can go without water except in unusually hot, dry spells. Scatter a balanced, granular, organic or gradual-release fertilizer over the bed in early spring. Asters should be divided every two or three years in early spring or when the clumps die out in the

center. Replant fist-sized pieces at their same depth, then water.

Regional Advice and Care

Stake taller varieties in spring to prevent fall flopping. Or trim tall varieties in half in early June. This will delay flowering slightly but lead to a more compact late-season plant. Snip off spent flower stalks after the flowers brown. Cut plants to the ground after frost kills them in fall or at the end of winter before new growth begins. Asters sometimes attract aphids and lace bugs (usually cosmetic damage). Some types are prone to powdery mildew on the leaves (also usually cosmetic) and to wilt disease (potentially fatal).

Companion Planting and Design

Asters are good choices for the back of sunny perennial border gardens. Shorter ones are suitable for south- or west-facing foundations or sunny driveways. Pair with sedum, mums, and goldenrod in a fall garden. Or interplant asters with spring bulbs, which will pop up, flower, and be on the way out by the time asters get going.

Try These

I like the compact, 16-inch, purple-blooming New York aster (*Aster novi-belgii*) 'Sapphire'. Foot-tall New York aster 'Wood's Purple' and 'Wood's Pink' are also good. New England aster (*Aster novae-angliae*) 'Purple Dome' is a purple, 2-foot bestseller, and New England aster 'Alma Potschke' is a bright pink 3-footer. Heart-leaf aster 'Avondale' is a good light blue 2-footer.

Astilbe

Astilbe chinensis

Botanical Pronunciation
ah-STILL-bee chye-NEN-siss

Other Name Chinese astilbe

Bloom Period and Seasonal Color
July through August; pink, red, lavender, white

Mature Height × Spread
12 to 36 inches × 18 to 24 inches

  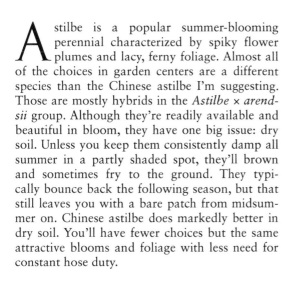

Astilbe is a popular summer-blooming perennial characterized by spiky flower plumes and lacy, ferny foliage. Almost all of the choices in garden centers are a different species than the Chinese astilbe I'm suggesting. Those are mostly hybrids in the *Astilbe × arendsii* group. Although they're readily available and beautiful in bloom, they have one big issue: dry soil. Unless you keep them consistently damp all summer in a partly shaded spot, they'll brown and sometimes fry to the ground. They typically bounce back the following season, but that still leaves you with a bare patch from midsummer on. Chinese astilbe does markedly better in dry soil. You'll have fewer choices but the same attractive blooms and foliage with less need for constant hose duty.

When, Where, and How to Plant
Plant Chinese astilbe in spring or early fall, 18 to 24 inches apart in moist, mildly acidic, compost-enriched soil. A site with morning sun and afternoon shade is ideal. It'll take brighter sunlight if given consistently damp soil. One to 2 inches of mulch is plenty.

Growing Tips
Water once or twice a week throughout the first season to help the roots establish, then water weekly in hot, dry weather at the first sign of leaf-edge browning. Scatter a balanced, granular, organic or gradual-release fertilizer over the bed in early spring. Divide astilbe every three or four years, also in early spring.

Replant fist-sized divisions at their same depth, then water.

Regional Advice and Care
Chinese astilbe makes a good cut flower, so clip a few for a vase just as they're opening. Snip off spent flower stalks after the flowers brown in late summer. Then cut plants to the ground after frost kills them in fall or at the end of winter before new growth begins. Other than browning out in dry soil, astilbe is a trouble-free plant that seldom runs into any bug or disease problem. Astilbe also is *not* a deer-favorite meal.

Companion Planting and Design
Chinese astilbe is at its best in a band lining a partly shaded water garden or stream. It's also a good choice in a perennial shade garden, and its propensity for dampness makes it a top choice in a partly shaded rain garden. Hostas, bergenia, and false forget-me-nots are good round-leaf partners for astilbe's upright ferny foliage. Hydrangea is a good shrub partner along an eastern house foundation.

Try These
'Pumila' is a 12- to 18-inch lavender bloomer that's an oldie but goodie. Even better is the new Vision series, which comes in three colors and grows 18 inches tall ('Vision in Pink,' 'Vision in Red', 'Vision in White'). If you keep them damp, try one of the many June-blooming *Astilbe × arendsii* hybrids, such as 'Fanal' (red) or 'Snowdrift' (white), or *Astilbe japonica* 'Rheinland' (pink).

Black-Eyed Susan

Rudbeckia fulgida

Botanical Pronunciation
rood-BECK-ee-ah FULL-jih-dah

Other Name Orange coneflower

Bloom Period and Seasonal Color
July through September; gold, yellow

Mature Height × Spread
2 to 3 feet × 18 to 24 inches

Another familiar wildflower is this Southeast meadow native that has daisylike flowers with bright golden petals fanning out around a central black cone. Perennial black-eyed Susan is the winter-hardy cousin of the annual black-eyed Susan, or gloriosa daisy (*Rudbeckia hirta*), which reseeds itself throughout Pennsylvania meadows. Perennial black-eyed Susan also often reseeds itself, but it reliably survives Pennsylvania winters and colonizes via spreading root clumps. Birds appreciate a winter feast of dried black-eyed Susan seeds when you leave a few stalks standing over winter. This is one of our favorite and brightest midsummer flower choices, and it also makes a good cut flower. Black-eyed Susan handles drought well and is one of the toughest perennials in summer heat and humidity.

When, Where, and How to Plant
Plant black-eyed Susans in spring or fall, 18 to 24 inches apart, in moist, compost-enriched soil. Summer planting is fine if you keep the young plants well watered. Or start black-eyed Susans by scratching seeds directly into the soil surface in early to mid-spring. Full sun is best, but black-eyed Susans will tolerate light shade. One to 2 inches of mulch is plenty.

Growing Tips
Water once or twice a week during the first season, then water weekly in hot, dry weather. Although black-eyed Susan is drought-tolerant, it grows and flowers best in damp soil. Scatter a balanced, granular, organic or gradual-release fertilizer over the bed in early spring. Divide every three to five years in early spring or early fall. If you want to replant the divisions, cut fist-sized pieces, plant at the same depth, then water.

Regional Advice and Care
Black-eyed Susan usually reseeds if you let it stand all winter. If you don't want its offspring, cut the flower stalks after the flowers brown. Cut plants to the ground in fall after frost kills them or at winter's end before new growth begins. Rabbits and groundhogs sometimes gnaw on black-eyed Susan, especially young transplants. Repellents may discourage them. Leaf-spot disease occasionally blackens plants in late summer. Rake out fallen, diseased leaves, divide plants to improve air flow, and avoid overhead watering.

Companion Planting and Design
Black-eyed Susans make a good "skirt" around the base of tall evergreens. They also mass nicely on sunny banks and pair well with red flowers, such as beebalm, mums, or daylilies (perennials), or lantana, celosia, or zinnias (annuals).

Try These
'Goldsturm' was Perennial Plant of the Year and remains very popular. I like the golden yellow newcomer 'Little Gold Star' (*Rudbeckia fulgida* var. *sullivantii*) for its heavy bloom and compact size—16 inches vs. 'Goldsturm' at 2 feet. 'Viette's Little Suzy' is another compact type. Smooth coneflower 'Henry Eilers' (*Rudbeckia subtomentosa*) is 3 feet tall with tubular yellow flowers, and *Rudbeckia* × Denver Daisy™ has burgundy-tinged, sunflower-like flowers (hardy to Zone 6, but it can reseed itself).

Blanket Flower

Gaillardia × grandiflora

Botanical Pronunciation
gay-LARD-ee-ah gran-dih-FLOOR-ah

Bloom Period and Seasonal Color
June through October; red, gold, yellow,
burgundy, blends

Mature Height × Spread
8 to 24 inches × 15 to 18 inches

Blanket flower is one of the longest-blooming, most heat- and drought-tolerant perennials you'll find. It'll grow in your hottest, driest spots, including along roads, walks, and driveways since it's also salt-tolerant (think salt-based ice-melters in winter). The plants grow in mounded clumps with 3- to 4-inch, multi-petaled daisylike flowers of red, gold, and/or burgundy surrounding a red-gold pincushion center. Flowers nearly cover the mounds in early to midsummer. The narrow leaves are gray-green with toothy edges. Blooms may continue sporadically even into November some years. To come up with such a long bloom time, breeders crossed the southern U.S. native perennial *Gaillardia aristata* with the annual *Gaillardia pulchella*. That's the heritage of most blanket flower hybrid varieties you'll find these days in garden centers.

When, Where, and How to Plant
Blanket flower is best planted in early to mid-spring, 15 to 18 inches apart in full sun and well-drained, slightly alkaline and sandy soil. Good drainage is *imperative*. Wet soil in winter is the leading blanket flower killer. Planting in raised beds helps; improving your lousy clay with gravel or 25 percent coarse sand helps even more. Summer planting is okay if you keep new plants damp (but never soggy). One inch of mulch is enough. Some blanket flower varieties start well if you plant seed in April or May.

Growing Tips
Water weekly the first season to keep the young roots damp, then watering is usually never needed again. Spread a balanced, granular, organic or gradual-release fertilizer over the bed in early spring. Snip off browned flowers to neaten the plant and encourage continuing bloom. Divide fist-sized pieces every two to three years in early spring.

Regional Advice and Care
Don't be surprised if your blanket flowers die off in two or three years. Wet soil in winter contributes, but the genetic tradeoff for longer bloom (i.e. the *Gaillardia pulchella* genes) also shortens the longevity of *Gaillardia × grandiflora* hybrids. Watch for reseeded offspring though. You might not get the exact look you started with, but blanket flower "babies" can be transplanted in spring to keep your colorful planting going. Wait until end of winter to cut back frost-killed plants to the ground.

Companion Planting and Design
Blanket flower makes a good front-of-bed perennial in a sunny border garden or along a southern or western house foundation. A band of it also makes a bright "skirt" at the base of green- or gold-needled evergreens. Good perennial partners are Shasta daisy, daylily, black-eyed Susan, mum, and goldenrod.

Try These
'Goblin' is a common, compact, foot-tall choice with yellow-tipped red flowers. 'Bijou', 'Fanfare', 'Arizona Sun', and the Gallo® series are good red-gold 15-inchers. 'Frenzy' and 'Tizzy' have unusual fluted flowers on 18-inch plants. 'Oranges and Lemons' gives a new look with orange/gold flowers on a 2-foot upright plant.

Blazing Star

Liatris spicata

Botanical Pronunciation
lye-AY-triss spy-KAY-tah

Other Name Gayfeather

Bloom Period and Seasonal Color
July through August; pinkish purple, white

Mature Height × Spread
2 to 4 feet × 18 to 24 inches

This native, upright perennial adds a spiky, fine-textured look to the landscape in addition to its midsummer pinkish purple or white flowers. Blazing star produces slender stems with long, narrow, green leaves that are almost grassy in appearance. By early summer, flower buds line the top foot or so of the 2- to 3-foot-tall shoots, opening in July into fuzzy, pinkish purple, upright cigars or bottle brushes. The flower stalks open at the tips first and then flower their way down the ladder. Butterflies adore blazing star, and birds feed on the seeds over winter if you let at least a few flower stalks standing. Blazing star also makes an excellent cut flower, as you might tell by this U.S. wildflower's common use in the floral industry.

When, Where, and How to Plant

Plant blazing star 18 to 24 inches apart in moist, compost-enriched soil, in spring or fall. Summer planting will do if you keep young plants well watered. Plants also can be started by scratching seeds directly into the soil surface in early to mid spring. Blazing star loves full sun but will tolerate light shade. Cover the soil with 1 or 2 inches of mulch.

Growing Tips

Water once or twice a week during the first season, then weekly in hot, dry weather. Although blazing star is drought-tolerant, it grows best in damp soil. Scatter a balanced, granular, organic or gradual-release fertilizer over the bed in early spring. Stake plants if you find yours tend to flop in summer (a possible sign of excess fertilizer or not enough sunlight). Divide every three to five years in early spring. Once it's divided, replant fist-sized pieces at the same depth, then water.

Regional Advice and Care

The main precaution is to avoid wet soil in winter. Blazing star prefers *damp* soil and can tolerate temporary wet spells in the growing season, but soggy clay in winter crosses the line. Cut back to remove spent flower stalks after the flowers brown. Wait until end of winter or at least until after frost kills the foliage to cut plants back to the ground. Deer don't like blazing star, but voles occasionally eat the roots. Divide and spread out plantings if the leaves develop powdery mildew (whitish cast) after the flowers fade.

Companion Planting and Design

Blazing star is an excellent choice in a sunny bird or butterfly garden. It also mixes well in border gardens with rounded shrubs such as spireas, abelias, and boxwoods, or with other sun-loving pastel bloomers such as purple coneflower, balloon flowers, salvias, and sedums.

Try These

'Kobold' is a common 3-foot-tall variety that blooms rosy purple (some would say mauve). Two other good, slightly more compact varieties are 'Floristan Violet' (rosy lavender) and 'Floristan White' (white). The straight species does fine and grows 3 to 4 feet tall.

Bleeding Heart

Dicentra spectabilis

Botanical Pronunciation
dye-SEN-trah spek-TAB-ih-liss

Bloom Period and Seasonal Color
April through May; pink, rosy red, white

Mature Height × Spread
24 to 36 inches × 30 to 36 inches

B leeding heart is one of the most recognized and beloved perennial flowers, primarily because of its distinctively heart-shaped pink or white blooms that hang down clothesline-fashion all along the stems in April and May. It gets its nickname from the petals that protrude from the bottom of the puffy flowers, like blood drops dripping out the bottom of the hearts. Bleeding heart plants are bushy in habit and can grow 2 to 3 feet tall. The leaves are light bluish green and lobed, somewhat like small maple leaves. This Japanese woodland native is one of the most trouble-free, deer-resistant choices for springtime shady spots, but keep in mind it's an "ephemeral." That means it goes dormant and dies back to the ground in summer.

When, Where, and How to Plant
Bleeding heart does best in shady spots or at least in areas out of the hot, afternoon sun. Plant in early spring, 30 to 36 inches apart in moist, compost-enriched, mildly acidic to neutral soil. Mulch 1 to 2 inches deep after planting. Dormant root divisions can be planted or transplanted in early fall.

Growing Tips
Water once or twice a week throughout the first season to help its roots establish, then water weekly while bleeding heart is blooming if the weather is hot and dry. Stop watering when the leaves begin to yellow, which signals the beginning of summer dormancy. Feed with a balanced, granular, organic or gradual-release fertilizer over the bed in early spring. There's no need to divide bleeding heart unless the clump is spreading beyond where you like.

Regional Advice and Care
Bleeding heart fakes out many a rookie gardener by yellowing and apparently dying in early summer. This is normal. The plant goes dormant in summer heat (and for the rest of the year, for that matter), but it'll re-emerge the following spring. Set a flower pot, decorative urn, statue, or similar garden ornament over the bare spot in summer. Bleeding heart often reseeds itself; transplant or give away seedlings that pop up in spring. All parts of bleeding heart plants are poisonous if ingested; prevent pets or young children from eating them.

Companion Planting and Design
Bleeding heart overlaps bloom with two other shade-preferring, spring-flowering, blue perennials—Virginia bluebells and false forget-me-not. It pairs well with blue- or purple-blooming spring bulbs too, in particular hyacinth, Siberian squill, and glory-of-the-snow. But my favorite pairing is bleeding heart under-planted with a white-blooming groundcover of sweet woodruff. Lovely.

Try These
'Valentine' is a variation with rosy red flowers and red stems. 'Gold Heart' has golden foliage and pink flowers. 'Alba' is a good white-flowering variety. By all means, try our native fringe-leaf bleeding heart (*Dicentra eximia*), which stays green all summer and grows only 12 to 15 inches tall. Good varieties of those include 'Luxuriant', 'King of Hearts', and 'Dolly Sods'.

Blue Star Flower

Amsonia hubrichtii

Botanical Pronunciation
am-SONE-ee-ah hew-BRIK-tee-eye

Other Name Threadleaf bluestar

Bloom Period and Seasonal Color
May through June; pale blue

Mature Height × Spread
36 to 42 inches × 30 to 36 inches

This Arkansas native with the long, thready foliage is a multi-seasonal, trouble-free, tall perennial that's one of my favorite plants. Yet it's *way* underused in Pennsylvania landscapes, probably because it's just not well known. The Perennial Plant Association tried to change that by naming blue star flower as a Perennial Plant of the Year. Once people know blue star, they usually love it. Plants grow 3 feet tall and are bushy, almost looking like evergreens with their fine-textured leaves. Pale blue flower clusters bloom at the top of the stems in late spring, but the real show comes in fall when the foliage turns a rich golden yellow. The color holds for weeks, making it a long-lasting addition to the fall garden.

When, Where, and How to Plant
Plant blue star flower in spring when it's small and just getting started. But it'll also adapt to summer or fall planting if you keep the roots damp. This is *not* a finicky plant. It'll grow in damp to dry soil, accept a fair amount of clay, and tolerate some shade, although its best growth is in full sun. Blue star flower gets bushy, so allow 3 feet of space. One to 2 inches of mulch is fine.

Growing Tips
Water weekly when conditions are dry the first season, then water only in very hot, dry spells. A balanced, granular, organic or gradual-release fertilizer scattered over the bed in early spring is fine. Division is not needed unless you want to shrink the clump

or expand your planting. In that case, do the deed in early spring as new growth is just starting.

Regional Advice and Care
While you're trimming off the spent flowers after they brown in June, consider trimming the whole plant back by one-third to one-half if you want less flopping in fall. Corralling the plants by hammering bamboo stakes around the perimeter and wrapping jute around them is another way to keep the plants upright. Otherwise, enjoy their loose habit and brilliant fall foliage! Wait until end of winter to cut plants to the ground. It's virtually pest-free.

Companion Planting and Design
Take advantage of the tall, golden fall foliage by using red, orange, or purple fall-peaking plants in front. Examples are mums, asters, or dwarf goldenrod (perennials); dwarf zinnias, lantana, or marigold (annuals); or ornamental peppers with red fruits. Dark-leaf ninebark, purple smokebush, and St. Johnswort 'Albury Purple' are great shrub partners.

Try These
You'll likely only find the straight species of this in garden centers, which is perfectly fine. While you're there, try the Pennsylvania native common blue star (*Amsonia tabernaemontana*), which is shorter (18 to 24 inches), with medium blue spring flowers and slightly wider leaves than the Arkansas blue star. 'Blue Ice' is a common variety of that, but the straight species is just as good.

Catmint

Nepeta species and hybrids

Botanical Pronunciation
NEPP-eh-tah

Bloom Period and Seasonal Color
May through November; blue,
lavender-blue, white

Mature Height × Spread
10 to 24 inches × 24 to 30 inches

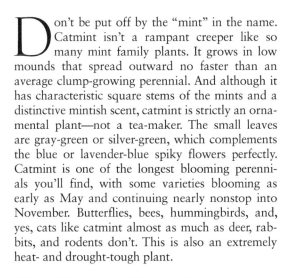

Don't be put off by the "mint" in the name. Catmint isn't a rampant creeper like so many mint family plants. It grows in low mounds that spread outward no faster than an average clump-growing perennial. And although it has characteristic square stems of the mints and a distinctive mintish scent, catmint is strictly an ornamental plant—not a tea-maker. The small leaves are gray-green or silver-green, which complements the blue or lavender-blue spiky flowers perfectly. Catmint is one of the longest blooming perennials you'll find, with some varieties blooming as early as May and continuing nearly nonstop into November. Butterflies, bees, hummingbirds, and, yes, cats like catmint almost as much as deer, rabbits, and rodents don't. This is also an extremely heat- and drought-tough plant.

When, Where, and How to Plant
Catmint thrives in hot, dry sites and isn't too picky about soil, including salty roadside territory. Given a choice, though, it would take slightly raised beds and sandy or gravelly soil that's damp, never soggy and slightly alkaline. Plant 24 inches apart in spring or fall. Summer planting is fine if you keep the young roots moist. Full sun yields best flowering, but catmint does tolerate light shade. One inch of mulch is enough.

Growing Tips
Water every week the first season to establish the roots, then you'll never need to water catmint again. Fertilizer usually isn't needed either. Prevent plants from looking floppy in late season by trimming back to 6 or 8 inches right after the first flush of flowering, usually in midsummer. This keeps growth compact and encourages fresh late-season growth and reblooming. Divide every three or four years in early spring or early fall.

Regional Advice and Care
Other than the midseason trim, catmint requires almost no work. Bugs and disease issues are nil. Just cut plants to 2-inch stubs in fall after frost kills the foliage or in early spring before new growth begins. *Nepeta racemosa* and most catmints self-sow new plants from dropped seed, so either transplant seedlings if you like that trait or trim off flowers right after bloom if you don't. *Nepeta × faassenii* hybrids are sterile and don't reseed.

Companion Planting and Design
Catmint makes an excellent mass planting on a sunny bank as well as a good edging plant in any hot, sunny, dry spot, including south- and west-facing house-foundation beds. It also plays well with other sun perennials and shrubs in a mixed border garden, especially dwarf butterfly bush, purple coneflowers, sedum, ornamental grasses, and shrub roses.

Try These
'Walker's Low' (a Perennial Plant of the Year) is long-blooming and the most popular variety, but it's not particularly low, growing 18 to 24 inches tall. I like the 10- to 15-inchers better, including 'Kit Cat', 'Blue Ice', 'Junior Walker', 'Little Titch', 'Purple Haze', and 'Little Trudy'.

Cheddar Pinks

Dianthus gratianopolitanus

Botanical Pronunciation
dye-AN-thus grah-tee-ah-no-po-lih-TAY-nus

Bloom Period and Seasonal Color
May through September; pink, red, white, bicolors

Mature Height × Spread
6 to 10 inches × 18 to 24 inches

Pinks and their *Dianthus* family members have been gracing gardens almost as long as there have been gardens. Although most flower pink, that's not why they're called "pinks." That comes from the fringed edges of the flowers, which look to be "pinked," as in pinking shears. My favorite of this clan is the European native cheddar pinks, which is a low, carpetlike plant with slender, gray-green, grasslike leaves and dime-sized flowers. This one blooms a long time (best in May, but sometimes into early fall), is tough in drought, and is evergreen in my Harrisburg-area garden. Some types are mildly fragrant too. I had less luck with cheddar pinks cousins, including sweet William (short-lived), carnations (rabbits ate 'em), and Chinese pinks (annuals that fried in summer heat).

When, Where, and How to Plant
Cheddar pinks are best planted in early to mid-spring, 18 to 24 inches apart in full sun in loose, slightly alkaline soil. Good drainage is a must. Planting in raised beds helps; improving clay soil with gravel or 25 percent coarse sand helps even more. Summer and early-fall planting is okay; just keep the roots damp but never soggy. One inch of mulch is plenty.

Growing Tips
Water weekly the first season to keep the young roots damp, then watering usually is never needed again. In early spring scatter a balanced, granular, organic or gradual-release fertilizer over the bed. Lightly trim off flowers after they brown in late spring. Cut up to one-third of the foliage then if the plants are too bushy or looking worn. Divide and replant fist-sized pieces every two to three years in early spring, especially if you see signs of dieback in the older center sections.

Regional Advice and Care
The foliage of cheddar pinks holds up well throughout most Pennsylvania winters. Wait until the end of winter to trim off or cut back growth that hasn't weathered the cold. Assuming plants are intact, just rake out any debris and trim back to maintain the spread. Sections growing beyond where you want also can be shoveled out anytime during the season.

Companion Planting and Design
Cheddar pinks make *excellent* edging perennials along driveways and sidewalks. They're also good front-of-the-bed choices in any west- or south-facing house-foundation bed. And they're naturals in a rock garden. Purple salvia is a good perennial partner that blooms at the same time and color coordinates nicely with the pink cheddar pinks.

Try These
'Bath's Pink' is a worthy, well-known, 8-inch pink bloomer. I like the eight-color 'Star' series and also the 6-inch, deep pink 'Tiny Rubies'; the 8-inch, magenta-flowered 'Firewitch'; and the 10-inch, pink-flowered 'Pixie'. The Scent First series is one of the most fragrant. Try Allwood pinks (*Dianthus × allwoodii*) if you like blue-gray leaves and a more mounded habit, and cottage pinks (*Dianthus plumarius*) for a more open and upright habit.

Coralbells

Heuchera species and hybrids

Botanical Pronunciation
HEW-ker-ah

Other Name Alumroot

Bloom Period and Seasonal Color
May through July; white, pink, red, yellow
flowers; endless foliage colors

Mature Height × Spread
12 to 24 inches × 18 to 30 inches

Beginners, begin here. Few plants offer so many upsides with so little on the downside as the coralbell. I'll just rattle them off: not picky about soil; will do sun to shade and everything in-between; willing to take on tree roots; good drought tolerance; mostly U.S. natives; flowers attract hummingbirds and butterflies; cut flowers do well in a vase; foliage colors come in almost any imaginable shade; makes an excellent container plant; usually evergreen for winter interest; almost no chance of any bug or disease problems; deer don't like them; they come in a huge menu of choices. Whew! Just plant with the roots pointing down, and there's a good chance you'll succeed. The biggest problem is trying to figure out which one(s) to buy.

When, Where, and How to Plant
Coralbells do best in rich, moist, compost-enriched, well-drained soil in a site that gets ample morning sun and some shade in the afternoon. That's the ideal. But unlike some garden divas, coralbells are versatile enough and forgiving enough to do reasonably well in all sorts of extremes. Just avoid soggy spots. Plant 18 to 24 inches apart in spring or early fall.

Growing Tips
Water weekly the first season to keep the young roots damp, then water is needed only in hot, dry spells. Scatter a balanced, granular, organic or gradual-release fertilizer over the bed in early spring. Snip off flower stalks after flowers finish blooming. Division isn't needed but can be done in early spring to expand a planting.

Regional Advice and Care
Most coralbells hold their leaves in Pennsylvania winters. Wait until winter's end and clip off cold-damaged leaves, up to *all* of them if winter was particularly cold. Some types do better in summer heat and sun than others. Check the plant tags for variety specifics, and don't be afraid to move coralbells that are losing their leaf color or otherwise suffering in a too-hot, too-sunny spot. Voles occasionally eat coralbell roots.

Companion Planting and Design
Such a versatile plant can be used most anywhere, but especially these sites: north- and east-facing foundation beds, edging a water garden, massed under trees along with liriope or Japanese forest-grass, paired with annuals in a flower pot, clustered throughout a border garden on the east side of shrubs, and spotted throughout a bird or butterfly garden.

Try These
Where to begin? A coralbell breeding frenzy has brought us countless foliage colors, including silver, purple, burgundy, gold, lime, caramel, near black, and shades I can't even describe. Many of them change color in fall and winter. Most varieties are at least good, so go with what grabs your eye. Me? I like 'Caramel', 'Hollywood', 'Lime Marmalade', 'Gypsy Dancer', 'Green Spice', 'Dale's Strain', 'Silver Scrolls', and 'Rave On'.

Daylily

Hemerocallis hybrids

Botanical Pronunciation
hem-er-oh-KAL-liss

Bloom Period and Seasonal Color
June through October; gold, yellow, red, burgundy, orange, white, assorted pastels

Mature Height × Spread
6 inches to 3 feet × 18 to 24 inches

And you thought coralbells came in an overwhelming glut of choices. The American Hemerocallis Society recognizes 58,000 daylily varieties—and counting. Plant sizes range from 6 inches to more than 3 feet. Flowers come in nearly every shade except true black and blue, with bright reds, golds, and oranges leading the parade. The two most sought-after traits lately are compact sizes (1- to 2-footers) and varieties that rebloom or produce new flower buds from June to fall. All daylilies have strappy leaves with flower stalks that hold flower-bud clusters. Buds open sequentially into trumpet-shaped flowers that last only a day each (hence the plant's name). Daylily is so durable and long-living that it's the perennial of choice in mall parking lots and office-building gardens everywhere.

When, Where, and How to Plant
Daylily tolerates heat, drought, variable sunlight, poor soil (rock, clay, salt) and virtually any abuse you throw at it—except soggy soil. The ideal situation is moist, compost-enriched soil in sun, with a few hours out of direct afternoon sun. Plant in spring or fall, 18 to 24 inches apart. Summer planting is okay if you keep young plants well watered. One to 2 inches of mulch is plenty.

Growing Tips
Water weekly during the first season, then water is needed only in hot, dry spells. Even without water, daylily survives drought. Feed a balanced, granular, organic or gradual-release fertilizer in early spring and early fall. Daylily is easy to divide in spring or

early fall. Just pull or split its root sections apart. Divide every two or three years or if flowering wanes.

Regional Advice and Care
Many daylilies suffer from a fungal leaf-streak disease that causes rust-colored markings and eventual leaf browning. Rust is another disease that causes spotting with dusty orange spores on the leaves and browning. Pick off and remove diseased leaves (don't compost them). If the whole plant browns, cut foliage to a stub and allow fresh growth to emerge. Wait until early spring to rake or pull off the season's dead foliage. Deer is the daylily's main enemy, and rabbits like the edible flower buds.

Companion Planting and Design
Daylily is a summer staple in any low-care, sunny or part-sun garden, especially paired with earlier and later perennials to create a three-season symphony. Dwarf rebloomers are good choices along house foundations. A band of daylilies adds color around the base of tall evergreens. Masses of them even stabilize soil on banks.

Try These
Some types are more disease-prone than others, but even they bounce back. Compact types that rebloom or bloom continuously make most sense to me. 'Stella de Oro' is the most common (and very good), but also check out the lemon-yellow 'Happy Returns', the red-blooming 'Red Hot Returns' and 'Ruby Stella', the taller orange-gold 'Primal Scream', and the yellow-throated, burgundy-blooming 'Ruby Spider'.

False Forget-Me-Not

Brunnera macrophylla

Botanical Pronunciation
BRUNN-er-ah mack-ro-FILL-ah

Other Name Siberian bugloss

Bloom Period and Seasonal Color
April through May; light blue

Mature Height × Spread
12 to 18 inches × 18 to 24 inches

The silver-leafed versions of this shade perennial are some of the most eye-grabbing plants you'll find, but proper siting is critical. False forget-me-not is at home in the moist shade of woodlands. That's what it wants to thrive in your yard. Give it too much sun or droughty conditions, and the beautiful, heart-shaped leaves brown around the edges—or worse. Even in fairly shaded conditions, false forget-me-not doesn't appreciate the heat and humidity of summer. It tends to do better in Pennsylvania's cooler regions. Yet the dainty, light blue spring flowers that resemble *real* forget-me-nots (*Myosotis* genus)—not to mention those silvery, heart-shaped leaves—make this plant well worth trying. Some of the new silver-leafed varieties actually do better in heat than the original green-leafed species.

When, Where, and How to Plant
The ideal site is loose, damp, compost-enriched, mildly acidic "woodsy" soil, ideally in morning sun but afternoon shade. Shade all day also is fine, although flowering will be less, but definitely avoid hot afternoon sun and dry sites. Plant in spring or early fall, spacing 18 to 24 inches. Top with 1 to 2 inches of mulch.

Growing Tips
Water every three or four days throughout the first season, then weekly in hot, dry weather. Avoid soggy soil, but false forget-me-not doesn't like dry roots either. Scatter a balanced, granular, organic or gradual-release fertilizer over the bed in early spring. Divide every three or four years in early spring or early fall. If plant centers are dying, dig the clump, discard the centers, and replant fist-sized pieces from around the perimeter.

Regional Advice and Care
Our summer heat and humidity can take a toll on false forget-me-nots, shortening their life span. They often do well for a few years, then suddenly don't show up one spring. Shady, moist locations help prevent that. So does watering once or twice a week in hot, dry weather. Slugs occasionally chew on leaves, but they're seldom a serious threat. Deer and bunnies let this plant alone.

Companion Planting and Design
Try a few bands or clusters of false forget-me-not in a north- or east-facing foundation bed. Silver-leafed types make good partners for blue-blooming hydrangeas and spiky pink astilbes. A moist, wooded garden is another good spot, especially paired with a shade-tolerant grassy plant, such as liriope, Japanese forest grass, or Pennsylvania sedge (or nearly any plant in the *Carex* family). Or line them along a shady water garden or shaded stream.

Try These
'Jack Frost' won a Perennial Plant of the Year for its green-veined, silver leaves. 'Looking Glass' is almost pure silver. Two newcomers have more leathery leaves that purportedly hold up better in heat and humidity. 'Sea Heart' is a 'Jack Frost' lookalike while 'Silver Heart' is an alternative to 'Looking Glass'. These are also more compact (12 inches versus 15 to 18).

Foamflower

Tiarella cordifolia

Botanical Pronunciation
tee-a-RELL-ah kor-dih-FOE-lee-ah

Bloom Period and Seasonal Color
April through May; white, pink

Mature Height × Spread
6 to 12 inches × 2 feet and beyond

This creeping native beauty is finally getting its due attention in shade circles. Foamflower's name comes from the pinkish white spring flowers that pop up in spikes, kind of like a foaming bottle brush. The plants grow in 6-inch mats that root as they go, making this a plant that could be lumped in with the groundcovers. The growth isn't invasive though; foamflower doesn't climb up walls or root out into the lawn. The foliage is as attractive as the flowers, sporting 3- to 4-inch lobed leaves (somewhat like maple) that have burgundy markings or variegation along the veins. Many foamflowers take on a bronzy hue in fall. Recent breeding has given this already good native even more varied leaf coloring and heavier blooms.

When, Where, and How to Plant
Plant in spring or early fall, 18 to 24 inches apart in damp, compost-enriched, slightly acidic soil. Morning sun and afternoon shade is perfect. Shade all day also is fine, although flowering may be less. Avoid hot afternoon sun and poorly drained spots. Although foamflower prefers moist soil, it's underrated in dry spots and usually holds its own in the root competition under trees. After planting, top the soil with an inch of bark mulch or leaves (keep it slightly away from the stems) and give a good soaking.

Growing Tips
Water weekly the first season to keep the young roots damp, then weekly in hot, dry spells. In early spring, feed with a balanced, granular, organic or gradual-release fertilizer. Snip off flower stalks after flowers finish blooming. Division isn't needed but can be done in early spring to expand a planting.

Regional Advice and Care
Foamflowers often hold their leaves in winter, at least in Pennsylvania's warmer regions. Wait until winter's end to clip off cold-damaged leaves, up to *all* of them if winter was particularly cold. Voles occasionally eat foamflower roots. Use repellents or traps if they become a problem. At least deer, rabbits, and groundhogs don't care for the taste of foamflowers.

Companion Planting and Design
Take advantage of the spring flowers and colorful foliage to use a band of foamflowers at the front of north- and east-facing foundation beds. Boxwoods, azaleas, and cherrylaurels make good backdrop evergreens, and hydrangeas and fothergilla are flowering shrub pals. Foamflower also can be massed as a shady groundcover under trees, where it pairs well with ferns, hostas, and Solomon's seal.

Try These
The straight species is good, but I especially like the varieties 'Sugar and Spice' (pinkish white flowers and burgundy-variegated leaves) and 'Spring Symphony' (heavy white flowering and bronzy leaves). Also excellent is the River series, named after five eastern Pennsylvania rivers ('Brandywine', 'Delaware', 'Lehigh', 'Octoraro', and 'Susquehanna'). Wherry's foamflower (*Tiarella wherryi*) is a related native foamflower that's a tad taller, more upright, and less running in its habit than *Tiarella cordifolia*.

Foamybell

× *Heucherella alba*

Botanical Pronunciation
hew-ker-ELL-ah AL-bah

Bloom Period and Seasonal Color
May through June; white, pink

Mature Height × Spread
8 to 16 inches × 18 to 24 inches

     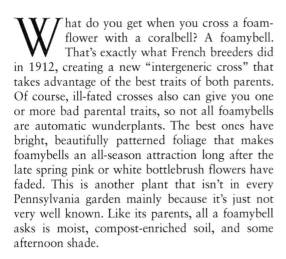

What do you get when you cross a foam-flower with a coralbell? A foamybell. That's exactly what French breeders did in 1912, creating a new "intergeneric cross" that takes advantage of the best traits of both parents. Of course, ill-fated crosses also can give you one or more bad parental traits, so not all foamybells are automatic wunderplants. The best ones have bright, beautifully patterned foliage that makes foamybells an all-season attraction long after the late spring pink or white bottlebrush flowers have faded. This is another plant that isn't in every Pennsylvania garden mainly because it's just not very well known. Like its parents, all a foamybell asks is moist, compost-enriched soil, and some afternoon shade.

When, Where, and How to Plant
Foamybells do well in all-day shade, although flowering typically drops off. Just avoid direct, hot afternoon sun and parched spots. Plant in spring or early fall, 18 to 24 inches apart. Foamybells will tangle with tree roots if you're willing to give them some water in hot, dry weather. After planting, mulch the soil with an inch or so of bark or leaves (keep it slightly away from the stems), and give a good soaking.

Growing Tips
Water once or twice a week the first season to keep the young roots damp, then weekly in hot, dry spells. Scatter a balanced, granular, organic or gradual-release fertilizer over the bed in early spring. Snip off flower stalks after flowers finish blooming.

If you want to expand your planting, divide in early spring, but it's not really necessary.

Regional Advice and Care
Foamybells often hold their leaves in winter, at least in warmer regions. Wait until winter's end and clip off cold-damaged leaves, up to *all* of them if winter was particularly cold. Leaf color often brightens or deepens in fall and winter. Voles occasionally eat foamybell roots. Use repellents or traps if they become a problem. Deer, rabbits, and groundhogs don't like them, though.

Companion Planting and Design
Foamybells work well everywhere you'd use coralbells or foamflowers, such as at the front of north- and east-facing foundation beds, massed or spotted in damp wooded gardens, or as a groundcover under trees, especially paired with more upright, dry shade perennials such as liriope, Pennsylvania sedge, hosta, hellebore, and Solomon's seal.

Try These
'Stoplight' and 'Alabama Sunrise' are excellent varieties that grow in 10- to 12-inch-tall clumps and have golden leaves with red veining. 'Tapestry' is lower and more spreading with burgundy-veined green leaves and long-lasting pink flowers. Two of the showiest are the 10-inch 'Gold Zebra' (neon yellow with dark red veining) and the 18-inch 'Brass Lantern' (brassy red-gold in spring, deeper and richer in fall). Although it doesn't sound all that great, the peach/apricot-leafed 'Sweet Tea' is my favorite; the leaves turn tea-colored in fall.

Gaura

Gaura lindheimeri

Botanical Pronunciation
GAW-rah LIND-hye-mer-eye

Other Name Wand flower

Bloom Period and Seasonal Color
July through October; white, pink, rosy red

Mature Height × Spread
14 inches to 3 feet × 2 to 3 feet

Although native to the southern United States (Louisiana and Texas), gaura didn't become a widely sold garden perennial until the pink-blooming 'Siskiyou Pink' hit the market in 1995. Since then, even heavier-blooming and more compact varieties have come along. Gaura plants have slender leaves that are often tinted red. Wiry flower stems poke up above the 2- to 3-foot foliage to produce dainty, open-petal flowers with long stamens that look a bit like little butterflies fluttering on skinny wands. That's where the plant's two nicknames—"wand flower" and "whirling butterflies"—come from. The flowers might look dainty, but gaura is a tough plant, tolerating rocky and clayish soil as well as brutal heat and humidity. If gaura is okay with Dallas, Philadelphia is a breeze.

When, Where, and How to Plant
Gaura does best in hot, sunny spots. It'll grow in half-day sun, but it'll flower less and grow taller and leggier. Gaura isn't picky about rocky, gravelly, sandy, or even compacted soil—just keep it away from wet spots. Plant 24 to 30 inches apart in spring or fall. Summer planting is fine if you keep the young roots moist. One inch of mulch is enough.

Growing Tips
Water weekly to establish the roots, then you'll never need to water gaura again. Fertilizer usually isn't needed either. Keep plants neat and more compact by shearing them back by one-third after flowering takes a break in late summer. A lighter

rebloom often occurs into frost, making this a long-blooming perennial. Gaura has a large taproot and doesn't transplant or divide well once it's established. To enlarge a planting, either dig up offshoots or watch for self-sown volunteers. Move both of those in early spring.

Regional Advice and Care
Don't be surprised if gaura disappears one winter after three or four years of doing well. It tends to be a short-lived perennial. Increase its winter survival by avoiding wet soil and by waiting until the end of winter to cut the browned-out foliage back to a stub. Protecting the base of plants with 2 to 4 inches of fallen tree leaves helps insulate the roots in colder Zone 5 winters.

Companion Planting and Design
Gaura looks most at home in a sunny butterfly garden. It's also a good choice in a perennial border, mixed with other cool-colored perennials such as purple coneflower, salvia, aster, mum, catmint, sedum, and Russian sage. Try compact varieties along sunny walks or driveways.

Try These
The original breakthrough variety 'Siskiyou Pink' is still popular and a good choice. I particularly like 'Crimson Butterflies' for its 18-inch, compact sized, hot pink flowers, and red-tinged foliage. Stratosphere Pink Picotee™ is another compact pink bloomer. And 'Whirling Butterflies' is one of the best white bloomers (3 feet tall).

Goldenrod

Solidago species and hybrids

Botanical Pronunciation
soll-ih-DAY-go

Bloom Period and Seasonal Color
September into October; gold, yellow

Mature Height × Spread
1 to 4 feet × 2 to 3 feet

Most people know goldenrod as the tall, yellow flower that grows in roadside ditches and that makes everyone sneeze in fall. The truth is that lots of better-looking, garden-bred goldenrods have come along, and *ragweed* is the culprit behind most of the sneezing. Ragweed blooms at the same time as goldenrod but is a lot less conspicuous, thus goldenrod takes the rap. Most of the goldenrods in garden centers are 1- to 2-foot plants that send up bright gold or yellow flower spikes to add fall color to the garden. They bloom fuller and denser than wild goldenrods, which flower mostly at the top of "bare legs." One of the best attributes of goldenrod is that it's highly attractive to numerous pollinating insects.

When, Where, and How to Plant
Goldenrod is easy to grow and tolerates of a variety of soils, ranging from dry, rocky gardens to damp meadows. The best flowering is in full sun, but it does reasonably well in light shade. Goldenrod is best planted in early spring, although early summer also works if young roots are kept damp. Space 24 to 30 inches apart. One to 2 inches of mulch is plenty.

Growing Tips
Goldenrod is drought-tolerant once established, but water weekly during the first season, then water is needed only in hot, dry spells. Scatter a balanced, granular, organic or gradual-release fertilizer over the bed in early spring. Divide clumps every three or four years in early spring or whenever they've spread beyond where you want.

Regional Advice and Care
Goldenrod is a Pennsylvania native that's well adapted to our erratic temperatures and rainfall. Taller types benefit from staking in spring, or cut back plants by one-half to one-third in late May to make them less prone to fall flopping. Let browned-out plants stand over winter (birds like the seeds as winter food). Cut them to the ground in early spring. To prevent unwanted seeding though, cut plants to the ground when foliage browns in fall. Leaves occasionally get mildew or rust disease; divide clumps to increase air flow and remove diseased foliage if that happens.

Companion Planting and Design
Mix goldenrod with mums, asters, and sedum for a fall-peaking perennial border garden. A good shrub partner is winterberry holly; its fall red berries look good with yellow goldenrod flowers. Another good use is to add fall interest and attraction to a butterfly garden.

Try These
I'm partial to the denser-blooming, compact varieties, such as the 12- to 15-inch 'Little Lemon' and the 2-foot 'Baby Gold'. *Solidago sphacelata* 'Golden Fleece' is another good one with lots of arching spikes on 24- to 32-inch plants. If you're okay with a taller type, check out the popular *Solidago rugosa* 'Fireworks', which is loaded with arching bright yellow spikes on 3- to 4-foot plants.

Hardy Geranium

Geranium species and hybrids

Botanical Pronunciation
jer-AYE-nee-um

Other Name Cranesbill

Bloom Period and Seasonal Color
May through September; pink, blue, purple, violet, magenta, white

Mature Height × Spread
6 inches to 3 feet × 18 to 30 inches

These are the *true* geraniums, ones that come back every year in Pennsylvania gardens and that are mounding, spreading, and usually pink, blue, or violet in flower color. That's much different than the bushy, much-used, red-balled annuals that most people call "geraniums." (Those are *Pelargonium*, an entirely different species.) Geraniums themselves come in about 250 species, growing over most of the Earth. One of them, the spotted geranium (*Geranium maculatum*), is a Pennsylvania native with a low, spreading habit and pink flowers. But many species and their crosses and hybrids grow well here, giving long-lasting spring to summer color on low-care plants that deer and bunnies don't eat. Flowers are nickel-sized with five petals, the leaves of most are dissected, and some have colorful fall foliage.

When, Where, and How to Plant
Most hardy geraniums do best in morning sun with some afternoon shade. Many do fine in full sun (especially bigroot geranium, *Geranium macrorrhizum*, and bloody cranesbill, *Geranium sanguineum*), while our native spotted geranium is one of the most shade-tolerant types. Plant in spring or fall in moist, compost-enriched soil, 18 to 30 inches apart. Avoid soggy spots and excess mulch (1 to 2 inches is plenty).

Growing Tips
Water weekly during the first season, then water is needed only in hot, dry spells. Scatter a balanced, granular, organic or gradual-release fertilizer over the bed early each spring. Division isn't necessary, but if you want to expand your number of plants, dig and divide fist-sized pieces in early spring.

Regional Advice and Care
Although May and June are the two big months for hardy geranium blooms in Pennsylvania, many new types bloom continuously for much of the season. To rejuvenate a tired, scraggly-looking plant or to encourage repeat bloom, shear back after the first flush of flowering by about one-half. Wait until end of winter to do your end-of-season cleanup. Either rake out dead foliage or clip it back to 2 to 3 inches. Never cut these plants to the ground.

Companion Planting and Design
Hardy geranium adds a long-blooming choice to any sunny or part-shade perennial garden. It also masses well on banks or in large gardens. And it's well behaved enough for use in east, south, or west house-foundation beds. Shrub roses and ornamental grasses are good low-care partners.

Try These
The long-blooming, blue-violet 'Gerwat' (better known as 'Rozanne') brought fame and glory to this previously underused species when it was named as a Perennial Plant of the Year. 'Jolly Bee' is almost identical. 'Johnson's Blue' (18 inches, blue-violet) and *Geranium* × *oxonianum* 'Wargrave Pink' (18 inches, pink) are other exceptionally long-bloomers. I like pinkish white *Geranium cantabrigiense* 'Biokovo' for its compact size (12 inches) and ability to deal with dry shade and root competition.

Hellebore

Helleborus species and hybrids

Botanical Pronunciation
hell-eh-BORE-us

Other Name Lenten rose

Bloom Period and Seasonal Color
February through May; white, rose,
green, lavender

Mature Height × Spread
12 to 24 inches × 18 to 24 inches

Here's a perennial catching on big-time with the public, in part because of the many new introductions from breeders. Hellebores are among the earliest blooming perennials, typically starting to flower in late winter along with the earliest spring bulbs. The flowers look like nodding lampshades to me. Most types hold their leathery green leaves all winter, adding life to a snowless December and January garden. Lenten rose hybrids (*Helleborus × hybridus*) are easiest to grow (lots of new ones to pick from too), while the white-blooming Christmas rose (*Helleborus niger*) is becoming a popular potted holiday plant. All hellebores are poisonous though, so keep them away from nibble-prone pets and children. The sap also causes a skin irritation in some people. Wear gloves when handling as a precaution.

When, Where, and How to Plant
Hellebores do best in shade or a site that gets morning sun and afternoon shade. Plant in spring or early fall, 18 to 24 inches apart, in moist, compost-enriched, well-drained soil. Avoid poorly drained locations. Once its roots are established, Lenten rose varieties perform well in the dry shade and root competition under trees.

Growing Tips
Water weekly the first season to keep the young roots damp, then water is needed only in hot, dry spells. Scatter a balanced, granular, organic or gradual-release fertilizer over the bed in early spring and early fall. Snip off flower stalks after flowers finish blooming, especially if you don't want plants to seed themselves (some types do). Division typically isn't needed but can be done in spring after flowering or in early fall.

Regional Advice and Care
Hellebores hold their leaves in Pennsylvania winters, although they may look a bit tattered by the end. Snip off badly browned leaves but let green ones alone until flowering finishes and new leaves are emerging from the base. Then cut off all of last year's leaves to make way for the fresh new foliage. Since hellebores are poisonous, animals avoid them.

Companion Planting and Design
Hellebores make an excellent, early-flowering, weed-choking groundcover under trees. They're also at home in any shade garden, lining a woodland path or grouped with other shade perennials, such as liriope, sedges, sweet woodruff, hosta, crested iris, astilbe, or Japanese forestgrass. Interplant with early spring bulbs, such as snowdrop, crocus, *Iris reticulata*, Siberian squill, or glory-of-the-snow for a season-beginning show.

Try These
My favorite is 'Pink Frost', a rosy pink hybrid with outward-facing flowers that's one of the excellent Gold Collection® series. But you won't go too wrong with just about any variety. Particularly check out the Brandywine® series from Pennsylvania's own David Culp as well as 'Sunshine Selections' and the Lady, Winter Jewels, and Winter Thrillers series. Hellebores earned Perennial Plant of the Year honors.

Hosta

Hosta species and hybrids

Botanical Pronunciation
HOSS-tah

Bloom Period and Seasonal Color
June through September; white, lavender flowers; grown for foliage

Mature Height × Spread
6 inches to 3 feet × 2 to 3 feet

Who *doesn't* have a hosta in the yard? This leafy plant is king of the Pennsylvania shade, showing up under trees and along shady house foundations everywhere. Although hostas send up summertime flower stalks that hold lily-like and sometimes fragrant white or lavender blooms, the foliage is the main attraction. Hosta leaves come in all sorts of variations from mouse-ear miniatures to fat, wide, 3-footers that look like something from the rain forest. Leaves also come in a variety of colors, including green, gold, lime, and blue-green, not to mention an endless selection of blends and variegations (white-edged green, blue-and-gold striped, lime with gold edges, and on and on). Hostas are hard to kill and easy to divide, making them a leading pass-along plant.

When, Where, and How to Plant
Hosta prefers morning sun and afternoon shade but it's content in your heaviest-shade spot. Some thicker-leaf types grow in full sun if soil is kept damp, but way too many hostas fry every summer next to suburban driveways. Plant hostas in spring or early fall, 24 to 36 inches apart, in moist, compost-enriched soil. Though that's the ideal, they grow well in the dry shade and root competition under trees. Cover the ground with 2 inches of mulch after planting.

Growing Tips
Water weekly throughout the first season to help the roots establish, then water is needed only in hot, dry spells (or at the first sign of wilting leaves). Scatter a balanced, granular, organic or gradual-release fertilizer over the bed in early spring. Hostas divide well in early spring or early fall, but dividing isn't necessary unless you want to expand a planting or give some away. Cut off flower stalks after flowers brown, or when they first emerge if you decide the flowers detract from the foliage.

Regional Advice and Care
Deer *love* hosta leaves, so use fencing, repellents, or (supposed) deer-resistant varieties if deer lurk nearby. Slugs often chew holes in leaves. Sprinkle slugs with salt at night or use slug traps or slug pellets. Voles also occasionally eat hosta roots. Care-wise, cut browned foliage to the ground after frost in fall or wait until winter's end when the decaying leaves can be raked off. Hosta Virus X (HVX) is a rare but fatal disease.

Companion Planting and Design
Interplant spring bulbs (daffodils or hyacinths especially) for early color while hosta is still thinking about emerging. Use short hostas for edging north and east house foundations. The #1 use is clumps or masses in the shade of trees, where hosta's wide leaves and mounded habit pair well with grassy liriope, sedge, or Japanese forest grass and heart-shaped barrenwort.

Try These
With nearly 4,000 varieties to pick from, you'll have no trouble finding ones you like. My favorites are 'June' and 'Sagae' (blue-green), 'Krossa Regal' and 'Elegans' (blue), 'Patriot' (white-edged), and 'Frances Williams' (gold-edged blue).

Iris

Iris species and hybrids

Botanical Pronunciation
EYE-riss

Other Name Flag

Bloom Period and Seasonal Color
March through October; purple, blue, lavender, yellow, white, burgundy, assorted pastels

Mature Height × Spread
6 inches to 3 feet × 18 to 24 inches

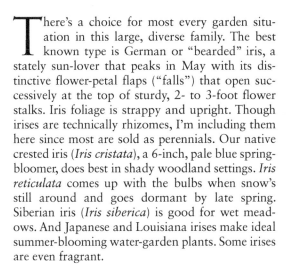

There's a choice for most every garden situation in this large, diverse family. The best known type is German or "bearded" iris, a stately sun-lover that peaks in May with its distinctive flower-petal flaps ("falls") that open successively at the top of sturdy, 2- to 3-foot flower stalks. Iris foliage is strappy and upright. Though irises are technically rhizomes, I'm including them here since most are sold as perennials. Our native crested iris (*Iris cristata*), a 6-inch, pale blue spring-bloomer, does best in shady woodland settings. *Iris reticulata* comes up with the bulbs when snow's still around and goes dormant by late spring. Siberian iris (*Iris siberica*) is good for wet meadows. And Japanese and Louisiana irises make ideal summer-blooming water-garden plants. Some irises are even fragrant.

When, Where, and How to Plant
Dormant rhizomes can be planted in fall or early spring. Don't plant them too deeply; just the tops should be visible at the soil line. Potted plants can be planted spring through fall. Just keep their roots damp. Know what type you're planting since soil needs vary. Common bearded types do best in full sun and well-drained, compost-enriched soil, especially in raised beds. They *hate* soggy soil. Plant irises 12 to 24 inches apart, depending on type. Mulch lightly; one inch is enough.

Growing Tips
Keep the soil damp but never soggy. Bearded iris is best fertilized with a balanced, granular, organic or gradual-release fertilizer in early spring and again right after bloom. Divide rhizomes every three or four years by digging clumps and pulling apart the "fans." For bearded iris, the best month for division is July.

Regional Advice and Care
Clip off flower stalks after blooming finishes. Many iris varieties hold their leaves through part of winter, so early-spring cleanup is best. Cut browned foliage to just above the soil surface. The biggest threat to bearded iris is rotting in wet clay soil. A second threat is the iris borer, a bug that tunnels down the leaves (watch for whitish streaks in summer) and into the rhizomes, where larvae can eat and kill the plants. Try cutting infested foliage before the borers reach the rhizome, or use an insecticide labeled for borer control. Iris is mildly poisonous (causing nausea) if eaten.

Companion Planting and Design
Iris is ideal in any old-fashioned perennial garden and works especially well around Victorian-style homes. Bearded types make good backdrop plants in border beds. Siberian, Japanese, and Louisiana types are good choices in wet spots. Native crested iris is a good groundcover in damp shade locations.

Try These
I'm partial to the deep, dark, velvety bearded iris, such as the nearly black 'Superstition' and 'Satin Satan'. I also like the white-speckled purple variety 'Batik', the blue-blooming 'Blue Suede Shoes', and the white rebloomer 'Immortality'.

Joe-Pye Weed

Eupatorium maculatum

Botanical Pronunciation
yew-pah-TORE-ee-um mack-yew-LAY-tum

Bloom Period and Seasonal Color
July through September; rosy purple

Mature Height × Spread
2 to 8 feet × 2 to 3 feet

This Pennsylvania native perennial needs a better name. The "weed" part means Joe-Pye can be found in its species form growing in roadside ditches and wet meadows, but it *doesn't* mean it's ugly and invasive. The "Joe-Pye" part comes from the name of a North Carolina Native American who used this plant for medicinal purposes. Maybe we should call it "Joe-Pye flower." While the species Joe-Pye weed can rocket up to 8 feet tall, garden-center varieties have been developed with heavier flowering and heights as low as 2 to 3 feet, although most of the so-called "dwarf" Joe-Pyes are still 4- to 5-foot-tall plants. The puffy, rosy purple, bee-attracting flower clusters grow at the top of the tall stems from July into early fall.

When, Where, and How to Plant
Plant Joe-Pye weed in spring, 24 to 30 inches apart, in moist, compost-enriched soil. Summer planting works fine if you keep young plants well watered. In fact, this is a plant that prefers moist soil all of the time. It'll survive dry spells and drought, but it's likely to brown and even die back. Full sun is best; afternoon shade is okay. Cover the soil after planting with 1 to 2 inches of mulch.

Growing Tips
Water once or twice a week during the first season, then weekly whenever it's hot and dry to prevent summer dieback. Scatter a balanced, granular, organic or gradual-release fertilizer over the bed in early spring. Stake plants to prevent summer flopping or cut plants by one-third to one-half in late spring to encourage more compact growth. Divide every three to five years in early spring. Replant fist-sized pieces at their same depth, then water.

Regional Advice and Care
Steady moisture but not sogginess is the key to keeping Joe-Pye weed looking good. It's not a fan of heat and drought. Plants occasionally develop powdery mildew on the leaves (a whitish cast). Divide and spread out plantings if that happens. Stem tips can be cut back after the flowers brown, then the whole plant can be cut to the ground when frost kills it in fall. Or plants can be cut back at winter's end. You'll have no worries from deer, rabbits, or rodents.

Companion Planting and Design
Joe-Pye weed is a good backdrop perennial in a border garden and works well when planted in a mass in any sunny, open area with damp soil. Include it in a pollinator garden or in any native-plant garden.

Try These
'Gateway' was an early dwarf form that's still around, but it grows 5 to 6 feet tall. A variety of the related species *Eupatorium dubium* called 'Little Joe' is a notch down at 4 feet and also is more tolerant of shade and blooms slightly earlier. Smaller still is 'Baby Joe' at about 3 feet tall.

Lavender

Lavandula species

Botanical Pronunciation
lah-VAN-dew-lah

Bloom Period and Seasonal Color
June through September; purple, blue, white, pink

Mature Height × Spread
12 to 30 inches × 18 to 24 inches

Zones Some types reliably hardy only to Zone 6

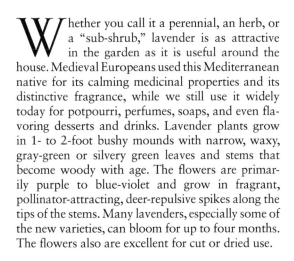

Whether you call it a perennial, an herb, or a "sub-shrub," lavender is as attractive in the garden as it is useful around the house. Medieval Europeans used this Mediterranean native for its calming medicinal properties and its distinctive fragrance, while we still use it widely today for potpourri, perfumes, soaps, and even flavoring desserts and drinks. Lavender plants grow in 1- to 2-foot bushy mounds with narrow, waxy, gray-green or silvery green leaves and stems that become woody with age. The flowers are primarily purple to blue-violet and grow in fragrant, pollinator-attracting, deer-repulsive spikes along the tips of the stems. Many lavenders, especially some of the new varieties, can bloom for up to four months. The flowers also are excellent for cut or dried use.

When, Where, and How to Plant
The most important consideration is *excellent drainage*. Lavender is fine in dry spots with all the sun you can give it, but it'll rot in wet clay, especially in winter. If you don't have a naturally hot, sunny, rocky, gravelly, or sandy spot, plant lavender in raised beds amended with gravel or lots of coarse sand (25 percent of total soil volume). Plant spring through early fall, 15 to 18 inches apart, in neutral to slightly alkaline soil. An inch of gravel or stone mulch (instead of ground wood) is best.

Growing Tips
Water weekly the first season, then water only in very hot, dry spells. Fertilizer usually isn't needed. Shear plants by one-third to one-half after the first flush of flowers browns out in summer. If plants are floppy at season's end, wait until early spring to shear back as low as to 8 to 10 inches. Lavender doesn't divide well, but new plants start easily from tip cuttings that are rooted in spring or early fall.

Regional Advice and Care
English lavender (*Lavandula angustifolia*) is usually cold-hardy throughout Pennsylvania (especially with good drainage and a wall-sheltered site in colder Zone 5 areas). Spike lavender types (*Lavandula latifolia*) are usually rated for Zones 6 and 7. You'll also see crosses of those two called "lavandins" (*Lavandula × intermedia*), which are usually winter-hardy throughout Pennsylvania. All want great drainage.

Companion Planting and Design
There are lots of potential lavender design uses around the yard in herb gardens, lining driveways and walks (it's salt-tolerant), mixed with other perennials and shrubs in a sunny border garden, in a cut-flower garden, in rock gardens, and especially clustered on a sunny, rocky slope. Lavender looks particularly good paired with roses or purple coneflowers. (Did I mention that lavender demands great drainage?)

Try These
'Hidcote' (18 inches) and 'Munstead' (14 inches) are two oldie-but-goodie English types. I like 'Blue Cushion' (16 inches) and 'Lady' (12 inches) too. For lavandin types, give me 'Grosso' (24 to 28 inches), 'Provence' (20 to 24 inches), or 'Dilly Dilly' (12 to 14 inches).

Mum

Dendranthema × *grandiflorum*

Botanical Pronunciation
den-DRAN-theh-mah gran-dih-FLORE-um

Other Name Chrysanthemum

Bloom Period and Seasonal Color
August through October; red, gold, yellow, orange, pink, white, lavender

Mature Height × Spread
1 to 3 feet × 18 to 30 inches

Mum is the word when it comes to fall flowers. This Oriental native has been hybridized for centuries, resulting in nearly every flower color except blue and flower shapes ranging from daisies to cushions to buttons to petals that are spoon-shaped at the tips. By far the most used mum is the so-called "hardy mum" or "garden mum," which comes in dense balls of bright color at stores everywhere in early fall. Many Pennsylvanians grow them in pots out front along with pumpkins, straw bales, and dried corn stalks, then toss them by Thanksgiving. Others plant them in the ground and get them to come back year after year with varying degrees of success. Either way, the mum is undisputed queen of our fall landscape.

When, Where, and How to Plant
Mums do best in full sun and well-drained locations. Plant them in spring, summer, or early fall, 18 to 24 inches apart in loose, compost-enriched soil. One to 2 inches of mulch is plenty.

Growing Tips
Water once or twice a week during the first season, then water weekly in hot, dry spells. Feed a balanced, granular, organic or gradual-release fertilizer in early spring and early fall. Divide and replant fist-sized pieces every three years to prevent die-outs in the center and to encourage mums' best growth and flowering.

Regional Advice and Care
Getting mums to come back—and preventing them from flopping—are the two big issues. Start with a winter-hardy type, not a "florist's mum" sold as a gift plant which is usually hardy only to Zone 7. For best winter survival, plant in spring or early September and *don't* clip off the frost-killed foliage until early spring. Growers typically treat mums with growth regulators to encourage compact growth for retail sales. Don't be surprised if yours grow bigger and floppier in the garden. For compactness, shear mums by one-third in mid- to late May and again in late June to early July.

Companion Planting and Design
Locate mums in sunny border or foundation beds for fall interest. Try planting a band of them around tall evergreens, such as arborvitae, holly, and spruce. Or pair them with ornamental grasses or with goldenrod, aster, and/or sedum for a fall-peaking display. A good shrub partner is winterberry holly with its fall red berries. And, of course, display a few in fall pots.

Try These
New names bump out old ones every fall, if you even find variety names listed. I've had good luck with the bloom and survivability of the Igloo® series. But pick the colors and flower types you like, stick with the care tips above, and you'll do fine with most mums. Try *Dendranthema rubellum* 'Clara Curtis' for her pink, late summer, daisylike flowers. And try a few Korean mums (*Dendranthema zawadsii*) for something different.

Phlox

Phlox paniculata

Botanical Pronunciation
FLOCKS pah-nick-yew-LAY-tah

Other Name Garden phlox

Bloom Period and Seasonal Color
July through September; pink, white, lavender, salmon, rosy-red

Mature Height × Spread
2 to 4 feet × 24 to 30 inches

This perennial phlox is in the same genus as moss pinks and similar creeping, ground-cover phlox, but you'd never know it. Garden phlox, as it's often called, is an upright perennial with mid-sized leaves and clusters of open-petaled, nickel-sized flowers at the top of the flower stalks. Plants can go as high as 4 feet, although most varieties have been bred for more compact 2- to 3-foot heights and bigger flowers. Garden phlox is a U.S. native that usually blooms for six to eight weeks in mid- to late summer, attracting ample butterflies and sometimes adding mild fragrance to the garden. It makes a nice cut flower and comes in an expanding array of colors (mostly pastels), including a few types with variegated green-and-white leaves.

When, Where, and How to Plant
Plant phlox in spring or fall, 18 to 24 inches apart in moist, compost-enriched soil. Summer planting is fine if you keep young plants well watered. Full sun is best, but light shade is okay and even preferable for the variegated-leaf types. Cover the soil with 1 to 2 inches of mulch after planting.

Growing Tips
Water weekly during the first season, then weekly in hot, dry weather. Water the ground, never over the plants. In early spring and early fall scatter a balanced, granular, organic or gradual-release fertilizer over the bed. Stake taller varieties if you find them prone to flopping. Divide clumps into fist-sized pieces every three to five years in early spring. Replant at their same depth, then water.

Regional Advice and Care
Garden phlox has one big Achilles heel: powdery mildew. This common fungal disease causes a whitish cast on the leaves that progresses into total browning. The disease seldom kills phlox, but it can ruin late-season performance after the flowers peak. Fight it by avoiding overhead watering, by giving plants good air circulation (divide dense patches), and by removing diseased leaves. Better yet, use a mildew-resistant variety (see "Try These"). Snip off flower clusters after they brown, but allow green foliage to stand until frost kills it. Then cut everything to the ground. This also can be done at winter's end. Dead shoots can be removed in summer if mildew kills them.

Companion Planting and Design
Phlox is an excellent back-of-row choice in a sunny border garden or butterfly garden. It pairs well with shorter or rounded purple or blue bloomers, such as lavender, salvia, catmint, balloon flower, and dwarf butterfly bush.

Try These
Almost every new variety claims to be mildew-resistant, but some deliver better than others. I like the lavender-blooming 'Jeana' and 'Katherine' varieties, the lavender-magenta 'Robert Poore', the hot pink 'Shortwood', and its pale pink cousin 'Blushing Shortwood'. The Flame® series is the shortest yet, checking in at about 1 foot.

Purple Coneflower

Echinacea purpurea

Botanical Pronunciation
ek-ih-NAY-see-ah pur-PUR-ee-ah

Bloom Period and Seasonal Color
June through September; mauve, pink-purple, white, red, gold, orange

Mature Height × Spread
18 to 36 inches × 24 to 30 inches

Purple coneflower is a mildly fragrant U.S. prairie native that has seen widespread use in Pennsylvania gardens, and for good reason. It takes heat, survives drought, tolerates lousy soil, is one of our best plants for attracting pollinators, *and* makes a good cut flower. What's fueled a recent coneflower craze is the arrival of bright bloomers in red, gold, and even orange—a whole new color range from the original mauve-pink-purple shades. Purple coneflower produces drooping petals that grow out in ray-like fashion from a central pincushion disc (the "cone"). Many newer varieties have petals that grow straight out as opposed to drooping. The leaves are dark green and grow in a foot-tall cluster from which the flower stalks emerge, much like black-eyed Susan.

When, Where, and How to Plant
Summer planting will work if you keep young plants well watered. But purple coneflower is usually planted in spring or fall, 18 to 24 inches apart in moist, compost-enriched soil. Full sun is best. After planting, cover the soil with 1 to 2 inches of mulch. Some varieties can be started by planting seed directly into the garden in spring.

Growing Tips
Water weekly during the first season, then weekly in hot, dry weather. Early spring is the time to feed a balanced, granular, organic or gradual-release fertilizer. Taller varieties benefit from staking. Divide clumps into fist-sized pieces every three to five years in early spring or early fall. Replant at the same depth, then water.

Regional Advice and Care
Purple coneflowers tolerate occasional wet soil, but prolonged soggy soil, especially in winter, will kill them. Some of the new varieties tire after a few years so don't be surprised if they fail to report for duty one spring. The straight species reseeds itself to keep going; sterile hybrids don't. Groundhogs like purple coneflowers, so use repellents (or traps) if any lurk. Cut flower stalks to the base after flowers fade, then cut browned-out foliage to the ground at winter's end.

Companion Planting and Design
Purple coneflower is a must in a sunny butterfly garden, and it plays well with most any perennial or shrub in a mixed border garden especially now that color choices run from cool pastels to hot reds and yellows (not to mention neutral whites). Purple coneflowers also look at home in meadow gardens as well as massed on sunny banks.

Try These
My favorites are the new 'PowWow Wild Berry' (vibrant raspberry) and 'PowWow White' (creamy white). But you'll find lots of winners, including 18-inch Pixie Meadowbrite™; the dark-stemmed 'Fatal Attraction'; the double-flowered 'Pink Double Delight'; bright bloomers such as 'Tomato Soup', 'Mac 'n Cheese', and 'Tiki Torch'; and pretty much the whole Big Sky and Sombrero™ series. Also try the native pale coneflower (*Echinacea pallida*) and the native Tennessee coneflower (*Echinacea tennesseensis*).

Russian Sage

Perovskia atriplicifolia

Botanical Pronunciation
per-OV-skee-ah at-rih-pliss-ih-FOE-lee-ah

Bloom Period and Seasonal Color
July through October; bluish purple, violet

Mature Height × Spread
2 to 4 feet × 2 to 3 feet

    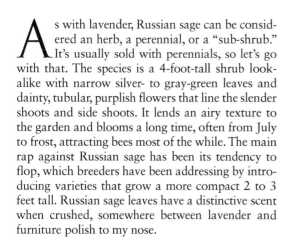

As with lavender, Russian sage can be considered an herb, a perennial, or a "sub-shrub." It's usually sold with perennials, so let's go with that. The species is a 4-foot-tall shrub look-alike with narrow silver- to gray-green leaves and dainty, tubular, purplish flowers that line the slender shoots and side shoots. It lends an airy texture to the garden and blooms a long time, often from July to frost, attracting bees most of the while. The main rap against Russian sage has been its tendency to flop, which breeders have been addressing by introducing varieties that grow a more compact 2 to 3 feet tall. Russian sage leaves have a distinctive scent when crushed, somewhere between lavender and furniture polish to my nose.

When, Where, and How to Plant
Also like lavender, Russian sage demands excellent drainage. Plant it in hot, sunny, gravelly/sandy/rocky spots. Although Russian sage does well in dry soil, it prefers slightly damp conditions . . . just not wet or soggy ones. Create raised beds by adding compost and gravel or coarse sand if drainage is doubtful. Plant spring through early fall, 2 to 3 feet apart. An inch of gravel or stone mulch suits better than wood mulch.

Growing Tips
Water weekly the first season, then water is useful only in very hot, dry spells. Fertilizer usually isn't needed. Division isn't necessary either, but plants can be divided in early spring if they are getting too big. Young, rooted "offsets" that emerge from around the base of plants can be severed from the "mother" plant and transplanted in early spring to expand a planting.

Regional Advice and Care
Russian sage is virtually bulletproof in Pennsylvania gardens, so long as drainage is good. Even deer have to be near starvation to eat this one. The main issue is "flop control," which can be accomplished by staking, cutting back growth by one-third to one-half in late spring, or, best of all, picking a compact variety in the first place. At the end of winter, cut plants back to 6 inches, not the whole way to the ground.

Companion Planting and Design
Russian sage adds as much in textural interest to a garden as it does for its long bloom. It's especially good in sunny mixed border gardens, where it partners well with shrub roses and purple coneflowers. It's useful in a pollinator garden (if you're not a native-plant purist), and it does well in any sunny, open area, including banks and in rock gardens.

Try These
If you're looking to stay compact, check out the new 2-foot 'Lisslit' ('Lacey Blue'). 'Little Spire' is a long-blooming 3-footer that still flops somewhat, and 'Peek-A-Blue' is a new 28-incher. If you like that happy-go-lucky habit, the straight species is fine and was good enough to earn Perennial Plant of the Year honors.

Salvia

Salvia species and hybrids

Botanical Pronunciation
SAL-vee-ah

Other Name Sage

Bloom Period and Seasonal Color
May through June; purple, blue-violet, white, pink, rose

Mature Height × Spread
12 to 24 inches × 18 to 24 inches

Salvia is another large family of plants (700 species!) with a lot of different looks. A majority of them aren't winter-hardy in Pennsylvania, some are hardy only in the warmer regions of the state, and a few are reliable perennials statewide. The two types commonly sold as perennials are violet sage (*Salvia nemerosa*) and meadow sage (*Salvia pratensis*), plus assorted crosses of those with others. The common denominator is square stems, opposite leaves, and small, tubular flowers that line slender, spiky flower stems. The flowers of the hardy types are mostly purple and highly attractive to hummingbirds. The leaves of most are green to gray-green, although a few are silvery; some are fuzzy. A few types are southwestern U.S. natives; most are from Mexico and Europe.

When, Where, and How to Plant
Especially in the state's cooler regions, plant salvia in spring. Early fall planting also is okay in warmer regions. Full sun and loose, compost-enriched soil is best. Hot and dry is better than wet; salvia is prone to rotting in poorly drained sites. Space 18 to 24 inches apart. After planting, cover the soil with 1 inch of wood or gravel mulch.

Growing Tips
Water weekly during the first season, then water is needed only in very hot, dry spells. Scatter a balanced, granular, organic or gradual-release fertilizer over the bed in early spring. Divide clumps into fist-size pieces every three to five years in early spring. Replant at the same depth, then water.

Regional Advice and Care
Zone 7 parts of Pennsylvania can grow many more "half-hardy" salvia types than Zones 5 and 6. Still, mild winters and good siting (wind protection, no wet clay, planting along west- and south-facing walls) are good salvia strategies statewide. Clip off flower stalks after the flowers turn brown and also any foliage that's looking tired or brown by early summer. Fresh foliage regrows, and some salvias rebloom in fall. Cut frost-killed foliage to the ground at winter's end.

Companion Planting and Design
Compact types add bands of color along a sunny house-foundation bed. Salvia also mixes well in sunny border gardens, rock gardens, pollinator gardens, and on sunny banks. Good shrub partners are pink spirea, shrub roses, and pink abelia. Good perennial partners are purple coneflower, pink dianthus, and ornamental grasses.

Try These
'May Night', an 18-inch purple bloomer and a Perennial Plant of the Year, is the most popular. 'Lubeca' and 'Caradonna' are similar good choices, and 'Marcus' is my favorite for its 12-inch size. *Salvia guaranitica* 'Black and Blue' (Zone 7) is the best hummingbird plant I've ever grown. Silver sage (*Salvia argentea*, Zone 7) has big, showy, silvery leaves. Purple, tricolor, and 'Berggarten' sages are all edible and good-looking (*Salvia officinalis*, Zones 5 to 7). And Mexican bush sage (*Salvia leucantha*, Zone 7) has eye-popping purple flower spikes in fall.

Sedum

Sedum spectabile

Botanical Pronunciation
SEE-dum speck-TAB-ih-lee

Other Name Showy stonecrop

Bloom Period and Seasonal Color
August through October; pink, rosy red, lavender-pink

Mature Height × Spread
15 to 36 inches × 18 to 30 inches

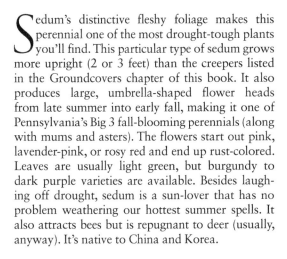

Sedum's distinctive fleshy foliage makes this perennial one of the most drought-tough plants you'll find. This particular type of sedum grows more upright (2 or 3 feet) than the creepers listed in the Groundcovers chapter of this book. It also produces large, umbrella-shaped flower heads from late summer into early fall, making it one of Pennsylvania's Big 3 fall-blooming perennials (along with mums and asters). The flowers start out pink, lavender-pink, or rosy red and end up rust-colored. Leaves are usually light green, but burgundy to dark purple varieties are available. Besides laughing off drought, sedum is a sun-lover that has no problem weathering our hottest summer spells. It also attracts bees but is repugnant to deer (usually, anyway). It's native to China and Korea.

When, Where, and How to Plant
Sedum is a good option for your hottest, driest territory. Although it'll tolerate brutal conditions (including fairly poor and even salty soil along paving), sedum prefers loose, damp, compost-enriched beds. Slightly raised beds are ideal. Most important is to give sedum lots of sun and avoid wet or soggy soil that'll rot its roots. Plant in spring, summer, or early fall, 18 to 24 inches apart. One to 2 inches of wood or gravel mulch is plenty.

Growing Tips
Water weekly the first season to establish the roots, then you'll probably never need to water sedum again. Scatter a balanced, granular, organic or gradual-release fertilizer over the bed in early spring.

Divide every three years in early spring. Replant the divisions at the same depth, and water.

Regional Advice and Care
The main complaint about upright, fall-blooming sedum is that the flower heads are so heavy that they cause plants to splay apart while they're blooming. One way to prevent that is to shear plants in half in late May or early June, à la mums. The plants will look butchered, but within a few weeks, they'll push new growth and bloom sturdier and bushier. Also, don't overfertilize; plant in full sun, and choose a compact variety to start with. Cut browned-out foliage to the ground in fall or at winter's end.

Companion Planting and Design
Sedum planted at the feet of ornamental grasses makes a fine fall display. Also, spot a few in sunny border gardens, in west- or south-facing foundation beds, in pollinator gardens, and in any hot, open area for fall interest. Goldenrod, mums, and asters make good perennial partners for a fall-peaking display.

Try These
'Autumn Joy' is the wildly popular variety that just about everybody sells. It's good, but 'Autumn Fire' is an improved version. I prefer a couple of more compact, 15-inch bloomers: 'Neon' and 'Brilliant'. 'Mr. Goodbud' is a 2-footer with a heavy bloom of rosy red flowers. 'Matrona' is a 3-footer with showy burgundy stems.

Shasta Daisy

Leucanthemum × superbum

Botanical Pronunciation
loo-KAN-the-mum soo-PER-bum

Bloom Period and Seasonal Color
June through July; white, yellow

Mature Height × Spread
12 to 42 inches × 18 to 24 inches

This cheery, upright perennial flower delivers that classic daisy look. A refugee of the chrysanthemum family, Shasta daisy sends up stiff flower stalks that open into 2- to 3-inch flowers of bright white petals surrounding central yellow-gold discs. A few types start out yellow and fade to creamy white. It blooms primarily in June and July. Compact varieties stay as low as a foot tall, while others top out at nearly 4 feet. The leaves are green and narrow with toothy edges. The Shasta daisy is a late nineteenth-century creation of the famous American breeder Luther Burbank, who named this European cross after California's Mt. Shasta. It makes one of the landscape's best cut flowers and is easily winter-hardy throughout Pennsylvania.

When, Where, and How to Plant
Plant Shasta daisy in spring or fall, 18 to 24 inches apart in moist, compost-enriched soil. Summer planting will work if you keep young plants well watered. Full sun is best, but Shasta daisy will grow in light shade, albeit with compromised flowering. One to 2 inches of mulch is plenty.

Growing Tips
Water once or twice a week during the first season, then weekly in hot, dry weather. Shasta daisy doesn't like wet soil, but it also will wilt in a dry spell. Plants usually survive droughts, but they may die back and go dormant in summer to achieve that. Scatter a balanced, granular, organic or gradual-release fertilizer over the bed in early spring. Divide every two or three years in early spring or early fall to maintain its vigor. Divisions can be replanted at the same depth they were growing; water after planting.

Regional Advice and Care
Shasta daisy tends to be a short-lived perennial in Pennsylvania. Give it good soil and regular water to aid first-year survivability. Cut back flower stalks after flowers finish blooming. If the foliage turns ratty in a hot summer, cut it back too. Then water the plant, and watch for fresh growth. Wait until end of winter to cut frost-killed foliage back to the ground. Rabbits and groundhogs sometimes eat Shasta daisy.

Companion Planting and Design
Shasta daisy is a must in a cut-flower garden. In border gardens or perennial gardens, pair it with salvia, daylily, and yarrow, which bloom at the same time. Or pair it with later bloomers that take over when the daisies are done, such as black-eyed Susan, coreopsis, and mums. Red or gold annuals, such as dwarf zinnias, celosia, lantana, and marigolds, also pair well.

Try These
'Becky' is the prized tall variety, topping 3 feet and winning a Perennial Plant of the Year award. 'Snowcap', 'Snow Lady', and 'Little Miss Muffet' are good 12- to 15-inch compact varieties. 'Goldfinch' is a new 2-footer that starts out yellow and fades to cream. 'Crazy Daisy' is an unusual 3-foot, double-petaled variety.

Spurge

Euphorbia species and hybrids

Botanical Pronunciation
yew-FOR-bee-ah

Bloom Period and Seasonal Color
May through June; yellow or chartreuse bracts

Mature Height × Spread
12 to 24 inches × 15 to 18 inches

The *Euphorbia* family has some wildly divergent members, from hot red poinsettias that grow into 15-foot-tall shrubs in their native tropics to the mounded, dainty white bloomers we grow as annuals under such names as Diamond Frost® and 'StarDust White Sparkle'. The versions worth trying as winter-hardy perennials are mainly *Euphorbia dulcis* (sorry, no nickname), the "cushion spurge" (*Euphorbia polychroma*), and a stable of hybrid varieties. They grow into 1- to 2-foot-tall mounds that offer two main attractions. One is the late spring, yellow to chartreuse "bracts" that look like flowers but are really small, colorful leaves. The actual flowers are yellow, budlike projections at the center of the bracts. The second attraction is showy, waxy leaves that turn maroon, burgundy, and/or purple as the season progresses.

When, Where, and How to Plant
Perennial spurges do best in locations with morning sun and afternoon shade, especially in the warmer regions of Pennsylvania. They'll handle full sun in cooler regions or if the soil is kept moist in hot, dry spells. Plant 15 to 18 inches apart in spring or fall, ideally in loose, damp, compost-enriched soil. Avoid soggy soil. Cover the soil with 1 to 2 inches of mulch after planting.

Growing Tips
Water weekly to establish the roots, then water is needed only in hot, dry spells. Scatter a balanced, granular, organic or gradual-release fertilizer over the bed in early spring. Plants can be sheared back by one-third to one-half for compactness after

blooming. Be aware that when cut, all euphorbias emit a milky sap that causes skin rash in some people. Wear gloves when handling. Perennial spurge doesn't divide well, but luckily division isn't necessary. Watch for offshoots or self-seeded "babies" that can be dug and transplanted in early spring instead.

Regional Advice and Care
Spurge tends to be a short-lived perennial. Help it survive winter by waiting until winter's end to cut back frost-killed foliage. At that time, cut back to live growth or the whole way back to the ground if cold has killed all top growth. Most types hold their leaves through part of winter, especially in warmer regions.

Companion Planting and Design
A subtle attraction of spurge is how raindrops bead and frost sticks to the waxy leaves. Try a few around patios or doors where that ephemeral bonus can be noticed. Plant a few near the front of eastern foundation beds or in the dappled sunlight of a cluster of small flowering trees. Daylily, black-eyed Susan, and dwarf Shasta daisy are good perennial partners.

Try These
My favorite is the foot-tall cushion spurge 'Bonfire', which has burgundy-tinged leaves and chartreuse spring bracts. 'Chameleon' (18 inches) is a variety of *Euphorbia dulcis* with purplish leaves and gold-orange bracts. 'Helena's Blush' is a 20-inch, Zones 6 to 7 *Euphorbia amygdaloides* hybrid with pinkish variegated summer leaves that turn purple/maroon in fall.

Tickseed

Coreopsis verticillata

Botanical Pronunciation
kor-ee-OP-siss ver-tiss-ih-LAY-tah

Other Name Threadleaf coreopsis

Bloom Period and Seasonal Color
Late May through July; gold, yellow, pink, rosy red

Mature Height × Spread
12 to 30 inches × 24 to 32 inches

You may find two or three species of tickseeds plus plenty of hybrids at the garden center. All are native to the United States. Try the "threadleaf" types; they're the ones with small, narrow, almost ferny leaves and flowers the size of buttons or dimes. This species is native to the eastern United States and also seems to be the longest-lived in Pennsylvania gardens. (Many of the big flower and lance-leaf types, *Coreopsis grandiflora* and *Coreopsis lanceolata*, tend to disappear after three or four years.) Threadleaf tickseed adds contrasting fine texture to the garden even when the long-lasting, early summer flowers finish. Some types rebloom into fall. Tickseed got its name because the shape, size, and color of its seed apparently reminded someone of a tick.

When, Where, and How to Plant
Tickseed is best planted in early to mid-spring, 24 to 30 inches apart in full sun and well-drained, compost-enriched soil. Wet soil in winter is a good way to shorten its life span. Raised-bed planting is a good idea. One inch of mulch added after planting is enough.

Growing Tips
Water weekly the first season to keep the young roots damp, then watering is needed only in hot, dry spells. Feed with a balanced, granular, organic or gradual-release fertilizer scattered over the bed in early spring and early fall. Trim off browned flowers after bloom in summer to neaten the plant and possibly encourage a repeat bloom. Divide every two to three years in early spring.

Regional Advice and Care
Some species and varieties of tickseed die out after several years. Minimize that by dividing every two to three years and avoiding compacted or wet soil. Also try trimming plants by one-third to one-half after the flowers fade in summer, then let frost-killed foliage in place as winter insulation. Cut it to the ground in early spring. Powdery mildew is a serious leaf-disease threat, especially in humid summers. Trim off diseased foliage and discard it, then divide and space out your clumps in early spring to improve airflow.

Companion Planting and Design
Tickseed pairs well with other brightly colored perennials (daylily, salvia, black-eyed Susan, Shasta daisy, and mums for example) toward the front of sunny border or flower gardens. Compact tickseeds are good choices for edging the front of west- and south-facing foundation beds. And bands of tickseed make colorful "skirts" at the base of green or gold-green evergreens.

Try These
The whole Big Bang™ series is good, but especially long-blooming is the 18-inch, rosy red 'Mercury Rising'. 'Zagreb' is my favorite of the classic gold-flowering threadleaf types (14 to 16 inches), and 'Golden Gain' is second (18 to 20 inches). 'Full Moon' (part of Big Bang™) and the popular 'Moonbeam' are good soft yellow bloomers. 'Show Stopper' is a long-blooming pink variety.

Turtlehead

Chelone species

Botanical Pronunciation
keh-LOE-nee

Bloom Period and Seasonal Color
August through September; white, pink

Mature Height × Spread
24 to 36 inches × 24 to 32 inches

Turtlehead gets its name from the shape of its hooded flowers that open sequentially from late summer into early fall at the tips of spiky flower stalks. Some say the flowers look more like big snapdragons. The leaves are green and lance-shaped. You might run across two different species. One is white turtlehead (*Chelone glabra*) with pink-tinged white flowers, and the other is pink turtlehead (*Chelone lyonii*), which has deeper rosy pink flowers. Both are natives to the eastern United States and are becoming more used in Pennsylvania gardens as natives have gained popularity. Turtlehead does best in damp spots, especially in our cooler Zones 5 and 6 regions. Keep it watered and plant in afternoon shade in the warmest spots of the state.

When, Where, and How to Plant
Turtlehead will grow in a range of light settings from full sun to fairly dense shade. In full sun, be ready to water to keep it from frying in summer drought. In shade, expect less flowering. Morning sun and afternoon shade is the ideal middle ground. Plant in spring, 24 inches apart in moist, compost-enriched, mildly acidic soil. Mulch the ground with 1 to 2 inches after planting.

Growing Tips
Water once or twice a week throughout the first season to help the roots establish, then water weekly whenever the weather is dry. Scatter a balanced, granular, organic or gradual-release fertilizer over the bed in early spring. Divide every four or five years in early spring or more often if you'd like to speed up the spread of a turtlehead patch.

Regional Advice and Care
Encourage compact growth (if desired) by pinching stalks or trimming back entire plants by one-third in May. The straight species usually self-sows seeds, so let browned-out flower stalks stand over winter if you want seedlings; cut off the stalks as soon as they brown if you don't. Sprouted seedlings can be transplanted in early spring. Cut frost-killed foliage to the ground at the end of winter. You'll likely run into no bug, disease, or animal troubles. White turtlehead is a favorite food source of the Baltimore checkerspot butterfly.

Companion Planting and Design
Because it prefers damp soil, turtlehead is a good choice in bog gardens, along stream banks, and in rain gardens. It also does well in the shade under trees, so long as you're willing to give it water if or when tree roots out-compete it for sparse moisture in dry times. Turtlehead is especially useful in native-plant settings since it's one of the few late-season-blooming native perennials.

Try These
Not many varieties are available. An exception is the pink turtlehead 'Hot Lips', which grows about 30 inches tall and has bronzy foliage and rich, rosy pink flower spikes. You'll likely find only the straight species of white turtlehead.

SHRUBS

FOR PENNSYLVANIA

Shrubs are woody-stemmed plants, generally grown with multiple trunks and used as seasonally changing workhorses throughout the landscape. Botanically, shrubs are akin to compact trees. They don't die back to the ground each winter as do herbaceous perennials.

There's no official distinction, though, on exactly when a plant goes from being a "tall shrub" to a "small tree." To my thinking, a tree has a single trunk and grows at least 10 or 12 feet tall. A shrub or "bush" has multiple branches and grows (or is kept) under that.

This chapter highlights twenty-six of the best flowering shrubs for Pennsylvania yards—ones that bloom mostly in spring or summer, offer bonuses such as fruits or colorful foliage, and then drop their leaves in fall.

Shrub-sized evergreens, which hold their leaves or needles all year, are included in the "Evergreens and Conifers" chapter.

Shrubs in the Landscape

Flowering shrubs give some of the best bang for the landscape buck, offering long-lasting, versatile interest for not a lot of care.

In the mix are "two-week wonders" with one-dimensional interest. I'm thinking here of the popular forsythia, which blooms gloriously golden for two weeks in spring and then goes gangly the rest of the season, or the burning bush (*Euonymus alata*), which is bare or boringly green for 50 weeks of the year but eye-popping, fire-engine red the other two in October.

Hydrangea paniculata 'Grandiflora'

I lean toward shrub choices that do more than one thing in one season. These include plants such as the viburnum, which flowers fragrantly white in spring and then develops both colorful fruits and brilliant foliage in fall, or the oakleaf hydrangea, which produces large, cone-shaped, pinkish white flowers in early summer, turns burgundy in fall, and then reveals peeling, cinnamon-colored bark after its leaves drop.

Even a few of these industrious choices around the yard give gardeners the changing, season-by-season interest they crave.

The color of hydrangeas depends on the amount of aluminum in the soil. It's not unusual for a plant to have several colors in the year after planting, as the shrub adjusts to its new environment.

Shrubs are best planted in spring or early fall, although container-grown plants (the most common offering) can be planted throughout summer, so long as the soil is kept moist. Some are sold bare-root (best planted in early spring), and some of the bigger ones are sold as field-dug, burlap-wrapped plants (best planted in spring or early fall).

Which Ones Where?

Shrubs are a diverse lot. Some are low and spreading and make good edging or front-of-the-border plants. Some are compact and rounded, making good choices for house-foundation beds. Still others are upright or columnar or weeping, making them valuable at house corners, flanking doorways, or as specimen stars in a mixed garden.

While the habit, size, and color will drive most of your selection, site consideration should trump everything. Some shrubs need moist soil or else they'll brown around the leaf edges or croak. Others prefer it on the dry side, lest their roots rot in wet clay. Some demand full sun to flower and thrive. Others are native to shady woodlands; give them something similar or they'll fry by your asphalt driveway.

Growers have made huge strides in recent years in breeding and selecting new varieties. Gardeners now have a broader choice of shrubs than ever and certainly many more than even a generation ago.

Much of the focus lately has been on compact sizes to reduce pruning efforts. But new choices also offer improvements such as longer bloom time, new flower colors, improved foliage textures and colors, and improved resistance to bugs, diseases, and drought.

The renewed interest in native plants also has brought a stream of new "nativars"– hybrids or selections of native plants that offer enough of an improvement to earn their own distinct variety names. These offer new options for gardeners who want to "go native" without being too "wild-looking."

Match your site to the plant needs smartly, and your shrub collection will give you decades of multiseasonal interest while asking little in return.

Abelia

Abelia × grandiflora

Botanical Pronunciation
ah-BEEL-eh-ah gran-dih-FLOR-ah

Other Name Glossy abelia

Bloom Period and Seasonal Color
June to October; white, pink

Mature Height × Spread
2 to 5 feet × 4 to 6 feet

Zones 6 and 7

Abelia has been planted in American gardens for more than a century, but recent compact, long-blooming, and variegated-leaf varieties earn this trouble-free flowering shrub a renewed look. In warmer areas, abelia often holds its inch-long, glossy leaves all winter, making it a flowering broadleaf evergreen. It sometimes does the same in warmer Zone 6 winters (semi-evergreen), although abelia is iffy altogether without winter protection in Zone 5. Plants grow 3 to 4 feet tall and are slightly wider than tall. Choices now come with yellow, rosy-burgundy, or white-variegated leaf color. The trumpet-shaped white or pink flowers are some of the longest lasting of any shrub, going from early summer to early fall. The flowers are mildly fragrant and attractive to hummingbirds and butterflies.

When, Where, and How to Plant

Abelia flowers best in full sun but also performs well in part-day shade. Plant early spring through early fall in loose, damp, mildly acidic soil. Pay attention to regular watering if you plant in the heat of summer. Fray out the roots of container-grown plants before planting. Plant an inch above grade and mulch after planting with 2 to 3 inches of wood chips or bark. Keep mulch at least 2 to 3 inches away from the trunk.

Growing Tips

Water deeply once or twice a week for the first full growing season, then weekly during hot, dry spells. Abelia is drought-resistant and very heat-tolerant once established. Spread a balanced, granular,

organic or gradual-release fertilizer formulated for acid-preferring plants over the bed in early spring.

Regional Advice and Care

Abelia needs some cold protection (such as planting along a heated wall and mulch) to survive Zone 5 winters. Even in Zone 6, abelia sometimes suffers diebacks in cold winters. Don't give up too soon! Cut back dead top growth, and you may be surprised to find that the roots are alive and able to push out new growth. Abelia flowers on new spring growth, so the time to thin out or shear back is the end of winter. This plant is a good choice if you've got deer lurking.

Companion Planting and Design

Abelia is compact and long-blooming enough to deserve greater use as a house-foundation shrub. It'll work along the eastern, southern, and western exposures. It also makes an attractive, informal, low hedge and is tough enough to be massed as a shrubby groundcover on sunny to partly shaded banks. Ornamental grasses are good textural partners.

Try These

I really like the new Pinky Bells™, a 3-footer with unusually large pink flowers and reddish new growth. 'Rose Creek' is similar with white flowers. 'Kaleidoscope' has white flowers and the best foliage, changing through shades of yellow, creamy white, green, and rosy red. 'Panache' (Silver Anniversary) is a good white-variegated type, and 'Minipan' (Golden Anniversary) is good yellow-variegated variety.

Bayberry

Myrica pensylvanica

Botanical Pronunciation
mih-RIKE-kah pen-sil-VAN-ih-kah

Other Name Northern bayberry

Bloom Period and Seasonal Color
Non-showy yellow-green spring flowers; waxy gray fall/winter berries are the main attraction

Mature Height × Spread
5 to 10 feet × 6 to 12 feet

Zones 5 and 6

You might recognize bayberry as a popular candle scent. This is the native plant that early settlers used to boil down fruits to make those familiar scented, blue-gray candles. What few people realize is that bayberry and its prolific clusters of waxy, blue-gray berries in fall and winter make an attractive landscape shrub—in the right spot. Female plants produce the berries. "She" plants need a "he" nearby for pollination. Bayberry can get big if left unpruned—10 feet tall and wide, or more. It also colonizes via spreading underground shoots. That's not an ideal trait around the house, but it's fine for borders, native-plant gardens, and especially in windy, open, salty, and lousy-soil areas, similar to bayberry's eastern U.S. coastal home.

When, Where, and How to Plant

Plant container-grown or field-dug, burlap-wrapped plants in spring or early fall. Container-grown plants can be planted throughout summer if roots are kept consistently damp. Bayberry adapts to sandy, clayish, salty, and infertile soil. It needs acidic soil to prevent leaf yellowing, so check the pH and add sulfur, if needed. Plant in full sun to part shade, an inch above grade. Mulch after planting with 2 to 3 inches of wood chips or bark, keeping at least 2 to 3 inches away from the trunk.

Growing Tips

Water deeply once or twice a week for the first full growing season, then water is needed only in droughts. Feed a balanced, granular, organic or gradual-release fertilizer formulated for acid-preferring plants over the bed in early spring. Additional sulfur may be needed to maintain acidic soil.

Regional Advice and Care

Bayberry doesn't like intense heat. It does best in the cooler Zones 5 and 6 regions of Pennsylvania and tends to suffer in Zone 7 (look for cooler, part-shade spots there). No pruning is needed so long as size is okay. If you need to control its size, thin out and/or shear back at winter's end. Shovel out spreading shoots that are emerging beyond where you want anytime.

Companion Planting and Design

This is a hefty, colonizing shrub, so give it elbow room. A sunny border is ideal for a line of bayberries (remember, you need at least one male near one or more females to get fruits). The plant's salt-tolerance makes it a good hedge choice along a road (think road-salt runoff). And it's effective in a large, mixed-plant border or island garden. Blue-needled junipers (spreaders and uprights) are ideal partners since they like similar sites and coordinate color-wise.

Try These

You'll likely only find males and females of the straight species; varieties are virtually unknown. Growers occasionally plant a male and female in the same pot for those with space for only one plant. Note to breeders: We could use a compact version of bayberry.

Beautyberry

Callicarpa dichotoma

Botanical Pronunciation
kal-ih-KAR-pah die-KOT-oh-mah

Other Name Purple beautyberry

Bloom Period and Seasonal Color
Small pink flowers in July and August; main attraction is magenta, violet, white fall fruits

Mature Height × Spread
4 to 6 feet × 5 to 6 feet

Yeah, this is pretty much a one-dimensional plant. But that one dimension—the BB-sized fruit clusters of fall—is so *striking* that beautyberry is worth a look. This is a shrub that most people don't know but love when they see it fruiting. Many a surreptitiously snipped branch is taken to garden centers by inquiring gardeners wanting to know, "What *is* this plant?" The purple beautyberry (*Callicarpa dichotoma*) is a Chinese/Japanese native that produces ho-hum little pink flowers in late summer. By September, the branches are magically lined with those little jewels of glowing metallic violet or magenta. Separate males and females aren't needed; you'll get fruits even with one beautyberry. This bird-friendly plant was good enough to earn a Pennsylvania Horticultural Society Gold Medal Award.

When, Where, and How to Plant
Plant container-grown or field-dug, burlap-wrapped plants in spring or early fall. Container-grown plants can be planted throughout summer if roots are kept consistently damp. Beautyberry fruits best in full sun but performs well in part shade and even in fairly dry conditions. Avoid soggy spots. Plant an inch above grade, and mulch after planting with 2 to 3 inches of wood chips or bark. Don't let mulch touch the trunk.

Growing Tips
Water deeply weekly the first season to establish the roots, then water is needed only in droughts. Fertilizer usually isn't needed, but a scattering of balanced, granular, organic or gradual-release fertilizer over the bed in early spring may give the plant a boost. Although beautyberry is self-fruiting, you'll get better fruiting by planting more than one.

Regional Advice and Care
The Oriental *Callicarpa dichotoma* is winter-hardy throughout Pennsylvania, but there's a native American beautyberry (*Callicarpa americana*) that's slightly bigger and hardy in Zones 6 and 7 (with bigger but fewer violet fall fruits). For the best compact growth of all beautyberries, cut plants back mercilessly to 6 to 12 inches at the end of each winter. Pruning isn't needed if size and rangier growth habit aren't issues.

Companion Planting and Design
Beautyberry makes an attractive, loose, informal, fall-peaking hedge along a sunny or partly shaded border. Use one or more as specimens as a fall attraction in a four-season design or near a water garden. Masses of beautyberry make low-care, tall-shrub groundcovers on a bank. And beautyberries tolerate dry shade and root competition well enough to work under tall trees.

Try These
'Issai' and 'Early Amethyst' are more compact and better-fruiting versions of the species. 'Albifructus' produces white fruits. 'Duet' has beautiful white-variegated foliage but not a lot of white fruits. Japanese beautyberry 'Leucocarpa' (*Callicarpa japonica*) is a similar beautyberry species with white fruits. Bodinier beautyberry 'Profusion' (*Callicarpa bodinieri*) is a heavy violet fruiter hardy to Zones 6 to 7.

Blueberry

Vaccinium corymbosum

Botanical Pronunciation
vack-SIN-ee-um kor-im-BOE-sum

Other Name High-bush blueberry

Bloom Period and Seasonal Color
Bell-shaped white flowers in late spring; red, orange, or golden fall foliage

Mature Height × Spread
2 to 5 feet × 2 to 3 feet

What's a fruit bush doing here? Edible though it is, the high-bush blueberry also happens to make a snazzy landscape plant with its hanging, white, bell-shaped late-spring flowers, followed by its dark blue, early-summer fruits, and capped off with surprisingly showy red, orange, or golden fall foliage. Wow! Blueberry is a plant that's seldom bothered by bugs or disease, a particularly unusual trait for a fruit bush. It's also a U.S. native shrub. If you'd like to keep the tasty and nutritious berries for yourself, plant at least three plants for best cross-pollination and figure on netting them near ripening time, lest birds eat every last fruit. Of course, if you're interested in *attracting* birds to the landscape, blueberry is a top choice.

When, Where, and How to Plant
Most important—blueberries demand acidic soil, ideally a pH of 4.5 to 5. Add sulfur if a soil test indicates acidifying is needed. Plant in spring, 3 feet apart in loose, damp soil. Blueberries prefer sandy soil; good drainage is essential. Improve your soil (especially clay) by working 2 inches of compost, aged sawdust, and/or peat moss into the top 10 to 12 inches. Mulch with 2 to 3 inches of bark after planting. Keep mulch at least 2 to 3 inches away from the trunk. Its best fruiting and fall color is in full sun, but plants tolerate light shade.

Growing Tips
Water deeply twice a week for the first season then whenever it's dry otherwise. Blueberries are shallow-rooted and need consistent moisture. Scatter a granular, organic or gradual-release nitrogen-rich and acidifying fertilizer (10-5-5 or similar) over the bed in early spring. You may need to supplement with sulfur annually to keep the pH low. Maximize harvest by planting a mix of early, middle, and late-maturing varieties.

Regional Advice and Care
Besides netting out birds, protect young plants with wire or hardware-cloth cylinders to prevent rabbit gnawing. No pruning is needed for the first four to five years. Then early each spring, remove two to three of the oldest canes to the ground, thin out excess twiggy growth, and shorten overly long remaining branches. Ultimately, keep ten to fifteen canes per bush each year.

Companion Planting and Design
Blueberries make a colorful (and tasty) border planting or hedge. Line them around a vegetable garden. Add a few to a sunny, bird-friendly garden. Or spot a few along southern or western house foundations. Leadwort makes a color-coordinated, blue-blooming groundcover companion.

Try These
'Sunshine Blue' won an award for looks and production. 'Top Hat', 'Peach Sorbet', and 'Jelly Bean' are dwarfs that grow into 2-by-2-foot balls. Good standard producers are 'Bluejay', 'Blueray', 'Duke', and 'Patriot' (early producers); 'Bluecrop' and 'Toro' (midseason); and 'Jersey', 'Herbert', and 'Elliott' (late). Native low-bush blueberry (*Vaccinium angustifolium*) is a foot-tall, groundcover blueberry for Zones 5 to 6.

Blue Mist Shrub

Caryopteris × *clandonensis*

Botanical Pronunciation
kar-ee-OP-ter-iss klan-doh-NEN-siss

Other Name Bluebeard

Bloom Period and Seasonal Color
August through September; light or dark blue

Mature Height × Spread
2 to 3 feet × 3 to 4 feet

Zones 6 and 7

Blue mist shrub is one of those few woody plants that waits until late season to start its flower show. It's one of the last shrubs to bloom, sending up clouds of dainty light or dark blue flowers in August and September. Plants grow into rounded mounds that are slightly wider than tall. Older varieties generally grow 3 feet tall and 4 feet wide, but recent introductions have been bred for heavier and longer bloom as well as a tighter 2-by-3-foot mound size. The inch-wide leaves are gray-green. A few yellow-variegated options are available. The foliage has a bug- and animal-repelling scent that to me smells something like a mix of lavender, santolina, and furniture polish . . . not bad, just unusual.

When, Where, and How to Plant
Plant container-grown or field-dug, burlap-wrapped blue mist shrubs in spring. Ones grown in containers can be planted throughout summer if roots are kept damp. Plant in full sun, 3 to 4 feet apart and an inch above grade in loose, well-drained or even sandy soil. Avoid soggy sites. Improve clay soil by working 2 inches of compost into the top 10 to 12 inches of existing soil. Once it's planted, mulch with 2 to 3 inches of wood chips or bark kept at least 2 to 3 inches away from the trunk.

Growing Tips
This is a shrub you'll likely never need to water after the roots establish its first season with weekly soakings whenever it's hot and dry. Blue mist shrub is exceptionally drought-hardy. Fertilizer usually isn't needed. Self-sown seedlings may pop up in spring; yank them if you don't want them, transplant them if you do.

Regional Advice and Care
Blue mist shrub thrives in heat, but it's borderline winter-hardy in Zone 5 regions. Plant there in protected sites, such as along a heated wall. Other than cold, the main threat is root-rot in wet soil. Prevent that by improving the soil, avoiding low-lying spots, and not over-mulching. Cut back plants to 6 to 8 inches at the end of winter. Be patient in spring because blue mist shrub is one of the last shrubs to leaf out.

Companion Planting and Design
This is a good shrub for hot spots such as along the driveway, in southern and western house-foundation beds, in rock gardens, or on sunny banks. Although it's not a native plant, blue mist shrub is attractive to bees and butterflies, so it's useful in a sunny pollinator garden. Blue-needled evergreens, especially juniper, fir, and blue spruce, are good partners.

Try These
Good 3- to 4-footers with medium to dark blue flowers are 'Dark Knight', 'Longwood Blue', and Grand Bleu™. Good compact choices (about a foot smaller) are Petit Bleu™ and 'First Choice'. The closely related species and variety *Caryopteris incana* Sunshine Blue® is an option with yellow-variegated foliage and blue flowers.

Butterfly Bush

Buddleia hybrids

Botanical Pronunciation
BUDD-lee-ah

Other Name Nectar bush

Bloom Period and Seasonal Color
July through November; purple, blue-purple,
white, pink, orange, yellow

Mature Height × Spread
3 to 8 feet × 4 to 6 feet

     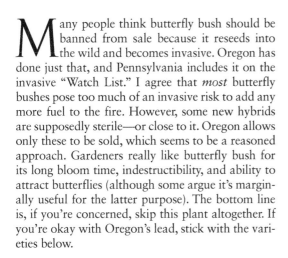

Many people think butterfly bush should be banned from sale because it reseeds into the wild and becomes invasive. Oregon has done just that, and Pennsylvania includes it on the invasive "Watch List." I agree that *most* butterfly bushes pose too much of an invasive risk to add any more fuel to the fire. However, some new hybrids are supposedly sterile—or close to it. Oregon allows only these to be sold, which seems to be a reasoned approach. Gardeners really like butterfly bush for its long bloom time, indestructibility, and ability to attract butterflies (although some argue it's marginally useful for the latter purpose). The bottom line is, if you're concerned, skip this plant altogether. If you're okay with Oregon's lead, stick with the varieties below.

When, Where, and How to Plant
Butterfly bush thrives in heat, full sun, and poor rocky, sandy, or even clayish soil. In other words, it takes considerable abuse, which is why it's popular with home gardeners, and why it's so effective elbowing its way into unwanted territory. About all that discourages butterfly bush is wet soil. Plant early spring through early fall in soil that's been dug down 10 to 12 inches. Mulch after planting with 2 to 3 inches of wood chips or bark. Keep mulch at least 2 to 3 inches away from the trunk.

Growing Tips
Water deeply once a week for the first growing season, then you'll likely never need to water again. Fertilizer usually is never needed either. Limit unwanted seeding by snipping off flowers as soon as they finish blooming. This is even a good safeguard for the low- or no-viable-seed types.

Regional Advice and Care
Besides unwanted seeding, the other rap against butterfly bush is super-fast growth and overgrown sizes. Control size by cutting all growth back to 1 foot at the end of winter. Branches can be shortened to desired lengths in season as you're deadheading the flowers. You're not limited to removing just the branch tips. Yank and toss any seedlings that pop up, and consider replacing existing butterfly bushes with non-invasive alternatives.

Companion Planting and Design
Most people use butterfly bush along borders, in butterfly gardens, and sometimes at sunny house corners. Most any hot, sunny spot with adequate space works. Purple coneflower, tall pink garden phlox, and blazing star are good butterfly-attracting perennial partners.

Try These
Lo and Behold® members 'Blue Chip' (blue-purple), 'Ice Chip' (white), and 'Purple Haze' (purple) are not only on Oregon's low-fertility list, they're compact 3- by 4-footers. Flutterby Petite™ 'Snow White' is similar to 'Ice Chip' except that it's slightly taller than wide. All five colors in the Flutterby Grande™ series made Oregon's approved list (these are mostly 8 feet tall and 6 feet wide), and 'Asian Moon' is another Oregon-approved, 6- to 7-foot purple bloomer.

Crapemyrtle

Lagerstroemia indica and hybrids

Botanical Pronunciation
lag-ur-STREE-mee-ah IN-dih-kah

Bloom Period and Seasonal Color
July to October; pink, rose, red, white, lavender, violet

Mature Height × Spread
3 to 20 feet × 3 to 18 feet

Is crapemyrtle a shrub or a tree? Yes. This Southern classic comes in forms and sizes from 3-foot mounds to 20-foot-tall, single-trunk trees—and everything in between. They all produce showy, cone-shaped flower clusters of pink to violet to red for up to three months in late summer. Breeding efforts paid off with cold-tough types that are reliably winter-hardy throughout Pennsylvania's Zones 6 and 7. A few might even make it in protected Zone 5 spots. Although the flowers are the main attraction, crapemyrtle is underrated for its yellow, orange, or red fall foliage and for its patchy, Dalmatian-like, tan-and-brown bark. The small to mid-sized shrub types are the most common and hardiest types that are becoming increasingly popular in Pennsylvania landscapes.

When, Where, and How to Plant
Any container-grown or field-dug, burlap-wrapped plants can be planted in spring. Container-grown plants can still be planted throughout summer if their roots are kept damp. but fall planting is slightly riskier. Site in full sun an inch above grade in loose, well-drained, mildly acidic soil. Avoid soggy sites. Improve clay by working 2 inches of compost into the top 10 to 12 inches of existing soil. Mulch after planting with 2 to 3 inches of wood chips or bark, keeping it away from the trunk by 2 to 3 inches.

Growing Tips
Crapemyrtle is drought-tough once its roots are established. Water deeply once or twice a week for the first growing season; then water as needed only during very hot, dry spells. Feed a balanced, granular, organic or gradual-release fertilizer in early spring.

Regional Advice and Care
Crapemyrtle is one of the last plants to leaf out in spring. Be patient. In cold years, the top growth may die to the ground, but new growth emerges from the roots. Many a crapemyrtle has been dug out for dead prematurely. Planting along a heated wall or other protected spot is a must in Zone 5, a nicety for nervous Zone 6'ers. In early spring, prune winter-killed wood, then thin out excess growth, then shorten overly long branches. Powdery mildew and Japanese beetles are potential problems.

Companion Planting and Design
Eight- to 12-foot uprights are superb specimens at sunny house corners. Small, mounded types make good southern- and western-foundation shrubs. Tall types are better used as small trees in open, sunny sections. Upright crapemyrtles tend to develop "bare legs," so underplant with low shrubs (spreading juniper, deutzia, dwarf boxwood) or perennials (leadwort, liriope, hardy geranium).

Try These
Good "shorties" are the Dazzle® series (3 to 5 feet in multiple flower color choices), 'Pocomoke' (rosy pink 3-footer), and 'Victor' (red 5-footer). Good bushy 6- to 12-footers include the heavy-blooming Magic™ series (6 feet, multiple colors), 'Tonto' (magenta-blooming 8-footer), and Rhapsody in Pink® and the award-winning Pink Velour® (dark foliage, pink-blooming 12-footers). Taller types include Red Rocket® (cherry red 15-footer) and Dynamite® (red 20-footer).

Deutzia

Deutzia gracilis

Botanical Pronunciation
DEWTZ-ee-ah grah-SILL-us

Other Name Slender deutzia

Bloom Period and Seasonal Color
April to May; white

Mature Height × Spread
2 to 4 feet × 3 to 5 feet

Plant connoisseurs often turn their noses up at deutzia, a long-used and arguably overused shrub that's one of those two-week wonders. Small, bell-shaped, hummingbird-attracting, snow white flowers nearly cover the arching branches in mid-spring (unarguably beautiful then). But frankly deutzia can then turn into an overgrown, gangly has-been the rest of the year. A few new varieties that offer compact growth, lime-green leaf color, and even some fall color make this old-fashioned workhorse worth a new look. After all, it *is* a largely trouble-free and reasonably drought-tough shrub that deer seldom eat. Slender deutzia (*Deutzia gracilis*) is the main type you'll find in garden centers. It has narrow leaves and grows slightly wider than tall, typically 2 to 3 feet tall and 3 to 4 feet wide.

When, Where, and How to Plant
Plant container-grown deutzia early spring through early fall an inch above grade in full sun or part-shade locations. Tease out the roots before planting. Pay attention to regular watering if you plant in summer's heat. Deutzia grows best in loose, damp, mildly acidic soil but will tolerate somewhat dry or clayish soil; avoid soggy spots. Mulch after planting with 2 to 3 inches of wood chips or bark. Keep mulch off the trunk.

Growing Tips
Water deeply once or twice a week for the first full growing season, then weekly during hot, dry spells. Deutzia is drought-resistant once its roots are established. It's a light feeder, so you'll likely need to do nothing more than scatter a balanced, granular,

organic or gradual-release fertilizer over the bed in early spring—if even that.

Regional Advice and Care
Deutzia sometimes comes out of winter looking a bit bedraggled with snow-snapped or dead branches. Cut out dead or injured wood at winter's end, but wait until after the plant is done flowering to thin out overly dense growth or to cut back to control size. At that time, cut back to as low as 6 inches to give a tired deutzia new life. Bug, disease, and animal troubles are unlikely.

Companion Planting and Design
Low, spreading types make a good choice for massing on sunny to partly shaded banks. Those are also compact enough for use in eastern, southern, or western foundation beds and for underplanting trees that are limbed up enough to allow in partial light. More upright varieties can be used in border gardens, foundation beds, or next to water gardens.

Try These
'Nikko' is an award-winning 2-foot-tall spreader (4 to 5 feet across) that develops burgundy fall foliage. Yuki Snowflake™ is newer, similar, and slightly heavier in bloom. Chardonnay Pearls™ is more upright (3 to 4 feet tall) and has lime green foliage in addition to the springtime white flowers. Give it afternoon shade. *Deutzia × hybrida* 'Magicien' is another Pennsylvania Gold Medal Award-winner with pinkish purple spring flowers and a 6- to 8-foot bushy habit.

Elderberry

Sambucus species

Botanical Pronunciation
sam-BOO-kuss

Bloom Period and Seasonal Color
White or pink flowers May to July; black or red early fall fruits

Mature Height × Spread
6 to 12 feet × 6 to 12 feet

Elderberry is another plant that breeders are morphing from a gangly big bush into an attractive landscape option. Breeders are working with three types. One is the native American elder (*Sambucus canadensis*), usually found growing 10 to 12 feet tall in roadside ditches and damp wooded areas. This is better known for its jelly- and wine-making black fall fruits than its shape or color. The European elder (*Sambucus nigra*) grows even bigger and has black fruits, while the European red elder (*Sambucus racemosa*) is the smallest of the three with red fruits. All produce pink or white umbrella-like flower clusters in early summer and those bird-attracting fruits. What's bringing them to the home landscape are black and gold leaf colors, finely textured foliage, and more compact sizes.

When, Where, and How to Plant
Elderberry does best in damp, sunny spots. It'll tolerate somewhat drier spots and some shade. Variegated and gold-leafed versions prefer morning sun and afternoon shade. Plant early spring through early fall in loose, damp, slightly acidic soil. Prepare the bed by digging down 10 to 12 inches and planting an inch above grade. Mulch after planting with 2 to 3 inches of bark kept at least 2 to 3 inches away from the trunk.

Growing Tips
Water deeply twice a week for the first full growing season and from then on whenever the soil is dry. Elderberry suffers in drought and prefers consistently moist soil. Early each spring, scatter a balanced, granular, organic or gradual-release fertilizer over the bed. Plant at least two plants for improved fruit production.

Regional Advice and Care
Elderberry does best in the cooler Zone 5 and 6 regions of Pennsylvania. Plant in a site where it gets afternoon shade or a cooler microclimate in Zone 7. Even compact varieties can grow 6 feet or more in one season, so cut plants as low as 1 foot at the end of winter, then shorten overly long branches back to joints as needed during the season. Varieties bred for ornamental leaves often produce little to no fruit, especially if you're growing just one.

Companion Planting and Design
Use native elderberry or varieties of it along sunny borders as an edible or bird-attracting hedge. Dark-leafed and golden types make good specimens at house corners, next to water gardens, or in mixed-used island gardens. Dark-leafed types pair especially well with white-flowering plants, such as white shrub roses, the annual Diamond Frost® euphorbia, or perennial dwarf Shasta daisy.

Try These
My favorite is Black Lace®, a cut-leaf and nearly jet black European elder reminiscent of a cut-leaf Japanese maple. It's got great texture and unusual leaf color, plus pink-white, early-summer flowers. Just keep it snipped. 'Sutherland Gold' is a golden cut-leaf European red elder (8 feet tall, 6 feet wide). 'Nova' and 'York' are compact, fruit-producing American varieties (6 by 6 feet).

Forsythia

Forsythia × intermedia

Botanical Pronunciation
for-SITH-ee-ah in-ter-MEED-ee-ah

Bloom Period and Seasonal Color
March to April; gold, yellow

Mature Height × Spread
3 to 10 feet × 5 to 12 feet

Personally, I'm not a forsythia fan—not since I hurt my back digging out an inherited, overgrown one at my front house corner. But so many people *love* the golden flower explosion forsythia puts out for two weeks in very early spring that it earns obligatory mention. What might be the deciding factor for you is the arrival of compact, 3- to 5-foot choices, which solves one of the criticisms of this bulletproof shrub: its super-fast and unkempt growth habit. A few new forsythia varieties even offer purplish fall foliage, adding a second season of interest to this previously one-dimensional shrub. Still, forsythia's main attribute is that it has the good sense to flower prolifically at a time when Pennsylvanians can use it most.

When, Where, and How to Plant
Plant container-grown or field-dug plants in spring or early fall. Container-grown plants can be planted throughout summer if roots are kept damp. Forsythia flowers best in full sun but also performs well in part shade. It likes damp, loose, and well-drained soil but tolerates hot, dry, rocky, or clay sites. Loosen soil down to 10 to 12 inches, and plant 1 inch above grade. Mulch after planting (2 to 3 inches). As always, keep that mulch off the trunk.

Growing Tips
Water deeply once a week for the first full growing season, then you'll likely never need to water this camel of a shrub again. Forsythia is deep-rooted and drought-tough. There's no need to fertilize. Its growth rate needs no encouragement.

Regional Advice and Care
Abnormal cold snaps can kill forsythia flower buds before they open. You might notice flowers low on the plant but none higher up, a result of snow insulating the lowest buds. Guys with chainsaws like to buzz forsythia to within a foot of the plant's life, seemingly with no ill effect. Others use hand pruners to thin and shorten branches to maintain the arching habit. Give forsythia plenty of room or buy a compact type so you don't have to prune much. The timing is soon after the plant finishes flowering so you don't cut off next year's flower buds.

Companion Planting and Design
Forsythia makes a dense, informal hedge along sunny borders. It's excellent for tall cover on a big bank. In smaller yards, use it at the back of the yard or garden so its flowers can be seen in spring, then fade into the background as showy foreground plants take over. Daffodils and hyacinths are good bulb partners that overlap bloom time.

Try These
'Lynwood Gold' and 'Meadowlark' are good standard-sized varieties (8 to 10 feet tall and wide). Gold Tide™ is a 3-by-5-foot, mid-sized spreader. Show Off Sugar Baby® and Goldilocks™ are two of the smallest at 3 to 4 feet tall and wide. 'New Hampshire Gold' is a 6-footer with red-purple fall foliage.

Fothergilla

Fothergilla species

Botanical Pronunciation
fah-thur-GILL-ah

Other Name Witch alder

Bloom Period and Seasonal Color
White flowers April to May; red, orange, gold, yellow fall foliage

Mature Height × Spread
3 to 6 feet × 3 to 6 feet

For a U.S. native shrub, fothergilla is surprisingly little known and underused in Pennsylvania landscapes. That's slowly changing as gardeners realize what a multi-season and trouble-free shrub it is. Fothergilla is a compact plant, typically growing about as tall as it is wide, about 3 to 6 feet, depending on the species. White, licorice-scented, bottlebrush flowers appear in spring as the leaves are forming. The plant has blue-green, quarter-sized leaves through summer, then it goes out in a blaze of red, orange, or gold foliage in late fall. It's one of the last shrubs to turn color in fall. *Fothergilla gardenii* is the smallest of the species (3 to 4 feet), *Fothergilla major* is the biggest (6 to 8 feet), and *Fothergilla × intermedia* is in the middle.

When, Where, and How to Plant
Spring or early fall are the two best times to plant container-grown or field-dug fothergilla. Container-grown plants can be planted throughout summer if roots are kept consistently damp. Fothergilla does well both in full sun or part shade and prefers moist, well-drained, and slightly acidic soil. Once established, it tolerates dry soil. Loosen the soil to 10 to 12 inches, work an inch or two of compost into it, and plant an inch above grade. Mulch after planting with 2 to 3 inches of wood chips or bark kept away from the trunk.

Growing Tips
Water deeply once or twice a week during the entire first season to establish fothergilla's roots. Then water is needed only in hot, dry spells. Feed with a balanced, granular, organic or gradual-release fertilizer formulated for acid-preferring plants scattered over the bed in early spring.

Regional Advice and Care
Fothergilla appreciates an afternoon-shade site in the warmer Zones 6 and 7 parts of Pennsylvania. It's a slow grower that seldom needs pruning. Thin out excess branches and shorten overly long branches with hand pruners right after the plant finishes flowering in spring. Some types colonize by runners that go out and then poke up. To stop that creep (if desired), sever the runners with a shovel and remove anytime.

Companion Planting and Design
Fothergilla is most at home in a wooded garden with dappled sunlight, but it's compact and attractive enough for use as a house-foundation shrub (ideally the east exposure, but north works too). Foamflowers, fringe-leaf bleeding heart, and hellebores are good part-shade perennial partners. Hyacinths and daffodils are bulbs that overlap bloom time.

Try These
Fothergilla gardenii 'Blue Mist' is a compact, 3- to 4-footer that was good enough to earn a Pennsylvania Horticultural Society Gold Medal Award. My favorite is the 5- to 6-foot 'Mt. Airy', which virtually glows golden in fall. It's also a Gold Medal Award-winner. 'Blue Shadow' is similar to 'Mt. Airy' but with bluer summer foliage and slightly less showy fall foliage.

Hydrangea

Hydrangea species

Botanical Pronunciation
hi-DRANE-jah

Bloom Period and Seasonal Color
June to October white, rose, pink, blue, purple flowers; yellow, burgundy fall foliage

Mature Height × Spread
3 to 8 feet × 4 to 6 feet

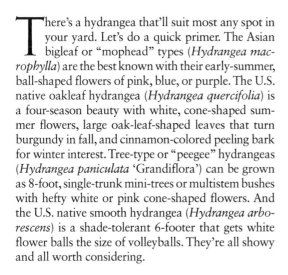

There's a hydrangea that'll suit most any spot in your yard. Let's do a quick primer. The Asian bigleaf or "mophead" types (*Hydrangea macrophylla*) are the best known with their early-summer, ball-shaped flowers of pink, blue, or purple. The U.S. native oakleaf hydrangea (*Hydrangea quercifolia*) is a four-season beauty with white, cone-shaped summer flowers, large oak-leaf-shaped leaves that turn burgundy in fall, and cinnamon-colored peeling bark for winter interest. Tree-type or "peegee" hydrangeas (*Hydrangea paniculata* 'Grandiflora') can be grown as 8-foot, single-trunk mini-trees or multistem bushes with hefty white or pink cone-shaped flowers. And the U.S. native smooth hydrangea (*Hydrangea arborescens*) is a shade-tolerant 6-footer that gets white flower balls the size of volleyballs. They're all showy and all worth considering.

When, Where, and How to Plant
Bigleaf and oakleaf hydrangeas are best in morning sun and afternoon shade, although they'll handle full sun if kept watered. Tree-type hydrangeas are the most sun-tolerant. Smooth hydrangea prefers shade. Plant all from spring through early fall. Keep summer-planted ones regularly damp. Loosen the soil to 10 to 12 inches, work in an inch or 2 of compost, and plant an inch above grade. Mulch after planting, and keep that mulch a few inches back from the trunk.

Growing Tips
Bigleaf types are the most water-needy, so soak them whenever the ground is dry. Water all types deeply once or twice a week the first full season. Then weekly in hot, dry weather is enough for most. The bigleaf species' flower color can change based on soil acidity (blue in acidy soil, pink in alkaline soil, both or a purple blend in-between). White flowers stay white no matter what. You'll likely need to add sulfur to get vibrant blues. Fertilize with a balanced, granular, organic or gradual-release fertilizer early each spring.

Regional Advice and Care
Bigleaf types are the least cold-hardy and benefit from a warm, protected site in Zone 5 regions. The other three are cold-hardy throughout Pennsylvania. Pruning varies by species. Prune tree-type hydrangeas and smooth hydrangeas at the end of winter; oakleafs and bigleafs right after they finish flowering.

Companion Planting and Design
Bigleaf hydrangea is ideal along an eastern house foundation. Tree-type hydrangeas make good house-corner specimens. Use an oakleaf hydrangea along borders or in a grove of trees that allows some sun. Try smooth hydrangea along shady borders, on shady banks, or clustered in shady spots under trees.

Try These
The Forever and Ever™ and Endless Summer® series are reblooming bigleaf types. I also like the Cityline™ and Edgy™ series of compact bigleafs. 'Ruby Slippers' is an excellent new compact oakleaf type; 'Snow Queen' is a good standard one. Pinky Winky® (pink) and 'Limelight' (white) are my favorite tree-types (and Little Lime™ and Bobo® are dwarf tree-types). I'll take Incrediball® (white), Bella Anna™ (pink), or Invincibelle Spirit® (pink) in smooth hydrangeas.

Lilac

Syringa species

Botanical Pronunciation
sur-ING-gah

Bloom Period and Seasonal Color
Purple, lavender, pink, white flower clusters late
April into June; some yellow fall foliage

Mature Height × Spread
5 to 14 feet × 5 to 10 feet

Lilac has been a popular landscape shrub since Colonial days mainly for its large, showy, cone-shaped flower clusters that are powerfully fragrant (usually). May is the peak bloom month. The old-fashioned French or common lilac (*Syringa vulgaris*), however, has a variety of drawbacks, such as powdery mildew leaf disease, tending to get overgrown, and developing "bare legs" as it ages. If you're not keen on any of that, check out some of the compact types, which grow denser, bushier, and with much better disease resistance while retaining that sweet, distinctive lilac fragrance. A few types ('Josee', Bloomerang®, and Bloomerang Purple®, to name three) rebloom for several more weeks into early summer. Fall color isn't spectacular, but some offer a bit of yellow fall foliage.

When, Where, and How to Plant
Spring or early fall is the time to plant container-grown or field-dug, burlap-wrapped plants. Container-grown plants can be planted throughout summer if roots are kept consistently damp. Lilac is best planted in full sun. It tolerates dry sites but prefers slightly damp conditions. No soggy spots! Loosen soil to 10 to 12 inches, plant an inch above grade, and mulch after planting with 2 or 3 inches of wood chips or bark kept back away from the trunk.

Growing Tips
Water deeply once a week for the first growing season, then water is needed only in very hot, dry spells, if even that. Lilac is drought-tough once established. Scatter a balanced, granular, organic or gradual-release fertilizer over the bed in early spring, but avoid overdoing the nitrogen, which can limit flowering.

Regional Advice and Care
Lilac can suffer in intense heat, so keep it watered in a Zone 7 heat wave. Summer humidity increases the odds of powdery mildew, especially on common lilac. Proper pruning improves airflow, decreases diseases, and keeps the plant looking good and flowering best. Right after bloom each spring, remove one-third of the shoots to the ground and shorten overly long branches. Do that each spring so you'll end up with a "new" bush every fourth year. Young branches flower best.

Companion Planting and Design
Common lilacs work best as tall flowering hedges along a sunny border (give them ample room). Compact types are better for pairing with perennials in island beds or at house corners and along southern or western house foundations. Place one or more near a patio or window to take advantage of the fragrance.

Try These
Besides the rebloomers, try the small-leafed 'Tinkerbelle' (6- by 5-foot, pink), the Manchurian lilac (*Syringa pubescens patula*) 'Miss Kim' (6- by 5-foot, lavender), or the dwarf Korean lilac (*Syringa meyeri*) 'Palabin', a 6-by-6-foot lavender bloomer that earned a Pennsylvania Horticultural Society Gold Medal Award. 'President Grevy' (double lilac) and 'Charles Joly' (double magenta) are good, tall common lilacs. 'Prairie Petite' is a super-dwarf, 3- to 4-foot common lilac that blooms light pink.

Ninebark

Physocarpus opulifolius

Botanical Pronunciation
fizz-oh-KAR-pus op-you-lih-FOE-lee-us

Bloom Period and Seasonal Color
Pinkish white flowers in May and June; coppery fall foliage

Mature Height × Spread
4 to 10 feet × 4 to 10 feet

American gardeners largely ignored this gangly, green-leafed shrub before European breeders came up with a dark burgundy-leafed type (Diabolo®) that gave us a "new" cutting-edge landscape plant. Diabolo® earned a Pennsylvania Horticultural Society Gold Medal Award and provided the genetics that led to numerous other burgundy, gold, and copper-colored varieties, including several compact, 5- to 6-foot choices. It all adds up to a cold-tough, drought-tough, deer-resistant, multiple-season native shrub that's gaining deserved interest. The late-spring flowers are pinkish white, quarter-sized, and shaped like mini pincushions. Clusters of BB-sized red fruits follow the bloom in summer. Then comes coppery to red-burgundy fall foliage. Finally, the leaves drop to reveal cinnamon-colored bark that peels off in the shape of the name-inducing numeral 9 (they look like brown Doritos to me).

When, Where, and How to Plant
Ninebark grows best in full sun and tolerates both damp and dry sites as well as fairly poor soil. Plant container-grown or field-dug, burlap-wrapped plants in spring or early fall. Container-grown plants can be planted throughout summer if roots are kept consistently damp. To plant, dig down 10 to 12 inches, plant an inch above grade, and mulch after planting with 2 or 3 inches of wood chips or bark. No mulch against the trunk!

Growing Tips
Once you get the roots established by watering deeply weekly whenever it's dry that first season, you'll likely never need to water a ninebark again. It's a deep-rooted and drought-tough native species. Fertilizer is usually not needed.

Regional Advice and Care
Ninebark's main Achilles heel is powdery mildew leaf disease. It can disfigure foliage in a humid summer but is unlikely to kill the plant. Remove fallen, diseased leaves in fall, prune out any infected or dead branches as they occur, and cut whole plants to 6 inches at the end of winter through early summer to rejuvenate a chronically diseased plant. To control size, thin out excess branches and shorten overly long branches after the plant finishes blooming. End-of-winter pruning won't hurt the plant but it will limit flowering that season.

Companion Planting and Design
The large 8- to 10-foot types are best used as border hedges or specimens. Tall, dark-leafed types also can be used as backdrop shrubs or centerpieces in a sunny mixed garden. Compact types are better size-suited if you want a ninebark at a house corner or along southern or western house foundations.

Try These
Diabolo® is good but gets big and may get mildew. Summer Wine® is a notch down size-wise (6 by 5 feet) and has good burgundy color but also gets occasional mildew. The new dark-leafed Little Devil™ is smaller still (about 4 by 3 feet) and more resistant to mildew. 'Center Glow', Coppertina™, and Amber Jubilee® are 6- to 8-footers with golden or coppery summer foliage.

Shrub Dogwood

Cornus species

Botanical Pronunciation
KOR-nus

Other Name Redtwig dogwood

Bloom Period and Seasonal Color
Late-spring white flowers; purple, yellow fall foliage; red, gold bare branches in winter

Mature Height × Spread
5 to 8 feet × 4 to 6 feet

Dogwoods that grow as upright multi-stemmed bushes aren't nearly so well known as dogwood trees. While not as spectacular in flower or fall foliage, shrub dogwoods offer interesting seasonal change. The show starts in late spring with creamy, umbrella-shaped flowers, followed by white, dark blue, or black berries in summer. Fall brings burgundy-purple foliage in some types. But the main attraction is winter when the leaves drop revealing brilliant red or gold stems that brighten as temperatures drop. You'll mainly find three species: Tatarian dogwood (*Cornus alba*), an Asian species with white berries and red stems; bloodtwig dogwood (*Cornus sanguinea*), a European native with black berries and crimson/gold stems; and red osier dogwood (*Cornus sericea*), a U.S. native with blue berries and red winter stems.

When, Where, and How to Plant

Plant container-grown or field-dug, burlap-wrapped plants in spring or early fall. Container-grown plants can be planted throughout summer if roots are kept consistently damp. Shrub dogwoods grow in full sun to part shade and appreciate loose, damp soil. They'll even tolerate occasionally wet sites. Work an inch or two of compost into your loosened lousy clay, plant an inch above grade, and mulch after planting with 2 to 3 inches of wood chips or bark, kept several inches away from the trunk.

Growing Tips

You should've watered yesterday if your dogwood leaves are drooping or browning around the edges. Soak them at least weekly during the first season to establish the roots, then you may need to water deeply every week or two during hot, dry spells. Feed balanced, granular, organic or gradual-release fertilizer formulated for acid-preferring plants over the bed in early spring.

Regional Advice and Care

Shrub dogwoods can suffer in intense summer heat, so afternoon shade is best in Zone 7. Leaf spot is a possible disease problem, especially on variegated-leaf varieties. Remove fallen, diseased leaves or spray a fungicide labeled for leaf spot control if that's a problem. Deer are possible threats. Get the best winter stem color by pruning plants to within a few inches of the ground early each spring before new growth begins.

Companion Planting and Design

Plant shrub dogwoods out your favorite winter-view window so you can enjoy their golden or red stems from the warmth inside. Backdrop the dogwoods with taller evergreens to accent the stem color. This grouping is especially nice after a snow. Shrub dogwoods also are useful as a tall hedge along a sunny or partly shaded border.

Try These

My favorite is bloodtwig dogwood 'Midwinter Fire' with its glowing yellow and red winter stems. It earned a Pennsylvania Horticultural Society Gold Medal Award. 'Cardinal' and 'Arctic Fire' are native red-osier types with purple fall foliage and 5- to 6-foot sizes. 'Sibirica' is a compact Tatarian dogwood with red winter stems. Ivory Halo™ and 'Elegantissima' are variegated versions of that species.

Shrub Rose

Rosa species

Botanical Pronunciation
ROE-sah

Bloom Period and Seasonal Color
June through November; pink, red, white, salmon, coral

Mature Height × Spread
2 to 6 feet × 3 to 6 feet

By all means, try a few classic hybrid tea, floribunda, or grandiflora roses—if you're up for spraying to fight the bugs and diseases that threaten these types. Novices and those interested in low-care landscape plants are better off starting with "shrub" roses, which grow in a more spreading or bushy habit with lots of smaller flower clusters as opposed to sleek, upright shrubs with fragrant, queen-of-the-vase divas gracing the tips of slender single stems. The Knock Out® series brought this type of rose to the forefront and is now one of the most widely used landscape shrubs. This "no-fear" rose touched off a breeding wave that has brought innumerable new compact, disease-resistant, and spreading shrub roses. Besides long-lived flowering beauty, rose petals are edible.

When, Where, and How to Plant
Shrub roses thrive in heat and sun. They grow best in loose, rich, damp, and mildly acidic soil but tolerate dry sites and poor, rocky, sandy, or clayish soil. Just avoid poorly drained spots. Light shade is passable, but flowers go downhill with less light. Plant bare-root roses in early spring; plant container-grown plants spring through early fall. Work 1 to 2 inches of compost into the loosened top 10 to 12 inches of soil, plant an inch above grade, and mulch after planting.

Growing Tips
Water deeply weekly for the first season, then water weekly during hot, dry spells. Shrub roses may not show signs of drought stress, but they'll flower best with adequate moisture. In early spring and early summer scatter a fertilizer formulated for roses over the bed.

Regional Advice and Care
Shrub types are winter-hardy throughout Pennsylvania. Winter protection isn't necessary. Control size by cutting all growth back to 6 to 10 inches at winter's end. Plants can be cut back by one-third after the first round of flowering in early summer. If size is okay, lightly trim off spent flowers as desired or skip in-season pruning altogether. There's no need to spray for minor leaf disease issues or temporary Japanese beetle damage.

Companion Planting and Design
Knock Out® and similar upright types are excellent situated along southern and western house foundations and as colorful sunny border hedges. They pair well with liriope, lavender, hardy geranium, salvias, and nearly any blue, purple, or white annuals or perennials. Spreading types are useful as a groundcover on sunny banks or as 2-foot-tall edging plants along paths, patios, and driveways (kept back enough so thorns don't grab passersby).

Try These
The original red Knock Out® (5 by 4 feet) is as good as any. So is the pink and the double-petaled pink and red versions. The seven color Drift® series is my favorite spreading type (2 by 3 feet). Meideland™, Oso Easy™, Easy Elegance®, and Flower Carpet® series offer assorted other colors, sizes, and habits. *Rosa glauca* (5-foot pink bloomer) is an old-fashioned but trouble-free shrub type.

Smokebush

Cotinus coggygria

Botanical Pronunciation
ko-TIE-nus kog-GIG-ree-ah

Other Name Smoketree

Bloom Period and Seasonal Color
Dusky rose flower puffs from late May through July; red, red-purple, orange, yellow fall foliage

Mature Height × Spread
6 to 15 feet × 8 to 12 feet

Smokebush and smoketree are the same; the difference is in the pruning. Either way, the main attraction is the airy, dusky pink flower structures that look like puffs of smoke in early summer. It's an unusual, eye-grabbing sight to the beginner who's never seen one, even though smokebush was a highly popular small tree in Victorian times. These days, the foliage color competes with the smoke-puffs for gardeners' attention. Several varieties have burgundy-purple leaves all season, while at least one (Golden Spirit™) has lemony golden leaves. Left unpruned, a smokebush grows into a multi-stemmed smoketree that can reach 15 to 20 feet tall. Some gardeners prefer it more as a 6-foot shrub and whack the whole thing down to 4 to 6 inches at each winter's end.

When, Where, and How to Plant
Field-dug, burlap-wrapped smokebush can be planted in spring or early fall. Container-grown plants can go in the ground spring through early fall, including summer, so long as you keep the roots well watered. Smokebush prefers full sun to light shade and loose, damp soil. However, it tolerates dry sites and poor soil. To plant, loosen the top 10 to 12 inches of existing soil, plant an inch above grade, and mulch with 2 to 3 inches of wood chips or bark after planting. Don't pack mulch up against the trunk.

Growing Tips
Water deeply once a week for the first full growing season, then once every week or two during hot, dry spells. Smokebush is reasonably tough in droughts. Fertilizer isn't mandatory, especially with mulch breaking down to supply nutrients, but an annual spring dose of a balanced, granular, organic or gradual-release fertilizer may aid bloom.

Regional Advice and Care
If you're growing smokebush mainly for its foliage and want to keep the size down, cut the whole plant back nearly to the ground at winter's end. This likely will reduce or eliminate the smoke-puffs that season. If you want maximum flowers and tree-size growth, wait until *after* the blooms fade to make your thinning and shortening cuts. Smokebush can suffer in intense summer heat, so afternoon shade is best in Zone 7. Rodents may eat the base of trunks; wrap with hardware cloth as a precaution.

Companion Planting and Design
Purple-leaf types add spots of eye-high dark color to border and island gardens. Many people like smokebush enough to use it as house-corner specimens. Unpruned, tree-form plants are best used as you would a small tree in a more open spot of the front or back yard.

Try These
'Royal Purple' and 'Velvet Cloak' are the most common dark-leafed types (possibly one and the same). 'Daydream' has green leaves and is exceptionally showy in flower. Our native smokebush (*Cotinus obovatus*) is a small tree well worth trying for its brilliant yellow/orange/red fall foliage alone. 'Grace' is a 15-foot hybrid with red new growth and red/orange/gold fall foliage.

Spirea

Spiraea species

Botanical Pronunciation
spy-REE-ah

Bloom Period and Seasonal Color
Late March to June; white, pink, rose

Mature Height × Spread
2 to 8 feet × 4 to 10 feet

Spirea is a virtually bulletproof family of shrubs—sometimes too much so for its own good. The most popular type is the Japanese spirea (*Spiraea japonica*), a 3- to 4-foot rounded pink-, rose- or white-bloomer that garden centers offer in numerous varieties. The problem is that species is prone to unwanted seeding, earning it a spot on Pennsylvania's Invasive Plant List. The complication is that not all varieties are equally fertile, ranging from rampant ('Little Princess', 'Shibori', 'Anthony Waterer') to almost sterile ('Neon Flash', 'Crispa', 'Dart's Red'), according to Montana State University research. An alternative is to plant the non-invasive, willowy, gold-leafed *Spiraea thunbergii* 'Ogon' (Mellow Yellow®), a 5-by-5-footer with bronze fall foliage and stems that are covered with white flowers in early spring.

When, Where, and How to Plant
Spirea is almost always sold as container-grown and can be planted spring through early fall. Keep summer-planted plants well watered. Plant in full sun to light shade. Spirea prefers loose, damp, and mildly acidic soil but tolerates dry sites and sandy, rocky, or clay soil. Avoid soggy sites. Loosen soil to 10 to12 inches deep, set plants an inch above grade, and mulch with a few inches of wood chips or bark after planting. I'll repeat: Keep mulch *at least* 2 to 3 inches away from shrub trunks.

Growing Tips
Water deeply once a week for the first full growing season, then you'll likely never need to water a spirea again. This is a very drought-tolerant plant family. Fertilizer usually is never needed either, especially if you're mulching around the plants.

Regional Advice and Care
If you have one of the more behaved Japanese types, I'd still suggest pruning or shearing at the end of winter and then shearing off the spent flower heads right after bloom to further limit seeding. Prune 'Ogon' right after flowering, if needed to control size. 'Ogon' is best hand-pruned as opposed to shearing to maintain its arching habit. Vanhoutte and *Spiraea nipponica* 'Snowmound' are also pruned right after flowering.

Companion Planting and Design
'Ogon' is a colorful and textural winner most *everywhere*—massed along a sunny or partly shaded border, spotted along house foundations, as a specimen next to a water garden, or paired with bright perennials in an island bed or Asian garden. Rounded Japanese types are survivors in your hottest, driest sites, such as along sidewalks, driveways, and western or southern house foundations.

Try These
Vanhoutte spirea (*Spiraea × vanhouttei*) is a bigger, 8-by-10-footer with a fountainlike habit and white flowers. *Spiraea nipponica* 'Snowmound' is an arching 5-by-5 footer covered with small white flowers in May and June. Avoid the Japanese and *Spiraea × bumalda* types, except possibly for varieties testing as sterile (or almost so). In Zones 5 to 6, try the native steeplebush (*Spiraea tomentosa*), a colonizing 4-footer that blooms rosy pink in late summer.

St. Johnswort

Hypericum species

Botanical Pronunciation
hi-PERR-ih-kum

Bloom Period and Seasonal Color
Yellow flowers June to September; red, golden orange fruits late summer to fall

Mature Height × Spread
2 to 3 feet × 3 to 4 feet

You may recognize St. Johnswort more as an herbal antidepressant than a compact, yellow-flowering shrub. Although this genus produces pills, St. Johnswort offers gardeners a deer-resistant shrub with multiple-season interest. The five-petaled yellow flowers open in early summer and can keep going for three months, ultimately progressing into pea-sized fruits. The fruits (mostly red or gold-orange blends) are attractive enough that florists use St. Johnswort branches in arrangements. Some types add colorful, season-long foliage to the mix, in particular the blue-green leaves of native *Hypericum kalmianum* Blue Velvet™ and the burgundy-tinted leaves of non-native *Hypericum androsaemum* 'Albury Purple' (winter-hardy in Zones 6 to 7). Most St. Johnsworts grow into 3-by-4-foot bushes, but *Hypericum calycinum* is a foot-tall, non-native, creeping shrub best used as a groundcover.

When, Where, and How to Plant
Plant container-grown St. Johnswort spring through early fall in full sun (where it flowers best) to part shade. It prefers loose, damp, and mildly acidic soil, but most types tolerate dry, rocky, or clay soil and even tree-root competition. Loosen the soil 10 to 12 inches deep, work in an inch or two of compost, and plant an inch above grade. After planting, cover the ground with 2 to 3 inches of wood chips or bark. Keep mulch 2 to 3 inches or more away from the trunk.

Growing Tips
Water deeply once a week for the first full growing season, then water is needed only in hot, dry spells.

Some St. Johnsworts self-sow, so yank seedlings you don't want. Feed a balanced, granular, organic or gradual-release fertilizer formulated for acid-preferring plants over the bed in early spring.

Regional Advice and Care
St. Johnswort often dies back to the ground over winter, especially in Zones 5 to 6. New growth usually pushes up from the roots by early May. If that happens, cut off dead wood and let new shoots take over. Prune back dead tips to live buds at this time too. Prune to control size in early spring. St. Johnswort's main drawback is that some types really *do* die after three or four years in the ground. Replace them or switch to something else if that happens.

Companion Planting and Design
Use St. Johnswort as foundation flowering shrubs along south, west, or east exposures. It's one of the best shrubs for dry shade under trees. Daylilies, mums, and coreopsis make good perennial partners in a border or island garden.

Try These
Start with Blue Velvet™, a 3-by-4-foot, cold-hardy native that earned a Pennsylvania Horticultural Society Gold Medal Award. I like 'Albury Purple' for its burgundy-tinted leaves, but it probably won't do Zone 5 and seems to be short-lived everywhere. *Hypericum frondosum* 'Sunburst' is a bushy, 4-foot native; the native *Hypericum prolificum* is a foot shorter and durable in poor soil, and the new Mediterranean-native Mystical™ series has some of the nicest fruits.

Sumac

Rhus species

Botanical Pronunciation
RUSS

Bloom Period and Seasonal Color
Small yellow flowers April to July; red fruits; yellow, orange, red fall foliage

Mature Height × Spread
2 to 6 feet × 5 to 8 feet

Don't turn up your nose at this one . . . yet. Sumac, admittedly, is one of those love-or-hate plants. Some view sumacs as "those weed trees" that invade roadside ditches and rocky banks. Others view sumac as a hard-to-kill, deer-resistant native plant with brilliant fall foliage and fruits that feed birds. Two varieties bridge that gap. One is a compact version of native staghorn sumac (*Rhus typhina*) called Tiger Eyes®, which has deeply toothed, golden foliage that turns golden scarlet in fall. It grows much smaller (6 feet) than the species (20 feet or more). The other is 'Gro-Low', a 2-foot-tall native fragrant sumac (*Rhus aromatica*) that colonizes out to 8 feet, gets red fall fruits, and has lobed leaves that turn deep gold-burgundy in fall.

When, Where, and How to Plant
Sumac is extremely tough and adaptable in all kinds of soil, except soggy ones, and in light ranging from full sun to shade. Plant container-grown plants in spring or early fall. Loosen soil (there's usually no need to improve it unless it's atrocious), plant an inch above grade, and mulch with 2 to 3 inches of wood chips or bark after planting.

Growing Tips
Water deeply once a week for the first growing season, then you'll likely never need to water again, although Tiger Eyes® appreciates a drink to head off browning around the leaf edges in hot, dry spells. Fertilizer is usually not needed.

Regional Advice and Care
Sumac is comfortable in Pennsylvania's coldest cold and hottest heat. No pruning is needed, unless plants are outgrowing the space. 'Gro-Low' and other *Rhus aromatica* cultivars colonize by "suckers," so sever and remove any of those anytime they are extending beyond where you want. Plants can be pruned back or sheared to 1 foot at the end of winter. Tiger Eyes® is best pruned like a mini-tree—cut back branches to joints as needed at the end of winter.

Companion Planting and Design
'Gro-Low' is best used massed as a shrubby groundcover, especially on a rocky, sunny bank where lesser plants will fry. It'll also grow in the dry shade under trees. Fall foliage is best in sunnier spots. Tiger Eyes® works best as a standalone specimen, ideal for texture and bright color in a mixed island garden or along a border. It's also effective as a focal-point plant next to a water garden or in a large pot.

Try These
Both Tiger Eyes® and 'Gro-Low' won Pennsylvania Horticultural Society Gold Medal Awards for their color, durability, and improved growing manners. But if you've got a big property with lots of space to fill and bad soil, the bigger and more aggressive straight species of staghorn sumac, fragrant sumac, and native smooth sumac (*Rhus glabra*) might suit as well.

Summersweet

Clethra alnifolia

Botanical Pronunciation
KLETH-rah al-nih-FOE-lee-ah

Other Name Sweet pepperbush

Bloom Period and Seasonal Color
White, pink flowers June to August; yellow, gold fall foliage

Mature Height × Spread
3 to 6 feet × 4 to 6 feet

I'm not sure why summersweet isn't in more yards, given that it's got so much going for it. The main attraction is the spicy-fragrant white or pink bottlebrush flowers that poke up for four weeks or more, mainly in July when few other shrubs are blooming. Butterflies, bees, and hummingbirds are all attracted to this native plant then. Come fall, the green leaves turn gold or yellow. Summersweet hardly ever runs into any bug or disease problems, and it'll grow in sun to almost all-day shade. Though it's regarded as a plant that prefers damp or even wet soil, it'll adapt to dry sites. And varieties are available that stay under 3 feet tall, making it a compact enough option for even small yards.

When, Where, and How to Plant
Plant container-grown or field-dug plants in spring or early fall. You can plant container-grown summersweet even in summer, but pay special attention to keeping the soil always damp. A damp spot with loose, mildly acidic soil and some afternoon shade is ideal, but summersweet also does well in full sun (especially if the soil is damp). Shade is okay, although flowering is less. Dig down to loosen soil to 10 to 12 inches, work an inch or two of compost into it, and plant an inch above grade. Mulch with 2 to 3 inches of wood chips or bark, and keep all mulch back away from the trunk.

Growing Tips
Water deeply once or twice a week to establish roots during the first season. Weekly watering during hot, dry weather from then on will maximize flowering and minimize browning around the leaf edges. Fertilize at the beginning of each season by scattering a balanced, granular, organic or gradual-release fertilizer formulated for acid-preferring plants over the bed.

Regional Advice and Care
Summersweet easily handles our winter cold and summer heat without any special precautions. No pruning is needed so long as size is okay. Summersweet blooms on each season's new growth, so the time to thin out and shorten branches is at the end of winter. Summersweet colonizes by sending out running shoots; sever and remove any that spread beyond where you want anytime.

Companion Planting and Design
Summersweet's tolerance for sun and dampness make it a natural in a rain garden or any open spot that's usually damp and occasionally wet. Upright types make good border shrubs or specimens in hummingbird and butterfly gardens. Compact types are useful as foundation shrubs or for underplanting small to mid-sized trees.

Try These
'Compacta' is a compact, white-blooming 3-footer highly rated in Longwood Gardens testing. 'Hummingbird' is similar in color, habit, and size. 'Ruby Spice' is a 6-by-5-foot upright that flowers rosy pink. All three earned Pennsylvania Horticultural Society awards. Another good choice is 'Sixteen Candles', a white bloomer that grows 3 to 4 feet tall.

Viburnum

Viburnum species

Botanical Pronunciation
vye-BURR-num

Bloom Period and Seasonal Color
Pink, white flowers in April to May; red, black, blue, or gold fall fruits; red, purple-burgundy fall foliage

Mature Height × Spread
5 to 10 feet × 6 to 12 feet

Viburnum is a large family of tough, hefty shrubs, mostly 6- to 10-footers, that come in numerous variations. The common denominator is snow-cone-like white or pink spring flowers, clusters of pea-sized fruits in late summer, then red to burgundy-purple fall foliage. The Koreanspice viburnum (*Viburnum carlesii*), Judd viburnum (*V. × juddii*), and Burkwood viburnum (*V. × burkwoodii*) are some of the most fragrant types. The native cranberrybush (*V. trilobum*) has showy red fruits. The native smooth witherod (*V. nudum*) has great dark blue fruits and glossy burgundy-purple fall foliage. The native arrowwood viburnum (*V. dentatum*) is a good shade performer. And doublefile viburnum (*V. plicatum* var. *tomentosum*) is a heavy bloomer with a graceful habit.

When, Where, and How to Plant
Spring or early fall are the best times to plant container-grown or field-dug viburnums. Container-grown plants can be planted in summer as long as you're careful to keep the roots damp throughout that first season. Most viburnums do best in full sun or light shade, but some are reasonably shade-tolerant. Most also aren't picky about soil (except sogginess). To plant, loosen soil 10 to 12 inches deep. Soil amendments usually aren't needed unless site conditions are atrocious. Plant an inch above grade, mulch after planting with 2 to 3 inches of wood chips or bark, kept away from the trunk.

Growing Tips
Most viburnums are very drought-tolerant once their roots are established. Water deeply once a week for the first growing season, then you'll likely not need to water again, except in extended droughts. Fertilizer is usually not needed either. If flowering and fruiting is poor or declining, scatter a balanced, granular, organic or gradual-release fertilizer over the bed in early spring

Regional Advice and Care
Know your site and then match the best viburnum to it. Pick well, and viburnum can become a no-care plant, other than pruning. As long as size is okay, even that's not needed. Thin out excess or crossing branches and shorten too-long or too-wide branches at the end of winter before new leaves emerge. For maximum flowering, wait until after bloom to prune. Avoid shearing, which causes excess twiggy growth and reduces flowering and fruiting.

Companion Planting and Design
Viburnums are big, so give them room, such as at house corners, along the back of the yard, or massed underneath large trees or on a large bank. Fragrant ones are nice near a patio or window.

Try These
'Winterthur' and Brandywine™ are two multi-season beauties. They're both native smooth witherod types. Chicago Lustre® and Blue Muffin™ are native arrowwoods with blue fruits and glossy leaves. 'Mohawk' (Burkwood type) has pink buds that open a very fragrant white. Koreanspice viburnum is hard to beat for fragrance and nice fall foliage.

Virginia Sweetspire

Itea virginica

Botanical Pronunciation
eye-TEE-ah vur-JIN-ih-kah

Bloom Period and Seasonal Color
White flowers in May to June; red, burgundy fall foliage

Mature Height × Spread
3 to 5 feet × 4 to 6 feet

Virginia sweetspire is another relatively unknown native shrub that deserves greater use in home landscapes. In nature, it's found in damp, sunny areas, especially along stream banks. But it's an adaptable plant that grows even in dry, heavy "builder's soil" and mostly shaded spots. Virginia sweetspire is particularly striking in bloom in late spring. The mildly fragrant flowers are white and shaped like drooping tassels or slender, 6-inch-long, arching bottlebrushes. The effect is a bit like an exploding star. The leaves are light green in summer. The plant form is loosely arching. In October and November, Virginia sweetspire puts on an encore show with brilliant red to burgundy-purple fall foliage that holds into early December some years. It's also a bird-favorite shrub.

When, Where, and How to Plant

You'll usually find container-grown plants, which can be planted spring through early fall. Keep summer-planted sweetspires particularly well watered. Field-dug plants are best planted in spring or early fall. Virginia sweetspire grows in full sun to mostly shade, but it does best with consistently damp soil no matter the light. It tolerates dry soil; occasionally wet sites are okay. Loosen the soil down 10 to 12 inches, work some compost into it, and plant at grade. After planting, cover the ground with 2 to 3 inches of wood chips or bark, and keep mulch a few inches away from the trunk.

Growing Tips

You're more likely to under water than over water it. Soak well once or twice a week for the first growing season, then soak weekly in hot, dry weather. Moisture-stressed sweetspires may brown around the leaf edges and fail to put on a peak fall-foliage show. Fertilizer usually isn't needed, especially if you're mulching.

Regional Advice and Care

Virginia sweetspire is a "suckering" shrub, meaning it colonizes by sending out runners that shoot up into new branches. Let that happen if you're growing a mass of sweetspires, but if you want to corral the spread, sever and dig runners anytime. These transplant easily if you want to start a new colony. Pruning isn't necessary, but to keep the height compact, prune or shear plants by up to one-third right after the flowers fade in late spring.

Companion Planting and Design

Virginia sweetspire is made to order for rain gardens, along sunny stream banks, and in any sunny, low-lying, damp to wet spot in the yard. It makes a good 3- to 4-foot informal hedge, is compact and attractive enough to use along house foundations, and is excellent for massing on shady to partly shaded banks or in damp areas under trees.

Try These

The 4- to 5-foot-tall 'Henry's Garnet', discovered at Swarthmore College, won a Pennsylvania Horticultural Society award. Little Henry™ is slightly more compact at 3 to 4 feet tall with shorter flower tassels. Pink varieties are in the works.

Weigela

Weigela florida

Botanical Pronunciation
wye-JEE-lah FLORE-ih-dah

Bloom Period and Seasonal Color
May and June; pink, rose, red, white

Mature Height × Spread
2 to 8 feet × 3 to 10 feet

Old-fashioned weigela has long been used for its stunning show of tubular flowers (most often pink- or rose-colored) that nearly cover the arching branches in May. But after that, you end up with, some would say, a gangly or rangy big, green, boring bush the rest of the year. Ah, but the breeders have been working on weigela lately, introducing more compact varieties, ones with dark leaves and even a new line that reblooms in fall (the Sonic Bloom™ series). Also nice are varieties with creamy-edged, variegated leaves. Flower colors include red and white in addition to pink and rose, and the flowers' tubular shape makes them hummingbird favorites. Despite the *"florida"* in the species name, weigela is a Japanese native.

When, Where, and How to Plant
Weigela flowers best in full sun and grows well in loose, damp soil (no soggy spots). But it's a tough species that tolerates dry sites and rocky or clayish soil. Plant container-grown or field-dug, burlap-wrapped plants in spring or early fall. Container-grown plants can be planted throughout summer if roots are kept damp. To plant, loosen soil down 10 to 12 inches, work in an inch or two of compost if the soil's not good, plant an inch above grade, and mulch with 2 to 3 inches of wood chips or bark kept 2 to 3 inches away from the trunk.

Growing Tips
Weigela is one of the more drought-resistant shrubs. Water deeply once a week the first season to establish the roots, then water only in very hot, dry spells. Fertilizer isn't usually necessary if you're mulching, but an annual spring feeding may give flowering a boost.

Regional Advice and Care
Variegated types do best in afternoon shade to avoid browning around the leaf edges. To control size, thin branches and cut back overly long ones right after the plant finishes blooming. You can shear overgrown weigelas back to 1 foot, but shearing encourages twiggy growth and alters the natural arching shape of the plant (at least temporarily). In spring, thin out dead branches that fail to leaf out after winter.

Companion Planting and Design
Dark leaf types make color-contrasting specimens along sunny borders, along western or southern house foundations, and in sunny island gardens. Use a line of them as an informal hedge that's especially showy in spring. Compact types are ideal for house-foundation beds, next to water gardens, or in hummingbird gardens.

Try These
Wine and Roses® is a popular, 4- to 5-foot dark leafed variety with rosy blooms, good enough to win a Pennsylvania Horticultural Society award. Fine Wine® is dark leafed and more compact, about half the size of Wine and Roses®. Midnight Wine® is even smaller (2 feet tall and wide). 'Variegata' is a variegated 6-footer, and My Monet™ is a cutie, 2-foot variegated type that needs afternoon shade.

Winterberry Holly

Ilex verticillata

Botanical Pronunciation
EYE-lecks vur-tiss-ih-LAY-tah

Bloom Period and Seasonal Color
May to June white flowers; yellow fall foliage;
red, gold, orange fall/winter berries

Mature Height × Spread
5 to 10 feet × 6 to 8 feet

Most people know hollies as those spiny-leafed evergreens that sometimes get red berries in fall. Far fewer know this holly, which has smooth-edged leaves that drop in fall. Like evergreen hollies, winterberry holly females get red berries (and in some varieties, gold or orange berries) in fall. These are especially big and showy, standing out not only for their sheer quantity but also because they're held on bare stems (no leaves to compete for attention from November on). Birds eventually polish off the fruits of this 6- to 10-foot multistemmed native shrub, but usually not until well into winter after we've enjoyed the show for months. The leaves turn yellow before dropping. Note that hollies are moderately toxic to people and pets.

When, Where, and How to Plant
Plant container-grown or field-dug plants in spring or early fall. Summer planting of container-grown plants also is okay if you keep the roots well watered in the heat. Winterberry holly produces the best fruits in full sun but also grows in part shade. It prefers damp, acidic soil and even grows in wet areas where many shrubs rot. Work an inch or two of compost into the loosened top 10 to 12 inches of existing soil, plant above grade, and mulch. Keep mulch 2 to 3 inches away from the trunk.

Growing Tips
Water deeply once or twice a week for the first full growing season, then weekly during hot, dry spells. Winterberry holly likes it on the damp side. Scatter a balanced, granular, organic or gradual-release fertilizer formulated for acid-preferring plants over the bed in early spring. Additional sulfur (an acidifying mineral) might be needed if the leaf color is yellowish.

Regional Advice and Care
The main trick is matching the right male to the right female. Bloom times must overlap. Some growers plant a female and suitable male in the same pot so you get fruits with "one" plant. Give ample room to avoid pruning, which can limit flowering and fruiting. Avoid shearing. To control size, thin and shorten branches at winter's end. Sever and remove any undesired colonizing shoots anytime.

Companion Planting and Design
Winterberry holly is a plain-Jane green bush until those berries begin ripening in September. Use them as backdrop or border shrubs so they come into play when foreground plants drop leaves or die back in fall. Backing them with tall evergreens helps show off the berries. Their tolerance for wet soil makes them good choices in any sunny or partly shaded damp, wet, or low-lying area.

Try These
Three 8- to 9-foot females won Pennsylvania Horticultural Society Gold Medal Awards: 'Scarlet O'Hara' (pollinate with 'Rhett Butler'), 'Winter Gold' ('Southern Gentleman'); and my favorite, Winter Red® ('Southern Gentleman'). Good 5- to 6-foot females are Berry Nice® ('Jim Dandy', 'Southern Gentleman'), 'Red Sprite' ('Jim Dandy', 'Apollo'), and 'Maryland Beauty' ('Jim Dandy').

Witch Hazel

Hamamelis species

Botanical Pronunciation
hahm-uh-MEE-liss

Bloom Period and Seasonal Color
February to March yellow, orange, red flowers;
yellow, gold, bronze, red-orange fall foliage

Mature Height × Spread
10 to 20 feet × 10 to 20 feet

Whether you consider it a small tree or a large shrub, witch hazel is another nearly trouble-free plant that's scarcely seen locally. This one is explainable, though. Witch hazel is such an early bloomer, even before forsythia in late winter, that it's long done flowering by the time people see it at the garden center in May. The fragrant flowers are unique; airy clusters of yellow, red, or bronze twisted fringes that some describe as "spidery." The other interest is brilliant fall foliage of yellow, gold, or red-orange. Two available species are U.S. natives, the common witch hazel (*Hamamelis virginiana*), which grows about 20 feet tall and flowers yellow in late fall, and vernal witch hazel (*Hamamelis vernalis*), a 10-foot colonizer with yellow late winter flowers.

When, Where, and How to Plant
Witch hazel flowers best in full sun but does well in part shade. It prefers damp, humus-rich, acidic soil but adapts to dry sites and heavier soil. Container-grown or field-dug plants are best planted in spring or early fall, but container-grown witch hazel can be planted throughout summer if roots are kept consistently damp. Work an inch or two of compost into the loosened top 10 to 12 inches of existing soil, plant an inch above grade, and cover the ground with 2 to 3 inches of wood chips or bark after planting. Keep mulch a few inches back from the trunk.

Growing Tips
Establish the roots by soaking weekly the whole first growing season, especially when it's dry. Then you'll likely need to water witch hazel only during extended hot, dry spells. It's fairly drought-tough. Feed a fertilizer formulated for acid-preferring plants in early spring.

Regional Advice and Care
You might see witch hazel blooming as early as late January. Give plants ample room and you may get away with no care after watering enough to establish the roots. If size control is needed, wait until flowers finish blooming, then remove excess or crossing branches and shorten overly long ones back to joints.

Companion Planting and Design
The 10- to 12-foot types are a good size for house corners. Bigger ones can be used as small, stand-alone trees in small front or back yards. Ideal sites for any are at back corners, borders, and other back-of-garden spots where witch hazel will stand out when most everything else is bare in front then fade into the background when the flower show begins in spring.

Try These
Hybrid witch hazel (*Hamamelis × intermedia*) offers some of the best bloomers and fall foliage, such as 'Arnold Promise' (yellow-red flowers, yellow-orange fall foliage, 18 to 20 feet), 'Jelena' (orange-gold flowers, yellow-red fall foliage, 12 to 15 feet), and 'Pallida' (light yellow flowers, yellow fall foliage, 15 to 18 feet). 'Early Bright' is a showy, 15-foot, yellow-blooming Chinese witch hazel (*Hamamelis mollis*) with orange-gold fall foliage.

TREES
FOR PENNSYLVANIA

Trees are the yard's framework, the biggest, most enduring living features that guide the rest of your landscaping.

Trees determine where you'll have shade, what views will be blocked (or highlighted), and what other plants will suit best nearby. Healthy, well placed trees are worth thousands of dollars each and add immeasurably to a house's curb appeal. Struggling trees in a wrong spot, however, can be a liability that can *cost* you thousands of dollars.

So more than any other plant, trees are a long-term investment worthy of astute homework.

A line of white oaks (*Quercus alba*)

Planning Your Trees

The most common tree mistake involves size—usually too big of a choice in too small of a space. You might adore oak or beech, but in a tiny yard, you're better off sticking with smaller species.

Pay close attention to *ultimate* sizes. Crabapple, dogwood, and redbud are examples of trees that stay in the 20- to 30-foot range. Most oak, maple, beech, and even birch can grow to double that.

Trees outgrowing the space can be pruned, but that gets expensive. It's also a leading source of neighbor spats when one person's branches or roots invade the other's yard.

The lessons? Err on the small side, stay back from property lines, and give adequate grow space near your own home.

Leaf-dropping or "deciduous" trees (the ones we'll discuss in this chapter) are excellent choices in the southern and western sections of the yard. There they'll shade the house (or patio) in summer while letting the sun through to warm the house in winter.

Trees also are useful for blocking unwanted views, such as streetlights, homes on the hill behind, or your neighbor's billboard collection. On the other hand, trees can accent views you like, such as framing a lake or mountain.

Those are all practical benefits. Just as important is the beauty trees offer, from fragrant spring flowers to bird-attracting fruits to brilliant fall foliage to interesting bark that embellishes the winter landscape.

Acer griseum (paperbark maple)

Planting Trees

You'll find trees in three forms: bare-root (no soil around the roots), balled-and-burlapped (field-grown, dug, and wrapped in burlap), or container-grown (in pots).

Plant bare-root trees in early spring, ideally just before the branches leaf out. Balled-and-burlapped trees are best planted in spring or early fall, while container-grown trees can be planted spring through early fall.

Loosen your soil before planting—at least three to five times the width of the rootball, but wider is even better. Dig no deeper than the depth of the ball to prevent the tree from sinking as the soil settles underneath. Too-deep planting is the leading cause of newly planted tree death.

To get it right, find the "root flare," which is where the trunk widens as it transitions into the roots. Note that the flare already might be covered by soil in the pot or burlap sack. Remove excess soil until you locate the flare. Then plant with the flare 1 to 2 inches *above* the soil grade.

Don't overimprove existing soil. It's fine to work an inch or two of compost into the loosened top 10 to 12 inches of your atrocious clay, but limit amending to 10 percent.

Once a tree is positioned in a hole, remove all wires, baskets, ropes, burlap, and anything else that could constrict its root growth. Backfill with soil, soak well, and cover the planting bed with 2 to 3 inches of wood chips or bark kept 3 to 4 inches away from the trunk.

Staking isn't necessary unless you're planting on a slope or very windy area. If you stake, remove it within a year.

Keep the soil consistently damp all around and to the bottom of the rootball for at least the first three years until the roots establish. It's better to soak deeply every week or two than to sprinkle every few days.

Site well, plant well, and you'll create beauty that generations to come will appreciate.

American Fringe Tree

Chionanthus virginicus

Botanical Pronunciation
key-oh-NAN-thus ver-JIN-ih-kus

Other Name Old man's beard

Bloom Period and Seasonal Color
White spring flowers; yellow fall foliage

Mature Height × Spread
15 to 20 feet × 15 to 20 feet

Despite being a trouble-free U.S. native, the American fringe tree is seldom used in Pennsylvania landscapes. When people see one in bloom, they're drawn by its shaggy, white, confetti-like flowers and usually exclaim, "What *is* that tree?!?" It's just not well known. The unusual blooms are reason enough to try one, but fringe trees also are a good size for small yards and have attractive yellow foliage in fall. Female trees produce blue fruits that birds like, but if you're just planting one female tree with no males nearby, expect little to no fruits. Fringe trees can be grown as single-stemmed small trees or as multiple-stemmed tall shrubs. Those shaggy flowers, which give the plant its nickname of "old man's beard," are also mildly fragrant.

When, Where, and How to Plant

Plant container-grown or field-dug, burlap-wrapped plants in spring or early fall. Container-grown trees can be planted throughout summer if roots are kept damp. Fringe trees are happy in full sun, part shade, and even in mostly shaded spots in the understory of taller shade trees. They prefer damp, loose, acidic soil, although they'll adapt to dry sites and somewhat rocky or clayish soil. Loosen soil as deep as the rootball and three to five times as wide, plant with the root flare just above grade, and mulch with 2 to 3 inches of wood chips or bark. Keep mulch at least 2 to 3 inches away from the trunk. Add sulfur if the soil is too alkaline.

Growing Tips

Water deeply once or twice a week for the first growing season, then soak weekly during hot, dry spells for the next two to three years. After that, watering usually isn't needed. Fertilizer also usually isn't needed if you're maintaining a 2-inch layer of mulch. Topdress with sulfur or an acidifying granular fertilizer if the leaves show signs of chlorosis (yellowing between the veins).

Regional Advice and Care

Shaping is critical in the early years because fringe trees can grow gangly when left to their own whims. Thin out misdirected, excess, and crossing branches back to their junction with larger branches or the trunk at the end of winter, then shorten overly long branches. For maximum flowering, wait until after bloom to prune.

Companion Planting and Design

Fringe trees are nice front-yard specimens or if sited at the corner of houses. Their skinny flowers and small leaves also make a non-messy choice next to patios and water gardens. Fringe-leaf bleeding heart, lamium, and creeping veronica are colorful perennial underplantings that overlap its bloom time.

Try These

'Emerald Knight' is a non-fruiting male with an upright habit. 'Spring Fleecing' is an improved bloomer. Chinese fringe tree (*Chionanthus retusus*) is a related non-native species that's also small, trouble-free, and similar in bloom, although two to three weeks earlier. It sometimes produces unwanted seedlings though.

Beech

Fagus species

Botanical Pronunciation
FAY-gus

Bloom Period and Seasonal Color
Summer, green, purple foliage; gold, bronze fall foliage

Mature Height × Spread
40 to 60 feet × 40 to 60 feet

If you've got space for a big shade tree, put this one on the list. Beech is a muscular tree with a classic, rounded canopy and brilliant gold to bronze fall foliage. It's a slow grower but ultimately works its way to 60 feet tall and wide. My favorite feature is the smooth gray trunk that reminds me of an elephant's leg. American beech (*Fagus grandiflora*) graces many a forest but isn't nearly as used in landscapes as European beech (*Fagus sylvatica*). One reason is that purple-leafed and weeping versions are available of European beech as well as one most everyone loves when they see it—the tricolor beech (*Fagus sylvatica* 'Roseomarginata'), a 30-footer with rose, cream, and green leaves in spring.

When, Where, and How to Plant
Plant container-grown or field-dug plants in spring or early fall. Container-grown trees can be planted throughout summer if its roots are kept damp. Beech needs lots of space, at least 40 to 50 feet across, which means locating them 20 to 25 feet from buildings and property lines. Full sun is best in damp, mildly acidic soil, but beech adapts to most sites, except soggy ones. Loosen soil as deep as the rootball and three to five times as wide, plant with the root flare just above grade, and mulch 2 to 3 inches deep. Keep the wood chip or bark mulch at least 2 to 3 inches away from the trunk.

Growing Tips
Water deeply once or twice a week for the first season, then soak weekly during hot, dry spells for the next two to three years. After that, watering usually isn't needed. Fertilizer also usually isn't needed if you're maintaining a 2-inch layer of mulch.

Regional Advice and Care
Avoid extra-hot sites (such as next to an asphalt parking lot or surrounded by brick buildings and concrete), especially in Zone 7 parts. American beech is more heat-tolerant. Prune to shape in the early years, mainly to eliminate multiple leaders (one main trunk only) and misdirected, excess, and crossing branches. Prune at the end of winter. Remove the lowest limbs as the tree ages to expose its smooth gray trunk.

Companion Planting and Design
Beech is a specimen shade tree for big yards only. Place one at a back corner with a bench underneath for a future shady getaway spot. Purple-leaf ones add color as well as shade, and weepers are ideal front-yard specimens. Grass dies out as the big roots grow, so underplant with a groundcover, such as leadwort, periwinkle, or liriope.

Try These
'Riversii' is an excellent 50-foot, purple-leaf European beech. 'Purple Fountain' is a beautiful, narrow, purple-leaf weeper (about 20 by 8 feet). Tricolor beech does best in afternoon shade to prevent leaf-edge browning. 'Fastigiata' is a columnar type that grows 20 to 30 feet tall and 6 feet around.

Black Gum

Nyssa sylvatica

Botanical Pronunciation
NISS-ah sil-VAT-ih-kah

Other Name Black tupelo

Bloom Period and Seasonal Color
Yellow, orange, red, maroon fall foliage

Mature Height × Spread
30 to 50 feet × 25 to 30 feet

Glowing fall foliage is the highlight of this U.S. native shade tree. Black gum leaves turn assorted shades of yellow, orange, red, or maroon in early fall. Every tree seems to color differently, and even the same tree can take on different shades in different autumns. It's one of the first trees to change color in fall, usually starting in September. Although the spring flowers are barely noticeable, they're attractive to bees. Female trees produce small oval fruits that ripen dark blue and provide food for birds, so besides the fall foliage, it's wildlife-friendly. Black gum is a slow-grower that can reach 50 feet tall. It tends to grow broadly pyramidal when young but then, like people, becomes more round with age.

When, Where, and How to Plant
Black gum has a deep taproot and is usually grown and sold in pots. Plant spring through early fall, and keep the roots damp through that first summer. Black gum prefers damp, mildly acidic soil and even grows in wet, poorly drained soil. It adapts to dry sites as well. Give this species ample room; black gum might grow slowly, but it'll eventually get big. Loosen soil as deep as the rootball and three to five times as wide. Make sure the root flare is planted just above grade, and mulch with 2 to 3 inches of wood chips or bark kept at least 2 to 3 inches away from the trunk.

Growing Tips
During the first season, water deeply once or twice a week, then soak weekly during hot, dry spells for the next two to three years. After that, watering usually isn't needed. Fertilizer also usually isn't needed if you're maintaining a 2-inch layer of mulch.

Regional Advice and Care
Black gum tolerates both heat and cold well. Leaves occasionally get fungal leaf-spot disease, which doesn't harm the tree but lessens the fall foliage show. Prune to shape in the early years, mainly to eliminate multiple leaders and any misdirected, excess, and crossing branches. Prune at the end of winter. Remove the lowest limbs as the tree ages to expose more of the trunk.

Companion Planting and Design
Black gum's tolerance for poor drainage makes it one of the best shade trees for a large, open, sunny area that stays wet or even soggy for days after a rain. It's ideal in a rain garden but adaptable enough to be a fall focal point in average to dry soil; just give it room to spread out. Underplant with daffodils for spring color. Sweet woodruff is a wet soil-tolerant groundcover.

Try These
'Wildfire' has purple-red new leaves and orange-red fall foliage. It won a Pennsylvania Horticultural Society Gold Medal Award. Green Gable™ is dense, upright, and resistant to leaf-spot disease. 'Zydeco Twist' is a novelty plant with twisted, contorted branches and leaf-spot resistance.

Carolina Silverbell

Halesia carolina

Botanical Pronunciation
hah-LEE-zee-ah kar-oh-LINE-ah

Bloom Period and Seasonal Color
White flowers in April; yellow fall foliage

Mature Height × Spread
30 to 40 feet × 25 to 35 feet

Carolina silverbell is a Southeast U.S. native tree usually found growing along stream banks or in the dappled shade of taller trees in nature. It's at its best in April when the tree blooms profusely just as the leaves open. The flowers are white and bell-shaped and hang from the stems. In fall, the leaves turn pale yellow, and curious, inch-long, four-winged pods mature and turn brown, hanging from the stems where the flowers were in spring. Bees like the flowers, and squirrels gather the pods. Carolina silverbell is a mid-sized, single-trunk or multistem tree, topping out in the 30- to 40-foot range. It's big enough to offer shade but small enough to suit where oak, beech, and maple trees will overwhelm the site.

When, Where, and How to Plant
Field-grown Carolina silverbell trees don't transplant well, so it's usually sold in pots. Plant spring through early fall in damp but well-drained, mildly acidic soil. Some shade protection from taller trees or buildings is perfect, but silverbell will grow in open sun to daylong shade. Loosen soil as deep as the rootball and three to five times as wide, plant with the root flare just above grade, and mulch with 2 to 3 inches of wood chips or bark. Don't pack mulch against the trunk.

Growing Tips
Soak your new silverbell once or twice a week for the first season then weekly during hot, dry spells for the next two to three years. After that, watering and fertilizer usually aren't needed if you're maintaining a 2-inch layer of mulch. Leaves may yellow between the veins if the soil is too alkaline; sulfur corrects it.

Regional Advice and Care
Site silverbells away from patios, walks, or anywhere you don't want seedpods dropping. Most seeds never sprout. Ones that do should be pulled *immediately* when they come up easily. Prune to shape in the early years to eliminate multiple leaders (if you want just one trunk) and to get rid of misdirected, excess, and crossing branches. Prune to where two branches meet. The best times are at the end of winter (when it's easiest to see what you're doing) or right after bloom (for maximum flowers).

Companion Planting and Design
Carolina silverbell serves as a good shade tree for smaller back yards. Place it out a window where the showy white bells can be seen in April. On larger lots, try a triangle of silverbells in the dappled shade near large trees or toward the front of a wooded edge. Underplant with pink-blooming deutzia or azalea or a sweetbox groundcover. Pink and purple hyacinths are color-coordinated bulbs that overlap bloom time.

Try These
'Rosea' and 'Arnold Pink' are pink-blooming silverbells. Two-wing silverbell (*Halesia diptera*) is a similar native species that's slightly smaller and has two-winged fall seedpods instead of four wings.

Crabapple

Malus hybrids and selections

Botanical Pronunciation
MAL-us

Bloom Period and Seasonal Color
Spring in white, pink, rosy red flowers; orange, yellow, red fall fruits; yellow fall foliage

Mature Height × Spread
10 to 25 feet × 15 to 25 feet

Crabapple is one of our most popular small trees for its prolific pink, white, or rose flowers in late spring. A second interest is the fall fruits, which make a good jelly for us or a nutritious winter dessert for birds. It's not a tree without trouble though. Several diseases and bugs threaten and there are complaints of "messy fruits." Thanks to widespread breeding efforts, new varieties sidestep almost all of those drawbacks. So if you're gun-shy due to leafless or ragged older crabapples you've seen, rethink your opinion with the varieties named here. Most types you'll find are hybrid selections with berry-sized fruits, many with U.S. native heritage. Compact, narrow, and burgundy-leafed varieties are all in the mix, and a few even have weeping habits.

When, Where, and How to Plant
You'll find crabapples in container-grown and field-dug, balled-and-burlapped versions. Spring and early fall are the best planting times, but if roots are kept damp you can still plant container-grown trees through summer. Crabapple flowers best in full sun in moist, mildly acidic soil. It'll tolerate rocky, heavier soil so long as drainage is good. Just avoid poorly drained spots. Loosen soil as deep as the rootball and three to five times as wide. Be sure the root flare is just above grade. After planting, mulch with 2 to 3 inches of wood chips or bark kept back away from the trunk.

Growing Tips
Crabapple is a drought-tough species. Just keep the roots damp the first three years until they mine their way into the soil, then you'll probably never need to

water again. If mulch is maintained fertilizer usually isn't necessary, but scattering balanced, granular organic or gradual-release fertilizer may help its first few springs.

Regional Advice and Care
Cut off "suckers" from around the trunk as soon as you see them. Japanese beetles and tent caterpillars sometimes cause cosmetic leaf damage (Neem oil and Bt are spray options, respectively). Rust, scab, and fireblight are diseases best prevented by picking disease-resistant varieties (see "Try These"). Prune out misdirected, excess, and crossing branches at the end of winter or right after bloom. Shorten branches after bloom. Finish all pruning by early June.

Companion Planting and Design
Crabapples are ideal front-yard specimens for sunny small to mid-sized landscapes. Narrower types can be used at house corners. Tulips make good bulb partners (bloom times overlap), and liriope, coralbells, and creeping phlox are good perennial partners.

Try These
These have won Pennsylvania Horticultural Society awards: 'Donald Wyman' (25-footer, white flowers, red fruits); 'Jewelberry' (12-footer, white flowers, red fruits); and 'Adirondack' (18-by-10-footer, white flowers, red fruits). 'Prairiefire' is a 20-footer with burgundy-tinged leaves, magenta flowers, and red fruits. Sugar Tyme® is another excellent, slender white-bloomer, and Centurion® is similar in size with rosy red flowers. Sargent crabapple (*Malus sargentii*) grows 8 to 10 feet tall and twice as wide.

Dogwood

Cornus species and selections

Botanical Pronunciation
KOR-nus

Bloom Period and Seasonal Color
White, pink, yellow flowers March to June; red, orange, black fruits; red, burgundy fall foliage

Mature Height × Spread
15 to 25 feet × 15 to 20 feet

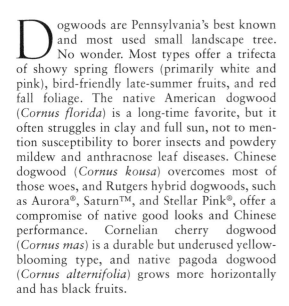

Dogwoods are Pennsylvania's best known and most used small landscape tree. No wonder. Most types offer a trifecta of showy spring flowers (primarily white and pink), bird-friendly late-summer fruits, and red fall foliage. The native American dogwood (*Cornus florida*) is a long-time favorite, but it often struggles in clay and full sun, not to mention susceptibility to borer insects and powdery mildew and anthracnose leaf diseases. Chinese dogwood (*Cornus kousa*) overcomes most of those woes, and Rutgers hybrid dogwoods, such as Aurora®, Saturn™, and Stellar Pink®, offer a compromise of native good looks and Chinese performance. Cornelian cherry dogwood (*Cornus mas*) is a durable but underused yellow-blooming type, and native pagoda dogwood (*Cornus alternifolia*) grows more horizontally and has black fruits.

When, Where, and How to Plant
A site in loose, rich, damp, and mildly acidic soil and morning sun and afternoon shade are the ingredients for dogwood's success. Chinese and cornelian cherry types are better choices for full sun and poor soil. Plant container-grown or field-dug, burlap-wrapped plants in spring or early fall. Container-grown trees can be planted throughout summer if roots are kept damp. Loosen soil as deep as the rootball and three to five times as wide. Work in an inch or 2 of compost, plant with the root flare just above grade, and mulch with 2 to 3 inches of wood chips or bark kept 2 to 3 inches away from the trunk.

Growing Tips
Water deeply once or twice a week for the first season, then weekly during hot, dry spells for the next two to three years, then every two weeks during hot, dry spells from then on. Fertilizer usually isn't needed if a mulch layer is maintained, but a scattering of balanced, granular organic or gradual-release fertilizer formulated for acid-preferring trees is helpful the first few springs.

Regional Advice and Care
Most dogwoods are woodland understory trees and suffer in the frying summer sun and poor soil of an open yard. Well-sited trees are less likely targets of the bugs and diseases that affect stressed dogwoods. Thin out misdirected, excess, and crossing branches and shorten overly long branches at the end of winter or right after flowering (to maximize the bloom).

Companion Planting and Design
Plant specimens in prime spots out of afternoon sun, such as in the shade or dappled light of taller trees or to the east of tall evergreens. Rutgers hybrids are good fruitless choices for patios. Tulips and azaleas bloom about the same time as American dogwoods.

Try These
'Appalachian Spring' (white) and 'Cherokee Chief' (pink) are disease-resistant American varieties. 'Greensleeves' and 'Moonbeam' are heavy-blooming Chinese types. For something different, try Japanese cornel dogwood 'Kintoki' (*Cornus officinalis*), which flowers yellow in March and is among the most durable dogwoods.

Flowering Cherry

Prunus species and selections

Botanical Pronunciation
PROO-nus

Bloom Period and Seasonal Color
March to June white, pink flowers; yellow, bronze fall foliage

Mature Height × Spread
15 to 35 feet × 20 to 35 feet

Along with crabapple and dogwood, flowering cherry is part of Pennsylvania's Big 3 small-tree triumvirate. Few trees are showier in bloom. After all, the flowering cherry is a huge tourist draw to Washington's Tidal Basin every spring. April is the main show month for the white or pink flowers, some of which are double-petaled and fragrant. Flowering cherries differ from edible cherries in that they flower more heavily and have much smaller or no fruits. The yellow or bronze fall foliage is nice, although not as eye-popping as a maple or stewartia. The metallic dark bronze bark with horizontal striping adds winter interest. Growth habits are mostly vase-shaped. Some types are more rounded (especially with age), while weeping forms make popular front house-corner specimens.

When, Where, and How to Plant
Plant container-grown or field-dug plants in spring or early fall. Plant container-grown trees throughout summer; just keep those roots damp. It flowers best in full sun with moist, mildly acidic soil. Flowering cherries tolerate rocky, heavier soil so long as drainage is good. To plant, loosen soil three to five times as deep as the rootball and work in an inch of compost if your soil is poor, plant so the root flare is just above grade, and mulch with 2 to 3 inches of wood chips or bark. Always keep mulch away from plant trunks.

Growing Tips
Flowering cherry is reasonably drought-tough once the roots become established in three to four years. Keep the root zone damp but never soggy in those

years. As with crabapple, cherry usually doesn't need supplemental fertilizer, especially if mulch is maintained, but it won't sulk if you scatter a balanced fertilizer the first few springs.

Regional Advice and Care
Flowering cherries tend to live shorter lives due to borer insects and diseases such as canker and black knot. Japanese beetles and tent caterpillars often cause cosmetic leaf-chewing damage. Treat or accept these as a floral-show tradeoff. Cut off "suckers" that shoot up around the trunk whenever you see them. If needed, thin branches at the end of winter and shorten branches after bloom. Or do all pruning right after flowering for maximum bloom.

Companion Planting and Design
Flowering cherry makes a striking allée when lining driveways or walks. It's also a good specimen in a small, sunny front yard. Try a weeper next to a water garden or patio. Hyacinths, Siberian squill, and glory-of-the-snow are good bulb partners.

Try These
Prunus × *yedoensis* 'Yoshino' is the pink-blooming 30-footer that dominates D.C's Tidal Basin. It's happy in Pennsylvania too. *Prunus serrulata* 'Kwanzan' is a double-petaled, pink 30-footer. *Prunus* × *incam* 'Okame' is an early bloomer (pink) and won a Pennsylvania Horticultural Society Gold Medal Award. Higan cherry 'Snow Fountain' (*Prunus subhirtella*) is a 12-foot, white-blooming weeper, and 'Autumnalis' is a vase-shaped Higan variation that reblooms pinkish white in fall.

Ginkgo

Ginkgo biloba

Botanical Pronunciation
GINK-oh by-LOE-bah

Other Name Maidenhair tree

Bloom Period and Seasonal Color
Golden fall foliage

Mature Height × Spread
40 to 60 feet × 20 to 40 feet

If you did one of those leaf-hunting projects in elementary school, odds are the fan-shaped leaf of the ginkgo was in the collection. This isn't a showy tree in bloom, but the telltale leaves, the upright habit, and the brilliant golden fall foliage make it a nice mid-sized addition to the landscape. While ginkgo can grow 50 feet tall and almost as wide, narrow varieties stay within a 20-foot span. This is also an extremely durable tree as evidenced by its survival along New York City streets and the fact that it's been around since dinosaur times. Ginkgo's main downside is the very smelly odor of fruits that fall from female trees, which is usually not a concern since garden centers sell only males.

When, Where, and How to Plant
First, make sure you're buying a male. Then plant in spring or early fall (container-grown or field-dug plants) or even in summer (if you're going with a container-grown tree). Ginkgo does best in full sun to light shade but handles nearly any soil. Just avoid soggy sites. Loosen soil as deep as the rootball and three to five times as wide. Be sure to set the plant so that the root flare is just above grade, and finish off with 2 or 3 inches of wood chips or bark (but not right up against the trunk).

Growing Tips
Ginkgo has excellent drought-tolerance once its roots establish. Water deeply weekly the first year and every couple of weeks during hot, dry spells for the next two to three years. After that, you're off the hook. Fertilizer also usually isn't needed if you're maintaining a 2- to 3-inch layer of organic mulch.

Regional Advice and Care
Give ginkgo enough space to spread out, and water it to establish the roots; it'll outlive you without asking anything else in return. Bugs and diseases are unlikely. Prune to shape in the early years, mainly to eliminate multiple leaders (one main trunk is best) and any misdirected, excess, and crossing branches. Prune to joints (where two branches meet). The best time to prune is the end of winter before new leaves emerge.

Companion Planting and Design
Ginkgo's ability to tolerate urban stress makes it a good street tree or specimen near asphalt or concrete as well as a standalone specimen in a sunny, open yard. Narrow types are good choices for lining driveways or borders. Barrenwort, hostas, and hellebores are good perennial underplantings. Russian cypress is a good evergreen groundcover.

Try These
'Autumn Gold' is a fruitless male that grows 50 by 30 with rich gold fall foliage. 'Princeton Sentry' and Golden Colonnade™ are fruitless (male) narrow varieties, growing 45 to 50 feet tall but only 20 feet across. 'Jade Butterflies' is a slow-growing, compact ginkgo (12 by 10 in 20 years)—if you can get your hands on one.

Golden Rain Tree

Koelreuteria paniculata

Botanical Pronunciation
kole-roo-TEER-ee-ah puh-nick-you-LAY-tah

Bloom Period and Seasonal Color
June to September yellow flowers;
orange-yellow fall foliage

Mature Height × Spread
30 to 35 feet × 25 to 35 feet

Golden rain tree is one of the few summer-flowering trees (and mid- to late summer at that). The blooms of this Chinese/Japanese native consist of small yellow flowers that hang in clusters. To me, they look like exploding stars. The petals drop (the "golden rain" part) to make a golden carpet underneath. The toothy-edged leaflets are green in summer and orange-yellow in fall. Golden rain tree is a tough customer that'll take most anything you throw at it: heat, drought, clay, sand, wind, acidic or alkaline soil, and polluted air. The deal-killer for some is the lantern-shaped pods that turn brown in late summer and emit pea-sized black seeds that can sprout. The look can be ratty, and the seeding may create work to pull them out.

When, Where, and How to Plant
Container-grown trees can go in the ground spring to early fall. Field-dug, burlap-wrapped ones are best planted in spring *or* early fall. Golden rain tree grows best in full sun to light shade in damp, loose soil. Loosen soil three to five times as wide as the rootball but only as deep. Improve lousy soil by working in an inch of compost. Then plant with the root flare just above grade, and mulch with 2 to 3 inches of wood chips or bark kept 2 to 3 inches away from the trunk.

Growing Tips
Soak the rootball every week or two for the first three years until the roots establish. After that, watering usually isn't needed. Neither is fertilizer if a 2- to 3-inch mulch layer is maintained.

Regional Advice and Care
The main tradeoff for the durability and summer color is raking up the fallen pods and/or pulling self-sowed seedlings. The sooner you get them, the better. The "pop-ups" occur mainly right underneath the canopy, not all over the yard or neighborhood. Other than that, just prune to shape the tree in the early years. Eliminate multiple leaders so you end up with a single trunk, and thin out any misdirected, excess, and crossing branches at the end of winter.

Companion Planting and Design
Golden rain tree is attractive enough to be used as a specimen in open yards and tough enough to grow as a street tree in urban settings. Its 30-foot, mid-range size also makes it compact enough for all but small yards. St. Johnswort is a good shrubby underplanting. Red daylilies, red coreopsis, or red mums are color-coordinated perennials.

Try These
You'll likely run into only the straight species, which is fine. One variety, 'September', is a particularly late-season (September) bloomer that won a Pennsylvania Horticultural Society Gold Medal Award. It's slightly less winter-hardy than the species, though, and is best limited to Zones 6 and 7. Golden Candle™ is a columnar variety, growing 30 feet tall and 4 feet across, but it's not widely available.

Hawthorn

Crataegus species

Botanical Pronunciation
krah-TEE-gus

Bloom Period and Seasonal Color
May to early June white flowers; red, orange-red fruits; burgundy, gold, bronze fall foliage

Mature Height × Spread
20 to 30 feet × 25 to 35 feet

Hawthorn is a family of mostly native mid-sized trees offering three seasonal interests: small white flowers in May, attractive burgundy to red-gold fall foliage, and red to orange-red berry-sized fruits that mature in early fall and feed birds in winter. Hawthorn is also durable in heat and drought and isn't picky about soil. With all of that going for it, you'd think there would be a hawthorn in every yard. But as the name suggests, most species have thorns . . . some big, sharp ones too. And most types are susceptible to potentially fatal rust and fireblight diseases. Fortunately a few hawthorn varieties are disease-resistant *and* thornless, or nearly so. Stick with these, and you'll get the pros without the cons.

When, Where, and How to Plant

Hawthorn is best suited for full-sun locations in damp, mildly acidic soil, although it'll tolerate rocky, heavy, or dry soil and urban conditions. Plant container-grown or field-dug plants in spring or early fall. Container-grown trees can be planted throughout summer if roots are kept damp. To plant, loosen soil as deep as the rootball and three to five times as wide, and then set the tree with the root flare just above grade. Cover the ground with 2 to 3 inches of wood chips or bark kept back off the trunk.

Growing Tips

Water deeply once a week for the first season then weekly during hot, dry spells for the next two to three years. After that, watering usually isn't needed. Neither is fertilizer if a 2- to 3-inch mulch layer is maintained.

Regional Advice and Care

The main disease threat of cedar/hawthorn rust has dual hosts, so avoid Eastern red cedar (*Juniperus virginiana*) nearby. Cut off suckers as soon as they appear around the base. Eliminate competing leaders when the tree is young, and thin out misdirected, excess, and crossing branches at the end of winter or right after bloom. Shorten branches, if needed, after bloom, being careful to leave enough flower clusters to create fruits later.

Companion Planting and Design

Hawthorn's tough-site tolerance makes it a good choice as a street tree or for lining driveways or hot, rocky banks. It's showy enough as a specimen in sunny front or back yards or as a centerpiece of a bird-attracting garden. Golden creeping sedum is a colorful and equally durable underplanting.

Try These

Everybody's favorite is the 20-foot native 'Winter King' (*Crataegus viridis*), which resists disease, has few thorns, and plenty of red fruits. It won a Pennsylvania Horticultural Society Gold Medal Award. English hawthorn 'Crimson Cloud' (*Crataegus laevigata*) has red flowers and few thorns. Native cockspur hawthorn 'Crusader' (*Crataegus crus-galli*) is thornless and especially heat- and drought-tough. Washington hawthorn (*Crataegus phaenopyrum*) is native but has long, stiff thorns and limited rust-resistance.

Hornbeam

Carpinus species

Botanical Pronunciation
kar-PINE-us

Other Name Musclewood

Bloom Period and Seasonal Color
Non-showy yellow-green flowers in March;
yellow, orange-red fall foliage

Mature Height × Spread
20 to 50 feet × 20 to 40 feet

You'll find two species of this mid-sized shade tree, a European version (*Carpinus betulus*) and the native American hornbeam (*Carpinus caroliniana*), sometimes called "musclewood" for its smooth gray trunk that looks like it's flexing its thigh muscles. Both are slow growing, a bit taller than wide, and trouble-free. European hornbeam grows bigger (40 to 50 feet) and has yellow fall foliage, while American hornbeam stays closer to 25 to 30 feet and has orange-red fall foliage. The early spring flowers aren't showy, but the early fall winged nutlets offer late-season wildlife interest. Hummingbird fans take note: Hornbeams are a favorite nesting species of these little birds. Hornbeam leaves are 3 to 4 inches long with distinctive ribs. It tolerates frequent, heavy pruning and is sometimes sheared into hedges or tunnels.

When, Where, and How to Plant
Field-dug plants are best planted in spring. Plant container-grown trees spring through early fall. Keep roots consistently damp the first summer. American hornbeam is usually found in moist, partly to mostly shaded sites, so similar landscape spots are ideal. Both European and American types adapt to sun or shade, to acidic or alkaline soil, and to moist or dry sites. Loosen soil as deep as the rootball and three to five times as wide, work in an inch or two of compost, and plant with the root flare just above grade, and mulch. Keep mulch at least 2 to 3 inches away from the trunk.

Growing Tips
During the first season, water deeply once or twice weekly to encourage consistent root growth. Then soak weekly the next two to three years during hot, dry spells. After that, water is needed only during drought. Fertilizer usually isn't needed if you're maintaining a mulch layer.

Regional Advice and Care
Prune to shape in the early years to eliminate multiple leaders (assuming you want just one trunk) and to get rid of misdirected, excess, and crossing branches. This is one of the few trees that tolerates shearing, which encourages denser growth for screening. Prune or shear at the end of winter before the leaves emerge.

Companion Planting and Design
Hornbeam is an ideal mid-sized shade tree where the soil is damp or where the light is less than full sun. Use as a shade tree when the yard isn't big enough to support an oak, beech, or large maple. Narrow types are good choices at house corners, patio corners, and as a backdrop to water gardens. Plant a line of hornbeams 6 to 8 feet apart and shear for a European-style tree hedge. Underplant with crocus, Siberian squill, or glory-of-the-snow for spring color.

Try These
'Fastigiata' and 'Columnaris' are narrow (30 by 20 feet) European hornbeams. Emerald Avenue™ is more pyramidal and has dark green leaves. Ball O'Fire™ is a compact American hornbeam with showy red fall foliage. Try a 25-foot Japanese hornbeam (*Carpinus japonica*) if you can find one.

Japanese Tree Lilac

Syringa reticulata

Botanical Pronunciation
sur-ING-gah reh-tick-you-LAY-tah

Bloom Period and Seasonal Color
White flowers in May to June

Mature Height × Spread
20 to 30 feet × 15 to 20 feet

Japanese tree lilac is not nearly so well known as old-fashioned French lilacs (*Syringa vulgaris*), the big, multistemmed bushes with the fragrant and usually purple May flowers. This Asian native grows taller and is most often used as a single-trunk small tree, topping out around 20 to 30 feet tall and 15 to 20 feet across. Japanese tree lilac blooms two to three weeks later than French lilacs with snowy clusters of creamy white flowers. It's not quite as fragrant as French types, and not everyone agrees the scent is pleasant. The big plus, though, is that Japanese tree lilac is a tough, durable, survivor plant that largely overcomes the powdery mildew and borer threats of French types. Its size also makes it a good choice for small yards.

When, Where, and How to Plant

Japanese tree lilac flowers best in full sun and prefers damp, mildly acidic soil, although it'll tolerate rocky, heavy, sandy, or dry soil, and urban conditions. Just avoid soggy sites. Container-grown trees can be planted spring through early fall. Field-dug plants are best planted in spring or early fall. To plant, loosen soil three to five times as wide as the rootball but only as deep, and plant with the root flare just above grade. Mulch with 2 to 3 inches of wood chips or bark kept a few inches away from the trunk.

Growing Tips

Water deeply once a week for the first season then weekly during hot, dry spells for the next two to three years to establish the roots. After that, neither water nor fertilizer is usually needed, especially if you're maintaining a 2- to 3-inch mulch layer underneath. The browned-out flower clusters detract from the summer look of this tree, so if that bugs you, cut off the flowers anytime after peak bloom.

Regional Advice and Care

Zone 7 is at the southern end of Japanese tree lilac's range, so a cooler, slightly shaded spot is best in the hottest parts of the state. Cut off any "suckers" that pop up from around the base. Eliminate competing leaders when the tree is young to maintain a single trunk, and thin out misdirected, excess, and crossing branches at the end of winter or right after bloom. Shorten branches, if needed, immediately after bloom.

Companion Planting and Design

Japanese tree lilac's durability and adaptability make it a good choice as a street tree or for lining driveways. It's showy enough in bloom as a specimen in sunny front or back yards. Catmint is a blue-flowering, sun-loving perennial that blooms at the same time and makes a good underplanting.

Try These

'Ivory Silk' is the most available choice and is a 20-footer that flowers heavier than the species. It won a Pennsylvania Horticultural Society Gold Medal Award. 'Summer Snow' is slightly smaller and even heavier in bloom, if you can find it.

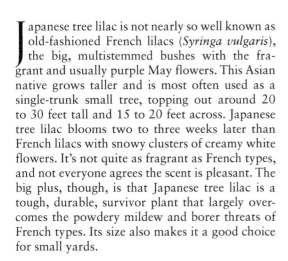

Katsura

Cercidiphyllum japonicum

Botanical Pronunciation
sur-sid-ih-FILL-um jah-PON-ih-kum

Bloom Period and Seasonal Color
Non-showy reddish green spring flowers;
yellow to orange-gold fall foliage

Mature Height × Spread
40 to 60 feet × 35 to 60 feet

Looking for something a little different in shade trees? Katsura is an Asian species that offers a troublefree option with a stately, rounded habit, and 40 to 60 feet tall and wide size. It's underused mainly because it's just not well known. The leaves are heart-shaped and emerge reddish purple in color, turning to light green in summer and then to yellow or orange-gold in fall. A curious side feature is that the fall leaves have a sweet scent when crushed that most describe as something akin to burnt sugar or cotton candy. Spring flowers are reddish green but not significantly showy. Particularly graceful are several weeping versions of katsura tree, which grow more like 15 to 25 feet tall and 12 to 15 feet across.

When, Where, and How to Plant
Field-dug, burlap-wrapped plants are best planted in spring. Container-grown trees can be planted spring through early fall, but be careful to keep summer-planted ones especially well watered. Katsura does best in loose, damp soil and in areas protected from wind and direct afternoon sun. That prevents scorching and browning of young leaf margins. However, katsura usually adapts well to full sun and clayish soil. To plant, loosen soil as deep as the rootball and three to five times as wide, plant with the root flare just above grade, and cover ground with 2 to 3 inches of wood chips or bark kept back away from the trunk.

Growing Tips
Young katsuras appreciate regular water but become more tolerant of dry soil once their roots establish. Water deeply once or twice a week for the first season, then cut back to weekly soakings when it's hot and dry for the next two to three years. Fertilizer usually isn't needed if you maintain a 2- to 3-inch layer of mulch.

Regional Advice and Care
With wind protection to avoid leaf-browning and adequate water in the early years, katsura can go on to become a long-lived, no-care specimen tree. Prune to shape in the early years by eliminating multiple leaders and any misdirected, excess, and crossing branches. The best time to prune is at the end of winter. Remove the lowest limbs as the tree ages to expose the brown, slightly shaggy bark.

Companion Planting and Design
Weeping katsura is one of the most elegant specimen trees for front yards, house corners, water gardens, and other prominent focal points. Standard katsuras make a good shade tree for large back yards, especially in a back corner with a bench underneath. Japanese forest grass, liriope, or sedge are good grassy partners that contrast texturally.

Try These
The straight species is the only option you'll likely find for a full-sized, rounded katsura tree. 'Morioka Weeping' is a graceful, 35- by 20-foot weeper that won a Pennsylvania Horticultural Society award. 'Pendulum' and 'Amazing Grace' are other good weeping forms that are slightly shorter and skinnier.

Littleleaf Linden

Tilia cordata

Botanical Pronunciation
TILL-ee-ah kor-DATE-ah

Bloom Period and Seasonal Color
Creamy yellow flowers in June; yellow fall foliage

Mature Height × Spread
60 to 80 feet × 30 to 45 feet

Here's another shade tree choice to expand diversity beyond overworked maples and pin oaks. Littleleaf linden is a European species that grows into a dense, pyramidal form, about one-third taller than wide (plan for 60 by 40 feet). The creamy yellow, hanging, and mildly fragrant June flowers attract both bees and butterflies. Small nutlets form by late summer. While the wide, dark green, toothy-edged leaves are smaller than other lindens, they're not exactly little . . . nearly the size of a saltine cracker. The leaves turn a mellow shade of yellow in fall. Littleleaf linden's best trait is that it's a survivor. It tolerates heat, clay, and drought better than most trees. It also takes frequent and heavy pruning and is sometimes used as a tall hedge.

When, Where, and How to Plant
Plant container-grown or field-dug plants in spring or early fall. Container-grown trees can be planted throughout summer if its roots are kept damp. Full sun is best. Littleleaf linden is adaptable to most soils—moist or dry, acidic or alkaline, and sandy to clayish. Dig a hole three to five times as wide as the rootball but only as deep. Set the tree with the root flare just above grade. Then mulch, keeping the mulch back away from the trunk.

Growing Tips
Soak deeply once a week for the first growing season then weekly the next two to three years whenever it's hot and dry. After that, linden is drought-tough enough to make it on natural rainfall alone.

Fertilizer usually isn't needed if you're maintaining a mulch layer.

Regional Advice and Care
Linden is a Japanese beetle favorite. Chewing damage is cosmetic and temporary, but you can apply Neem oil to repel beetles in bad years. Aphids are another occasional cosmetic bug problem; soap sprays usually control bad outbreaks. Prune to shape in the early years by eliminating multiple leaders and any excess or wayward branches. The best time to prune is end of winter. Remove the lowest limbs as the tree ages to expose the grayish brown trunk.

Companion Planting and Design
Littleleaf linden is a good, big-yard shade tree, but since its spread isn't quite as broad as many other shade trees, it's doable in mid-sized yards. Consider one at a back corner with a bench underneath. Or plant a grove or three or more in a large, open, sunny field. Boxwood and cherry laurel are good broadleaf evergreens for underplanting.

Try These
Greenspire® is a nicely shaped, slightly smaller version with good fall color. Corinthian® is a tad smaller, and Summer Sprite® checks in at around 20 feet. If you're going native, try the similar American linden or basswood (*Tilia americana*) or a handsome, 60-foot hybrid of it called 'Redmond'. Silver linden (*Tilia tomentosa*) is a 50-footer with silvery leaf undersides and less interest to Japanese beetles.

Magnolia

Magnolia species and hybrids

Botanical Pronunciation
mag-NO-lee-ah

Bloom Period and Seasonal Color
March to June white, pink, rose, lavender, yellow flowers; some have glossy evergreen foliage

Mature Height × Spread
12 to 60 feet × 10 to 60 feet

Where to begin? Let's just say magnolias aren't only for the South. Saucer magnolia (*Magnolia × soulangeana*) is most common, grows 30 feet tall and wide, and produces rosy pink, fragrant, tulip-shaped flowers in April. It's hardy statewide. Star magnolia (*Magnolia stellata*) is earliest to bloom (white in March), grows a compact 12 to 15 feet and is hardy statewide. Loebner magnolia (*Magnolia × loebneri*) is a statewide-hardy, 20-foot hybrid with pinkish white March flowers. Zones 6 and 7 can do native, 40- to 60-foot evergreen southern magnolias (*Magnolia grandiflora*) with their colossal, fragrant pink to purplish late spring flowers. The native sweetbay magnolia (*Magnolia virginiana*) is a statewide-hardy, 20-footer with semi-evergreen leaves, shade and wet-soil tolerance, and fragrant creamy yellow flowers in early summer.

When, Where, and How to Plant

Most magnolias grow best in full sun to light shade, although some (especially sweetbay) tolerate shade and damp soil. Ideal soil is loose, rich, well drained, and slightly acidic. Plant field-dug, burlap-wrapped trees in spring and container-grown trees spring through early summer. Keep the roots consistently damp the first summer. Loosen soil before planting as deep as the rootball and three to five times as wide. Work in an inch or two of compost. Then plant with the root flare just above grade, and finish by mulching 2 to 3 inches with wood chips or bark. Keep mulch 2 to 3 inches away from the trunk.

Growing Tips

Water deeply once or twice a week for the first season, then soak weekly during hot, dry spells for the next two to three years, especially sweetbay types. After that, watering and fertilizer usually aren't needed if you're maintaining a 2- to 3-inch mulch layer.

Regional Advice and Care

In colder parts of Pennsylvania, look for sites that offer wind protection and the least likelihood of a late frost, which can kill magnolia flower buds. Prune off any dead wood at the end of winter, but wait until after flowering to make shaping, thinning, or shortening cuts.

Companion Planting and Design

Magnolia is as showy in bloom as any tree, so this is a front-and-center species for your prime real estate. Most are fragrant too. Bigger ones need big yards, but some types are as small as 12 to 15 feet and suitable for small yards. Underplant with blue, purple, or deep pink bulbs (Siberian squill, hyacinth, tulip) for a coordinated spring show.

Try These

Little Girl hybrids, such as 'Ann', 'Betty', and 'Jane' are three diminutive 15-footers. 'Butterflies' is an 18-foot yellow-bloomer (May to June). 'Daybreak' is a deep pink 30-footer (May). 'Bracken's Brown Beauty' (Zones 6 to 7) and 'Edith Bogue' are evergreen southern types with tan leaf undersides. 'Little Gem' is a 20-foot compact southern magnolia. Moonglow® is an improved, heavier-blooming sweetbay variety, and 'Centennial' is a white, double-petaled star magnolia.

Maple

Acer species

Botanical Pronunciation
ACE-er

Bloom Period and Seasonal Color
Yellow, creamy-green, or red flowers in March to June; red, orange, or yellow fall foliage

Mature Height × Spread
3 to 60 feet × 6 to 50 feet

While flaming fall color is the main attraction of maple, it's not the only interest. Smaller ones offer intriguing forms and branch structure, bigger ones give great shade, and a few have colorful or peeling bark for winter interest. This is a large and diverse family. Native red maples (*Acer rubrum*) are classic 50-foot shade trees with red fall foliage and a tolerance for wet soil. Japanese maples (*A. palmatum*) make some of the showiest small specimens, especially cut-leaf, umbrella-shaped beauties such as 'Tamukeyama', 'Crimson Queen', and 'Waterfall'. Paperbark maple (*A. griseum*) is my favorite for its cinnamon-colored peeling bark, red/orange/gold fall foliage, and slow-growing 30-foot size. Trident maple (*A. buergerianum*) and three-flower maple (*A. triflorum*) are compact enough for small-yard shade and fall glory.

When, Where, and How to Plant
Plant container-grown or field-dug plants in spring or early fall. Container-grown trees can be planted throughout summer if roots are kept damp. Most maples prefer full sun to light shade in loose, moist, slightly acidic soil. Loosen soil as deep as the rootball and three to five times as wide, plant with the root flare just above grade, and mulch with 2 or 3 inches of wood chips or bark. Keep mulch a few inches away from the trunk.

Growing Tips
Water regularly the first three to four years to help roots establish. Japanese types are thin-leafed and appreciate water during hot, dry spells even beyond the fourth year. If you see leaf edges browning in summer, you've probably been lax in the hose department. Fertilizer usually isn't needed if you maintain mulch.

Regional Advice and Care
Many Japanese types are borderline winter-hardy (at best) in Zone 5. Thin-leaf types (especially Japanese cut-leafs) appreciate a wind-protected site in all zones. Aphids, scale, borers, and Japanese beetles are potential bug problems. Anthracnose, root rot, and verticillium wilt are possible diseases. Prune to shape in the early years, mainly to eliminate multiple leaders and misdirected, excess, and crossing branches. The best time to prune is January or February before the sap flows. Remove the lowest limbs as trees age.

Companion Planting and Design
Japanese types are small enough for house corners, water gardens, and courtyards. Place great "barkers" like paperbark maple and coralbark maple (*A. palmatum* 'Sango Kaku') where you can see them out a favorite window in winter. Use red maples for shade in larger yards; trident and three flower maples for shade in smaller ones.

Try These
Redpointe®, Red Sunset®, and October Glory® are some of the best red maples, and 'Columnare', 'Armstrong', and 'Bowhall' are columnar forms. 'Autumn Blaze' is a durable 50-foot hybrid good for hot, dry, open spots. 'Red Feather' and 'Viridis' are two excellent weeping, cut-leaf Japanese maples. Full-moon maple (*A. japonicum*) is a 20-foot maple for shadier spots.

Oak

Quercus species

Botanical Pronunciation
KWERK-us

Bloom Period and Seasonal Color
Tan catkins in spring; red, gold, bronze
fall foliage

Mature Height × Spread
50 to 80 feet × 50 to 80 feet

If you've got space, oak is the shade tree king. Oaks tower over all else, usually reaching 50 feet tall and wide—and beyond. Most home landscape oaks are U.S. natives that provide food (acorns) to birds and mammals as well as shade, privacy, and fall foliage for people. Native pin oak (*Quercus palustris*) is our most-used shade tree, but there are better oaks. The native red oak (*Quercus rubra*) runs into fewer bug and disease troubles, has reddish new leaves, and red fall foliage. The native white oak (*Quercus alba*) has rounded leaf edges, burnt-red fall foliage, and is a Pennsylvania Horticultural Society Gold Medal Award. Native willow oak (*Quercus phellos*) has narrow leaves and yellow fall foliage, but it isn't reliably winter-hardy in Zone 5.

When, Where, and How to Plant
Some oaks don't transplant well; start with smaller ones and be patient. Container-grown or field-dug plants are best planted in spring. Early fall is second best. Keep roots consistently damp the first season. Oaks prefer sunny, open locations with moist, slightly acidic, and well-drained soil. Loosen soil as deep as the rootball and three to five times as wide, plant with the root flare just above grade, and mulch. Keep mulch back away from trunks.

Growing Tips
Soak weekly the first season then weekly during hot, dry spells for the next two to three years. Once established, most oaks are drought-tough and won't need supplemental water. Fertilizer usually isn't needed, but watch for chlorosis (leaves yellow

between the veins) as an indication that the soil isn't acidic enough.

Regional Advice and Care
Stick with types sold locally or mentioned here since not all oaks are winter-hardy in Pennsylvania. Surround trunks of young oaks with hardware-cloth (wire) cylinders to prevent deer and rodent damage. Many oaks are susceptible to a host of occasional and mostly non-fatal bugs and diseases, including gypsy moths, midges, wasps that cause bumps ("galls") on the leaves, scale, oakworm, root rot, and bacterial leaf scorch. Prune young trees in mid- to late winter to eliminate multiple leaders and excess or wayward branches. Remove the lowest limbs as trees age.

Companion Planting and Design
An oak in a large back yard will give shade and enclosure for generations to come. A grove of them will create your own eventual mini-forest and a perfect site for a future shade garden. Gradually eliminate lawn as their shade spreads, and incorporate oakleaf hydrangea, fothergilla, viburnum, hosta, liriope, and other dry-shade species.

Try These
Few named varieties exist. One is Green Pillar®, a 50- by 15-foot columnar pin oak with red fall foliage. Besides the above-named species, the Asian sawtooth oak (*Quercus acutissima*) is a smaller option (40 feet). Native swamp white oak (*Quercus bicolor*) tolerates wet soil, and native scarlet oak (*Quercus coccinea*) has nice red fall foliage.

Parrotia

Parrotia persica

Botanical Pronunciation
pah-ROE-tee-ah PUR-sih-kah

Other Name Persian ironwood

Bloom Period and Seasonal Color
Small, rosy red flower clusters in March and April; orange-gold to purple fall foliage

Mature Height × Spread
20 to 35 feet × 20 to 25 feet

A *what*? Few people have ever even heard of this trouble-free, densely leafed mid-sized tree with four seasons of interest. Parrotia hails from Iran but finds Pennsylvania's soil and weather to its liking. Button-sized, pincushion clusters of rosy red flowers start the season, followed by reddish purple, slightly toothed new leaves that turn glossy green in summer, sometimes with faint maroon edges. Fall is prime time when the foliage turns neon orange-gold with occasional hints of purple. It's one of the last woody plants to turn color and holds those brilliant leaves into December most years. As the tree ages, bark flakes off in a mottled, Dalmatian-like pattern for winter interest. Parrotia can be grown either as a single-trunk, 30-foot tree or as a large, multistemmed "bush."

When, Where, and How to Plant
Parrotia grows best in full sun to light shade in loose, damp, mildly acidic soil but adapts well to rocky, heavy, sandy, or dry soil, and the heat and air pollution of urban sites. Avoid soggy sites. Plant container-grown trees spring through early fall. Field-dug, burlap-wrapped plants are best planted in spring *or* early fall. To plant, loosen soil three to five times as wide as the rootball but only as deep and set the tree with the root flare just above the soil grade. Mulch after planting with 2 to 3 inches of wood chips or bark kept 2 to 3 inches away from the trunk.

Growing Tips
Parrotia has good drought-tolerance and usually doesn't need supplemental water once the roots establish. For the first three to four years, water deeply once a week whenever rain doesn't moisten the soil all around and to just below the rootball. Fertilizer usually isn't needed if the 2- to 3-inch mulch layer is maintained.

Regional Advice and Care
Parrotia is winter-hardy throughout Pennsylvania and needs no special treatment. It's unlikely to encounter bug or disease troubles, except possibly for some early-summer leaf-chewing by Japanese beetles. Neem oil is an organic spray that may repel them if the cosmetic damage exceeds your tolerance. Cut off "suckers" that pop up around the base and eliminate competing leaders if you're trying to grow parrotia as a single-trunk tree. Otherwise, thin out suckers and misdirected, excess, and crossing branches as desired at winter's end.

Companion Planting and Design
Parrotia is tough enough for punishing duty, such as a street tree, along driveways and sidewalks, or in sunny, open yards. It's small enough to serve as a fall-interest, front- or backyard specimen, even in limited-space suburban landscapes. A line of parrotia makes a good border planting in larger yards.

Try These
Not all garden centers even carry this underused species, much less any of the few varieties (including a narrower and a weeping type) that are floating around the trade. The straight species is perfectly fine. Grab one if you see one.

Redbud

Cercis canadensis

Botanical Pronunciation
SUR-siss kan-ah-DEN-siss

Other Name Judas tree

Bloom Period and Seasonal Color
Pink, rosy pink, lavender, white flowers March to April; yellow, yellow-orange fall foliage

Mature Height × Spread
15 to 25 feet × 20 to 25 feet

Along with dogwood, redbud is one of Pennsylvania's top two small-tree choices for shadier spots and for underplanting along edges of woods. Redbud is a native tree that flowers in March or April before the leaves emerge. Magenta buds appear first, then open all along the branches to cover the otherwise bare tree in pink, rosy pink, lavender, or white petals. Both buds and flowers are edible if you want a colorful salad accent. The distinctive heart-shaped leaves open gold, maroon, or gold-orange on some varieties. A few retain golden or burgundy shades all summer. Fall foliage is nice too, usually yellow but yellow-orange in some varieties. Redbud has an open habit and tends to grow a bit wider than tall, maxing out in the 20- to 25-foot range.

When, Where, and How to Plant
Spring planting is best for both container-grown and field-dug, burlap-wrapped trees. Keep roots damp the first season. Afternoon shade is ideal as is loose, damp, well-drained soil, but redbud adapts to full sun or shade and to sandy, clayish, acidic, or alkaline soils. Prepare it by loosening the soil as deep as the rootball and three to five times as wide. Work in an inch or two of compost, plant with the root flare just above grade, and mulch with 2 to 3 inches of wood chips or bark. Keep mulch several inches away from the trunk.

Growing Tips
Soak weekly the first season, weekly during hot, dry spells for the next two to three years, then every two weeks in drought, especially in full-sun planting. Fertilizer usually isn't needed if a mulch layer is maintained.

Regional Advice and Care
Redbud produces hanging, brown seed capsules that often self-sow. It's nearly impossible to pick them all off the tree if you don't like the look or don't want seeding; just dig seedlings that pop up. Protect young plants from deer. Canker and verticillium wilt are diseases that can reduce redbud's life span; good soil and correct planting help prevent them. Prune after flowering to eliminate competing leaders, to thin out excess and wayward branches, and to shorten long branches.

Companion Planting and Design
Plant specimens in prime spots out of afternoon sun, such as in the dappled light of taller trees, to the east of tall evergreens, or in an east-facing yard. Siberian squill and glory-of-the-snow are short bulbs that overlap redbud's bloom time. Foamflowers, hellebores, and hardy geraniums make good perennial underplantings.

Try These
'Forest Pansy' is my favorite for its burgundy leaves (pink-blooming 20-footer), but it's iffy in Zone 5. The Rising Sun™ has gold-orange new foliage (rosy pink 18-footer) and won a Pennsylvania Horticultural Society Gold Medal Award. 'Ace of Hearts' is a compact 12- to 15-foot lavender-pink bloomer. Lavender Twist™ and 'Ruby Falls' are small (8 to 10 feet) weeping types.

River Birch

Betula nigra

Botanical Pronunciation
BET-you-lah NYE-grah

Bloom Period and Seasonal Color
Tan catkins in April; yellow fall foliage

Mature Height × Spread
40 to 60 feet × 30 to 45 feet

Earlier generations planted lots of paper birch trees for their peeling, snow white bark, and we've watched most of them suffer from leaf-spot disease and leaf-miner attack, then die from borer damage. The borer-resistant native river birch has largely replaced white birch in Pennsylvania landscapes. The rangy, almost weeping growth habit is similar, but the main difference is the bark—river birch has cinnamon-colored and even more pronounced peeling bark. The toothed green leaves turn yellow in fall, fair in color impact although not up to maple standards. River birch starts out narrow but widens with age and grows fast, easily ending up 40 feet tall and 30 feet wide and counting. River birch is also one of the most heat-tolerant members of the birch family.

When, Where, and How to Plant
Plant container-grown or field-dug plants in spring or early fall. Container-grown trees can be planted throughout summer if roots are kept damp. River birch grows in full sun to light shade and prefers damp or even wet sites and slightly acidic soil. Loosen soil as deep as the rootball and three to five times as wide. Plant with the root flare just above grade, and mulch with 2 to 3 inches of wood chips or bark. Keep mulch several inches away from the trunk.

Growing Tips
This is one tree you'll likely never overwater. Water deeply twice a week for the first season, then soak weekly during hot, dry spells for the next two to three years to establish roots. Watering in drought from then on helps prevent premature leaf drop. Fertilizer usually isn't needed if you're maintaining a mulch layer. Leaves may yellow between the veins if the soil is too alkaline; sulfur corrects it.

Regional Advice and Care
River birch can be "messy" when the catkins drop in spring, so keep away from patios. Although resistant to borers, river birch can suffer from leaf-spot disease in humid years. That's generally not life-threatening but can lead to premature leaf drop. Prune out "suckers" that emerge from the base to maintain an ideal count of three trunks. Thin out misdirected, excess, and crossing branches in the early years. Prune in January or February or in midsummer when the sap isn't heavily flowing.

Companion Planting and Design
Birches make good standalone specimens but need plenty of space; too many are overgrown next to house corners. Triangular groves of three river birches look nice in an open yard, especially in spots that get or stay wet. Virginia sweetspire makes a good, moisture-tolerant shrubby underplanting.

Try These
Heritage® is the most available variety with improved disease resistance, good fall color, and a Pennsylvania Horticultural Society Gold Medal Award. Dura-Heat® is heat-tolerant as well as disease-resistant. 'Little King' (Fox Valley®) is compact, growing 12 to 15 feet and usually wider than tall. 'Summer Cascade' is a weeping form.

Serviceberry

Amelanchier species

Botanical Pronunciation
am-ul-LANK-ee-ur

Other Name Shadblow

Bloom Period and Seasonal Color
White flowers in March to April; yellow, gold, red, gold-orange fall foliage

Mature Height × Spread
15 to 25 feet × 15 to 25 feet

Another under-used small flowering tree is this group of U.S. natives that offers multiseason interest. Serviceberry blooms white in early spring, producing tight clusters of cherry blossom-like flowers close to the stems. In June, small fruits that look and taste like blueberries ripen dark blue and make an excellent pie or jelly—if the birds don't get them first. In fall, the oval leaves turn from gray-green to gold, blood red, or assorted blends between. Two very similar types are downy serviceberry (*Amelanchier arborea*) and Allegheny serviceberry (*Amelanchier laevis*), which differ mainly in the leaf texture. The shadblow species (*Amelanchier canadensis*) is slightly more upright and tolerant of damper soil. All can be grown as multistemmed small trees or as single-trunk specimens.

When, Where, and How to Plant
Serviceberries grow best in some afternoon shade in loose, damp, mildly acidic soil. But they'll also grow in full sun to mostly shade and in dry, rocky, clayish, and/or slightly alkaline soils. Container-grown trees can be planted spring through early fall; field-dug ones are best planted in spring *or* early fall. Work an inch or two of compost into the planting bed after loosening soil three to five times as wide as the rootball (but only as deep). Plant with the root flare just above the soil grade, and mulch with wood chips or bark, kept a few inches away from the trunk.

Growing Tips
Soak weekly the first season, weekly during hot, dry spells for the next two to three years, then every two weeks in drought, especially in full-sun sites. Fertilizer usually isn't needed if a mulch layer is maintained, although scattering balanced, granular, organic or timed-released fertilizer is often helpful the first few springs.

Regional Advice and Care
Serviceberry is prone primarily to cosmetic leaf diseases such as rust, powdery mildew, and leaf spot. Fireblight is a rare but potentially fatal disease. Sawfly, scale, and borers are occasional bug problems. Prune "suckers" that emerge from the base whenever you see them, and prune to control size or to eliminate excess or crossing branches after the berries are gone. Pruning can be done at end of winter, although that reduces flowering and fruiting.

Companion Planting and Design
Serviceberry is at its best in partly shaded, damp parts of a back yard or as an understory tree near a woods edge. It's also a natural next to a water garden or along a stream. Yet it's durable enough to serve as a sunny front-yard specimen. Siberian squill and glory-of-the-snow are short bulbs that overlap serviceberry's bloom time. Leadwort makes a good groundcover.

Try These
Two of the best are hybrids of the downy and Allegheny types: 'Autumn Brilliance' and 'Princess Diana'. Both bloom heavily and end the season in a blaze of red. 'Rainbow Pillar' is a narrow form (20 by 10) of shadblow.

Snowbell

Styrax species

Botanical Pronunciation
STYE-racks

Bloom Period and Seasonal Color
White, pink flowers in April to June;
yellow fall foliage

Mature Height × Spread
8 to 25 feet × 12 to 30 feet

Snowbell is a good option if you're looking for a small, easy-to-grow flowering tree other than the common crabapples, cherries, and dogwoods that dominate Pennsylvania landscapes. The most likely type you'll find is Japanese snowbell (*Styrax japonicus*), a rounded, 20- to 25-footer that produces a prolific display of hanging, white, bell-shaped flowers in May and June. The flowers are mildly fragrant. By late summer, the flowers morph into hanging, creamy gray, berry-sized fruits ("drupes"), which are of some interest to birds but which can also self-sow where they drop. (The potential for invasiveness is considered low.) Fall foliage is pale yellow at best. In Zones 6 to 7, native American snowbell (*Styrax americanus*) can be trained from its natural shrubby habit into a single-trunk, 10-foot tree.

When, Where, and How to Plant
Snowbell is best planted in spring, either as a container-grown or field-dug, burlap-wrapped young tree. It'll grow in full sun to part shade and prefers loose, damp, and mildly acidic soil. Loosen soil as deep as the rootball and three to five times as wide. Work in an inch or two of compost, plant with the root flare just above grade, and mulch with 2 to 3 inches of wood chips or bark. Keep mulch at least 2 to 3 inches away from the trunk.

Growing Tips
Water deeply once or twice a week for the first season, then soak weekly during hot, dry spells for the next two to three years. After that, watering is needed only during drought. Fertilizer usually isn't needed if you're maintaining a 2- to 3-inch layer of mulch.

Regional Advice and Care
Japanese snowbell is iffy in Zone 5, though possibly a protected site near a building would work. The slightly more cold-hardy fragrant snowbell (*Styrax obassia*) is a better bet there. In Zone 7, Japanese snowbell is best sited in part shade or at least away from hot spots. Yank any unwanted seedlings that pop up *immediately*, and don't plant snowbell near a patio where you don't want dropping drupes. Borers (rare) are the only known bug threat. Prune to shape in the early years to eliminate multiple leaders (assuming you want just one trunk) and to get rid of misdirected, excess, and crossing branches. The best times are end of winter (easiest to see what you're doing) or right after bloom (for maximum flowers).

Companion Planting and Design
Snowbell is most effective as a standalone specimen in such sites as front yards, out a back window, next to a water garden, or lining a wooded border. Late pink tulips overlap snowbell's bloom time. Compact hydrangeas flower in summer after snowbell finishes.

Try These
'Pink Chimes' is a 20-foot, pink-blooming Japanese snowbell that's winter-rated to withstand even Zone 5 cold. 'Fragrant Fountain' and 'Carillon' ('Pendula') are 10- to 12-foot weeping versions that make eye-grabbing specimens at house corners.

Stewartia

Stewartia species

Botanical Pronunciation
stoo-AR-tee-ah

Bloom Period and Seasonal Color
White flowers in June to July; red, gold, orange-red, purple, bronze fall foliage

Mature Height × Spread
10 to 30 feet × 12 to 25 feet

Stewartia is my favorite landscape tree, especially the similar Japanese (*Stewartia pseudocamellia*) and Korean (*Stewartia koreana*) types that develop flaking, Dalmatian-like gray, tan, and brown bark as they age. Even better than that winter interest feature is the long-lasting fall foliage. The October colors change daily in a kaleidoscope of gold, red, orange-red, purple, and bronze. Stewartia flowers in early summer after most trees are done, white petals around a golden center, reminiscent of camellia. This species also is slow-growing and tight in form, making it a good option for small to midsized yards. It seldom runs into disease or pest problems, including deer. Stewartia has a reputation of being somewhat hard to grow, but I haven't found that to be the case.

When, Where, and How to Plant
Stewartia likes loose, damp, and slightly acidic soil in full sun to light shade. It's best planted in spring, either as a container-grown or field-dug, burlap-wrapped young tree. Loosen soil as deep as the rootball and three to five times as wide. Work in an inch or two of compost, plant with the root flare just above grade, and mulch with 2 to 3 inches of wood chips or bark. Keep mulch a few inches back from the trunk.

Growing Tips
Watering in the early going is critical to success. Soak deeply once or twice a week for the first season then weekly during hot, dry spells for the next two to three years. Once the roots establish, stewartia is reasonably tolerant of dry weather. Make sure the soil is acidic at planting (a pH of 6 is good). Fertilizer usually isn't needed if you're maintaining a 2- to 3-inch layer of mulch. Topdress with sulfur if the leaves yellow between the veins.

Regional Advice and Care
Almost all stewartias are winter-hardy throughout Pennsylvania. The exception is the native, 15-foot silky stewartia (*Stewartia malacodendron*), which isn't hardy in Zone 5. Shape in the early years to eliminate multiple leaders and to get rid of excess, crossing, or other wayward branches. Then shorten remaining branches only as needed. End of winter is the best time to prune.

Companion Planting and Design
Stewartia is a "clean," root-behaved tree that's excellent near a patio or water garden and beautiful enough in all seasons as a front-yard specimen or wherever it can be appreciated in fall and winter. Stick with low groundcovers as partners (barrenwort, foamflower, or coralbells) to avoid hiding the great bark.

Try These
Look for Korean or Japanese stewartia, or 'Skyrocket', a particularly narrow choice in tight areas. Mountain stewartia (*Stewartia ovata*) is a U.S. native that's more of a tall shrub and doesn't have quite the stunning fall foliage or mottled bark of the Asian types. Tall stewartia (*Stewartia monadelpha*) is a Japanese 25-footer with decent fall foliage and good heat- and dry-soil tolerance.

Sweetgum

Liquidambar styraciflua

Botanical Pronunciation
lick-wid-AM-bar stye-rah-SIFF-loo-ah

Other Name Gumball tree

Bloom Period and Seasonal Color
Non-showy creamy yellow flowers in April to
May; red-purple to gold fall foliage

Mature Height × Spread
60 to 75 feet × 35 to 50 feet

No other tree gets alternatively praised and cursed as the native sweetgum. This is a 60- to 75-foot-tall pyramidal tree with handsome, glossy green, star-shaped summer leaves, turning glossy purple-red to gold for weeks in fall. But along with that showy fall foliage comes brown, golfball-sized, spiky "gumballs" that drop in seemingly never-ending numbers through winter. The tree's roots also tend to grow near the surface, eventually out-competing a lawn. That adds up to a tree worth considering toward the back of a large yard where you can enjoy it from the patio without the need for spiky-ball raking. It's *not* the choice for next to the patio or anywhere you plan to walk barefoot. On the plus side, crafters find lots of uses for the balls.

When, Where, and How to Plant
Plant field-grown, burlap-wrapped young sweetgums in spring. Plant container-grown ones spring through summer. Either way, keep the roots consistently damp through the first summer. Sweetgum prefers loose, damp, mildly acidic soil and full sun. Occasionally wet soils are okay. Loosen soil as deep as the rootball and three to five times as wide, plant with the root flare just above grade, and mulch with wood chips or bark. Keep mulch at least 2 to 3 inches away from the trunk.

Growing Tips
Water deeply once or twice a week for the first season, then soak weekly during hot, dry spells for the next two to three years until the roots establish. After that, watering and fertilizer usually aren't needed, especially if you're maintaining a mulch layer. Leaves may yellow between the veins if the soil is too alkaline; sulfur corrects this.

Regional Advice and Care
Most important is siting to avoid trouble from the dropping balls and surface roots. Those balls contain seeds that sometimes sprout, so yank seedlings that pop up (if you're not already raking the balls as they drop). Prune in mid- to late winter in the early years to eliminate multiple leaders, to get rid of misdirected, excess, and crossing branches, and to shorten overly long branches. Webworms are occasional cosmetic pests that chew on leaves. Leaf-spot disease discolors the foliage in some summers.

Companion Planting and Design
Site in large lots only, and even then, plant well away from property lines, wherever the balls can drop in peace. A cluster of sweetgums looks nice backdropping a large pond or lining a stream. Underplant with Pennsylvania sedge or native Allegheny spurge.

Try These
'Slender Silhouette' is a Pennsylvania Horticultural Society Gold Medal Award-winning, limited-fruiting, columnar form that can grow 50 to 60 feet tall but only 4 to 6 feet across. A triangular trio of these makes an interesting vertical grouping. 'Rotundifolia' is a full-sized, mostly fruitless variety with rounded leaf lobes instead of pointed, starlike ones. It's reliably winter-hardy only in Zones 6 to 7.

VINES

FOR PENNSYLVANIA

V ines are plants that appreciate our support in their growing efforts.
They're plants happiest on some sort of wall, fence, or trellis/arbor/
pergola contraption so they can strut their stuff at eye level . . . and beyond.
Some vines pull themselves up with twining stems or curly "tendrils" that
latch onto any nearby support like skinny little arms. Others do their climbing via
rootlets that suck themselves onto surfaces as they go.

Vines also can be divided by whether they're "annuals" (they grow just one summer and then die off with frost) or "perennials" (ones that come back year after year).

Either way, most vines flower in spring or summer, but a few have attractive
enough foliage to stand (climb) on that merit alone.

Vines in the Landscape

Vines are woefully underused in Pennsylvania yards. A visiting troupe of European
garden-center owners once told me that the likely reason is that we're blessed here
with so much horizontal space that we don't have to think about milking every last
inch out of vertical space as do so many European gardeners with smaller yards.

Clematis trained to a trellis

Nonetheless, vines are extremely
useful for offering privacy screening in tight side yards where even
narrow evergreens will eat up too
much space. Vines on a trellis also
give quick privacy, and they can do
so with as little as a foot or two of
border space.

Even more practical is using
vines to add life and color to large,
bare, side-facing house walls or barren garage or barn walls—especially
when a sidewalk has left you with
one of those skinny 3- or 4-foot beds
that's too confining for most other
tall-growing plants.

Another good use for vines is
softening corners, hiding "uglies,"
and accenting existing vertical features around the house. Examples

Climbing roses, catmint, and lady's mantle

include: downplay a house corner and its drainage pipe by erecting a tall, narrow trellis and planting a clematis vine; screen a heat pump by erecting a three-sided, vine-covered lattice wall around it; and dress up a front-yard light post by adding netting for hyacinth beans or golden sweet potato vines to clamber up.

The spreading habit of vines doesn't mean they *have* to go up. If you don't give, say, a clematis or a honeysuckle anything to climb on, it'll ramble across the ground to make a groundcover.

The best way to find good spots for vines around your house is to look *up* instead of down as you walk around. Where is it bare up there? What's already skinny and sticking up that would look better with a little color? And what "uglies" (trash cans, utility boxes, pool pumps, and so forth) do you see that could disappear behind a vine-covered wall?

Which Vine Where?

First figure out whether you want a perennial or annual species. The tradeoff is that most annuals will bloom nonstop all season in exchange for having to replant them each spring.

Next, assess your site to determine whether to opt for a sun-lover or a choice that prefers (or at least tolerates) a bit of shade.

Third, decide whether you want a twiner or a sucker. You might have to help guide the twiners, but they can be removed for size control, painting, and such without any trace. Suckers are more permanent growers and usually leave behind rootlet remnants if you let them attach and try to remove them later.

Finally, consider size and aggressiveness. Some vines grow big and bulky, such as a Chinese wisteria or a trumpet vine that can pop apart a flimsy lattice support within a few years. Others, such as ivy or climbing hydrangea, can cover a house (windows included) if not kept in check. Still others, morning glory for example, can seed themselves throughout the yard for years to come.

Do your homework, choose wisely starting with the dozen choices that follow, and let vines take your landscape to new heights.

Black-Eyed Susan Vine

Thunbergia alata

Botanical Pronunciation
thun-BURR-gee-ah ah-LATT-ah

Bloom Period and Seasonal Color
May to October; yellow, orange, rosy pink,
creamy white, pastel flowers

Mature Height × Spread
6 to 8 feet × 1 to 2 feet

Black-eyed Susan vine gets its name from its nickel-sized flowers—golden yellow petals around a black throat, reminiscent of the familiar perennial flower black-eyed Susan (*Rudbeckia fulgida*). This plant, though, is a tropical East African native grown as an annual in Pennsylvania. It can be direct-seeded into the garden in May or bought as a small plant from the garden center. Frost kills it in fall. The stems twine themselves around string, netting, or stakes as they climb 6 to 8 feet. Black-eyed Susan vine blooms throughout summer but often performs best late in the season after summer's worst heat dissipates. The 3-inch leaves are green and shaped like slightly elongated shields. Recent varieties have expanded the flower color range into orange, rosy red, cream, and assorted pastels.

When, Where, and How to Plant

Wait until all danger of frost is past to plant seeds or transplants. Seeds also can be started inside 6 to 8 weeks ahead of transplanting, then seedlings can be planted outside after frost. Plant in loose, damp, compost-enriched, well-drained soil in full sun to part shade. Space 12 to 18 inches apart along a trellis, wall, or similar mass-planted setting. An inch of mulch is plenty.

Growing Tips

Water two or three times a week for the first six weeks then weekly the rest of the season when rain doesn't wet the soil for you. Work a gradual-release fertilizer or granular, organic fertilizer into the soil at planting according to package directions. Then fertilize monthly with a liquid fertilizer formulated for flowers. In a pot, fertilize at half-strength weekly, and water every day or two. Yank when frost kills them in fall.

Regional Advice and Care

Black-eyed Susan vine performs best with some afternoon shade, especially in the warmer Zone 6 and 7 regions of Pennsylvania. Avoid soggy spots, and don't rush planting in spring since this tropical vine is sensitive to cold temperatures. Some varieties self-sow, so watch for "babies" the following spring and yank or transplant them as desired. Bug, disease, and animal problems are unlikely.

Companion Planting and Design

Black-eyed Susan vine is a well behaved vine that's suited for smaller supports, such as narrow, decorative trellises next to a front door or growing up a light post or mailbox. It's amenable to snipping if you like your vines neat. Black-eyed Susan vine also is reserved enough to grow up an obelisk or stake as a pot centerpiece, and it'll trail nicely out of a hanging basket.

Try These

'Susie Mix' produces a blend of creamy white, yellow, and orange flowers. 'Blushing Susie Mix' produces creamy white, rosy red, and apricot flowers. The 'Superstar' series has some of the largest flowers—almost the size of quarters. 'Lemon A-Peel' (yellow) and 'Orange A-Peel' (orange) are two new types with heavy flowering.

Clematis

Clematis species

Botanical Pronunciation
KLEM-ah-tiss

Bloom Period and Seasonal Color
May to September; purple, pink, yellow, white,
lavender-blue, rosy red flowers

Mature Height × Spread
8 to 20 feet × 2 to 4 feet

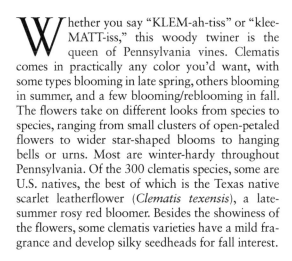

Whether you say "KLEM-ah-tiss" or "klee-MATT-iss," this woody twiner is the queen of Pennsylvania vines. Clematis comes in practically any color you'd want, with some types blooming in late spring, others blooming in summer, and a few blooming/reblooming in fall. The flowers take on different looks from species to species, ranging from small clusters of open-petaled flowers to wider star-shaped blooms to hanging bells or urns. Most are winter-hardy throughout Pennsylvania. Of the 300 clematis species, some are U.S. natives, the best of which is the Texas native scarlet leatherflower (*Clematis texensis*), a late-summer rosy red bloomer. Besides the showiness of the flowers, some clematis varieties have a mild fragrance and develop silky seedheads for fall interest.

When, Where, and How to Plant
Plant container-grown clematis spring through early fall. Keep roots consistently damp the entire first season. The best flowering is in full sun, but most types do fine in afternoon shade and with cooled roots (by mulch or planting on the east side of a trellis). Clematis is best planted at or slightly below grade. Avoid soggy areas. Plant in loose, damp, mildly acidic, compost-improved soil. Mulch after planting with 1 to 2 inches of wood chips or bark kept at least 2 to 3 inches away from the trunk.

Growing Tips
Water deeply once or twice a week for the first full growing season then weekly during hot, dry weather. Scatter a balanced, granular, organic or gradual-release fertilizer over the bed in early

spring. Don't be surprised if plants suddenly turn black after flowering. This is a condition known as clematis wilt, and large-flowered, spring-blooming types are particularly prone to it. Cut back dead wood, and plants usually regrow. The best prevention is to buy wilt-resistant varieties in the first place (see below).

Regional Advice and Care
Pruning varies by type. Spring bloomers are thinned out and cut back by one-third to one-half right after blooming. Varieties that bloom on new spring growth (June and after) can be cut back to 6 inches at winter's end. Not sure? Wait until buds start to emerge in early spring and remove any dead wood above them; then thin and shorten after flowering. Avoid sweet autumn clematis (*Clematis terniflora*), which is becoming an invasive seeder in Pennsylvania.

Companion Planting and Design
Anywhere there's something to grab onto is fair game—up trellises by bare walls, over arbors, up netting on mailboxes and light posts, even clambering up trees. New compact "patio clematis" are good choices for containers.

Try These
Good Texas types are 'Gravetye Beauty' (red), 'Princess Diana' (deep pink), and 'Duchess of Albany' (two-tone pink). Good wilt-resistant Italian clematis (*Clematis viticella*) varieties are 'Madame Julia Correvon' (rose), 'Etoile Violette' (purple), and 'Betty Corning' (pinkish blue). 'Helios' is one of the best yellow-bloomers (*Clematis tangutica*).

Climbing Hydrangea

Hydrangea anomala ssp. *petiolaris*

Botanical Pronunciation
hye-DRANE-gee-ah ah-NOMM-ah-lah
pet-ee-oh-LAY-russ

Bloom Period and Seasonal Color
June to July; white flowers

Mature Height × Spread
20 to 35 feet × 20 to 35 feet

Other than the flower clusters that look like a lacecap-type hydrangea, climbing hydrangea is a different animal from the blue-ball-blooming round bushes that most people think of as a hydrangea. Climbing hydrangea is a hefty climber that sends out arms that grow little rootlets to pull the plant ever upward and outward—30 feet or more if it's not snipped! The leaves are green and heart-shaped, growing densely enough to make a solid green wall covering. Budlike 8-inch-wide creamy flower clusters form in June and produce white petals around the perimeter that can last for six weeks. The leaves drop in fall to reveal peeling tan bark in winter. Climbing hydrangea is slow to start, so give it three years to hit its blooming stride.

When, Where, and How to Plant
Plant container-grown climbing hydrangea vines spring through early fall at or slightly above grade in loose, damp, compost-enriched soil. They'll grow in full sun to mostly shade, although they're happiest with morning sun and afternoon shade. Keep roots consistently damp the entire first season. Mulch after planting with 2 to 3 inches of wood chips or bark located at least 2 to 3 inches away from the trunk.

Growing Tips
Water deeply once or twice a week for the first full growing season then weekly during hot, dry weather for the next year or two. After that, climbing hydrangea won't need water, except in a prolonged drought. Fertilizer usually isn't needed if a 2-inch mulch layer is maintained.

Regional Advice and Care
Grow on a sturdy pergola or trellis or along a stone, brick, or other wall where you're okay with the arms sticking and staying. It's possible to pull off and prune back arms later, but the rootlets will remain stuck to the surface. Thin out excess or crossing arms and shorten overly long ones at the end of winter before new leaves emerge. Once it spreads to the size you want, prune annually to keep it that size. Flowers can be cut off after they brown, and long arms can be lightly snipped as needed throughout summer. Japanese beetles are occasional pests that can be repelled with sprays of Neem oil.

Companion Planting and Design
Climbing hydrangea is a muscular, woody vine and is ideal on a sturdy support, such as a big, bare wall or a pergola over a patio. It's also a good, self-climbing chimney plant. Left without a support, the arms will ramble across a bank or over the ground to make a wavy groundcover.

Try These
'Skylands Giant' is a denser-growing, improved-blooming variety discovered by Pennsylvania's Barry Yinger. 'Firefly' has spring green and yellow variegated foliage and was developed at Chanticleer gardens in Wayne, PA, by horticulturist Dan Benarcik.

Climbing Rose

Rosa species and selections

Botanical Pronunciation
ROZE-ah

Bloom Period and Seasonal Color
May to June (and sometimes beyond); pink, red, yellow, white, orange, apricot, bicolor flowers

Mature Height × Spread
6 to 15 feet × 4 to 6 feet

Climbing roses aren't really climbers. They don't twine themselves up or grab onto surfaces with sucking rootlets but instead depend on the gardener to tie up their long canes. Climbing roses also aren't a distinct species but rather versions of many rose types grouped by the trait of extra-long canes. They range from large-flowered, single-bloomers to clusters of smaller flowers and come in a wide selection of colors. Late spring is prime time for flowering, but many rebloom later in summer and fall, especially if they're cut back after spring flowering. Some have decent fragrance, and almost all have thorns, which is the main consideration if you're the pruner or in charge of making sure thorny arms don't grab passersby walking under that rose-covered arbor.

When, Where, and How to Plant
Plant bare-root roses in early spring; boxed or container-grown ones from spring to early summer. Plant in loose, rich, slightly acidic, well-drained, and compost-enriched soil in a site with at least six hours of sun a day. Avoid soggy sites. Keep roots consistently damp the entire first season. Mulch after planting with 2 to 3 inches of wood chips or bark. Keep any mulch a few inches away from the trunk.

Growing Tips
Water deeply once a week, especially during hot, dry spells. Water the *ground*, not over the foliage, to limit leaf disease. Scatter an organic or gradual-release fertilizer formulated for roses in early spring, again right after the first round of flowering, then in early August.

Regional Advice and Care
Some types are more disease-resistant than others and need little or no treatment. Others get blackspot or cane diseases without fungicides. Repel Japanese beetles with Neem oil sprays. Aphids and mites are other bug possibilities. In cold areas, add an extra 2 inches of leaf or bark mulch over the roots in winter; remove in spring. Prune in mid- to late winter by first removing dead or damaged wood, then by thinning crossing branches. Keep evenly spaced main canes unless bloom deteriorates; then remove old canes and allow younger ones to replace them. Finally, shorten evenly spaced side shoots to three to five buds each. After flowering, snip back flowering tips to the second set of stems with five leaves.

Companion Planting and Design
Climbing roses look best on open fences, large stone walls, arbors, and trellises. They can also be trained up pillars, porch posts, or trees. Just keep arms tied so thorns don't scratch people walking by. Climbing roses also can be interplanted with clematis vines.

Try These
Pinks are 'New Dawn', 'William Baffin', and 'Berries 'n Cream'. 'Zephirine Drouhine' is a pink-blooming thornless climber. Yellow ones are 'Golden Showers' and 'Abraham Darby'. Reds include 'Altissimo', 'Blaze', 'Dublin Bay', and 'Don Juan'. A red-white bicolor is 'Fourth of July'. *Rosa banksiae* 'Lutea' is a thornless, double-yellow climber for Zone 7.

Honeysuckle

Lonicera species

Botanical Pronunciation
lonn-ISS-er-ah

Bloom Period and Seasonal Color
May to August; red, orange, yellow, coral flowers

Mature Height × Spread
10 to 15 feet × 4 to 6 feet

Honeysuckle is a twining, woody, winter-hardy plant with skinny, tubular flowers. Some types are shrubby, but we'll look at the two kinds that make good climbers for Pennsylvania landscapes. One is the native trumpet honeysuckle (*Lonicera sempervirens*), which flowers from late spring into midsummer in red, orange, yellow, and blends of those. The other is goldflame honeysuckle (*Lonicera × heckrottii*), a hybrid of trumpet and European honeysuckles that blooms the same time but in coral to yellow. The latter has mild fragrance; the former doesn't but sometimes gets small red berries in fall. Both are hummingbird favorites that make a showy, vining plant for about two months, sometimes longer. Climbing honeysuckle grows by twining itself up supports, ideally with a little guidance.

When, Where, and How to Plant
Plant container-grown honeysuckle spring through early fall at or slightly above the soil grade in loose, damp, compost-enriched soil. Full sun is best, but honeysuckle also flowers reasonably well in part shade. Mulch after planting with 2 to 3 inches of wood chips or bark kept away from the trunk.

Growing Tips
Water deeply once or twice a week for the first growing season then weekly during hot, dry weather for the next two to three years until the roots are established. After that, honeysuckle is drought-resistant and needs water only in a prolonged drought. Fertilizer usually isn't needed if a mulch layer is maintained.

Regional Advice and Care
Aphids are a common bug pest. They won't kill the plant, but they can discolor leaves and short-circuit flowering. Spray with insecticidal soap or horticultural oil if they're troublesome. Honeysuckle sometimes gets powdery mildew disease on the leaves. Pruning for good air circulation helps prevent it. Thin out dead or excessive branching at the end of winter, but do shortening and most size-control pruning right after flowering. Spent flowers can be snipped off after they brown in summer to neaten the plant. Some additional flowers may keep appearing from late summer into early fall.

Companion Planting and Design
Honeysuckle is a good choice for arbors, pergolas, trellises, and other supports near people. No worries about thorns as with climbing roses. Goldflame types offer mild fragrance and are effective near patios and windows. With the help of attached netting or string, honeysuckle also will grow up pillars and porch columns for eye-level color. Underplant with bright perennials such as coreopsis, black-eyed Susan, daylilies, or mums.

Try These
'Major Wheeler', 'Alabama Crimson', and 'Cedar Lane' are three of the longest-blooming red-flowered trumpet honeysuckles. Pink Lemonade™ is a good coral-pink type of goldflame honeysuckle. 'Dropmore Scarlet' is a heavy-blooming hybrid that has red-orange flowers with yellow throats.

Hyacinth Bean

Lablab purpureus

Botanical Pronunciation
LAB-lab pur-PUR-ee-us

Other Name Purple hyacinth bean

Bloom Period and Seasonal Color
June through October; violet flowers

Mature Height × Spread
8 to 15 feet × 3 to 6 feet

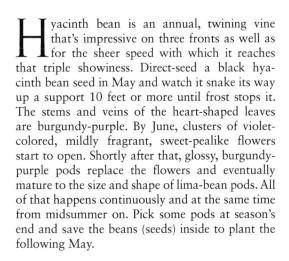

Hyacinth bean is an annual, twining vine that's impressive on three fronts as well as for the sheer speed with which it reaches that triple showiness. Direct-seed a black hyacinth bean seed in May and watch it snake its way up a support 10 feet or more until frost stops it. The stems and veins of the heart-shaped leaves are burgundy-purple. By June, clusters of violet-colored, mildly fragrant, sweet-pealike flowers start to open. Shortly after that, glossy, burgundy-purple pods replace the flowers and eventually mature to the size and shape of lima-bean pods. All of that happens continuously and at the same time from midsummer on. Pick some pods at season's end and save the beans (seeds) inside to plant the following May.

When, Where, and How to Plant
Garden centers sell pots of young hyacinth beans in spring, but it's easy and cheaper to start your own by planting seeds directly in the ground. Seeds also can be started inside four to six weeks ahead of time. In all cases, wait until all danger of frost is past to get plants going outside. Plant in loose, damp, compost-enriched, well-drained soil, avoiding soggy spots, in full sun to light shade. Space 10 to 12 inches apart to create a wall of beans. An inch of mulch is plenty.

Growing Tips
Water daily until the seeds come up (or two or three times a week for young transplants) for the first six weeks. Then water weekly the rest of the season whenever it's hot and dry. Fertilizer usually isn't needed.

Regional Advice and Care
Hyacinth beans are conditionally edible, *but only after boiling them well twice*, changing the water after the first boil. The twining arms grow best up "skinny" supports such as string, netting, or narrow posts. Help guide the arms in the early going. Hyacinth beans sometimes self-sow themselves, so watch for "babies" in the spring and pull or transplant them as desired. Rabbits or groundhogs may eat young shoots (erect low netting or fencing around young plants until they take off). Japanese beetles may eat holes in leaves in early summer (spray with neem oil if they become intolerable). Yank bean plants when frost kills them in fall after drying several large pods to save the seeds inside for next year.

Companion Planting and Design
Hyacinth bean is at its best billowing up both sides of an arbor. It'll also cover a patio or border trellis by midsummer. Kids love these, so read them *Jack and the Beanstalk* and be sure to plant a few in any child's garden.

Try These
The straight species is perfectly fine and usually all that you'll find in plant or seed form. 'Ruby Moon' is one of the few varieties developed for its darker foliage and nearly purple-black pods.

Japanese Hydrangea Vine

Schizophragma hydrangeoides

Botanical Pronunciation
skiz-oh-FRAG-mah hye-drane-gee-OY-deez

Bloom Period and Seasonal Color
June to July; white, pink flowers

Mature Height × Spread
20 to 35 feet × 20 to 35 feet

My favorite vine, Japanese hydrangea vine, is very similar to climbing hydrangea, except that it blooms slightly later with single white petals and has more pronounced toothy edges to its leaves. What I especially like is the foliage, at least on the 'Moonlight' variety that's the most common variety. Its 8-inch-wide, heart-shaped leaves have a silvery sheen that's particularly beautiful paired with the white-petaled flowers that bloom in June and July. The new leaves also are rosy-tinted in spring. Like climbing hydrangea, Japanese hydrangea vine is a muscular vine that grabs onto rough surfaces as it climbs and spreads. It's shade-tolerant and can grow to make a dense surface covering of 35 feet up and out if not clipped smaller.

When, Where, and How to Plant
Plant container-grown Japanese hydrangea vines spring through early fall at or slightly above grade in loose, damp, compost-enriched soil. The ideal site is morning sun and afternoon shade, although this vine tolerates most light from sun to deeper shade. Keep roots consistently damp the entire first season. Mulch after planting. Keep all mulch, about 2 to 3 inches of wood chips or bark, at least 2 to 3 inches away from the trunk.

Growing Tips
Japanese hydrangea vine is drought-tough and won't need water once its roots are established. Water deeply once or twice a week for the first season then weekly during hot, dry weather for the next two to three years. After that, you're off the

hook. Fertilizer usually isn't needed if a mulch layer is maintained.

Regional Advice and Care
Grow on a sturdy pergola or trellis or along a stone, brick, or other wall where you're okay with the arms sticking and staying. It's possible to pull off and prune back arms later, but the rootlets will remain stuck to the surface. Thin out excess or crossing arms and shorten overly long ones at the end of winter before new leaves emerge. Once it reaches the size you want, prune Japanese hydrangea vine annually to keep it at that size. Flowers can be cut off after they brown, and long arms can be lightly snipped as needed throughout summer. Bugs and disease are unlikely.

Companion Planting and Design
Japanese hydrangea vine needs a sturdy support, such as a big, bare wall or a pergola over a patio. It's also a good, self-climbing chimney plant. In its native wooded areas, Japanese hydrangea vine often is found climbing up trees. Without a support, it'll sprawl over the ground to make a wavy groundcover.

Try These
'Moonlight' is excellent and was discovered in Japan by Pennsylvania's Barry Yinger. 'Roseum' is a variety with pale pink flowers. Chinese hydrangea vine (*Schizophragma integrifolum*) has even bigger flower clusters and bigger leaves but is hardy only to Zone 7.

Mandevilla

Mandevilla species

Botanical Pronunciation
man-deh-VILL-ah

Bloom Period and Seasonal Color
May to October; pink, rose, red, white flowers

Mature Height × Spread
4 to 12 feet × 1 to 2 feet

    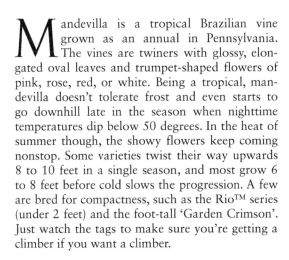

Mandevilla is a tropical Brazilian vine grown as an annual in Pennsylvania. The vines are twiners with glossy, elongated oval leaves and trumpet-shaped flowers of pink, rose, red, or white. Being a tropical, mandevilla doesn't tolerate frost and even starts to go downhill late in the season when nighttime temperatures dip below 50 degrees. In the heat of summer though, the showy flowers keep coming nonstop. Some varieties twist their way upwards 8 to 10 feet in a single season, and most grow 6 to 8 feet before cold slows the progression. A few are bred for compactness, such as the Rio™ series (under 2 feet) and the foot-tall 'Garden Crimson'. Just watch the tags to make sure you're getting a climber if you want a climber.

When, Where, and How to Plant
Don't rush; wait until all danger of frost is past to plant young transplants. Nighttime lows should be 50 degrees and up. Plant in loose, damp, compost-enriched, well-drained soil in a sunny spot or in a sunny deck pot. Plant 12 to 18 inches apart if you're making a mandevilla wall along a wide trellis or lattice wall. An inch of mulch is plenty.

Growing Tips
Water two or three times a week for the first six weeks then weekly the rest of the season when rain doesn't happen. Work a gradual-release fertilizer or granular, organic fertilizer into the soil at planting according to package directions, then fertilize every two weeks with a liquid fertilizer formulated for flowers. In a pot, fertilize at half-strength weekly, and water every day or two.

Regional Advice and Care
Mandevilla can be overwintered inside. Dig it up and pot it in lightweight potting mix when nights dip below 50, cutting back to about a foot, and hosing off well (or spraying it with insecticide soap) before moving inside to kill aphids or mites trying to hitch a ride. Grow inside near a bright window, water once or twice a week (no soggy soil), and skip fertilizer through winter. In early spring, fertilize monthly and gradually expose plants to increasing light outside on above-50-degree days before replanting after the danger of frost has passed.

Companion Planting and Design
Grow mandevilla in smaller vertical areas for summerlong color at eye level, such as up light posts, mailboxes, porch columns, and obelisks in garden beds. Mandevilla is one of the best vines for growing in pots. Underplant with purple or blue annual flowers, such as blue salvia, verbena, scaevola, angelonia, or heliotrope.

Try These
The Sun Parasols® series dominates the market with a wide assortment of colors, flower sizes, and vine heights. 'Cream Pink' from that series rates high in Penn State University trials. 'Alice du Pont' is a top-selling light pink bloomer with a red throat. 'Red Riding Hood' is a 4- to 6-foot rosy red bloomer with a yellow throat.

Ornamental Kiwi Vine

Actinidia kolomikta

Botanical Pronunciation
ak-tin-IDD-ee-ah koh-loh-MICK-tah

Other Name Variegated kiwi vine

Bloom Period and Seasonal Color
May to June; non-showy white flowers

Mature Height × Spread
15 to 20 feet × 8 to 15 feet

You're familiar with the fuzzy, egg-shaped kiwi fruits from the grocery store? This is a relative of that vining, not-so-hardy plant that produces those. Ornamental kiwi vine is winter-hardy throughout Pennsylvania and is a woody, twining viner that grows 15 to 20 feet within a few years. Female plants produce smooth, grape-sized, light green, edible fruits in early fall that taste like kiwi. Both the females and non-fruiting males of this kiwi species grow elongated heart-shaped leaves that are variegated green, white, and bubble-gum pink, patterned as if blotches of color were painted on randomly over the plant. The showy leaf color is most pronounced in spring. The rest of the year, ornamental kiwi vine makes a dense, green wall covering that doesn't attach onto surfaces.

When, Where, and How to Plant
Plant container-grown kiwi vines spring through early fall at or slightly above grade in loose, damp, compost-enriched soil. A bit of shade in the afternoon is ideal for best leaf spring leaf color and to avoid browning around the leaf edges in a hot, dry summer. Full sun to part shade is fine. Mulch after planting with 2 to 3 inches of wood chips or bark. Don't pack mulch against the trunk.

Growing Tips
Soak a new kiwi vine weekly the first season, then soak weekly during hot, dry weather for the next two to three years. After that, kiwi vine needs water only in a drought. Fertilizer usually isn't needed if a 2-inch mulch layer is maintained.

Regional Advice and Care
This type of kiwi vine is more cold-hardy than most people think and doesn't need special winter protection in any part of Pennsylvania. If you want fruit, grow one or more females with at least one male nearby (within 15 to 20 feet). Prune at the end of winter to eliminate dead wood and crossing or excess branches and to shorten overly long branches. Prune back to where two branches meet or to where a side shoot attaches to a main shoot. Help guide arms of young plants in the direction desired.

Companion Planting and Design
A male and one or more females make a tasty and good-looking planting over an arbor or pergola leading into a vegetable garden. A lattice wall of kiwis also makes a good backdrop to a vegetable garden. Use non-fruiting male ornamental kiwi vines on a pergola over a patio, or for growing up trellises along borders, or for screening heat pumps and electric boxes.

Try These
If you're not interested in fruits, go with the colorful male 'Arctic Beauty'. If you want fruit, 'Red Beauty' is an attractive and productive female that's pollinated by 'Arctic Beauty'.

Passion Vine

Passiflora species

Botanical Pronunciation pass-ih-FLOR-ah

Other Name Maypop

Bloom Period and Seasonal Color
June to October; lavender, purple-blue, white, rosy red flowers

Mature Height × Spread
10 to 20 feet × 4 to 6 feet

Passion vine is usually thought of as a tropical plant, which is true for the majority of South American siblings in this 500-member family. However, a type called "maypop" (*Passiflora incarnata*) is a U.S. native vine that's winter-hardy in Zones 6 and 7 and sometimes Zone 5 warm microclimates. Though native, maypop can spread aggressively by runners, so consider containing it in a sunken pot if you try it. Less hardy (to Zone 7) is the blue passion vine (*Passiflora caerulea*), which can be grown as a fast-growing, blooming annual vine throughout Pennsylvania. Passion vine's main attraction is the unusual, multipart flowers that get their nickname from their resemblance to Christ's crown of thorns. Most have blooms with lavender to purplish blue filaments. Plants climb by tendrils.

When, Where, and How to Plant
Treat cold-hardy types in Zones 6 to 7 as you would a perennial flower. Wait until May to plant in loose, damp, compost-enriched, well-drained soil in a sunny spot. An inch of mulch is plenty. For tender types in cold areas, wait until frost is past and set out in pots or in a loose, damp, compost-enriched, well-drained bed in sun.

Growing Tips
Water in-ground passion vines twice a week for the first six weeks then weekly the rest of the season when it doesn't rain. Work a gradual-release fertilizer or granular, organic fertilizer into the soil at planting according to package directions, then fertilizer usually isn't needed (especially not for maypops). In a pot, fertilize at half-strength weekly and water every day or two.

Regional Advice and Care
Cut back winter-hardy passion vines to 2 to 3 inches after frost kills the top growth and add an extra 2 inches of leaves or bark mulch to insulate the roots over winter. Remove the extra mulch in spring. For tender types in cold zones, passion vine can be dug up before a killing frost, potted in lightweight potting mix, and moved inside for winter. Cut back vines to 8 to 12 inches before potting, and hose off any bugs. Grow inside near a bright window, water weekly (no soggy soil), and skip fertilizer through winter. In early spring, gradually expose plants to increasing light outside on above-50-degree days before replanting after danger of frost.

Companion Planting and Design
Passion vine grows fast—10 feet or more in a single season—so give it plenty of space. Train it up patio trellises, arbors, or pergolas. Plant the base with blue, purple, or pink annual flowers, such as blue salvia, verbena, scaevola, angelonia, or petunia.

Try These
You'll likely only find the straight species of maypop and possibly a few variations of blue passion vine, such as 'Grandiflora', which has blue-purple flowers larger than the species. You might also encounter red passion vine (*Passiflora coccinea*), which is an annual type with rosy red flowers.

Rex Begonia Vine

Cissus discolor

Botanical Pronunciation
SISS-suss DISS-kul-or

Other Name Painted cissus

Bloom Period and Seasonal Color
Usually non-flowering; main attraction is silver
and green variegated foliage

Mature Height × Spread
8 to 10 feet × 2 to 4 feet

This is one of the most attractive summer vines that nobody knows. It's also a vine that everybody loves once they see it. Rex begonia vine isn't a begonia at all but a colorful, vining grape relative that's native to the tropical rainforests of Java and Southeast Asia. In Pennsylvania, it's grown as an annual that can be overwintered as a houseplant. Rex begonia vine doesn't flower, but it's every bit as showy as a bloomer with its somewhat woolly-textured, arrowhead-shaped leaves of dark green. The leaves are painted throughout with silver variegation. The stems and leaf veins are rosy purple to add a third color to the mix. Rex begonia vine climbs by tendrils, thrives in heat and humidity, and prefers shadier spots.

When, Where, and How to Plant
Wait until nights have warmed consistently above 50 degrees to set outside. That means late May or even June. This is a plant that doesn't like cold weather. Rex begonia vine can be grown in pots or in the ground in loose, damp, compost-enriched, well-drained soil. Either way, plant in shade or at least in a spot out of direct afternoon sun. An inch of mulch is plenty.

Growing Tips
Water two or three times a week for the first six weeks then weekly the rest of the season–especially in dry weather. Rex begonia vine is a rainforest native and appreciates regular water, but not soggy soil. Work a gradual-release fertilizer or granular,

organic fertilizer into the soil at planting according to package directions, then in-season fertilizer usually isn't needed. In a pot, fertilize at half-strength weekly, and water every day or two.

Regional Advice and Care
Dig up, cut back, and pot your Rex begonia vine when end-of-season nights dip below 50 degrees. Hose off any spider mites or mealybugs that might be lurking on the leaves, then grow it inside near a bright window. Water once or twice a week, and skip fertilizer through winter. In early spring, fertilize monthly and gradually expose plants to increasing light outside until above-50-degree nights return. Rex begonia vine also readily roots from cuttings, so snip a few tips and root them in potting medium in late summer to create "babies" that you can grow inside.

Companion Planting and Design
This vine is perfect for a trellis along a shady section of a patio. It's also compact enough to be trained up an obelisk in a pot or up light posts and porch posts. Just watch that sunlight isn't too heavy. Silvery white flowers make good underplantings.

Try These
Your main challenge will be finding a Rex begonia vine in the first place. It's not well known even in the retail trade. Try looking at plant-geek haunts, or ask your favorite garden center if they can order one for you.

Sweet Potato Vine

Ipomoea batatas

Botanical Pronunciation
ih-poe-MEE-ah ba-TAH-tahz

Bloom Period and Seasonal Color
Occasional lavender flowers; main attraction is chartreuse, bronze, purple, black, green/pink/cream variegated foliage

Mature Height × Spread
6 to 10 inches × 3 to 4 feet

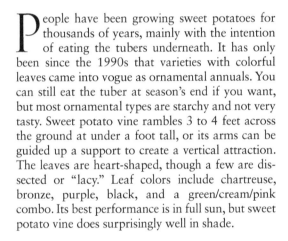

People have been growing sweet potatoes for thousands of years, mainly with the intention of eating the tubers underneath. It has only been since the 1990s that varieties with colorful leaves came into vogue as ornamental annuals. You can still eat the tuber at season's end if you want, but most ornamental types are starchy and not very tasty. Sweet potato vine rambles 3 to 4 feet across the ground at under a foot tall, or its arms can be guided up a support to create a vertical attraction. The leaves are heart-shaped, though a few are dissected or "lacy." Leaf colors include chartreuse, bronze, purple, black, and a green/cream/pink combo. Its best performance is in full sun, but sweet potato vine does surprisingly well in shade.

When, Where, and How to Plant
Wait until after danger of frost to plant. Sweet potato vine is a South American native that doesn't like cold. Grow it in pots, baskets, or in the ground in a sunny to shady spot. In the ground, plant in loose, damp, compost-enriched, well-drained soil. No soggy spots. An inch of mulch is plenty.

Growing Tips
Water two or three times a week for the first six weeks then weekly the rest of the season, especially in dry weather. Sweet potato vine appreciates regular water and will wilt in hot, dry conditions. Work a gradual-release fertilizer or granular, organic fertilizer into the soil at planting according to package directions. In-season fertilizer usually isn't needed.

In a pot, fertilize at half-strength once a month, and water every day or two.

Regional Advice and Care
Sweet potato tubers can be dug and stored inside over winter in peat moss, sawdust, or vermiculite. When the "eyes" sprout in spring, those pieces can be dug out of the tubers and potted for planting outside after frost. Eyes can be induced by placing a tuber in a vase with the bottom half in water. Tip cuttings also can be taken in late summer and potted for inside growth as a houseplant. Replant the following spring or take cuttings off of those in late winter.

Companion Planting and Design
Sweet potato vine is versatile enough for a variety of uses—draping down a hanging basket, flowing out around the edge of a large pot, rambling across a sunny garden, or growing up a trellis or arbor. Bright flowers, such as black-eyed Susan, marigolds, zinnias, coreopsis, and mums, are ideal partners.

Try These
'Margarita' was the first (and still one of the best) chartreuse varieties. 'Black Heart' and 'Blackie' are two nearly black-leafed types. The entire Sweet Caroline series (multiple colors) is excellent and more compact than most. The Illusion™ series comes in several colors and has lacy leaves. 'Tricolor' has green, cream, and pink foliage; is compact; and prefers shade.

PENNSYLVANIA AWARD-WINNING PLANTS

Pennsylvania has two state-specific plant-award programs in which local experts put their heads together and bestow honors on plants deserving greater use in Pennsylvania landscapes.

One is the Gold Medal Award program run by the Pennsylvania Horticultural Society, which operates the Philadelphia International Flower Show. Since 1988, PHS panels have awarded Gold Medals to between three and six trees or shrubs each year. Starting in 2014, perennial flowers were added to the program. More information on the Gold Medal Award program is available online at www.goldmedalplants.org.

The other program is the Green Ribbon Native Plants Award®, chosen by the staff and Horticulture Committee of Jenkins Arboretum in Devon, Pa. Each year since 2003, Jenkins has given a Green Ribbon to one native tree, one native shrub, and one native fern or wildflower deserving more use in Pennsylvania home gardens. All winners must be plants existing in eastern North America prior to European settlement. More information on Green Ribbon Native Plants is available online at www.jenkinsarboretum.org/greenribbon.html.

Here's the list of PHS Gold Medal Award-winners from 1988 to 2014:

Trees

American fringetree (*Chionanthus virginicus*)
Amur maackia (*Maackia amurensis*)
Black tupelo 'Wildfire' (*Nyssa sylvatica*)
Cornelia cherry dogwood 'Golden Glory' (*Cornus mas*)
Crabapple 'Adirondack' (*Malus* hybrid)
Crabapple 'Donald Wyman' (*Malus* hybrid)
Crabapple 'Jewelberry' (*Malus* hybrid)
Crapemyrtle Pink Velour® (*Lagerstroemia indica* 'Whit III')
Dogwood Aurora® (*Cornus* 'Rutban')
Dogwood Ruth Ellen® (*Cornus* 'Rutlan')
Dogwood Venus™ (*Cornus* hybrid)
Flowering cherry 'Hally Jolivette' (*Prunus* hybrid)
Flowering cherry 'Okame' (*Prunus* hybrid)
Golden rain tree 'Rose Lantern' (*Koelreuteria paniculata*)

Hawthorn 'Winter King' (*Crataegus viridis*)
Japanese cornel dogwood 'Kintoki' (*Cornus officinalis*)
Japanese cutleaf maple 'Tamukeyama' (*Acer palmatum* var. *dissectum*)
Japanese cutleaf maple 'Waterfall' (*Acer palmatum* var. *dissectum*)
Japanese hornbeam (*Carpinus japonica*)
Japanese tree lilac 'Ivory Silk' (*Syringa reticulata*)
Japanese zelkova 'Green Vase' (*Zelkova serrata*)
Korean stewartia (*Stewartia pseudocamellia* var. *koreana*)
Magnolia 'Bracken's Brown Beauty' (*Magnolia grandiflora*)
Magnolia 'Centennial' (*Magnolia stellata*)
Magnolia 'Daybreak' (*Magnolia* hybrid)
Magnolia 'Edith Bogue' (*Magnolia grandiflora*)

Magnolia 'Elizabeth' (*Magnolia* hybrid)
Magnolia 'Galaxy' (*Magnolia* hybrid)
Paperbark maple (*Acer griseum*)
Persian ironwood (*Parrotia persica*)
Pin oak Green Pillar® (*Quercus palustris* 'Pingreen')
Redbud 'Rising Sun' (*Cercis canadensis*)
River birch Heritage® (*Betula nigra* 'Cully')
Seven-son flower (*Heptacodium miconioides*)
Snowbell 'Emerald Pagoda' (*Styrax japonicus* 'Sohuksan')
Sweetbay magnolia Moonglow™ (*Magnolia virginiana* 'Jim Wilson')
Three-flower maple (*Acer triflorum*)
Trident maple (*Acer buergerianum*)
Two-winged silverbell (*Halesia diptera* var. *magniflora*)
Weeping katsura tree 'Morioka Weeping' (*Cercidiphyllum japonicum*)
White oak (*Quercus alba*)
Yellowwood (*Cladrastis kentukea*)

Shrubs

Beauty briar (*Eleutherococcus sieboldianus* 'Variegatus')
Beautyberry (*Callicarpa dichotoma*)
Bloodtwig dogwood 'Midwinter Fire' (*Cornus sanguinea*)
Blueberry 'Sunshine Blue' (*Vaccinium corymbosum*)
Bottlebrush buckeye (*Aesculus parviflora*)
Chastetree 'Shoal Creek' (*Vitex agnus-castus*)
Daphne 'Jim's Pride' (*Daphne* × *transatlantica*)
Deutzia 'Magicien' (*Deutzia hybrida*)
Deutzia 'Nikko' (*Deutzia gracilis*)
Doublefile viburnum 'Shasta' (*Viburnum plicatum* f. *tomentosum*)
Dwarf lilac 'Palabin' (*Syringa meyeri*)
Enkianthus 'J.L. Pennock' (*Enkianthus perulatus*)
Fothergilla 'Blue Mist' (*Fothergilla gardenii*)
Fothergilla 'Mt. Airy' (*Fothergilla intermedia*)
Fragrant sumac 'Gro-Low' (*Sumac aromatica*)
Hydrangea 'Annabelle' (*Hydrangea arborescens*)
Hydrangea 'Blue Billow' (*Hydrangea macrophylla*)
Hydrangea 'Limelight' (*Hydrangea paniculata*)
Ninebark Diabolo™ (*Physocarpus opulifolius* 'Monlo')
Oakleaf hydrangea 'Snow Queen' (*Hydrangea quercicifolia*)
Red buckeye (*Aesculus pavia*)
Red chokeberry 'Brilliantissima' (*Aronia arbutifolia*)

Redosier dogwood 'Silver and Gold' (*Cornus sericea*)
Rose-of-sharon 'Diana' (*Hibiscus syriacus*)
St. Johnswort 'Blue Velvet' (*Hypericum* hybrid)
Southern bush-honeysuckle Cool Splash™ (*Diervilla sessifolia*)
Spicebush (*Lindera glauca*)
Spirea Mellow Yellow® (*Spiraea thunbergii* 'Ogon')
Summersweet 'Hummingbird' (*Clethra alnifolia*)
Summersweet 'Ruby Spice' (*Clethra alnifolia*)
Summersweet Tom's Compact (*Clethra alnifolia* 'Compacta')
Staghorn sumac Tiger Eyes® (*Sumac typhina* 'Bailtiger')
Viburnum 'Conoy' (*Viburnum* × *burkwoodii*)
Viburnum 'Erie' (*Viburnum dilatatum*)
Viburnum 'Eskimo' (*Viburnum selection*)
Viburnum 'Mohawk' (*Viburnum* × *burkwoodii*)
Viburnum 'Winterthur' (*Viburnum nudum*)
Virginia sweetspire 'Henry's Garnet' (*Itea virginica*)
Weigela Wine and Roses™ (*Weigela florida* 'Alexandra')
Winterberry holly 'Harvest Red' (*Ilex* hybrid)
Winterberry holly 'Scarlet O'Hara' (*Ilex verticillata*)
Winterberry holly 'Sparkleberry' (*Ilex* hybrid)
Winterberry holly 'Winter Gold' (*Ilex verticillata*)
Winterberry holly 'Winter Red' (*Ilex verticillata*)
Witch hazel 'Diane' (*Hamamelis* × *intermedia*)
Witch hazel 'Pallida' (*Hamamelis* × *intermedia*)

Evergreens/Conifers

American holly (*Ilex opaca*)
Arborvitae 'Green Giant' (*Thuja* hybrid)
Baldcypress Debonair® (*Taxodium distichum* var. *imbricarium* 'Morris')
Blue holly Blue Maid™ (*Ilex* × *meserveae* 'Mesid')
Boxwood 'Dee Runk' (*Buxus sempervirens*)
Boxwood 'Green Velvet' (*Buxus* hybrid)
Boxwood 'Vardar Valley' (*Buxus sempervirens*)
Camellia 'Korean Fire' (*Camellia japonica*)
Carolina allspice 'Michael Lindsey' (*Calycanthus floridus*)
Dawn redwood (*Metasequoia glyptostroboides*)
Dawn redwood 'Gold Rush' (*Metasequoia glyptostroboides* 'Ogon')

Dwarf Japanese-cedar 'Globosa Nana'
  (*Cryptomeria japonica*)
Eastern redcedar Emerald Sentinel (*Juniperus virginiana* 'Corcorcor')
Eastern white pine 'Fastigiata' (*Pinus strobus*)
False-holly 'Goshiki'
  (*Osmanthus heterophyllus*)
Florida anise 'Halleys Comet'
  (*Illicium floridanum*)
Hinoki cypress 'Nana Gracilis'
  (*Chamaecyparis obtusa*)
Holly Red Beauty® (*Ilex* 'Rutzan')
Inkberry holly 'Densa' (*Ilex glabra*)
Japanese cedar 'Yoshino'
  (*Cryptomeria japonica*)
Japanese plum yew 'Duke Gardens'
  (*Cephalotaxus harringtonii*)
Japanese plum yew 'Prostrata'
  (*Cephalotaxus harringtonii*)
Japanese umbrella pine
  (*Sciadopitys verticillata*)
Juniper 'Silver Mist' (*Juniperus conferta*)
Korean fir (*Abies koreana*)
Korean white pine (*Pinus koraiensis*)
Leatherleaf mahonia (*Mahonia bealei*)
Nordmann fir (*Abies nordmanniana*)
Oriental spruce (*Picea orientalis*)
Portugal laurel (*Prunus lusitanica*)

Privet honeysuckle (*Lonicera pileata*)
Sweetbox (*Sarcococca hookeriana* var. *humilis*)
Viburnum 'Dart's Duke'
  (*Viburnum × rhytidophylloides*)

Vines
American wisteria 'Amethyst Falls'
  (*Wisteria frutescens*)
Carolina jasmine 'Margarita'
  (*Gelsemium sempervirens*)
Chinese trumpetcreeper 'Morning Calm'
  (*Campsis grandiflora*)
Clematis 'Betty Corning' (Clematis viticella)
Cross vine 'Dragon Lady'
  (*Bignonia capriolata*)
English ivy 'Buttercup' (*Hedera helix*)
Hydrangea vine 'Moonlight'
  (*Schizophragma hydrangeoides*)

Perennials
Barrenwort 'Frohnleiten'
  (*Epimedium × perralchicum*)
Christmas fern (*Polystichum acrostichoides*)
Japanese forestgrass (*Hakonechloa macra*)
Threadleaf bluestar (*Amsonia hubrichtii*)

Here's the list of Jenkins Arboretum Green Ribbon Native Plants winner from 2003 to 2013:

Trees
Alternate-leaf (pagoda) dogwood
  (*Cornus alternifolia*)
American fringetree (*Chionanthus virginicus*)
American holly (*Ilex opaca*)
Carolina silverbell (*Halesia carolina*)
Eastern redbud (*Cercis canadensis*)
Pawpaw (*Asimina triloba*)
Flowering dogwood (*Cornus florida*)
Franklinia (*Franklinia alatamaha*)
Sourwood (*Oxydendrum arboreum*)
Sweetbay magnolia (*Magnolia virginiana*)

Shrubs
Bottlebrush buckeye (*Aesculus parviflora*)
Dwarf fothergilla (*Fothergilla gardenii*)
Mountain laurel (*Kalmia latifolia*)
Oakleaf hydrangea (*Hydrangea quercifolia*)
Pinxterbloom azalea
  (*Rhododendron periclymenoides*)
Rosebay rhododendron
  (*Rhododendron maximum*)

Strawberry bush (*Euonymus americanus*)
Sweet pepperbush (*Clethra alnifolia*)
Virginia sweetspire (*Itea virginica*)
Winterberry holly (*Ilex verticillata*)

Wildflowers/Ferns
Allegheny spurge (*Pachysandra procumbens*)
American wisteria (*Wisteria frutescens*)
Bluestem goldenrod (*Solidago caesia*)
Cardinal flower (*Lobelia cardinalis*)
Christmas fern (*Polystichum acrostichoides*)
Cinnamon fern (*Osmunda cinnamomea*)
Foamflower (*Tiarella cordifolia*)
Indian pink (*Spigelia marilandica*)
Largeflower heartleaf
  (*Hexastylis shuttleworthii*)
Northern maidenhair fern
  (*Adiantum pedantum*)
White wood aster (*Eurybia divaricata*)
Wild bleeding heart (*Dicentra eximia*)
Wild columbine (*Aquilegia canadensis*)

WHEN THINGS
GO WRONG
IN THE GARDEN

Much can go awry in dressing up the outside of your property. Plants are living, breathing objects that react sensitively to their always changing (sometimes shockingly so) surroundings. That's why landscaping is more, shall we say, "challenging" than interior decorating. Inside at least you don't have to worry about the wallpaper outgrowing the wall or a groundhog eating the coffee table.

Bugs, diseases, animal pests, droughts, hurricane-remnant downpours, surprise frosts, 100-degree summer days, minus-20 winter nights, and hailstorms are just some of the trials that torment Pennsylvania gardeners.

The good news is that plants are a resilient lot. They do their best to survive. Even though they may take a fleeting beating from a storm or Japanese beetle swarm, most live to bloom another day.

Even if the worst happens, consider it not a loss but an opportunity to try that pretty new shrub you just noticed.

Is Your Problem *Really* a Problem?

There's not much we can do about most of the troubles that come along, other than roll with the punches. Sometimes doing nothing really *is* a better idea than doing the wrong something.

When it comes to bugs and diseases in particular, many gardeners have been conditioned to apply something—a fertilizer, a bug-killer, or some sort of "anti-disease" spray. Some gardeners routinely use all of those—"just in case." That approach doesn't make good sense for a variety of reasons.

For one thing, you can't spray any old thing any old time to take care of whatever bug or disease might be ailing your plants. Certain insecticides kill certain bugs, so if you're guessing, you might apply an ineffective product.

Timing also is important. It'll do no good to spray the right insecticide at the wrong time, that is, long before the bug shows up or after it's already done its damage and left.

With fungicides, almost all of those are geared toward stopping the spread of a disease as opposed to killing pathogens or undoing damage that's already occurred. If you don't get the right product on before or at the beginning of an infection, those are useless too. (That raises the gardening conundrum, "How do I know I need a fungicide if the disease hasn't happened yet?")

Relying on hope-for-the-best troubleshooting not only is often ineffective, it needlessly pollutes, wastes money, wastes time, and sometimes makes problems worse. Overfertilizing, for example, can make plants *more* attractive to bugs.

A better approach is to first figure out if your problem really *is* a problem.

Dropping leaves or peeling bark is a normal part of some plants' growth, not a disease or deathknell at all. Many a rookie has fretted about the bark peeling off a crapemyrtle or needles dropping in fall from a larch, only to find out those are normal habits of those plants.

Beyond that, the majority of setbacks are either cosmetic, or temporary, or both.

Caterpillars may eat holes in your perennial leaves, but once they turn into butterflies or moths and fly away, the damage ends, and the plant moves on.

Or your tree leaves may discolor and drop prematurely in a wet year, only to resprout and return to normal the following drier season.

Or your boxwoods may brown around the edges after a notoriously cold and windy winter, only to "green" back up when new growth occurs in spring.

These are all "problems" that take care of themselves and don't threaten your plants' survival. So unless you're looking for perfection, you'll save a lot of time, effort, money, and aggravation by letting the cosmetic and temporary issues run their course.

How to Diagnose Actual Problems

So how do you separate those from the real problems that might kill your plants? Some ideas include:

1. **Get familiar up front with what's normal for your plants and what's not.**
2. **Become a backyard Sherlock Holmes.** Gather clues on signs and symptoms that will help you zero in on what's wrong.
   - Are the leaves chewed or spotted or just discolored?
   - Is there anything nearby that could be causing trouble, such as a walnut tree with its natural competition-repelling plant chemical or a neighbor's growing tree that's blocking sunlight?
   - Has the plant been getting enough water? Or maybe too much?
   - You didn't recently pack 6 inches of mulch up against the plant's bark, did you?
   - Have there been any significant weather events or changes recently?
   - Is it possible the bed got hit with herbicide spray drift or an excess of fertilizer runoff?
   - Have you fertilized lately? Maybe a soil test is in order.
   - Is there a pattern to the problem in that area or is the problem specific to just one particular plant or species?

   Virginia Tech Extension has an excellent tip sheet called "Diagnosing Plant Problems" that walks you through this process. It's available free online at www.pubs.ext.vt.edu/426/426-714/426-714.html.

3. **Nail down a diagnosis.**

     If you prefer to use a computer, one of the best tools is the University of Maryland's Landscape Problem Solver. This website walks you through a series of questions that eventually leads you to the likely problem, including photos and tips on what to do about it. It's a free service and available at www. plantdiagnostics.umd.edu.

     Another helpful resource is the University of Pennsylvania's Morris Arboretum, which not only provides one-on-one advice to walk-ins but has a "Diagnosing Your Plant" website at www.upenn.edu/paflora/plantclinic/diagnose.htm.

     Even general Internet searches, such as typing in "bugs on azalea" in a search engine, can yield a variety of help.

     If you like paper references, an excellent book that does much the same thing is *What's Wrong With My Plant? And How Do I Fix It* by David Deardorff and Kathryn Wadsworth.

     Also helpful for diagnosing disease and bug problems on trees, shrubs, and evergreens is Penn State University's "Woody Ornamental Insect, Mite, and Disease Management" manual, available at county Penn State Extension offices or online for free at www. pubs.cas.psu.edu/FreePubs/PDFs/agrs025.pdf.

4. **Seek professional help.**

     Start with your local county Penn State Extension office, many of which have trained Master Gardeners who can help you identify bugs, diseases, and assorted other mayhem.

     Many local garden centers also have experts on staff who can take a look at bagged bugs or damaged clippings.

     If you don't mind paying for the service, certified arborists, consulting horticulturists, and landscape pest-control companies are available to hire for an on-site examination.

     To check your soil, Penn State University's Agricultural Analytical Services Lab offers do-it-yourself, mail-in kits that give readings on acidity level and nutrient breakdowns as well as recommendations on what and how much to add. Those are available for a reasonable cost at most garden centers, county Penn State Extension offices, or online at www. agsci.psu.edu/aasl/soil-testing/soil-fertility-testing.

     Penn State's Plant Disease Clinic also offers free diagnosis to Pennsylvania homeowners of mailed-in plant specimens. More information on that is available online at www. plantpath.psu.edu/facilities/plant-disease-clinic or through county Penn State Extension offices.

Dealing with Troubles

Once you figure out what's wrong, determine whether it's something you want to treat or not. Factors influencing that include whether the problem is cosmetic or potentially fatal, your tolerance for imperfection, the cost and effectiveness of the treatment, and even the troubled plant's location. You may decide to treat, say, a valuable plant out front while letting a more ordinary plant fend for itself out back.

Rather than spray everything just in case, try to target any treatment to the exact problem, starting with whatever does the least off-target damage first. That's the heart of a pest-control approach known as Integrated Pest Management (IPM).

Sometimes, a stiff spray or two of water is enough to control a mite or aphid outbreak. Horticultural oils, soaps, and other "soft" treatments can often control a target pest while having limited impact on the non-pests and environment.

If all else fails and the problem threatens to kill a plant you really don't want to lose, then IPM calls for "bringing out the big guns" (chemical sprays) as a last resort. At that point, you may even decide it's cheaper and preferred to just replace a struggling plant with one that seldom runs into trouble.

Getting bulletproof varieties in the right spot up front is the best way to sidestep problems. That's the gist of this book—steering you toward 170 of the best choices for Pennsylvania landscapes.

You might notice that some commonly used plants are *not* included in this book. A big reason is that many of the non-listed choices often run into one or more serious problems. Another reason is space; you can't plant everything, so we cut it off at the top 170.

What Didn't Make the Cut

Just because a plant you're considering isn't profiled here doesn't mean it's a "bad" plant or not worth using. Here's a list of some of the plants that didn't make our cut and why:

Prone to bug trouble: Ash, mugho pine, dwarf Alberta spruce, euonymus, pieris, cotoneaster, hemlock, white birch, honeylocust, purple plum, most roses.

Prone to disease trouble: Beebalm, hollyhock, purple-leaf sand cherry, elm, Douglas-fir, impatiens (*Impatiens walleriana*), peony, most roses, lily-of-the-valley, old-fashioned French lilac.

Wimpy in our heat, cold, humidity, or other less-than-ideal conditions: Daphne, mountain laurel, sourwood, heath, heather, lupine, lamb's ear, lady's mantle, delphinium, enkianthus, Oregon grape holly, annual lobelia, annual stock, sweet pea.

At least one potential deal-killing curse: Pyracantha (weapons-grade thorns), cactus (ouch), pansy (rabbits' favorite dessert), carnation (second on the rabbit list), mock orange (often just decides to stop blooming), mulberry (gobs of staining fruit if planted near walks and patios), female ginkgo (fruits smell like vomit), datura (hallucinogenic, toxic), foxglove (toxic), monkshood (toxic), walnut (kills off many other species nearby), weeping willow and poplar (leaders in branch breakage).

Invasive, overly aggressive, or just big and gangly: Barberry, bamboo (most), burning bush, butterfly bush (most), bush clover, rose-of-sharon, callery pear, mimosa, Norway maple, purple perilla, crown vetch, ivy, creeping jenny, bishop's weed, evening primrose, most mints, yellow archangel, maidenhair grass (*Miscanthus*), empress tree (*Paulownia*), ribbon grass, Japanese blood grass, Russian olive, privet, trumpet vine, Virginia creeper, Chinese wisteria, morning glory, silver lace vine, porcelain vine, chocolate vine.

The Problem with Invasives

That brings us to an increasing problem we've had in Pennsylvania with plants that escape our yards and start to choke out native vegetation along with the food and shelter those species provide to local wildlife.

Plants originally sold as garden plants have been the source of many a current weed problem. Tree-of-heaven, kudzu, multiflora rose, purple loosestrife, and Japanese honeysuckle are some of the most salient examples.

While the plant is already out of the bag on those invaders, an equal concern is, "What plants are we still buying, planting, and growing today that could become tomorrow's invaders?" A few common ones high on the concern list are barberry, burning bush, most butterfly bushes, and most Japanese spirea.

All of those are still sold despite being on one or more invasive-plant lists. Concern about the invasive potential of some non-native plants, as well as loss of natural habitats in general, has been fueling increased interest in native plants.

If you're interested in leaning to natives, that feature is spelled out in the descriptions and symbols in each of the plant profiles in this book.

Some other good online resources on Pennsylvania-native plants are:

- The Pennsylvania Native Plant Society at www.panativeplantsociety.org.
- iConserve Pennsylvania's native plant website at www.iconservepa.org/plantsmart/nativeplants.
- The University of Pennsylvania's Pennsylvania Flora Project Morris Arboretum website www.paflora.org.
- The New Hope, Pa.-based Bowman's Hill Wildflower Preserve website at www.bhwp.org.
- The Lady Bird Johnson Wildflower Center, which lists recommended natives for Pennsylvania at www.wildflower.org/collections/collection.php?collection=PA.
- The Hummelstown, Pa.-based Manada Conservancy's native plant site at www.manada.org/nativeplants.html.

Four good books on using native plants in the landscape:

- *Bringing Nature Home* by Douglas W. Tallamy www.bringingnaturehome.net
- *Native Alternatives to Invasive Plants* by C. Colston Burrell
- *Armitage's Native Plants for North American Gardens* by Allan M. Armitage
- *Native Plants of the Northeast: A Guide for Gardening and Conservation* by Donald J. Leopold

And to at least steer clear of potential invasives, the Pennsylvania Department of Conservation and Natural Resources Bureau of Forestry maintains a list of species already invading Pennsylvania as well as others on the "watch" list. That site can be found at www.dcnr.state.pa.us/forestry/plants/invasiveplants/index.htm.

Here's DCNR's list of invasive plants:

Invasive species

Grasses
Cheatgrass (*Bromus tectorum*)
Common reed (*Phragmites australis* ssp. *australis*)
Japanese stiltgrass (*Microstegium vimineum*)
Johnson grass (*Sorghum halepense*)
Poverty brome (*Bromus sterilis*)
Reed canary grass (*Phalaris australis*)
Shattercane (*Sorghum bicolor* ssp. *drummondii*)

Herbaceous Species
Beefsteak plant (*Perilla frutescens*)
Black knapweed (*Centaurea nigra*)
Bristled knotweed (*Persicaria longiseta*)
Brown knapweed (*Centaurea jacea*)
Bull thistle (*Cirsium vulgare*)
Canada thistle (*Cirsium arvense*)
Dames rocket (*Hesperis matronalis*)
Garlic mustard (*Alliaria petiolata*)
Giant hogweed (*Heracleum mantegazzianum*)
Giant knotweed (*Fallopia sachalinensis*)
Goatsrue (*Galega officinalis*)
Greater celandine (*Chelidonium majus*)
Goutweed (*Aegopodium podagraria*)
Hairy willow herb (*Epilobium hirsutum*)
Japanese knotweed (*Fallopia japonica*)
Jimsonweed (*Datura stramonium*)
Lesser celandine (*Ranunculus ficaria*)
Moneywort (*Lysimachia nummularia*)
Musk thistle (*Carduus nutans*)
Narrowleaf bittercress (*Cardamine impatiens*)
Poison hemlock (*Conium maculatum*)
Purple loosestrife (*Lythrum salicaria*)
Smallflower hairy willowherb (*Epilobium parviflorum*)
Spotted knapweed (*Centaurea stoebe*)
Star-of-Bethlehem (*Ornithogalum nutans*, *O. umbellatum*)
Wild chervil (*Anthriscus sylvestris*)
Wild parsnip (*Pastinaca sativa*)
Yellow flag iris (*Iris pseudacorus*)

Shrubs
Amur honeysuckle (*Lonicera mackii*)
Autumn olive (*Elaeagnus umbellata*)
Bell's honeysuckle (*Lonicera × bella*)
Border privet (*Ligustrum obtusifolium*)
Burning bush (*Euonymus alata*)
Chinese bushclover (*Lespedeza cuneata*)
Chinese privet (*Ligustrum sinense*)
Common buckthorn (*Rhamnus cathartica*)
Common privet (*Ligustrum vulgare*)
European barberry (*Berberis vulgaris*)
Glossy buckthorn (*Frangula alnus*)
Guelder rose (*Viburnum opulus*)
Japanese barberry (*Berberis thunbergii*)
Japanese privet (*Ligustrum japonicum*)
Japanese spiraea (*Spiraea japonica*)
Jetbead (*Rhodotypos scandens*)
Morrow's honeysuckle (*Lonicera morrowii*)
Multiflora rose (*Rosa multiflora*)
Russian olive (*Elaeagnus angustifolia*)
Shrubby bushclover (*Lespedeza bicolor*)
Standish honeysuckle (*Lonicera standishii*)
Tartarian honeysuckle (*Lonicera tatarica*)
Wineberry (*Rubus phoenicolasius*)

Trees
Callery pear (*Pyrus calleryana*)
Empress tree (*Paulownia tomentosa*)
European black alder (*Alnus glutinosa*)
Japanese angelica tree (*Aralia elata*)
Mimosa (*Albizia julibrissin*)
Norway maple (*Acer platanoides*)
Siberian elm (*Ulmus pumila*)
Sycamore maple (*Acer pseudoplatanus*)
Tree-of-heaven (*Ailanthus altissima*)

Vines
Black swallow-wort (*Vincetoxicum nigrum*)
Chocolate vine (*Akebia quinata*)
English ivy (*Hedera helix*)
Japanese hops (*Humulus japonicus*)
Japanese honeysuckle (*Lonicera japonica*)
Kudzu (*Pueraria lobata*)
Mile-a-minute (*Persicaria perfoliata*)
Oriental bittersweet (*Celastrus orbiculatus*)
Pale swallow-wort (*Vincetoxicum rossicum*)
Porcelain berry (*Ampelopsis brevipedunculata*)
Wintercreeper (*Euonymus fortunei*)

PENNSYLVANIA GARDENS TO VISIT

Public gardens are a valuable aid to anyone trying to figure out what to plant. These gardens show what plants look like in real settings, throughout different seasons, at mature sizes, and for gardens close to home, in the same soil and climate you're facing.

Pennsylvania is loaded with public gardens. The Philadelphia area in particular offers America's richest cluster of them—some two dozen within an hour of the city.

Here are twenty of my favorite Pennsylvania public gardens to get you started:

Arboretum of the Barnes Foundation
Merion, Pa.
www.barnesfoundation.org

Arboretum at Penn State and H.O. Smith Botanic Gardens
University Park, Pa.
www.arboretum.psu.edu

Awbury Arboretum
Philadelphia, Pa.
www.awbury.org

Bartram's Garden
Philadelphia, Pa.
www.bartramsgarden.org

Bowman's Hill Wildflower Preserve
New Hope, Pa.
www.bhwp.org

Chanticleer
Wayne, Pa.
www.chanticleergarden.org

Conestoga House
Lancaster, Pa.
www.conestogahouse.org/Old_Index_Page.html

Erie Zoo
Erie, Pa.
www.eriezoo.org

Henry Schmieder Arboretum of Delaware Valley College
Doylestown, Pa.
www.devalcol.edu/offices-services/arboretum

Hershey Gardens
Hershey, Pa.
www.hersheygardens.org

Jenkins Arboretum & Gardens
Devon, Pa.
www.jenkinsarboretum.org

Landscape Arboretum of Temple University, Ambler Campus
Ambler, Pa.
www.ambler.temple.edu/arboretum

Longwood Gardens
Kennett Square, Pa.
www.longwoodgardens.org

Morris Arboretum
Philadelphia, Pa.
www.morrisarboretum.org

Phipps Conservatory
Pittsburgh, Pa.
www.phipps.conservatory.org

PHS Meadowbrook Farm
Meadowbrook, Pa.
meadowbrookfarm.org

Scott Arboretum of Swarthmore College
Swarthmore, Pa.
www.scottarboretum.org

Shofuso Japanese House and Garden
Philadelphia, Pa.
www.shofuso.com

Tyler Arboretum
Media, Pa.
www.tylerarboretum.org

Wyck, Historic House, Garden, Farm
Philadelphia, Pa.
www.wyck.org

GLOSSARY

Acidic soil: On a soil pH scale of 0 to 14, acidic soil has a pH reading of 6.0 and lower. Mildly acidic is 6.0 to 7.0.

Alkaline soil: On a soil pH scale of 0 to 14, alkaline soil has a pH higher than 7.0.

Allee: A walkway lined with trees or tall shrubs.

Annual: A plant that germinates (sprouts), flowers, and dies within one year.

Anti-transpirant: A product that thinly coats plant leaves to slow the loss of moisture. Often used to prevent browning on evergreens over winter when plants are unable to take up moisture from frozen ground. Also called anti-desiccant. Examples: Wilt-Pruf, Wilt Stop.

Bacillus thuringiensis (Bt): *Bt* is an organic pest control made from naturally occurring soil bacteria, often used to control harmful caterpillars such as cutworms, leaf rollers, and webworms.

Balled and burlapped (B&B): Plants that have been grown in field rows, dug up with their soil intact, wrapped with burlap, and tied with twine.

Balanced fertilizer: A fertilizer with equal (or close to it) amounts of the three main plant nutrients—nitrogen, phosphorus, and potassium. A product with a nutrient percentage breakdown of 10-10-10 or 20-20-20 on the label is considered "balanced."

Bare root: Plants that are shipped dormant, without being planted in soil or having soil around their roots.

Beneficial insects: Insects that perform valuable services such as pollination and pest control. Examples: ladybugs, spiders, and bees.

Biennial: A plant that blooms during its second year and then dies.

Botanical name: A two-word, Latin-based, plant-identification system comprised of the genus and species of a plant, such as *Rudbeckia fulgida*. Also called "scientific name."

Bract: A modified leaf that resembles a flower petal and is often colorful. The best known example is the colorful bracts of poinsettia.

Bud: An undeveloped shoot nestled between the leaf and the stem that will eventually produce a flower or plant branch.

Canopy: The overhead branching area of a tree, including foliage.

Cell packs: Multi-compartment containers, usually made out of thin plastic and used to sell small plants. They're most often used for annual flowers and vegetables and come in 3-packs, 4-packs, and 6-packs.

Chlorosis: Yellowing of the leaf tissue between the veins, usually caused by soil that's too alkaline to allow sufficient iron uptake (and sometimes by lack of iron in the soil).

Common name: A name used to identify a plant in everyday language in a particular region as opposed to its botanical name. Redbud, for example, is a common name for *Cercis canadensis*.

Conifer: A plant that produces cones. The large majority of them are needled evergreens, such as spruce, pine, and fir.

Container: Any pot or vessel that is used for growing plants. These can include ceramic, clay, steel, or plastic pots as well as buckets, barrels, or even an old bathtub.

Cool-season annual: A flowering plant, such as snapdragon or pansy, that thrives in cooler weather.

Cross-pollinate: The transfer of pollen from one plant to another.

Cultivar: A CULTivated VARiety. A plant that has been bred or selected for having one or more distinct traits from the species and then given a name to set it apart. 'Pardon Me', for example, is a cultivar of daylily.

Crown: The part of a plant at or near the soil surface from which the stems emerge. Sometimes referred to as the "growth point" of a plant.

Dappled: Refers to open or light shade created by high tree branches or tree foliage in which patches of sunlight and shade intermingle.

Deadhead: To remove dead flowers in order to encourage further bloom, neaten the plant, and prevent the plant from self-sowing.

Deciduous: A plant that loses its leaves seasonally, typically in fall or early winter.

Dissected leaves: Leaves that are divided into deep, narrow segments, sometimes described as "cut" or "lacy."

Divide: The process of digging up clumping perennials, separating the roots, and replanting the pieces.

Dormancy: The period when plants stop growing in order to conserve energy, usually in winter but also in summer in the case of spring-blooming bulbs and some cool-season perennials.

Dwarf: Describes a plant whose size is less than that of the species' standard or usual size.

Ephemeral: A short-lived or limited-appearance plant. A "spring ephemeral," for example, is one that appears in spring and then dies or goes dormant before summer.

Evergreen: A plant that keeps its leaves year-round instead of dropping them seasonally. These can be needled plants as well as broad-leaf ones.

Established roots: Refers to the stage after transplanting when roots have grown and recovered enough to resume normal growth.

Forcing bulbs: The process of potting dormant bulbs, then giving them the necessary chilling time before taking them into warmth to encourage earlier-than-usual bloom.

Frost: Ice crystals that form when the temperature falls below freezing. Tender plants die when frost kills their leaf cells.

Full sun: Areas of the garden that receive direct sunlight for at least six to eight hours a day.

Fungicide: A compound used to control fungal diseases.

Genus: The main classification of a plant and the first word in its botanical name. The "*Cornus*" in *Cornus florida* is the genus, and "*florida*" is the species.

Germination: The process by which a plant emerges from a seed or a spore.

Gradual-release fertilizer: A fertilizer that releases its nutrients slowly over time, meaning less-frequent applications are needed.

Grafted: A plant that has two parts—a lower section with strong roots and a top part (the "scion") that has been attached for a desired growth habit, such as dwarf size, disease resistance, or improved flowering or fruiting.

Graft union: The point where a grafted plant's rootstock and scion have been joined. This point must be planted above ground.

Granular fertilizer: A type of fertilizer that comes in a dry, pellet-like form rather than a liquid or powder.

Hand pruners: A hand tool that consists of two sharp blades that perform a scissoring motion to clip stems and branches.

Hardening off: The process of gradually acclimating seedlings and young plants grown in an indoor environment to the outdoors.

Hardiness zone: A numeral system developed by the U.S. Department of Agriculture to designate an area's average annual low temperature. Plants are then given ratings according to the temperatures they'll survive. Pennsylvania comprises six zones (5a to 7b).

Heirloom: A plant whose origin dates approximately to pre-World War II.

Herbaceous: Plants with fleshy or soft stems. Opposite of woody plants.

Hybrid: A plant produced by crossing two genetically different plants, usually to achieve a desired trait, new color, or some other perceived improvement.

Inflorescence: A cluster of flowers on a branch or network of branches. The blooming parts of ornamental grasses are usually called this as opposed to flowers.

Insecticide: A compound used to kill or control insects.

Intergeneric cross: A plant that has been created by merging plants of different genera (plural of genus), such as combining *Heuchera* and *Tiarella* to come up with *Heucherella*.

Leader: The term for the center or main trunk of a tree.

Liquid fertilizer: Plant fertilizer in a liquid form; some types need to be mixed with water, and some types are ready to use from the bottle.

Microclimate: Small sections of a property that deviate slightly from the prevailing, surrounding climate. A courtyard with stone walls, for example, likely will have warmer, less windy conditions than the rest of a yard.

Mulch: Any type of material that is spread over the soil surface, generally to suppress weeds and retain soil moisture.

Nativar: A cultivated variety of a native plant.

Native plant: In terms of U.S. native plants, these are species that were growing here before the arrival of European settlers.

New wood: The current year's growth. Usually used in reference to a plant "flowering or fruiting on new wood," meaning the flower buds form on the new growth.

Old wood: Growth that's more than one year old. Some plants produce fruits or flowers only on older growth, not that season's.

Organic: Technically, organic refers to any carbon-based material capable of decomposition and decay. It's usually used to mean a fertilizer, spray or product derived from naturally occurring materials instead of those synthesized in a lab or factory.

Panicle: A shape of flower in which buds are clustered along a single stem and open into a cone or bottle-brush form.

Part sun/part shade: Areas of the garden that get direct sunlight for part of the day (less than six hours) and that are in shade for part of the day (at least three hours of sunlight at some point). More than six hours of direct sunlight a day is full sun, and less than three hours is considered shade.

Perennial: A plant that lives for more than two years. Usually used to describe herbaceous plants.

Perennialize: A term usually used in growing bulbs, meaning species adept at coming back year after year as opposed to fizzling out in a year or two.

pH: A figure designating the acidity or the alkalinity of soil as measured on a scale of 0 to 14, with 7.0 being neutral.

Pollination: The transfer of pollen for fertilization from the plant's male pollen-bearing organ (stamen) to the female organ (pistil), usually by wind, bees, butterflies, moths, or hummingbirds.

Powdery mildew: A fungal disease characterized by white powdery spots on plant leaves and stems.

Pre-emergent herbicide: A weed-control product that works by preventing weed seeds from sprouting as opposed to killing plants after they're growing.

Rootball: The network of roots and soil clinging to a plant when it is lifted out of the ground or pot.

Root flare: The point at the base of a tree where the trunk transitions into the roots. This point starts to widen and should be visible just above grade if a tree is planted at the correct depth.

Runner: A stem sprouting from a plant that roots itself as it goes.

Self-fertile: A plant that does not require cross-pollination from another plant in order to produce fruit.

Species: A plant that's a variation or sub-group of a genus. It's the second word in its botanical name. The "*florida*" in *Cornus florida*, for example, is the species, while "*Cornus*" is the genus. The two together make up the botanical name of American dogwood.

Stippling: A description of damage to leaves. Stippled leaves are discolored due to loss of chlorophyll removed by tiny insects that insert small feeding holes throughout the leaf.

Silt: A granular, mineral component of soil that's sized between that of smaller clay particles and larger sand particles.

Soil test: An analysis of a soil sample, most often to determine its level of nutrients and pH (acidity) reading.

Sucker: Twiggy growth emerging from roots around the base of tree and tall shrubs. In most cases, suckers divert energy from more desirable tree growth and should be removed.

Tendril: Skinny, curled projections that grow out of vining stems and grab onto nearby supports like little arms to pull the plant up.

Thinning: In the context of pruning, it's the process of removing excess branches from woody plants to improve air flow, let more sunlight into the inner branches, and remove conflicts from branches that are rubbing one another.

Transplants: Plants that are grown in one location and then moved to and replanted in another.

Tropical plant: A plant that's native to a tropical region of the world and typically not able to survive frost.

Turfgrass: Short grasses that are mowed and used in lawns as opposed to ornamental grasses, which are left to grow as landscape plants.

Variegated: The appearance of differently colored areas on plant leaves, usually white, yellow, or a brighter green.

Water sprout: A vertical shoot that emerges from tree branches. These should usually be pruned off.

Weeping: A growth habit in plants that features drooping or downward curving branches.

Wood chips: Small pieces of wood made by cutting or chipping and used as mulch in the garden.

Woody plant: A perennial with bark that thickens each year and whose stems do not die back to the ground in winter.

REFERENCES

Armitage, Allan M. *Armitage's Garden Annuals: A Color Encyclopedia*. Timber Press: Portland, Oregon, 2004.

Armitage, Allan M. *Armitage's Manual of Annuals, Biennials, and Half-Hardy Perennials*. Timber Press: Portland, Oregon, 2001.

Armitage, Allan M. *Armitage's Native Plants for North American Gardens*. Timber Press: Portland, Oregon, 2006.

Armitage, Allan M. *Armitage's Vines and Climbers: A Gardener's Guide to the Best Vertical Plants*. Timber Press: Portland, Oregon, 2010.

Armitage, Allan M. *Herbaceous Perennial Plants: A Treatise on Their Identification, Culture and Garden Attributes*. Stipes Publishing L.L.C.: Champaign, Illinois, 2008.

Ball, Liz. *Pennsylvania Gardener's Guide*. Cool Springs Press: Nashville, Tennessee, 2002.

Bagust, Harold. *The Firefly Dictionary of Plant Names: Common and Botanical*. Firefly Books: Buffalo, New York, 2003.

Bitner, Richard L. *Conifers for Gardens: An Illustrated Encyclopedia*. Timber Press: Portland, Oregon, 2007.

Brickell, Christopher and Judith D. Zuk. *The American Horticultural Society A-Z Encyclopedia of Garden Plants*. DK Publishing Inc.: New York, New York, 1997.

Brown, George E. and Tony Kirkham. *The Pruning of Trees, Shrubs and Conifers*. Timber Press: Portland, Oregon, 2009.

Cohen, Stephanie and Nancy J. Ondra. *The Perennial Gardener's Design Primer*. Storey Publishing: North Adams, Massachusetts, 2005.

Darke, Rick. *The Color Encyclopedia of Ornamental Grasses*. Timber Press: Portland, Oregon, 1999.

Dirr, Michael A. *Dirr's Encyclopedia of Trees and Shrubs*. Timber Press: Portland, Oregon, 2011.

Dirr, Michael A. *Manual of Woody Landscape Plants*. Stipes Publishing L.L.C.: Champaign, Illinois, 2009.

DiSabato-Aust, Tracy. *The Well-Tended Perennial Garden: Planting and Pruning Techniques*. Timber Press: Portland, Oregon, 2006.

Longwood Gardens Plant Explorer database, Kennett Square, Pennsylvania. Available online at http://www.longwoodgardens.org.

MacKenzie, David S. *Perennial Ground Covers*. Timber Press: Portland, Oregon, 1997.

Manada Conservancy Native Plant Guides, Hummelstown, Pennsylvania. Available online at http://www.manada.org/nativeplantguides.html.

Mathew, Brian and Philip Swindells. *The Complete Book of Bulbs, Corms, Tubers, and Rhizomes*. Reader's Digest: Pleasantville, New York, 1994.

Missouri Botanical Garden Plant Finder plant database, St. Louis, Missouri. Available online at http://www.missouribotanicalgarden.org.

More, David and John White. *The Illustrated Encyclopedia of Trees.* Timber Press: Portland, Oregon, 2002.

Ondra, Nancy J. *The Perennial Care Manual.* Storey Publishing: North Adams, Massachusetts, 2009.

Pennsylvania Department of Conservation and Natural Resources native plant database, Harrisburg, Pennsylvania. Available online at http://www.dcnr.state.pa.us/forestry/plants/nativeplants.

Pennsylvania Horticultural Society Gold Medal Plants database, Philadelphia, Pennsylvania. Available online at http://www.goldmedalplants.org.

Pennsylvania State University Trial Gardens, Landisville, Pennsylvania. Plant evaluation information available online at http://www.trialgardenspsu.com.

Pennsylvania State University. *Woody Ornamental Insect, Mite, and Disease Management.* University Park, Pennsylvania. Book available online at http://pubs.cas.psu.edu/FreePubs/PDFs/agrs025.pdf.

Rhoads, Ann Fowler and Timothy A. Block. *The Plants of Pennsylvania: An Illustrated Manual.* University of Pennsylvania Press: Philadelphia, Pennsylvania, 2000.

Schmid, W. George. *An Encyclopedia of Shade Perennials.* Timber Press: Portland, Oregon, 2002.

INDEX

PHOTO CREDITS

Liz Ball: pp. 60, 63, 85, 95, 128, 170, 185, 188, 195, 199, 206

Cathy Wilkinson Barash: pp. 127, 189

Mike Dirr: pp. 212

Tom Eltzroth: pp. 22, 24, 25, 26, 27, 30, 34, 35, 37, 39, 40, 42, 48, 52, 54, 55, 58, 61, 64, 65, 70, 71, 72, 78, 84, 86, 90, 91, 93, 96, 97, 98, 99, 101, 105, 106, 107, 116, 117, 118, 120, 121, 123, 124, 125, 130, 132, 134, 137, 138, 141, 146, 147, 148, 150, 153, 154, 158, 166, 169, 173, 177, 179, 182, 186, 109, 191, 192, 194, 204, 213, 215

Flower Fields: pp. 83

Erica Glasener: pp. 200

Pam Harper: pp. 23, 88, 110, 151, 181, 221

Dave MacKenzie: pp. 69, 111

Charles Mann: pp. 46, 164

Melinda Myers: pp. 180

Jerry Pavia: pp. 6, 9, 10, 13, 16, 19, 20, 28, 29, 32, 33, 36, 41, 43, 44, 45, 49, 53, 59, 67, 73, 74, 75, 76, 81, 82, 87, 89, 94, 102, 104, 108, 109, 112, 113, 114, 119, 126, 131, 133, 135, 136, 139, 140, 142, 143, 152, 155, 160, 161, 165, 171, 172, 174, 175, 177, 178, 183, 184, 187, 193, 196, 197, 207, 208, 209, 210

Rick Ray: pp. 80

Shutterstock: pp. 38, 51, 56, 62, 103, 115, 144, 149, 156, 162, 168, 198, 201, 202, 203, 211

Ralph Snodsmith: pp. 47, 159

Georgia Tasker: pp. 122

Mark Turner: pp. 50

Andre Viette: pp. 205

George Weigel: pp. 31, 66, 77, 79, 92, 129, 145, 157, 163, 167, 214

Wikimedia Commons/CC-by-3.0, pp. 57

MEET
GEORGE WEIGEL

Geeorge Weigel is a garden writer, garden designer, and frequent lecturer best known for the garden columns he has written weekly for more than twenty years for *The Patriot-News* and Pennlive. com in Harrisburg, Pennsylvania.

Originally from Lancaster County, Pa, he earned a journalism degree from Penn State University and later became a Pennsylvania Certified Horticulturist through the Pennsylvania Landscape and Nursery Association.

Besides his newspaper column, Weigel has written for numerous magazines, including *Horticulture*, *Green Scene*, *Pennsylvania Gardener*, *Central Pennsylvania* magazine, and *People, Places and Plants*.

He also posts a weekly "e-column" on his own website, www.georgeweigel.net, which includes month-by-month garden tips, public-garden profiles, plant profiles, and a library of articles on a wide variety of gardening topics. Weigel is co-author with neurosurgeon Dr. Kenneth Casey of the medical book *Striking Back! The Trigeminal Neuralgia and Face Pain Handbook* (Trigeminal Neuralgia Association).

During the growing season, Weigel offers garden design and consultations to do-it-yourselfers through his Garden House-Calls business. He also leads numerous trips to gardens, both regionally and internationally, and he gives dozens of talks each year at the Pennsylvania Garden Expo, the Pennsylvania Garden Show of York, the Pennsylvania Home Show, and assorted garden clubs and Master Gardener programs.

Weigel is a member of the Pennsylvania Horticultural Society's Gold Medal Plant Committee, a long-time member of the Garden Writers Association, and a former board member of Hershey Gardens, where he helped design the one-acre Children's Garden.

He has taught classes at Harrisburg Area Community College, Hershey Gardens, and the Garden Club Federation of Pennsylvania's Landscape Design School.

Weigel says his best horticulture experience, though, comes from getting down and dirty with plants in the garden.

He once designed and planted a twenty-theme-bed Idea Garden for Country Market Nursery in Mechanicsburg, Pa, and he's an avid (his brother would say "wacko") life-long home gardener who's still trying to figure out how to outsmart the groundhogs.

Weigel and his wife, Susan, live and garden in suburban Cumberland County.

CPSIA information can be obtained
at www.ICGtesting.com
Printed in the USA
LVOW02s2108100216

474388LV00013B/15/P